THINGS OF THE
Spirit

THINGS OF THE Spirit

Women Writers Constructing Spirituality

edited by

KRISTINA K. GROOVER

University of Notre Dame Press
Notre Dame, Indiana

Copyright © 2004 by University of Notre Dame
Notre Dame, Indiana 46556
www.undpress.nd.edu
All Rights Reserved

Manufactured in the United States of America

Library of Congress Cataloging-in-Publication Data
Things of the spirit : women writers constructing spirituality / edited by
Kristina K. Groover.
p.   cm.
Includes bibliographical references and index.
ISBN 0-268-02961-X (alk. paper)
ISBN 0-268-02962-8 (pbk. : alk. paper)
1. Spirituality in literature.   2. Women authors.   3. Feminist theology.
I. Groover, Kristina K., 1961–
PN56.S7T48   2004
809'.9338204 — dc22

2004011324

This book is printed on recycled paper.

CONTENTS

ACKNOWLEDGMENTS

This collection is a true collaboration, not only of those whose names are listed in the table of contents, but of the many friends and colleagues who have helped me with this project.

I am most grateful to the group of scholars whose exciting, compelling work makes up this collection. They have been excellent correspondents and fellow travelers, and I thank them for their patience, good faith, and encouragement. I could not have asked for a better group of collaborators.

In the English Department at Appalachian State University, I work with the best of colleagues and friends. Among them are a number of excellent editors who have been generous in sharing their experience and advice; I am indebted especially to Chip Arnold, Tom McGowan, and Susan Staub. Many other colleagues have encouraged my work in various ways: reading drafts, offering advice, talking me through moments of perplexity, and celebrating my successes. Special thanks go to Betsy Beaulieu, Lynn Moss Sanders, Grace McEntee, Tom McLaughlin, Georgia Rhoades, Sandy Ballard, Cece Conway, Rosemary Horowitz, and Elaine O'Quinn; their generous collegiality and friendship sustain both my professional and personal life. I also thank David Haney and Daniel Hurley, present and former chairs of the Department of English at Appalachian, for their support of this project over the past four years.

I am indebted to Barbara Hanrahan at University of Notre Dame Press for her interest in this project and for her good humor, her expertise, and her support. Many thanks as well to editor Elisabeth Magnus and to the staff of the University of Notre Dame Press for their careful and thoughtful work and for their many kindnesses.

I am grateful to both of my families, the Groovers and the Peters, and to my wonderful circle of friends for their generosity, patience, and kindness. Finally, my deepest thanks go to Marian Peters, my partner in all things.

INTRODUCTION

KRISTINA K. GROOVER

My interest in women's literary representations of spirituality began with my background as a student of American literature. As
a reader of James Fenimore Cooper and Mark Twain, Ernest Hemingway
and John Updike, I couldn't help becoming interested in the quest. The
journey into a literal or metaphoric wilderness, with its promise of escaping society's shackles, conquering untamed territory, and achieving new
heights of freedom, is ubiquitous in the American canon. Equally as pervasive as the journey itself is the spiritual quest it implies. Famous questers
from Natty Bumppo to Nick Adams travel into the wilderness seeking not
only physical adventure and mastery but spiritual revelation.

In time, I was struck by the virtual exclusion of female protagonists
from the spiritual quest paradigm. A plot line that depends upon a flight
from home and family into an untamed wilderness not only limits the possibility of a female character being cast as the questing hero but also places
women in the role of entrapping domestic conservators whom the male
hero must flee. In *The Wilderness Within: American Women Writers and Spiritual Quest*,[1] my study of late-nineteenth- and twentieth-century texts by
American women writers, I posed the question of whether exclusion from
the quest also meant exclusion from the realm of spiritual experience or
whether, alternatively, American women writers might offer other patterns
for spiritual seeking. In that study I examined alternative paradigms to the
spiritual quest, tracing domesticity, female community, and storytelling as

realms of the spiritual, and the garden as a symbol that frequently substitutes for the untamed wilderness in women writers' texts.

In researching this earlier book, I found that scholars in many fields outside my own were also examining women's literary representations of spirituality. Throughout literary history, women have written of spiritual visions, insights, and transformations, and the past two decades have seen a surge of scholarship on women's spiritual writing: on medieval writers Hildegard of Bingen, Julian of Norwich, Christine de Pisan, and Margery Kempe; on early modern writers including Teresa of Ávila, Aemilia Lanyer, Lady Mary Wroth, Elizabeth Cary, Aphra Behn, Anne Hutchinson, and Anne Bradstreet; on nineteenth-century writers Elizabeth Barrett Browning, Sarah and Angelina Grimke, Sojourner Truth, Emily Dickinson, and Sarah Orne Jewett; and, among twentieth-century writers, E. M. Broner, Flannery O'Connor, Leslie Marmon Silko, Gloria Naylor, Alice Walker, and many others. As the diverse composition of this list suggests, much of women's spiritual writing is found not within theological or religious traditions but in fiction, poetry, autobiography, diaries, letters, and other literary forms.

Constructing spirituality through stories and poems is not unique to women's writing, of course, but it is perhaps uniquely important because women have traditionally been prohibited from taking part in official, church-sanctioned spiritual writing. Throughout religious history, men have been, almost exclusively, the writers of sermons, prayers, liturgies, hymns, and creeds. If naming is power, nowhere has that power been exercised so completely as in the development and exercise of religious language. Religion may in some sense be the final frontier for feminists who have worked for the past four decades to wrest language from patriarchal control. Although far greater gains have been made in some areas than others, feminists in virtually every field—history, science, linguistics, psychology, literature, education, business—have challenged and overturned beliefs and practices that treat patriarchal models of language as normative. Feminist theologians have been engaged in this same work, but resistance has been fierce. So total has been the patriarchal church's control of religious language that to refer to God in feminine terms, to speak the word of God as a female minister, or to question a creation myth that scapegoats women for original sin are still highly controversial speech acts in many quarters. Thus it is not surprising that women's spiritual writing often appears in genres that have, traditionally, been more accessible to women as writers.

This collection proposes that many women writers of poetry, diaries, autobiographies, and fiction, writing throughout literary history, have been engaged in the process of "doing theology"—that is, in exploring the nature of the sacred and the relationship of humans, especially women, to the sacred.[2] *Sacred* here refers not necessarily or exclusively to a transcendent God or a spiritual realm existing outside and apart from human experience. Rather, I am adopting a definition of the sacred or the spiritual shared by many feminist theologians and articulated by Carol Ochs as "coming into relationship."[3] Within this definition, spirituality is that which links us meaningfully with either an immanent or a transcendent other. Richard Grigg terms this "enactment theology," in which "the divine is a relation that human beings choose to enact."[4] Spirituality in this sense is thus located neither in an otherworldly realm nor within the individual but in the action of forming a relationship: whether with God, fellow human, nature, or an element of the self. According to Grigg, enactment theology thus "[reclaims] the whole of human experience and activity as the domain of divine influence."[5]

In this introduction, I draw on the works of feminist theologians to identify some of the central concerns of feminist theology and to show some of the striking parallels between the work of these theologians and that of the women writers represented here. While some readers may question this mingling of theological and literary discourses, I would argue that the terms *theological* and *literary* artificially separate and categorize disciplines that often have much to say in common. Nowhere is the falseness of this dichotomy illustrated more clearly than in the work of womanist theologians and literary critics. The term *womanist* comes from Alice Walker, who defines it in the epigraph to her collection of essays *In Search of Our Mothers' Gardens: Womanist Prose*.[6] Black feminist theologians have adopted this term and frequently apply Walker's definition to their own theological work; additionally, womanist theologians often look to the works of black women writers to illustrate points of their theology.[7] Thus I suggest that this easy collaboration of black women writers and black feminist theologians who share similar concerns provides an excellent feminist model for the cross-disciplinary work represented here.

Referring to feminist theology in the singular is problematic, for there are many feminist theologies reflecting the many and diverse experiences of women. As Susan Frank Parsons points out, although feminist theology largely grew out of the Western Christian tradition, "its bearings formed by the philosophical assumptions and political ideals of the Enlightenment," feminist theology has now "become something of a common discourse entered into by women of other faith and intellectual inheritance."[8] Nicola

Slee concurs: "Feminist spirituality . . . is a very broad-ranging movement, and takes expression in all of the major world religions, including Christianity, as well as in movements such as paganism and Wicca. There are also many women with no formal allegiance to any religious group who express their spiritual commitments in other ways, perhaps through work for justice, therapy, ecofeminism, or the arts. There is thus no *one* feminist spirituality, but many different traditions, movements, and forms."[9] Within feminist theologies and spiritualities, major movements arising since the early 1980s include womanist theology, lesbian spirituality, and *mujerista* theology. Likewise, despite feminist theology's roots in Western Christianity, feminist theologies and spiritualities reflecting other faiths, including Judaism, Buddhism, Islam, and Wicca and other earth-based religions, have emerged. All the feminist theologians I cite here, and almost all the writers represented in this collection, write out of some relationship to Christianity. While all of these writers challenge, revise, or dismiss aspects of Christian orthodoxy, they nonetheless struggle with this shared religious culture. I have selected these essays and these theologians knowing that this collection represents only an initial and very partial effort at bringing together the voices of feminist theologians and writers who are constructing their own forms of feminist god-talk.

In her essay "The Holy Spirit and Spirituality," Nicola Slee links the often unconventional forms of women's spiritual writing to the larger pattern of their traditional role in religion. As Slee points out, most of the women whose spiritual writings have been recognized and preserved as such have been mystics who conveyed their religious authority through reporting of supernatural visitations and other paranormal phenomena. "It is not difficult to see how these emphases [on mysticism] represent a kind of compensatory channeling of women's spirituality into permissible forms," Slee writes. "Denied liturgical office, authority had to come from supernatural sources rather than institutional ones; denied the possibility of consecrating the sacraments, women could nevertheless channel their adoration of the Eucharist into intense mystical devotion; denied overt expression, women's sexuality found shape in erotic devotion to Christ; denied official religious power, women could assume control over their bodies and food and thus tacitly transcend patriarchal rule."[10] More often, women's spiritual writing has not been preserved at all or, if preserved, not recognized as spiritual writing. "[U]ntil modern times," Slee writes, "women's spirituality was exercised mostly in the home (whether family or religious community) and thus took expression in the care and nurture of others and in what [Elizabeth] Johnson describes as 'the renewal of the fabric of life, the replenishment of physical and spiritual sustenance.' . . . [W]hen women did express their faith in more tangible form, it tended to be through small-scale and occasional means such as journals, letters, hymns, poems, or crafts which have not been accorded public recognition."[11] Thus women's spiritual writing has often been channeled into "minor" literary forms because women's spiritual work has, in general, been treated as marginal.

Just as traditional forms for spiritual writing have been inaccessible to many women writers, so too have common metaphors for spiritual experience often excluded women's knowledge, skills, and practices. Existing paradigms for spiritual experience are largely based on the metaphors provided by patriarchal religion. A fundamental task of feminist theology has been to demystify the origins of theological ideas and language by dissecting them as social constructs. As many feminist theologians have pointed out, all theology is rooted in human experience, but traditionally, patriarchal theology has not acknowledged this truth. "It has frequently been said that feminist theology draws on women's experience as a basic source of content as well as a criterion of truth," Rosemary Ruether writes. "There has been a tendency to treat this principle of 'experience' as unique to feminist theology . . . and to see it as distant from 'objective' sources of truth of classical theologies. This seems to be a misunderstanding of the experimental base of all theological reflection. What have been called the objective sources of theology, Scripture and tradition, are themselves codified collective human experience. . . . 'Experience' includes experience of the divine, experience of oneself, and experience of the community and the world, in an interacting dialectic."[12] Theologian Elizabeth Dodson Gray contends in *Sacred Dimensions of Women's Experience* that this process of sacred naming has resulted in "a strange landscape of the sacred. A few places, a few people, a few occasions are seen to concentrate and to embody the holy. . . . The only moments in time which become hallowed by an aura of holiness are those which involve these places, these people, these texts and these acts. The rest of life is perceived as a vast desert of the mundane, the *unholy*."[13] This spiritual paradigm is clearly reflected in the American story of the quest, in which the hero must flee home and community to achieve the sacred.[14]

Identifying and analyzing women's spiritual writing thus relies on redefining the sacred. In contrast to traditional theologies, which have frequently masked their basis in human experience, feminist theologians openly define spirituality out of their own life experiences. "The uniqueness of feminist theology lies not in its use of the criterion of experience," Rose-mary Ruether writes, "but rather use of *women's* experience, which has been almost entirely shut out of theological reflection in the past. The use of women's experience in feminist theology, therefore, explodes as a criti-cal force, exposing classical theology, including its codified traditions, as based on *male* experience rather than on universal human experience. Feminist theology makes the sociology of theological knowledge visible, no longer hidden behind mystifications of objectified divine and univer-sal authority."[15] In *Changing of the Gods: Feminism and the End of Tradi-tional Religions*, Naomi Goldenberg concurs: "Human beings of different sexes, ages, races, and environments have different experiences of spiritu-ality and religious phenomena. . . . Theologians are ignorant of what every anthropologist knows—i.e., that the forms of our thought derive from the forms of our culture."[16]

References to "women's experience" are of course fraught with prob-lems for feminists. Conflating the diverse experiences of women has some-times resulted in a false universalizing that has erased important elements of women's experience and at times served to mask privileges of race and class. However, in my view, this recognition of difference is misused if it makes impossible any discussion of sameness—that is, of shared experi-ence based on gender. Feminist scholars and writers are emerging out of virtually every religious tradition, and examination of the ways that these literatures and theological writings are linked is crucial to the develop-ment of a global feminist theology. "Feminist theologians . . . seek to re-construct the basic theological symbols of God, humanity, male and female, creation, sin and redemption, and the church, in order to define these sym-bols in a gender-inclusive and egalitarian way," Ruether writes.[17] Women writers are also engaged in this process of redefining the sacred. And de-spite the wide range and diversity of women's experience reflected in these texts, when they are deconstructed with regard to these basic theological symbols, strikingly similar patterns emerge.

Nearly all variations of feminist theology seek to undermine the dual-istic and hierarchical structures that dominate Christian tradition and, consequently, much of Western culture: as Rosemary Ruether expresses it, "[T]he alienation of the mind from the body; the alienation of the subjec-tive self from the objective world; the subjective retreat of the individual, alienated from the social community; the domination or rejection of na-ture by spirit—these all have roots in the apocalyptic-Platonic heritage of classical Christianity."[18] As many feminist theologians point out, this du-

alistic thinking has frequently led to privileging of characteristics and behaviors associated with maleness. Just as feminist theology has challenged
these dualisms, the writers represented here also challenge them in various
ways: by allowing for spiritualities that are heterogeneous and pluralistic,
embracing some aspects of religious tradition while rejecting others; by locating the sacred in the material world; by emphasizing the sacredness of
community instead of focusing on individual salvation; and by representing the body, and particularly the female body, as a site of the sacred. As
Carol Christ contends, "As women begin to question their historic subordination, they also challenge the adequacy of the dualistic, hierarchical,
and oppositional ways of viewing the world. If women are different from
but not inferior to men, then perhaps nature is different from but not inferior to spirit."[19]

One concern that unites the work of several writers represented here
is whether traditional religions can be meaningfully reformed to address
women's experience. Some of these authors write in dialogue with particular religious traditions; in doing so, they also critique and revise those traditions, particularly as they have been used to subordinate women. Others
draw on not one religious tradition but several, seemingly finding not conflict but harmony and understanding in the mingling of religious cultures.
While some religious writers and feminist theologians reject the idea that
traditional religions offer anything redeemable to women, Rosemary Ruether
finds reflected in this process of critique and revision a human need "to situate oneself meaningfully in history": "The effort to express contemporary
experience in a cultural and historical vacuum is both self-deluding and
unsatisfying. . . . To look back to some original base of meaning and truth
before corruption is to know that truth is more basic than falsehood. . . . To
find glimmers of this truth in submerged and alternative traditions through
history is to assure oneself that one is not mad or duped."[20] Several of these
writers thus seek to creatively reform oppressive religious traditions rather
than reject them outright.

In her study of Lady Mary Wroth's *Urania*, Sheila Cavanagh suggests
that one of the most remarkable aspects of Wroth's text is the unity of its
spiritual vision, which minimizes both divisions within Christianity and
tensions between Christianity and the occult. Wroth wrote at a time of
tensions between Protestants and Catholics that contributed to the Thirty
Years' War; but although her narrative is located in countries at the center of this conflict, Cavanagh writes, Wroth "suppresses the divisiveness
that characterized Protestant-Catholic relations during this period." Instead,

Wroth's narrative seems to support a "pan-Christian" worldview of the kind advocated by James I; in her narrative, "allied Christian rulers [unite] against non-Christian forces as they work to spread Christianity around the globe." Further, despite its positive portrayal of this quest to Christianize the world, the *Urania* also easily accommodates mysticism and the occult. "By incorporating such unfathomable entities and events into her text," Cavanagh argues, "Wroth extends her examination of the possibility of a 'unified universe.' Just as eliminating differences between Protestants and Catholics enables a vision of a united Christianity encircling the globe, ameliorating disjunctures between Christianity and the occult creates the space for a world where a wide range of previously competing spiritual forces can operate without undue friction. . . . Wroth appears to be imagining a universe that is unconstrained by conflicting spiritual powers."

In "Religious Reconstruction of Feminine Spirituality: Reading Past the Praise in *Salve Deus Rex Judaeorum*," Sue Matheson argues that Aemilia Lanyer's 1611 praise poem similarly appropriates and reconstructs religious tradition. Lanyer's text, Matheson argues, challenges "accepted and gendered notions of praise and blame" generated by the Judeo-Christian myth of the Fall. In doing so, Lanyer rewrites a theological history that has blamed women for the depravity of humankind. Further, Lanyer situates her reframing of this story in the midst of the *querelle des femmes* that began in the Middle Ages and still raged in the political arena in Lanyer's time. Moving this debate out of the political and into the religious arena, Lanyer ultimately argues "that women should be awarded a privileged but not a superior position in society." Lanyer, Matheson writes, "promotes the spiritual equality of the sexes rather than the elevation of one at the political expense of the other."

Roslyn Foy claims that modernist writer Mary Butts also sought spiritual enlightenment from a wide array of traditions. Like most modern artists, Butts experienced early-twentieth-century society as fragmented and chaotic; unlike most of her peers, however, she sought a spiritual answer to the troubles of the modern age. Prefiguring the concerns of ecofeminists much later in the century, Butts saw the destruction of nature as being closely linked to society's decline. Accordingly, she, like the romantics, immersed herself in the natural world in search of spiritual truths. Butts was also a student of mythology and the occult, and she experimented with drugs to try to induce a spiritual state. "What mattered for Butts," Foy argues, "was not the label of the spiritual revelation or connection. Rather, she drew from all sources to combat the spiritual failure of the world she inhabited."

In examining the poetry of Irish writer Nuala Ní Dhomhnaill, Kimberly Myers suggests that Ní Dhomhnaill usurps some of the mythology and iconography of Catholicism while rejecting aspects of it that have been used to oppress and control women. In particular, Myers argues that Ní Dhomhnaill critiques the way Catholicism has been used to repress female sexuality and to "[consign] women to either the role of virgin or that of mother." In response to this tradition, in some of her early poems Ní Dhomhnaill reframes the characters of Eve and Mary, re-creating icons neither guilty nor virginal but exultant in their fully human sexuality. In addition to revising Christian myths, Ní Dhomhnaill combines traditional religion with "pagan" elements that do not represent flesh and spirit as oppositional.

Also pervasive in the women's writings examined here are spiritualities that are engaged with the material and political world rather than withdrawn from it. Several of these texts show an intimate engagement between spirituality and politics. They locate spiritual truths not outside or above the physical world but in the midst of it; spiritual practices are frequently portrayed as vehicles for mending relationships and righting injustices. As Rosemary Ruether points out, feminist theologies reflect a similar focus on "this-worldly redemptive hope," which focuses less on the promise of life after death and more on "some combination of personal conversion and progressive or revolutionary reform of social structures that will overcome poverty, tyranny, and war. . . . Feminism sees patriarchy as a multilayered system of domination, centered in male control of women but including class and race hierarchy, generational hierarchy, and clericalism, and expressed also in war and in domination of nature."[21] Spiritual quest in these texts is thus intimately linked with social quest; they are, as Carol Christ writes, "two dimensions of a single struggle."[22]

In her essay on seventeenth-century diarist Jane Lead, Avra Kouffman argues that Lead frequently uses spiritual metaphors and Christian iconography to comment indirectly on economic and social practices of the time, particularly those that disadvantaged women. Kouffman suggests that Lead's concern with economic matters stemmed from her own precarious financial situation, first as a woman unmarried by choice and later as a widow. Throughout her diary, Lead laments her inability to focus solely on spiritual matters because she must be concerned with bodily survival and safety.

As Lead's text makes clear, while women may be powerful in the spirit world, in the material world they are at constant risk, in part because of social and economic injustice.

In "The Mirroring of Heaven and Earth: Female Spirituality in Elizabeth Prentiss's *Stepping Heavenward* and Elizabeth Stuart Phelps's *The Gates Ajar*," Rory Dicker discusses these two novels of the 1860s as responses to the nineteenth century's cult of domesticity, which recognized women's religious role primarily in terms of their obligations to husbands and children. Dicker argues that, despite contemporary views of ways that the cult of domesticity was used to limit and control women's autonomy, reigning over domestic life accorded women significant power and influence, if only within a limited realm. Further, the cult of domesticity valued women not only for "the domestic worlds they created and maintained" but also for their inner lives: "the moral qualities their minds and souls promoted." Dicker argues that Prentiss's and Phelps's novels place renewed emphasis on women's internal spiritual lives, depicting female religious experience as "a way for women to gain autonomy, self-worth, and self-determination."

In "The Spirit of a People: The Politicization of Spirituality in Julia Alvarez's *In the Time of the Butterflies*, Ntozake Shange's *sassafrass, cypress & indigo*, and Ana Castillo's *So Far from God*," Holly Blackford argues that modern ethnic women novelists counter the assertion of meaningless-ness that pervades the white male postmodern novel. These writers "fore-ground the presence of spiritual healers, oracles, saints, martyrs, visions, conjurings, and allusions to myth," Blackford writes; "In the view of these contemporary ethnic women writers, the work of the postmodern ethnic novel is to heal and transform the spirit of the ethnic community." Blackford asserts that Alvarez's novel condemns the Catholic Church for its traditional division of the material and spiritual worlds, charging this lack of political engagement on the part of the church with abetting the rise of an oppressive government. To avoid complicity with the church's nonengagement, her protagonist must merge her spiritual and political activities and take a stance for her people. In *sassafrass, cypress & indigo*, similarly, the Catholic Church resists activism in the everyday life of the community. The alternative spirituality that Shange's characters create blends magic and mythology from a wide range of cultures; its purpose is to heal the African American community from its history of oppression. In *So Far from God*, Ana Castillo creates female characters who "are simultaneously real women and saints, martyrs, and/or spirits," Blackford writes. The symbolic names of the sisters and mother at the center of Castillo's narrative—Fe (Faith),

Esperanza (Hope), Caridad (Charity), and Sophi (Wisdom) — suggest abstract qualities; however, Castillo translates these abstractions into activism as each of the women works to embody these qualities in her New Mexican community.

Several of these women writers' texts also emphasize not individual spiritual quest, but engagement with community as a source of spiritual truth. As Rosemary Ruether writes, one aspect of the dualism endemic in Western culture is "the subjective retreat of the individual, alienated from the social community."[23] In *Women and Spirituality,* Carol Ochs finds this same male-centeredness in the myth of the spiritual journey: "Since traditional spirituality has been male-centered, it has been regarded as an extension of the male maturational process that emphasizes individuation — coming into selfhood."[24] Conversely, most feminist theologies emphasize not solitary retreat but relationship as the source of the sacred. "Mystics have usually been pictured as struggling alone for their salvation," Ochs writes. "Women who are aware of the dependency of infancy and the mutuality of marriage can show that the spiritual struggle is shared and that salvation is the overcoming of separation."[25]

In her essay on Teresa of Ávila's 1577 *Interior Castle* (1577), Elizabeth Adams argues that Teresa's text is not only a "theological instruction manual" on prayer but "a persuasive argument for communal solidarity" in the time of the Spanish Inquisition. Although she writes as spiritual advisor to her sisters, Teresa assumes an equal status with them rather than the authoritative position of a religious leader. While granting the sisters a measure of independence to make their own decisions, however, Teresa encourages not merely the pursuit of their own salvation but their concern for their neighbors; this, she writes, is the true sign of spiritual progress. Resisting traditions of strict enclosure for nuns and of the mystic as solitary, Teresa travels freely throughout the countryside and grounds her spiritual concerns in the real social and historical problems of her time.

Similarly, Roxanne Harde argues that Emily Dickinson's poetry employs friendship as a theological construct that replaces a dominant concern with the self in relation to God. Although she employs a language "firmly tied to the discourse, doctrine, and rites of the Christian Church in which she was raised," Harde argues, the substance of Dickinson's faith was grounded in the material world and, particularly, in friendship. Dickinson's intimate relationship with her sister-in-law, Susan Gilbert Dickinson, Harde claims, "gave her the trust and mutuality necessary for a spiritual life." The influence of love and friendship on Dickinson's spiritual beliefs is particularly reflected in her poems about death, which mix the language of conventional Christian consolation with a message that real consolation is to be found in connection with others here on earth. While the church provided the language for Dickinson's religious poetry, it did not provide the answers to her eschatological concerns. Those answers were found in loving friendships, as her religious poetry makes clear.

Countering Western religious traditions that denigrate the physical body, particularly the female body, as impure, several of the women writers examined here explore a spirituality that is intimately connected to women's bodies and physical experiences. As Sharon Farmer writes in *Embodied Love: Sensuality and Relationship as Feminist Values*,

> These physical differences [between women and men] have served as primary reasons, in the Jewish and Christian traditions, for women's exclusion from the priesthood and from ritual functions. Theologians and philosophers, moreover, have cited these differences to support a gender dichotomy that associates women with the more physical side of human nature and men with the more spiritual or rational. Underlying this gender dichotomy is a dualism in Western thought that places mind and body, or the spiritual and material realm, in opposition to each other and values mind and the spiritual realm over body and the material realm.[26]

In her analysis of Christina Rossetti's 1859 poem "Goblin Market," Debra Cumberland likens Rossetti's appropriation of spiritual subject matter and bodily imagery to the practices of medieval women mystics. "Mysticism appealed to women such as Rossetti since it offered an alternative vocabulary that needed no interpretation from a higher authority," Cumberland writes. Interpreting Rossetti's poem as a religious allegory of temptation, fall, and redemption, Cumberland describes "Goblin Market" as a performative enactment of faith rather than a verbal statement of faith. Denied access to the "masculine discourse associated with the university and the pulpit, and forbidden to write in the traditional theological discourse," Cumberland writes, women "needed to seek out other means of interpreting Scripture." Thus Laura's seduction and violation by the "goblin men" is depicted as a "symbolic loss of virginity" that is restored by her sister Lizzie's offering of her own body as Eucharist. Like many of the medieval mystics, Rossetti eroticizes spiritual experience; in "Goblin Market," however, it is the *female* body that is eroticized and that symbolizes a promise of redemption.

A number of the twentieth-century writers examined here also locate spirituality in women's bodily experience. In "Faces of the Virgin in Sandra Cisneros's *Woman Hollering Creek*," Jacqueline Doyle argues that Cisneros and other contemporary Chicana writers are reclaiming the myth of the *Virgen* as it has been used by patriarchal theologies and institutions to enforce passive and subservient behavior in women. The *Virgen* has long been used by the Catholic Church as a symbol venerating virginity, chastity, motherhood, obedience, humility, and self-sacrifice. Conversely, the figure of *La Malinche*, Cortes's native mistress and interpreter who betrayed her people, has been established as the symbol of woman as sexual wanton, whore, traitor. In her fiction—replete with women who are neither virgin nor whore—Cisneros complicates this dichotomy, illustrating ways that images of both the virgin and the whore have been used to appropriate women's sexuality and control their lives. Cisneros's fiction undertakes the task of healing this artificial cultural split between *Virgen* and *La Malinche*, dispelling the notion that suffering is sacred and that spirituality is located outside and above the body. Cisneros thus reclaims the myth of the *Virgen* by re-creating her in the form of "real women": "The ones I've loved all my life. . . . Las girlfriends. Las comadres. Our mamas and tias. Passionate and powerful, tender and volatile, brave. And, above all, fierce."

In "Marvelous Arithmetics: Womanist Spirituality in the Poetry of Audre Lorde," Sharon Barnes analyzes Lorde's treatment of the erotic in her poetry as a deeply spiritual force that provides an essential connection between people. Barnes argues that "Lorde's understanding of the erotic shares deep connections with Alice Walker's concept of womanism, including her focus on immanental divinity in the physical world." Like much of Alice Walker's work, Lorde's poetry embodies a spirituality deeply connected to physical experience, to relationships, and to the earth. In the poems that explore her own experience of breast cancer, Lorde resists the medical establishment's desire to focus only on the physical and aesthetic loss of mastectomy. While the events Lorde recalls in these poems are deeply physical, recalling her diagnosis, mastectomy, and chemotherapy and the pain and exhaustion accompanying illness and treatment, these physical experiences are always intimately tied to spiritual issues: relationships with friends, enemies, lovers, and families; the meaning of her remaining life; the extension of her life and work into a spiritual life-beyond-death.

In her analysis of Linda Hogan's *Solar Storms*, Ellen Arnold points out that Hogan uses the scarred body of her protagonist, Angel, to construct a story about boundaries: between Euro-American and native cultures;

between history and the present; between spirit and the material world. Angel, a mixedblood young woman raised in foster care, embarks on a quest in search of her mother and her history. Symbols suggesting borders and boundaries abound in Hogan's text, but none is so prominent as the "boundary" of Angel's skin. Her dark skin and scarred face, reflecting an ethnic heritage and a violent past of which she knows nothing, "reflect back to her a history of violence and victimization," Arnold writes. By the novel's end, these scars come to represent a healing: "no seamless erasure of wounds, no restoration or harmonious balance," Arnold argues, "but a dynamic process grounded in the interdependency of destruction and creation."

These essays suggest broad commonality between the concerns of many feminist theologians and women writers constructing representations of women's spirituality. The writers discussed in these essays challenge definitions of spirituality that separate the sacred from embodied, interpersonal experience and from political life. In the work of these women writers, spiritual experience is clearly grounded in the physical and political realities of women's lives: in the female body, in an interdependent community, and in a material and political world. The shared themes that I have discussed here are by no means exhaustive; readers who bring different expertise than my own to their reading will surely see important themes that I have overlooked. I have therefore arranged the essays chronologically, allowing readers to discover connections among them. Although I aimed for broad representation, I selected these essays, ultimately, for their individual strengths. Thus, while readers will undoubtedly find gaps in the chronology, I hope that the broad selection of authors discussed here nonetheless suggests the scope of the history and diversity of women's spiritual writing.

In the nearly forty years since the beginning of the contemporary women's movement, patriarchal religious traditions have been increasingly interrogated for the ways in which their doctrines, writings, symbols, and rituals have been used to exclude, control, and silence women. While many women and men have worked to reform oppressive traditions from within, many have also turned to sources outside conventional religious practice for spiritual insights. At this intersection of literary and theological studies, readers and scholars have found a rich tradition of women's spiritual writing stretching back to the earliest women writers. In some cases, these texts have long been suppressed or discounted because they were written by women. In other cases, familiar texts are now being given a new reading because of new definitions of spirituality made possible by feminist theologies. Women writers have produced many sacred texts; we as readers are now learning to recognize them.

NOTES

1. Kristina K. Groover, *The Wilderness Within: American Women Writers and Spiritual Quest* (Fayetteville: University of Arkansas Press, 1999).

2. Endless distinctions between the concerns of theology and those of spirituality are possible; for example, some writers use the term *spirituality* to refer specifically to spiritual movements outside the established church; similarly, for some writers, *theology* refers only to the study of religious doctrines. I am using the terms more broadly and inclusively to suggest their shared concern with the sacred.

3. Carol Ochs, *Women and Spirituality*, 2d ed. (Lanham, Md.: Rowman and Littlefield, 1997), 10.

4. Richard Grigg, *When God Becomes Goddess: The Transformation of American Religion* (New York: Continuum, 1995), 55.

5. Ibid., 47.

6. Alice Walker, *In Search of Our Mothers' Gardens: Womanist Prose* (San Diego: Harcourt Brace Jovanovich, 1983), xi–xii.

7. The American Theological Library Association database lists more than two hundred entries published since 1987 whose titles include the term *womanist*.

8. Susan Frank Parsons, preface to *The Cambridge Companion to Feminist Theology*, ed. Susan Frank (New York: Cambridge University Press, 2002), xiii–xiv.

9. Nicola Slee, "The Holy Spirit and Spirituality," in Parsons, *Cambridge Companion*, 176.

10. Ibid., 174–75.

11. Ibid., 172–73.

12. Rosemary Radford Ruether, *Sexism and God-Talk: Toward a Feminist Theology*, 2d ed. (Boston: Beacon Press, 1993), 12–13.

13. Elizabeth Dodson Gray, *Sacred Dimensions of Women's Experience* (Wellesley, Mass.: Roundtable Press, 1998), 2.

14. Carol Christ's groundbreaking book *Diving Deep and Surfacing: Women Writers on Spiritual Quest*, 3d ed. (Boston: Beacon Press, 1995), has been formative in my own thinking about literature and feminist theology. I am indebted to her theological and literary insights and to her feminist vision of the sacred.

15. Ruether, *Sexism and God-Talk*, 13.

16. Naomi Goldberg, *Changing of the Gods: Feminism and the End of Traditional Religions* (Boston: Beacon Press, 1979), 115.

17. Rosemary Radford Ruether, "The Emergence of Christian Feminist Theology," in Parsons, *Cambridge Companion*, 4.

18. Rosemary Radford Ruether, "Motherearth and the Megamachine: A Theology of Liberation in a Feminine, Somatic and Ecological Perspective," in *Womanspirit Rising: A Feminist Reader in Religion*, ed. Carol P. Christ and Judith Plaskow (San Francisco: Harper and Row, 1979), 44.

19. Christ, *Diving Deep and Surfacing*, 25.

20. Ruether, *Sexism and God-Talk*, 18.

21. Rosemary Radford Ruether, *Women and Redemption: A Theological History* (Minneapolis: Fortress Press, 1998), 274.

22. Christ, *Diving Deep and Surfacing*, 8.

23. Ruether, "Motherearth," 44.

24. Ochs, *Women and Spirituality*, 2.

25. Ibid., 3.

26. Sharon A. Farmer, introduction to *Embodied Love: Sensuality and Relationship as Feminist Values*, ed. Paula M. Cooey, Sharon A. Farmer, and Mary Ellen Ross (San Francisco: Harper and Row, 1987), 1–2.

1

THE ARCHITECTONICS OF DESIRE

Pageantry, Procession, and Protagonists
in Teresa of Ávila's *Interior Castle* (1577)

ELIZABETH J. ADAMS

Scholars of philosophy and religion often liken Teresa of Ávila's *Interior Castle*, or *Las Moradas* (translated *Dwelling Places*), to other narratives of mystical experience by male writers from Cabala and Sufi as well as Christian mystical traditions to evaluate its worth as a spiritual masterpiece.[1] What is gained in such examinations is a broad appreciation of the writer's profundity. What is often lost, however, is the tangible sense of place and time that the work transmits to its readers, which could contribute toward even more insightful readerly interpretations of textual meaning than those gained by studies limited to comparative studies of mystical intellectual traditions. Feminist scholars struggle to reconstruct women's intellectual and bodily presences in human communities to better attempt a reconfiguration of "the whole story."

When she wrote this classic study of prayer, Teresa de Ávila, formerly Doña Teresa de Ahumada, signed her name simply Teresa de Jesús and wrote to specific audiences of nuns and other interested readers in the vernacular Spanish of Castile instead of the scholarly Latin of late medieval Europe. She had attended none of Spain's great universities such as Alcalá de Henares or the University of Salamanca.[2] Teresa's "degree" waited until 1970—four centuries—when the Roman Catholic Church awarded her the title "Doctor of the Church," thus verifying its official recognition of her relevance for modern readers. The same ecclesiastic authority had declared her a saint much earlier, in 1622.

Contextual renderings locate a writer inside her life's experiences. I "enliven" the text with its author and narrator and with historical communities of readers to show how Teresa of Ávila's narrative functions as a theological instruction manual of mystical experience for women *and* as an argument for communal solidarity. From the historical Teresa's point of view, both instruction and persuasive rhetoric were needed as the Spanish Inquisition knocked at her door to challenge her leadership of some fourteen convents of nuns.

MANU-SCRIPTING

Teresa de Jesús writes alone in her narrow cell. Her pen bites furiously into the thick, fibrous papers of a tablet that rests precariously on the window sill that serves as a desk in the sparsely furnished room. It is November 1577, and she is sequestered in Ávila behind the bare walls of San José; established in 1562, it is the first of seventeen Carmelite reform convents that she will have founded throughout Spain before her death in 1582. San José is situated on the side of a gently sloping hill, outside the medieval walls that surround the town of Ávila. A grand gate swings open to admit both citizens and strangers into the city's depths.

Unlike most other writers of her day, Teresa specifically addresses women readers, as she states in the Prologue to her new work. Certainly, on a few occasions, contemporary male authors write paternalistic advice to women regarding proper marriage and household manners.[3] Teresa, however, desires the attention of sister nuns who seek "marriage" to a divine "Spouse"; these potential audiences reside in convents she founded in Castile and Andalusia.[4] Her narrator in the *Interior Castle* chats easily with her women readers, addressing them as equals who have common concerns.

Teresa began the writing process at her convent in Toledo nearly six months ago in June, when religious processions thronged city streets and other public byways to celebrate the Feast of the Holy Trinity. Earlier, in April and May, the vernal season had stimulated a series of rogations and parades, formed to petition God's protection for the year's seedlings and crops.[5] Other celebrations had wound up and down the streets, stopping at various stations as they proceeded toward a local shrine or to a church. For instance, a priest led a Feast of Corpus Christi procession, with parishioners trailing behind as the celebration carried itself back to the altar at the center of the cathedral's nave where it began. But now, as Teresa completes her task at San José, the weather has changed to icy coldness. Soon, on the Feast of the Epiphany, scriptures read at communal celebrations will refer to the biblical account of the Magi's elaborate procession to the Christ Child's manger, and theatrical presentations held inside because of the cold will re-create the scene.

As she thus remembers the approach of the end of the liturgical year, Teresa might dwell for a moment too on other kinds of processions, but these would have affected her quite differently. Prisoners make their way in mule-drawn carts and by foot to an *auto-da-fé*, a public trial, including sentencing and sometimes an execution. Some of those people ascending the steps to the platform are accused of heresy. This fact strikes a chord in Teresa's being, but not a harmonious one. Just the year before she began writing, inquisitors in Seville had questioned her about her alleged connections to the *alumbrados*, who were thought to have promoted sexual freedom along with a kind of mysticism that disengaged them from sacraments and priests. Recently (1574), the Inquisition had tried members of this group in nearby Llerena for heresy, so any accounts of mystical experience are particularly scrutinized, especially those written by women.[6] The fact that several of Teresa's sisters were her accusers weighs heavily on her mind as she writes.[7]

As Teresa rests her pen for a moment to gaze out the window into the night,[8] she may be remembering her father, grandfather, and uncles, who in 1485 suffered public humiliation in an *auto-da-fé* for another act thought to be heretical, their alleged return to their Jewish faith. Her ancestors were forced to parade through the streets of Toledo wearing the yellow and red *sanbendito* or sign of the penitent.[9] After the family moved to Ávila, Teresa's father, Don Alonzo Sánchez de Cepeda, had appealed successfully for the status of a *hidalgo*, or lesser noble. Alonso, who died in 1543 when Teresa was twenty-eight, was known for his Christian piety, but in 1577 the racist *limpieza de sangre* (purity of blood) statutes keep some former Jews who have become Christian (referred to as *conversos*) from occupying positions of leadership in secular and religious circles. Teresa's convents do not honor these decrees, at least not in her lifetime. Furthermore, her reform efforts promote equality among members of the convent, in contrast to many other religious communities that separate women by class and social rank, giving the nobility separate quarters and permitting them servants.[10]

Although she is now enclosed behind convent walls, Teresa de Jesús is certainly not isolated from what lies outside them. She moves regularly about the countryside in a mule-drawn wagon, stopping at various locations to establish foundations for her sisters to inhabit; her perambulations gain her the nickname "gadabout" from Felipe de Sega, one of her detractors, who believes in the strict enclosure of all nuns. Teresa commandeers a unique procession of muleteer, mule, and wagon, sometimes sharing the tiny space inside the vehicle with other nuns. On these trips, her imagination connects "outside" scenic spaces with an interior geography of prayer; as she "sees" with the "outer" eyes of sense experience and with the "inner" eyes of the soul, processions unfold in mental and physical landscapes. In the *Interior Castle*, the concrete dramas of public and religious life become part of the narrative descriptions of the abstract "eternity" of the soul as it moves toward the divine presence in the center of the castle.

This "marriage" of materiality with immateriality is found as well in her political rhetoric, which depicts the author's struggle to maintain community in concrete social and historical realities. As her primary readers identify the narrator of this powerful story with the historical Teresa, they remember their common experiences through the narrator's many references to them in the story; as these readers learn to respect the narrator's capable guidance through the labyrinth of the soul, they may trust her leadership through other complicated and dangerous events, in this case, difficult times for the Carmelites in 1577.

The narrative's symbolic language supports the dominant metaphor of procession to reveal a pageantry of richly expressive words that "dress up" the account of the life of prayer and enhance the text's political argument. In depictions of nature and domestic settings that are familiar to her readers, an aesthetic of beauty supports the political rhetoric as the narrator's voice speaks with vibrant poignancy. The beautifully described dwelling places invite readers' active participation in solidarity with the narrator as they process with the hero-soul in her journey toward the central dwelling places where God resides. Through an act of transference, the journey with the story's protagonist becomes the reader's journey as well. God's grace extends to them as the "light" that emanates from the center to help guide them into the cavernous depths of the soul and as the "light" of wisdom emanating from the mind of the narrator as well.

My argument is not so ambitious as to attempt to solve the mystery of the text's language; neither does it claim to discern perfectly the writer's intent. It does not argue what must be the case, only what might reasonably be so, given a certain reading of the narrative. It asks a question and describes a possible interpretation in which the question may be heard and addressed: "Given certain events in 1577, how could readers interpret this text, surely an account of mystical experience, as also as a narrative used to build solidarity in women's communities?"

The language of the *Interior Castle* is political, where *political* connotes "the art or science of governing" (*Oxford English Dictionary*), as the term *politica* was probably understood in Teresa's day. Yet it is "political" in its theological usage as well. In early modern Spain, procession is a familiar theological motif to describe philosophical and theological principles.[11] Teresa could safely use the metaphor to help argue for her manuscript's orthodoxy in order to protect it, after its publication, from being placed on the Index of forbidden readings and to aid the text's safe passage through the scrutiny of the first round of male readers, the *letrados* or "learned men." The text is "political" in other ways as well, as its argument is extended to listening or reading audiences. The narrative exercises ethos, pathos, and logos to build the character of a narrator who reaches out to its women readers and listeners construed as fully capable of comprehending the message. These audiences respond to her appeals to both their reason and their emotions as they consider the rich rewards of living in community in pursuit of their common vocation.

While any reader may accept an invitation to participate in the story's plot, Teresa's narrator focuses on the author's contemporary sisters. The narrator uses a variety of rhetorical ploys to invite audience interest and participation in the text's argument. She applies digression to exit temporarily from the storyteller's description of the procession that propels the plot forward. She encourages, advises, apologizes for her unworthiness, confesses her sins, and presses readers to continue reading. She often speaks from the perspective of the first-person-singular "I," but she shifts to a focus on a third-person "it" (sometimes "she") to describe the soul's movement forward; this tactical move toward general pronouns promotes an inclusiveness, the possibility of any soul's participation. Shifts of mood are frequent and contradictory; for example, the timbre of the narrator's voice changes from confidence to contrition, from self-doubt to exhilaration, to portray a full range of human emotions.

References to her poor health and sense of impending death construct a persona that contradicts itself. The narrator, aware of her mortality and frustrated with the shortcomings of language to represent her experiences adequately, also worries about wasting the reader's time. Yet she continues to pepper the text with personal anecdotes and lessons learned from life experiences, thereby in a sense "wasting" narrative time. Eerily, her comments about her sense of impending death, her own sense of her limitations of time in her life's story, prepare the reader for the plot's demise as well, as it dwindles to nothing in the last pages. This *memento mori* or meditation on death extends the subject of limitations to her readers to prompt them to make choices. For instance, should they recommit themselves toward building communal solidarity when the order is experiencing such chaos? The narrative argues "yes," echoing the narrator's choice for community.

Through these excursions off the main path—through the digressions, for example—readers become increasingly aware of the narrator's character, and this awareness soon changes to the knowledge of her identity as a member of a community of women to whom she is uniquely and passionately connected. For instance, in the Prologue, before the story begins, the narrator drones on about her physical maladies, presenting a self-conscious, fearful self, not a persona that might confidently stride through the dwelling places of the *Interior Castle* with readers in tow. This readers' guide, who begins her assignment reluctantly, is someone plagued by physical and mental maladies. Lightheadedness, dizziness, and tinnitus (ringing in the ears) scatter her thoughts while she attempts to concentrate on her work: "Por tener la cabeza tres meses ha con un ruido y flaqueza tan grande que aun los negocios forzosos escrivo con pena" (For three months, I've had such noise in my head and dizziness that even writing about necessary business matters causes pain).[12] Furthermore, she worries that, in trying to remember what she has already said, she will repeat herself and make her headache worse. How should readers trust this worried self-doubter to lead them through the pages that follow?

Yet immediately the voice has become intimate, familiar. What reader, writer, or listener has not known sleepless nights, forgetfulness, pounding headaches, and other physical ailments that interrupt trains of thought? Such expressions of very human "failings" could serve the writer well: to set a mood in which to construct a pathos or empathy connecting reader to narrator, thus portraying the reader as "inside" rather than outside the circle of the narrator. Because the rhetoric thus implies a body-mind syncretism, it sets the stage for a reception of the story's argument that may be more deeply integrated into the psyche than that effected by dry intellectual discourse. While the narrator implies that her work is an act of self-sacrificial love as she overcomes many obstacles to benefit readers who ask questions about prayer, this kind of discourse about the bodily malaise that accompanies her writing efforts practically dissolves once the story gains momentum. While the voice strengthens in its resolve, she presents readers who have been softened by just enough pity to see the "other," or the narrator, as the "self."

The narrator thus invites any reader/listener/writer to join the interpreters' circle, even as she addresses herself in particular to a sixteenth-century community of nuns. As she weaves these "irregularities" of text into her account of the processional move toward the center, she sends a subliminal message to her primary audiences and others as well that reads something like this: "We're all in this together . . . for better or for worse, but, ultimately, for the better."

To continue pondering the subtleties of the text's political language in order to show how it argues for communal solidarity, I divide its audiences into four categories: primary, secondary, tertiary, and official, all constructed by the *Interior Castle*'s narrative language. The primary audience is sisters in Teresa's order who probably know about the substantial dangers confronting the community at the time. Secondary readers are all women, secular or religious, who wish to grow spiritually through prayer, yet who may have little knowledge of the work's contexts. Tertiary readers are men who wish to learn about prayer, possibly for their own spiritual health, but also perhaps because they are spiritual directors who wish to learn how to direct women, for example, in confession. Finally, the official audience is male readers who are charged with examining her work, most likely for its heretical content.

In the Prologue the narrator provides a basis for interpreting "degrees" of audiences in the text ("[I]t's nonsensical to think what I say could matter to other persons") as well as establishing the theme of humility, which is a main theme of the discourse:

> The one who ordered me to write told me that the nuns in these monasteries of our Lady of Mount Carmel need someone to answer their questions about prayer and that he thought they would better understand the language used between women, and that because of the love they bore me they would pay more attention to what I would tell them. I thus understood that it was important for me to manage to say something. So, I shall be speaking to them while I write; it's nonsense to think that what I say could matter to other persons. . . . And it should be very clear that if I manage to say something well the Sisters will understand that this does not come from me since there would be no foundation for it, unless the Lord gave it to me. (34)

By identifying "other persons" thus, she immediately challenges "others" to join the text's audiences and begins to create a space for their existences. What she says directly to her sisters about how her knowledge is derived from God, not directly from herself, serves as a "leveling" device to affirm her status as a sister among sisters. The text begins with hierarchical "power-over" patterns, simply because the author *is* an author and is "authorized" to write *to* them, which obviously privileges the voice that speaks. Yet this model is deconstructed early because the women all belong to an elite "club" whose membership converses in the "language used between women" in their acknowledgment of common dependence on God for their very existence.

Thus the narrator begins to construct her self-representation on the model of the Christian whose weaknesses of body and mind encourage her to rely not on her own strength but on God's, an account of Christian virtue that most of her readers would recognize. What Teresa's narrator says about her lowly status as a woman, which readers of a later generation might interpret simply as self-devaluation, is an example of a traditional way many Christian writers at the time affirmed God's goodness (in spite of my unworthiness, see what great things God does!). Teresa's narrator claims the virtue of humility to shield herself against critics who say she is usurping the prerogative of male theologians or those the Roman Catholic Church has officially designated as teachers of Christian doctrine. Male readers are not to presume that she writes for them; she argues that anything said well is a reflection of God's glory, not of her own personal strength as a writer or thinker. Furthermore, she writes not of her own free will but by the command of a superior male authority. Her hope is that this logic will disarm critical male readers, or her official audiences, as well as endear her to her primary readers whose attention she especially solicits. Jane Ackerman argues that the virtues of humility and obedience, especially cultivated in Teresa's convents as "feminine" assets, are described better as "shared qualities that bound women to each other than ones reinforcing hierarchical separations then usual between men and women."[13]

The narrator rather dutifully establishes the following elements of the narrative: her sisters are her primary readers, her purpose is to write about prayer, she writes because she is commanded to, and, finally, she is not in the mood to do it. However, there is one startlingly strong statement here: "because of the love they bear me," her sisters will pay more attention. Translation: "Sisters, if you love me, pay attention!" Teresa's narrator at once disarms unfriendly readers who might charge her with unseemly aggression through her insistence that she begins only at another's instigation (sheer duty), yet she nudges women audiences to continue reading the text in the light of friendship. In this Prologue no startling symbol or analogy enriches the writing. We meet a nonthreatening narrator who uses language familiar to different kinds of audiences to convince them that she is authorized for the task — and that they should thus, just as dutifully, begin reading.

Although the narrator wants to verify the status of her reading community of nuns as equal partners in a common endeavor and seems welcoming to other women readers as well as to nonthreatening male readers serious about studying prayer, her tone is often sarcastic and ironic when she considers male official readers who might prove dangerous to her reform efforts. But even these readers are included in a process of empowerment by the story's end because they are given theological and practical instruction about guiding women. Critical male readers who only skim the surface looking for heresy could also experience "conversion" to become more empathetic readers. Yet the narrative discourse constructs official male readers as quite possibly rejecting this kind of empowerment because it requires that they acknowledge the existence of a woman's spiritual wisdom that may be much more advanced and superior to their own. In fact, the *Interior Castle*, read from cover to cover, presents precisely that dilemma to male readers. Furthermore, since the text is obviously focused on women readers, male audiences may feel excluded as the "radical other" and may thus become reluctant or resistant readers, just as many women have felt excluded for centuries as they are left out of or barred from different kinds of public discourses.

Yet the situation of historical readers is even more complicated than this: some *women* readers are hypercritical, even if they are included automatically in the circle of privileged readers. In a more detailed discussion, below, of the events in Seville that occurred shortly before the *Interior Castle* was written, we will consider how Teresa's defiant sisters, those who turned her in to the Inquisition, are constructed by the text as having been shepherded back into the fold. One might say that they are "wooed" back. Whether they actually, historically felt restored to the community is another issue.

Now let us turn to how the narrator praises male readers' abilities to follow the text's advice, thus creating a reader who potentially acquiesces to the obvious fact of women's spiritual wisdom. If he chooses to stand in relationship to the text with that provision acknowledged and agreed to, he may feel welcomed (and become an asset to her reform movement):

In difficult matters, even though it seems to me that I understand and that I speak the truth, I always use this expression "it seems to me." For if I am mistaken, I'm very much prepared to believe what those who have a great deal of learning say. Even though they have not experienced these things, very learned men have a certain I don't know what; for since God destines them to give light to His Church, He enlightens them that they might acknowledge a truth when presented with it. And if they do not live a dissipated life but are God's servants, they are never surprised by His grandeur; they have come to understand well that He can do ever more and more. And finally, even though some things are not so well explained, these learned men will find others in their books through which they will see that these things could take place. I have had a great deal of experience with learned men, and have also had experience with half-learned ones, fearful ones; these latter cost me dearly. (88–89)

We could read this passage this way: if they are God's servants, my official readers will know that God can do things that they have not experienced personally. If these male readers read carefully and widely, and of course that is exactly what learned men do, they will find other men or male authors who concur. Agreeing with the narrator on this point means, in fact, that the male reader is listening to a woman's advice; however, this compliance with female guidance may be perceived as an affront to certain readers' masculinity.

The author confuses the male reader even more by at once both affirming and repudiating male advice giving. On the one hand, she directs male readers to consult books of wisdom before rashly judging women's spiritual experiences; on the other hand, she warns her sisters about male advisors who fail to understand and therefore belittle their accounts. Her sisters know that part of the trial of choosing life in a convent is putting up with men who cannot understand, so that it is best to attempt to find a guide who can hear them correctly. The narrator attempts to reconcile at least two audiences so that all her readers can proceed as one to the end of the story, or to what the narrator portrays as the center of God's love. In her attempts to reconcile these disparate audiences, she also points to her own authoritative guidance, but the tension in the text is never quite re-solved, at least as it regards her male audiences. By the time her sister read-ers, even the rebellious and reluctant ones, have finished the narrative discourse of the *Interior Castle*, all of them are constructed as having received its treasures and as having become brave and wise in the process.

"Centering" the Soul as Reader

I argue that the narrator's ability to divide her audiences into groups and to address them singly *as* groups is how she builds solidarity, especially among primary women readers, who then see clearly the narrator's obvious bias for them as she ushers all readers through the labyrinth of the soul. Teresa, the author behind the narrator's voice, appeals to her community through a choice of images they will recognize, images gleaned from particular geographical and historical locations. That recognition reinforces a sense of a common memory from which they may draw to build solidarity. The narrator's first image, the symbolic "clothing" the reader initially "puts on" for the journey, is the castle itself; an architectural wonder from the perspectives of some twenty-first-century travelers, it was a familiar sight in early modern Spain: "Today while beseeching our Lord to speak for me because I wasn't able to think of anything to say, nor did I know how to begin to carry out this obedience, there came to my mind what I shall now speak about, that which will provide us with a basis to begin. It is that we consider our soul to be like a castle made entirely out of a diamond or of very clear crystal, in which there are many rooms, just as in heaven there are many dwelling places" (35). Perhaps such rich language in the First Dwelling Place is part of an intentional strategy to invite readers into the story:

> Think of how a palmetto has many leaves surrounding and covering the tasty part that can be eaten. So here, surrounding this center room are many other rooms; and the same holds true for those above. The things of the soul must always be considered as plentiful, spacious, and large. The soul is capable of much more than we can imagine, and the sun that is in this royal chamber shines in all parts. It is very important for any soul that practices prayer, whether little or much, not to hold itself back and stay in one corner. Let it walk through these dwelling places which are up above, down below, and to the sides, since God has given it such great dignity. Don't force it to stay a long time in one room alone. Oh, but for the room of self-knowledge! (42)

What kinds of interests might "souls" now have in this text? The narrator constructs her sister readers or primary audiences as perhaps bored with a topic so simple, yet intrigued by their narrator's beautiful descriptive language. Secondary and tertiary audiences hope for inclusion in the text's story, no matter how little they actually practice prayer, and they see the narrator's promise, as she nudges them out of their corner, to instruct them about a subject of interest ("It is very important for any soul . . ."). Official audiences look for heretical error, but as "any souls" they are also invited to join the procession to learn its deepest secrets; yet if they remain only as critical observers they place themselves at the edge of the discourse, frozen in place and not moving toward the center. Here the narrator's subtle pastoral interest in her official readers seems evident. Inquisitors were also "souls" and sometimes pastors, and the narrator seems to counteract, briefly at least, her own tendency to construct cycles of opposition with male religious authorities often portrayed as the alien "other." Therefore, all audiences might be seen as now adhering to the text for one reason or another. In this dwelling place, the narrator sends out a strong invitation to any reader. It is not necessary to join a convent to participate: "each one should do this in conformity with [her] state of life" (45).

If the narrator seems to have created a hospitable space for all readers, it is to alert them to the primary objective of these dwelling places: to invite them to spend much time in the room of "self-knowledge," a place furnished with humility. The word in Spanish (*humildad*) as in English shares the Latin root for the word *humus*, organic matter that rests on or near the earth. Teresa and her sisters act out this principle through their choice to walk about without shoes (discalced) or with sandals that place them close to the earth, to the "ground" that sustains them. Readers are in effect warned that they will be left behind if they fail to circle back to these rooms of self-knowledge and humility. The traveler must return often, no matter how far she thinks she has progressed toward the center, for the knowledge of the self's dependence on God helps keep her from becoming "base" and "cowardly" and enables her to continue on this path (and to follow the narrative's logic as well). What might have been conceived as a linear path to God is deconstructed as the soul frequently "circles back" to inhabit the room of self-knowledge where this message is always parlayed: everything the soul does and is depends on the God who gives life and sustains it. To underscore this reality that the pilgrim must learn, the narrator selects a number of corresponding images. Here the soul becomes a tree, and God becomes life-giving water: "For just as all the streams that flow from a crystal-clear fount are also clear, the works of a soul in grace, because they proceed from this fount of life in which the soul is planted like a tree, are more pleasing in the eyes of both God and man. There would be no freshness, no fruit, if it were not for this fount sustaining the tree, preventing it from drying up, and causing it to produce good fruit" (40).

From Teresa's narrator's point of view, this essential knowledge of self keeps a person from wasting time in gossip and promotes community building and compassion for others. Although in the convent "there's not much occasion for gossip since such continual silence is kept," she warns all audiences but especially her primary readers that engaging in trivial backstabbing and gossip not only will delay the journey but may also ruin the whole process. This passage lends a certain poignancy to the text, for many readers know that the year before the *Interior Castle* was written, the Inquisition visited Teresa's convent to inquire about rumors that had spread beyond its cloistered walls. Alerted by a tip from Teresa's own sisters in Seville, they challenged her about her alleged participation in the *alumbrado* heresy, with its supposed connections to Luther and the Protestant Reformation. Her sisters had accused both Teresa and her advisor, Gracián, not only of heresy but also of a shared sexual indiscretion. People of *converso* lineage were especially vulnerable to these accusations since their allegiance to the Catholic Church was already suspect.

Much of the anxiety detected in the narrator's voice might have stemmed from such skirmishes with the Inquisition from the actions of Teresa's sisters. However, in this same dwelling place the narrator advises readers (and perhaps reminds herself as well) not to be so shocked by the behavior of others that they fail to progress in prayer and thus to grow spiritually. Memories of these events may stimulate the narrator's special focus on how promoting gossip and defamation of character can harm one's relationship with God and with others. But the authorial presence of the historical Teresa reminds rebellious sister readers that she is not so shocked by their behavior after all; in fact, she invites these "prodigal daughters" back into the circle of the primary readers.

The beauty of the narrative, with its crystal-clear streams and many-leafed palmettos, may entice readers away from such memories of regrettable events; perhaps this richly told story will help them refocus on prayer. But the narrator continues with a rather surprising comment about the use of analogy that seems to undercut her argument and undermine her efforts to construct an aesthetically appealing story: "Learned and wise men know about these things very well, but everything is necessary for our womanly dullness of mind; and so perhaps the Lord wills that we get to know comparisons like these" (41). While this comment seems to defer to her official audiences, through its presentation of the narrator and of all women readers as intellectual second-class citizens who must rely on figures of speech to understand theological concepts, it can also be read as a subtle and playful insult. What "dullness" of mind can create such beautiful prose? What "lack of intellect" in the reader marvels at the freshness of the imagery that will, perhaps, call to mind still other images to stimulate further reflection? The official reader, searching for theological error, might easily pass over this section of the book in his search for tasty heretical morsels. Other readers, however, enjoy the allusions to nature and a language that "dresses up" the narrative, further motivating them to move forward, even if only to experience what else the narrator will do with metaphor. For certain, the narrator thus gives herself permission to produce many more symbols and images to "dress up" her language, a language specifically addressed to women.

The narrative is "dressed up" to appeal to its women audiences in other ways as well. In the Second Dwelling Place, the narrator supplies this contract to her reader: "If I could present the matter to you in a variety of ways, I know well that you wouldn't be annoyed since we never tire of books—as many as there are—that deal with it" (48). In this passage, perhaps Teresa offers an inside joke as part of her explanation of intent: to present well-known matters "in a variety of ways." Kieran Kavanaugh translates the word *guisar* as "present"; E. Allison Peers, another renowned Teresian scholar, translates it as "arranged," yet footnotes the literal meaning as "dish up."[14] Somehow the image is just too "homely" to take seriously. If *guisar* implies a cooking metaphor, to "dish up" or to "cook up" food, Teresa's primary audiences may remember what she has often told them as she took turns with them cooking and cleaning up after meals: "God is to be found among the pots and pans as well."[15] The word *guisar* might stimulate a chuckle of recognition from some of her sisters, as it appears informally in a more or less "formal" teaching mode. Also, they remember here that she frowns on hierarchical patterns of living and supports egalitarian ones. The narrator's transparency, her lack of pretense, substantiates the lessons of humility she teaches throughout the discourse; such an earthy metaphor projects a narrator that playfully calls for that kind of community. The text's subtle reference to gaiety in the kitchen substantiates the point that readers should attend to God's presence at the hearth or in the heart of any circumstance of women in community.

Yet Teresa's narrator urges her women readers not to "nest" in any one spot but to move forward in the reading process to encounter the spaces constructed by the narrative and as practitioners of prayer to continue the procession into the depths of God's love. The narrator produces the image of the soldier to support her readers' progress in these early stages of the journey, to become "manly" in their pursuit of the Occupant dwelling in the central regions of the castle: "[L]et the soul be manly and not like those soldiers who knelt down to drink before going into battle (I don't remember with whom), but be determined to fight with all the devils and realize that there are not better weapons than those of the cross" (51). Readers of Teresa's day would have seen themselves as highly praised by this language; thus, through praise, Teresa begins to build a gender-inclusive community of readers, fortified with self-esteem, who will become proud of its efforts.[16]

The narrator praises her audience, but she continues to refer to her own weaknesses, in this case her lack of holiness, as she points to her dependency on God, who gives her and all her readers the courage to proceed. Such a confession, though, encourages all her sisters to place themselves not only in her narrative care as they continue along the way but also under the protection of God who fortifies her with the strength to write:

> Certainly, my daughters, I am so fearful as I write this that I don't know how I'm writing it or how I live when I think about it, which is very often. Pray, my daughters, that His Majesty may live in me always. If He doesn't, what security can a life as badly spent as mine have? And do not become sad in knowing that this life has been badly spent, as I have sometimes observed you become when I tell this to you; you continue to desire that I might have lived a very holy life—and you are right. I too would want to have so lived, but what can I do if I have lost holiness through my own fault! I will not complain about God who gave me enough help to carry out your desires. I cannot say this without tears and without being very ashamed that I am writing something for those who can teach me. Doing so has been a hard command to obey! (56)

So now the mantle of power shifts from narrator to audience. Her sisters hear her confession, and they teach her ("I am writing something for those who can teach me"). She asks them for their support in prayers: "Pray, my daughters, that His Majesty may live in me always." Perhaps this is also an indirect reference to official readers as well, a slightly confessional self-reproach for what happened or did not happen in the Seville episode, when she and Gracián were reported to the Inquisition. All this must have still been fresh in her memory, as the narrator affirms the reader's knowledgeable abilities and the student becomes the teacher in an exercise of role reversal, community building, and confession. We are given the image of a conscience heavily burdened with guilt even as it strengthens the resolve of all readers to continue the journey in solidarity with the community of primary readers. One might argue that indeed a sacramentlike transaction is performed between audiences and narrator, but in this case sympathetic and powerful audiences serve as the "priest," and a bond is formed between these protagonists as well, creating further unity between the attentive listener and the teller of the story. The narrator's confessions may have been generated as well as part of a general thrust toward transparency in order to create a reliable witness to the spiritual journey. In this reconstruction of a relationship between narrator and reader, what is left is "absolution" yet to be given.

The narrator is so aware of her sinful past that she declares that indeed it is only protection of the "true" mother of Mt. Carmel, Mary, the mother of Christ, that she has not ruined (*dilustrar en nada*)[17] the reputation of the order. Since it was so important to defend one's "honor" in early modern Spain, it must have been difficult or impossible for someone like Teresa to let go of these "worldly concerns" completely. The concept of honor indicates, of course, the possibility of dishonor, and a way to be dishonored at the time was to have been discovered to have engaged in what was socially constructed as improper sexual activity or to have *converso* lineage. Perhaps even an accusation of wrongdoing brings about a tone of shame in the narrative. Even so, her confession paints a pictorial image of the saint she insists she will never be, since she describes herself as a penitent in language an orthodox Christian saint would use to point to personal poverty in relationship to the goodness of God. Gillian Ahlgren in *Teresa of Ávila and the Politics of Sanctity* says that Teresa's placement of herself always in the position of a sinner helped her to make sure that she could not reasonably be accused, as the early *alumbrados* had been, "of believing that the soul in prayer was sinless."[18]

Certainly, holiness cannot be won by a soul who stubbornly positions herself outside a living community that nourishes her on her journey. Regarding audiences that are not her sister Carmelites, Teresa has this to say, in fact, something that applies to all: "And even if they are not members of a religious order, it would be a great thing for them to have—as do many persons . . . someone whom they could consult so as not to do their own will in anything . . . someone who is very free . . . someone who already knows the world for what it is" (65). While Teresa's narrator may prove herself as that trustworthy "someone," she points to her secondary and tertiary readers' need for a spiritual companion who can help them sort out the obstacles encountered in a life dedicated to prayer. Other readers readily claim themselves as free, worldly wise, and willing to guide a willful soul: the *letrados* or learned men who will read this work and who also have the sacramental role of the priest in the confessional. Perhaps the narrator flatters them into empathizing with other audiences in this community of readers as they begin to see themselves as the narrator wants to see them.

Toward the end of the description of the Third Dwelling Place, once again, Teresa's narrator urges her charges further ahead into the interior of the soul: "Entrad, entrad, hijas mias, en lo interior; pasad adelante de vuestras obrillas."[19] Enter into the interior of the castle, and leave these rooms: leave an inordinate focus on good works, pass on from the dryness of prayer in this place in which souls are so well ordered that "everything offends us because we fear everything" (63). Yet, while impatient with the duty of describing this space and pleased to leave it, the narrator has accomplished much. She reminds her sisters of her qualifications as a religious leader. She projects a persona of someone sincerely exposing her faults, who has nothing to hide, who looks out for the best interests of her community. Committed to a life of prayer and a concern for the other, she pushes forward, urging her readers past these comfortable habitats where reason alone rules, so much so that it could block the depth of mystery they will experience should they accompany her further along the way.

About halfway through the journey now, the narrator continues to study the element of water in its function in the narrative discourse as one of the most profound images that illustrates the mystery of the life of prayer. She humbly proclaims that recourse to this symbol is the best way for her to describe prayer "because I know little and have no helpful cleverness of mind and am so fond of this element that I have observed it more attentively than other things" (73). Many of her contemporary readers know these descriptions of waterworks through their activities in daily life. They are referred to in the Spanish as *arcaduce*,[20] a conduit for conveying water or a bucket for raising water in the well; getting water through such artificial means is hard work. Left over from the Roman occupation in the first four hundred years of the first millennium and maintained and improved upon by Muslim rulers of Spain, aqueducts may still function in some regions to help fill water receptacles.[21] At least, the ruins of these technologies would have reminded early modern Spaniards of their former uses. Yet the narrator also observes that a trough fed by a natural spring fills itself. Likewise, while a person in prayer can gain a sense of God's presence through reflecting on the Psalms, for example, sometimes the source of prayer (or God) replenishes the soul without any effort at all on its part, except to be still and listen. Teresa's narrator calls the effects of these latter prayers "spiritual delights" that "begin in God and end in ourselves" (74). A space in the soul expands to accommodate this infusion of God's presence, but the soul fails to understand how.

Spending much time in attempts to sort all this out will only distract the soul from its original purpose; thus the narrator prompts her sister readers not to think much but to love much. "I can be completely mistaken, but I would not lie" (76), she says about these kinds of prayers, which she calls prayers of union. The narrator adds this comment for the benefit, perhaps, of official readers as well, in case she sounds too sure of herself. Official readers and others will not accuse her of "deception," a word the Inquisition uses officially to sentence the accused to banishment or death. Now the narrator moves confidently yet cautiously into the dangerous regions of these "supernatural" spaces, with language that recalls her sisters' everyday communal life and that addresses other readers' different contexts. The souls hear God's voice so clearly that it seems to pierce the air of these cavernous spaces within the castle of the soul like a "shepherd's whistle"; in response they "abandon exterior things" to enter more deeply into the soul's interior (78). Even married people can experience this; however, they cannot leave "exterior things" except in their desire to leave them.

Probably the greatest asset for this state, which she also calls "recollection," is to function as a listener instead of a talker, which works well in the convent under the rule of silence. However, Teresa's narrator identifies the difficulty many readers experience when attempting to focus in spite of disruptive thoughts. She distinguishes between the rambling mind, which no one can ever pacify in prayer, and the intellect that somehow can attentively listen (although it can follow the mind in its chaos-making abilities as well). The mind is focused on busywork, a "mill clacking" that will not shut down its mechanical repetitiveness in spite of the will's efforts to stop it. Such a windmill might actually be engaging in its noisy business close by as Teresa writes or as her readers read. Such common remembrances of place help to build familiarity and unity between the text and its sixteenth-century Spanish readers. Cervantes immortalizes the landscape of "clacking" windmills in Don Quixote's famous joust with these mechanisms in nearby La Mancha.

These images are gleaned from familiar natural settings to beautify interior states as the soul proceeds even more deeply into the interior world of the castle. While the exterior world loses its "flavor" at this stage, the soul is still quite inexperienced, and so especially now, Teresa's narrator warns, it should not part itself from its Source. Like wild animals curling up into a ball as they rest or withdraw into a hiding place, souls "rest" in the knowledge of God. Teresa's narrator also applies mother and child imagery to explain this: "In this prayer the soul is not yet grown but is like a suckling child. If it turns away from its mother's breast, what can be expected for it but death? I am very much fearful that this will happen to anyone to whom God has granted this favor and who withdraws from prayer — unless [he] does so for a particularly special reason — or if [he] doesn't return quickly to prayer, for [he] will go from bad to worse. I know there is a great deal to fear in this matter" (82). Although the passage focuses here on the image of God as mother, the narrator may be recommending that readers having traveled thus far should also cling to the "mother" narrator of the text and perhaps trust the leadership abilities of the historical Teresa as well, the authorial presence behind the work. Teresa has defined herself in her Epilogue as a "mother" through addressing her "daughters" of Mt. Carmel. Readers should commit themselves even more strongly to seeing the journey through by clinging to support systems at their disposal. The narrator has shown her trustworthiness. She knows this place and has survived it; after all, she has promised to describe the Seventh Dwelling Place at some point. The implication here is that readers should continue to trust; as the soul adheres to God in this stage, so should the reader adhere to the narrator. According to the narrator, the soul puts itself in great peril if it proceeds this far only to quit; it will thus only find itself even more open to temptation and chaos.

However, sometimes people in this state remain *too* absorbed in the quiet "nothingness" of suspending in a mother's arms, especially women in general, she says to her sisters:

There is one danger I want to warn you about (although I may have mentioned it elsewhere) into which I have seen persons of prayer fall, especially women, for since we are weaker there is more occasion for what I'm about to say. It is that some have a weak constitution because of a great amount of penance, prayer, and keeping vigil, and

even without these; in receiving some favor, their nature is overcome. Since they feel some consolation interiorly and a languishing
and weakness exteriorly, they think they are experiencing a spiritual
sleep, which is a prayer a little more intense than the prayer of quiet,
and they let themselves become absorbed. (83)

The narrator maintains that "these people are doing nothing more
than wasting time and wearing down their health" (83). Furthermore, some
people are so full of illusion that "everything they think about they see";
in this dangerous natural/supernatural state too many souls are deceived.
Inasmuch as the narrator shows her audiences how to defy the darker elements of their imaginations, she adds one more role that she fills in the
text—that of the exorcist. She opposes negative forces that would inhibit
progress and freedom.[22]

Teresa's narrator reveals her depth of psychological knowledge about
the nature of deception; that is why she so ardently argues for a spiritual
director, perhaps to appease an official reader but also because she knows
the value of other opinions. Here the narrator again points to her trustworthiness to lead groups of readers through the passageways in the castle.
She knows what she speaks of and has survived it. She herself has been accused of being deceived. She knows spiritual directors who can attest to
her spiritual health as well as some who might accuse her of demonic possession. She has "seen" many of the rooms in the castle and "returns" to
show the readers the way.

While the spiritual director's important role has always officially been
filled by men, Teresa now writes a handbook for the spiritual journey that
could, in effect, free her sisters from those male advisors who often fail to
understand because they are not truly open to spiritual experiences.[23] Teresa
guides her sisters toward a freedom to make some of their own decisions in
their spiritual lives, and these decisions are never made in isolation. The
true sign that a soul has progressed in its journey toward God is love of the
neighbor, in this case "sister love": "If you see a sister who is sick to whom
you can bring some relief, you have compassion on her and do not worry
about losing this devotion, and if she is suffering pain, you also feel it, and
if necessary, you fast so that she might eat . . . and if you see a person
praised, the Lord wants you to be much happier than if you yourself were
being praised . . . and if we see some fault in the sister, it is also a very good
thing to hide the fault as if it were our own" (102). Teresa's experiences
with her sisters in Seville are probably freshly remembered at this point in

the narrative as the narrator warns her audiences not to dwell on others' faults but rather to "hide" them. Great acts of love are often needed to create a habit of being that finally overcomes many obstacles to loving in order to experience new life. Perhaps the narrator points to the historical Teresa's choice not to punish her sister critics in Seville in hopes that the whole episode will soon be forgotten.

Teresa's narrator demonstrates her ability to reach out to audiences in still other ways. Women's grief must have been present to members of the community, as indeed the historical Teresa suffers it as well. Readers who value the way their lives connect with others' and their abilities to grow in self-knowledge will identify with the struggles portrayed in this passage: "Don't think the matter lies in my so being conformed to the will of God that if my father or brother dies I don't feel it. . . . Here in our religious life the Lord asks of us only two things, love of His Majesty and love of our neighbor" (100). The narrator thus gives herself and her readers "permission" to grieve in a way not to be relegated to the category of "womanly weakness"; after all, all readers have now attained the Fifth Dwelling Place and have set their sights on the Presence located at the center of the castle, becoming more "manly" or courageous as they progress toward that meeting. Women then and now know the strength of grieving loss in community. In bringing grief into this discourse about prayer, in intimacy with God and with one's human neighbors, the text could be interpreted to recall the wailing and tears of the biblical Rachel in the wilderness, mourning for her lost children, and extended thus to characterize God's suffering for different kinds of losses, God's own and ours. Much is permitted and called for in the living out of the human life span in "divine" space, but "one should always strive for new life and move on," Teresa's narrator reminds her audiences.

What new life is gained without shedding the old? What "worm" that has not yet transcended its state knows what it is like to become a white butterfly? Still another image sparks a special interest in Teresa's primary readers: the soul emerging from its silken wrappings still "well-dressed." The nuns of San José wear a regionally produced coarse wool for which Ávila is famous, but they can imagine the feeling of silk against the skin in comparison to the roughness of their habit; thus the image may evoke a visceral response in some of the narrative's readers to prepare their imaginations for the descriptions of new life with their souls well dressed for the occasion. Conversely, other readers who may dress well exteriorly may imagine their "poverty" of spiritual life in light of this description. Teresa's narrator, however, wants to stress at this stage how the poverty of her sisters' clothing on the outside contrasts with the richness of their vesture on the inside.

While this prayer of union is possible for many, very few will actually experience it except through the experience of reading about it. Again, as in the Fourth Dwelling Place, a tone of trepidation is introduced as she warns readers to trust in what she says about spiritual events that they may never know: "And although I have said 'some,' there are indeed only a few who fail to enter this dwelling place of which I shall now speak. There are various degrees, and for that reason I say that most enter these places. But I believe that only a few will experience some of the things that I will say are in this room" (85). Thus she explores the perhaps puzzling possibility for some readers that some souls might know something without first experiencing it. The sisters here are especially called to this prayer, an inheritance from their original Carmelite founders whose rule Teresa adapts for her order; their goal is the contemplative life, but it is nothing like a "dreamy" state. Readers prepare themselves for it by not holding onto anything: "In sum, it is like one who in every respect has died to the world so as to live more completely in God. Thus, the death is a delightful one, an uprooting from the soul of all the operations the latter can have while being in the body" (86).

But the experience lasts only briefly, and then a person is left "with a thousand suspicions," which can be good since she should always remain alert to self-deception (87). Such a focus on certain readers' possible misunderstandings comes at an appropriate time in the argument, since in this dwelling place the narrator describes the phenomenon of religious ecstasy. On occasion, the soul is so "caught up in God" and "dead" to the things of the world that it has lost connection to the five external senses. Readers might be tempted to dwell in contemplation of this beautiful imagery that describes a richness of spiritual experiences and to stay awhile with the growing sense of accomplishment they might feel for having remained with the text this far. Yet, the narrator cautions, they should advance, because if they do not they could lose ground to "devilish intervention" (106). If readers glance outside a window, they might catch a split-second glimpse of a fragile butterfly, which could serve as an icon to contemplate the mysteriousness of these final dwelling places. The restless and fragile creature passes from flower to flower in the gardens of the convent, choosing not to light on any object for long. That image and their own desires and fears carry them forward.

As the soul waits impatiently for the final event, in the Sixth Dwelling Place the longing for union is described with erotic overtones. Yet one can reside in this state of interior joy and longing and suffer from real trials as well. Teresa's narrator returns to the issue of broken human relationships to show what she means. Here readers cannot help but think, once again, of the Seville incident:

> There is an outcry by persons a Sister is dealing with and even by those she does not deal with and who, it seems to her, would never even think of her; gossip like the following: "She's trying to make out she's a saint; she goes to extremes to deceive the world and bring others to ruin; there are other better Christians who don't put on all this outward show" (and it's worth noting that she is not putting on any outward show but just striving to fulfill well her state in life). Those she considered her friends turn away from her, and they are the ones who take the largest and most painful bite at her, "That soul has gone astray and is clearly mistaken; these are things of the devil; she will turn out like this person or that other that went astray, and will bring about a decline in virtue; she has deceived her confessors" (and they go to these confessors, telling them so, giving them examples of what happened to some that were lost in this way); a thousand kinds of ridicule and sayings like [this]. (109)

This storminess in exterior matters is contrasted with another kind of "pain": God's call, which now becomes urgent, persistent, and pervasive. Surpassing the gentle beckoning of shepherd's whistle at the beginning of the journey, it is now received as a "delightful pain," or "kindling," or fragrance softly "spreading over the senses" (118). Here the soul may also experience locutions, or actually hearing words spoken to it from the divine Being in the center. But again, to be safe, one should never act on what one thinks one has heard without consulting a "learned and prudent confessor" (123). In light of her audiences' different interests, the narrator's challenge to find just the right symbolic language is palpable.

Nearing the center of the castle, but still in the Sixth Dwelling Place, the soul perceives a wedding party of two; this section of the account of the journey is decorated with many sensual images of celebration and joy. The "spouse" closes all the doors to the castle, even the one of the outer wall. The soul feels as if it is locked in a wine cellar, drunken with joy. The "water" of recollection becomes a huge wave that carries the soul upward, and perhaps even the body will be carried off, as "we have read," says Teresa's narrator, who thus comments about what she expects her audiences already know (133). If they have only *read* about it, they have not experienced it, a state that lets official readers know that no one claims anything personally.

The soul practiced at letting go now physically experiences the sensation of not being tied to the earth, and it takes great courage to continue to endure this sense of weightlessness. In this dwelling place, she may experience a vision of Christ in his humanity; yet now Christ is dressed in white garments of fine Dutch linen ("como una holanda parace la vestidura"),[24] instead of the garments of a Galilean, and awaits her with jewels of surpassing beauty (156), with gold vessels, and with other presents—all metaphors chosen to describe the spiritual beauty of the place and the joy of the meeting. The writer chooses a surprising metaphor or conceit, also found in the metaphysical love poetry of some of her English contemporaries, that describes sexual orgasm: the soul now wants to "die."

To continue describing the experience as a kind of "death-in-life," Teresa's narrator refers to a passage from the Roman Breviary that she assumes many of her readers will know. She quotes St. Martin of Tours: "Lord, if I am still necessary to your people, I don't refuse to live: may your will be done." According to the liturgical calendar of Teresa's day, Teresa and her sisters may have recently recited the daily office that related these very words. It is quite possible that Teresa, who finished writing the *Interior Castle* only in late November, was describing this dwelling place at this time.[25] Here is yet another appeal to a common liturgical memory that could help build solidarity within her community of readers.

If earlier in the narrative she nudges and prods readers to enter one dwelling place at a time, now in the Sixth Dwelling Place the narrator hurries them along with a reference to the Song of Songs: "And if we hope to enjoy this blessing even in this present life, what are we doing? What is causing us to delay? What is enough to make us, even momentarily, stop looking for this Lord as did the Bride in the streets and in the squares?" (130). Here we encounter the image of the Bride, not cloistered or passively receiving the Bridegroom's attentions, but actively searching the public arena for the object of her desires. The provocative language that describes this stage illustrates the soul transcending many of the constraints of the sisters' particular contexts of enclosure. Yet Teresa hopes readers do not identify these erotic episodes in the narrative as excerpts from the historical Teresa's life story: "I have dealt with many holy persons who tell me about these experiences, but I want to limit myself in case you think I am talking about myself" (135). Teresa's narrator still addresses those readers linked to the Inquisition who might suspect that she tells of her own experiences; she would rather not admit it. Yet some readers might now think, "If this is an example of 'limited' language, what would its excesses look like?"

Thus a reader is left with a puzzle: exactly how much or how little of the text reflects the author's firsthand experience? In the *Interior Castle*, it is difficult to verify the connections among what might have been witnessed, what might have been experienced by the author herself, and what might have been gleaned from literary authorities. The historical Teresa's purposes are served well by this account of intertwining experiences; not only is the story itself enriched by the retelling of others' experiences, but also these examples obfuscate its author's firsthand experiences.[26]

In the final Seventh Dwelling Place, readers meet the desired end of prayer and the narrator's avoidance of taking credit for their descriptions. The following passage is a noteworthy example of the narrator's struggle with language that reveals as much as it hides: "It seems that a creature as miserable as I should tremble to deal with a thing so foreign to what I deserve to understand. And, indeed, I have been covered with confusion wondering if it might not be better to conclude my discussion of this dwelling place with just a few words. *For it seems to me that others will think I know about it through experience.* This makes me extremely ashamed; for, knowing what I am, such a thought is a terrible thing" (173, italics mine). The passage sounds like a disclaimer. If one of the assertions of the *alumbrados* is that, on reaching the highest stages of prayer, a person is sinless, then this passage answers official readers' concerns. Teresa's narrator continues, explaining that in spite of the dangers from certain readers, she must finish: "On the other hand, the thought of neglecting to explain this dwelling place seemed to me to be a temptation and weakness on my part, no matter how many of the above judgments you make about me. May God be praised and understood a little more, and let all the world cry out against me; how much more so in that I will perhaps be dead when what I write is seen" (173).

The "you" is obviously addressed to all her sisters, since the paragraph begins, "I hope, not for myself but for you, Sisters, that He may grant me this favor" (of helping her to reveal to them what she has learned about the last dwelling place), but the narrator especially targets sisters who are not empathetic audiences. The historical Teresa knows by now, in the aftershock of the Seville fiasco, that some members of her community may still gossip about her and reconsider her abilities to lead. Yet while some sisters may continue to challenge her leadership, the Inquisition will see her actions as obedient acquiescence to male counsel and adherence to her Rule (the Rule of St. Albert).[27] If the *Interior Castle* is published someday, hopefully sooner than later, it is sure to reach all her convents, even if only through a manuscript copy that is somehow discreetly released to be read aloud in community. Teresa wants to focus on prayer to return her sisters to the original intent of her reform of 1562 and to reduce their anxiety about recent disturbances in the order, those "exterior matters" that might prove to be stumbling blocks to their orderly progress in prayer. Her rhetorical choices at once defend her qualifications as a leader and invite community solidarity in these efforts. We may also perceive an indication of how much the historical Teresa wants her writings to live on after her death.

Last, the soul "sees" a vision of the Trinity, but not with the eyes; it is a perception more like a deep certainty or conviction than an event that can be described using the tools of sense experience, sight, sound, touch, taste, and smell. The Trinity speaks to the soul "some place very deep within itself"; this soul is even more occupied with serving God by serving her community: "O God help me! How different is hearing and believing these words from understanding their truth in this way! Each day this soul becomes more amazed, for these Persons never seem to leave it any more, but it clearly beholds, in the way that was mentioned, that they are within it. In the extreme interior, in some place very deep within itself, the nature of which it doesn't know how to explain, because of a lack of learning, it perceives this divine company" (175). The experiences of rapture are now taken away; rather, this quiet certainty rules over her senses. The "butterfly" dies at this stage because it is unified with the object of its longing, restless spirit.

Teresa ends the journey by saying, "[T]he Lord doesn't look so much at the greatness of our works as at the love with which they are done" (194), cautioning her readers once again about the primacy of love in community. Yet she herself has accomplished much since she and her audiences arrived together at the center. Having waged and won such furious narrative wars, she has connected herself with her audiences by the time the last battle has been fought. She ends her final pages by referring to other saintly women whose lives are also recorded in the gospels and read in the yearly cycles of liturgical prayers: Mary Magdalene and Mary and Martha of Bethany. Readers may now sense that, having traveled so far into their souls in prayer, and so deeply into the narrative's territory as well, they have become part of the historical community of women saints mentioned in the story who have known intimacy with God under the direct influence of the restless Holy Spirit, which in some early Christian traditions was considered feminine.[28] This focus on women as models surely reflects the narrator's desire to empower readers and to encourage growth and perseverance: "If you do not strive for the virtues and practice them, you will always be dwarfs. And, please God, it will be only a matter of not growing, for you know already that whoever does not increase decreases. I hold that love, where present, cannot possibly be content with remaining always the same" (191). Even now, as narrator and audiences dwell momentarily in the dwelling place that marks the end of the journey, the narrator recommends change and growth. As Teresa's narrator closes her complex, contradictory project, this somewhat incoherent text points toward the unfinished characters of the narrator, and of the author, and of audiences, still "happening," developing, being, beyond the pages of the text.

"Exiting" the Story

By the Epilogue, readers see that the action of storytelling itself has changed the narrator's frame of mind: now she loves what she has written, whereas when she started she was impelled by duty, not desire. She had begun the task dull-spirited and reluctant, but now, here in the work's Epilogue, she is well pleased. Her physical ailments seem healed, or at least she is now so much a part of her own narrative flow that she may have forgotten her sickness for a time. The narrator's persona has changed from a worried self-doubter to a more serene and confident navigator of the spiritual life. In fact, the task of writing seems to have helped her gain a voice, even as she encourages her readers to claim theirs. The narrator thus leaves a rich legacy of the time she has spent with her readers, and she hopes this will inspire their return to the text and perseverance in prayer. A storyteller's artfulness helps to ensure Teresa's fame even as her narrative technique "glues" readers to the text. She has kept the whole process—narrator, story, and audiences—moving toward the end.

While Teresa's narrator seems to protect herself from those who think she is too presumptuous and even dangerous, she wants to educate her sisters about what they might encounter experientially when no confessor is willing and able to decipher their accounts of spiritual experiences after she is gone. The narrator is caught in a double bind, but she has a legacy to leave behind. The irony here is that the traditional language of mystical union is a "language of unsaying."[29] One flounders in the attempt to express these experiences verbally. So her narrative discourse is, in a sense, at once a confirmation of her experiences of suspicious readers, a testimony to women who have often lost the opportunity to witness to their unique experiences in human communities, and a witness to the reality of mystical union. We might paraphrase the narrator as saying this: "How do I find the words to express what I'm not supposed to know, but do, but can't describe anyway?"

By the end of the story, the cumulative effect of all this sidetracking from specific examples back into general topics of the spiritual life, wrapped up in a processional motif, identifies the narrator as a Sophia-like persona, in charge of much of the knowledge inside the structure of the castle's story; thus the narrator's authority has been constructed by the story itself. Teresa's narrator leads readers through the streets of her fortified city-castle, stopping at various "stations" to reflect on the richness of the experiences discovered along the way, including the communion encountered as they traveled together. In circling back to the room of self-knowledge and in introducing many digressions and asides, the narrator transgresses the kind of formal narrative that doggedly tracks its way on a linear and straightforward path. As she freely engages in different kinds of discourse, one of the most attractive dimensions she presents of the place is the freedom a soul finds inside the castle. Her primary readers live behind convent walls, but their spirits move freely in this space. Here, after the tale has been spun, the author offers her blessing and a reminder to return to the soul's spaciousness once again: "Considering the strict enclosure and the few things you have for your entertainment, my Sisters, and that your buildings are not always as large as would be fitting for your monasteries, I think it will be a consolation for you to delight in this interior castle since without permission from the prioress you can enter and take a walk through it at any time. . . . [N]o one can take it from you" (195).

Similar to the way Shakespeare's narrator uses the "I and thou" language in Sonnet 73, "Love that well, which thou must leave ere long," Teresa's narrator urgently expresses her desire for her primary readers' love and trust, reminding them of the little time she has left and of the beauty that they have encountered together. She bids them farewell with an unofficial priestly blessing as a sign of her fidelity and trust and, in consideration of her official readers, rejects once again the perceived heresies of the *alumbrados*, which the Inquisition connects with Protestants, Jews, and other "heretics": "I ask that each time you read this work you, in my name, praise His Majesty fervently and ask for the increase of His Church and for light for the Lutherans. As for me, ask Him to pardon my sins and deliver me from purgatory, for perhaps by the mercy of God I will be in there when this is given for you to read—if it may be seen by you after having been examined by learned men. If anything is erroneous it is so because I didn't know otherwise; and I submit in everything to what the holy Roman Catholic Church holds, for in this Church I live, declare my faith, and promise to live and die" (196).

As the narrative proceeds and the narrator's voice strengthens, some "ideal" readers that the text constructs will become more capable of incorporating its instructions into their everyday lives. They will find themselves more disposed to the argument's rationality, more attuned to their own developing moral senses, and more refined in their abilities to connect empathetically to others. They may find their longing for God increased. While the zigzag quality of her prose at first glance makes her narrative language appear a model of inconsistency, another look shows us that we might characterize it as having a dialectic or logic of its own as it extends itself to multiplying audiences and encourages their many voices to take part in the journey. Finally, the text's "unity" is determined by its ability to connect with its audiences.

To link herself with her audiences, Teresa's narrator banks on what she has constructed as her readers' various desires: desire for right relations in community, desire for independence from hierarchical power plays, perhaps desire for a space to grieve in community with her sisters, desire for intimacy with God in prayer, an aesthetic desire for beauty and order. The narrator extends her own desires into the text as well: her desire for readers, her desire to tell a story well, her desire to relate what she knows, her yearning for the Presence at the center of the soul. The narrative records the death of desire as well: in the narrator's satisfaction with the end results of her efforts, in the blank page that represents the end of the discourse, in the handing over of the "interior life" to receptive audiences. The end result of her efforts is a narrative that illustrates audiences as co-producers and co-writers of the story, an interaction that continues past the conclusion in the manuscript.[30] Thus, through her narrative language, which embraces the realities of their physical and spiritual environments, Teresa constructs a political and spiritual fortress in which she, her sisters, and other interested audiences may thrive, in a way that transcends time and place.

Peter Rabinowitz explains how a postmodern reader can locate herself in relation to the text, fiction or nonfiction, by becoming one of its authorial audiences, or by imagining "What sort of person would I have to pretend to be—what would I have to know and believe—if I wanted to take this work of fiction (or non-fiction) as real?"[31] Rabinowitz argues that "distant texts" are "hard to understand," since "we do not possess the kind of knowledge required to join the authorial audiences."[32] Teresa's narrator invites into the text audiences who are not only able to understand the meaning of its words but also qualified to take pleasure in its aesthetics, sense of humor and play, openness to friendship, and descriptions of beauty.[33] The current cultural focuses on spiritualities throughout the world indicate that some "postmodern" readers will find the questions Teresa addresses as provocative and stimulating as did her early modern readers, and they may want to join its audiences. Teresa's story confronts ideologies that glorify power, the control of others, success in business, a preoccupation with honor, and competitive struggle with only one winner. These themes or ideologies still inhabit the thinking patterns of people living in postmodern technically developed and developing nations. Perhaps readers interested in women and spirituality study the *Interior Castle* to increase their own understanding of how a text constructs women's communities in history and to learn how a narrative discourse far removed from us in time may yet empower women's spiritual lives. Male readers may benefit from it as well. Such readings will stimulate conversations about how the *Interior Castle* is feminist, mystical, political, and spiritual.

One Teresian scholar energetically challenges the argument that Teresa's rhetoric is or can be liberating. She argues that Teresa's diminutive language or language that plays on the weaknesses of women may have "won a public voice for herself, if not for other women."[34] While it is true that Teresa's narrator often focuses on women's weaknesses in her digressions, she craftily links the prevailing images of the *mujercilla*, or little woman of no account, to another tradition within Christianity: the orthodox descriptions of the humility of the human being striving toward an authentic life in love with God and with others. These images thus become weapons against critics of her reform efforts. Language that is formulated in patriarchal societies must always be deconstructed and worked anew to evaluate its worth for women. We catch Teresa in the act of doing just that for her times, and it is up to us to continue the effort, to perhaps deconstruct hers. While the narrator does return to the theme of the stereotypical inferiority of women, quite jarring to the sensibilities of readers of later generations if not to those of her own, her rhetoric seen in its entirety, in the beauty of her descriptions, in the authoritative power of her voice as it banishes different kinds of "demons," and in its priestly blessings directed toward audiences, overshadows the haunting remnants of the language of women's self-hatred to demonstrate the powerful and liberating effect the entire story can have on its reading audience.

NOTES

1. For instance, the *Ascent of Mount Carmel* by St. John of the Cross, a contemporary, co-founder, and friend of "la Santa." See E. E. Trueman Dicken, "Teresa of Jesus and John of the Cross," in *The Study of Spirituality*, ed. Cheslyn Jones, Geoffrey Wainwright, and Edward Yarnold, S.J. (New York: Cambridge University Press, 1992), 373–76. For Cabala and Sufi mystical theologies that also describe how individuals may aspire to union with God through an "Ascent" in degrees, stations, or stages toward the presence of "the One," see Catherine Swietlicki, *Spanish Christian Cabala: The Works of Luis de León, Santa Teresa de Jesús, and San Juan de la Cruz* (Columbia: University of Missouri Press, 1986), and Luce López Baralt, "El simbolo de los siete castilos concentricos de alma en Santa Teresa y en el Islam," in *Huellas de Islam en la literatura española: De Juan Ruiz a Juan Goytisolol* (Madrid: Hiperión, 1985), 74–97.

2. Over one hundred years were to pass before any woman graduated from a European university: in 1678 a Benedictine oblate named Elena Carnaro matriculated at Padua University with a Ph.D. in philosophy. See Ann Kessler, O. S. B., "Oblate and Heroine: Elena Lucrezia Scholastica Cornaro Piscopia (1646–1684)," in *Benedict in the World: Portraits of Monastic Oblates*, ed. Linda Kulzer and Roberta Bondi (Collegeville, Minn.: Liturgical Press, 2002).

3. See Juan Luis Vives, *Libro llamado instruccion de la mujer cristiana* (Valencia: Impreso por Jorge Costilla, 1528), fol. 24 ss, and Fray Luis de León, *La perfecta casada* (Madrid: Ediciones Nuestra Raza, n.d.), both cited in Mariló Vigil, *La vida de las mujeres en los siglos XVI y XVII*, 2d ed. (México: Siglo Veintiuno Editores, 1994), 3, 18, 92.

4. Teresa of Avila, *Teresa of Avila: The Interior Castle*, trans. Kieran Kavanaugh, O.C.D., and Otilio Rodriguez, O.C.D. (New York: Paulist Press, 1979), 173. Subsequent page citations from this translation are given parenthetically in the text. All page citations to the *Interior Castle* are from this translation unless otherwise noted.

5. See William A. Christian, Jr., *Local Religion in Sixteenth-Century Spain* (Princeton, N.J.: Princeton University Press, 1981). In 1575 Phillip II commissioned a questionnaire that identified religious practices, including processions to shrines and outdoor religious dramas, in Toledo and in other places in New Castile as part of a description of the history of the area.

6. See Alastair Hamilton's excellent study *Heresy and Mysticism in Sixteenth-Century Spain: The Alumbrados* (Cambridge, England: James Clark, 1992), 27–29. By the time Teresa wrote the *Interior Castle*, Jews, Protestants, and *alumbrados* were seen as sharing similar heretical characteristics.

7. Especially a novice named María del Corro. See Enrique Llamas Martínez, O.C.D., "Delaciones y acusaciones ante el Tribunal de Sevilla (1575–1579)," in *Santa Teresa de Jesús y la Inquisición española* (Madrid: Instituto Francisco Suárez, 1972), 53–194.

8. A sister reports that she often wrote the *Interior Castle* between midnight and 2:00 a.m. See [Anon.], *San Jose de Avila: Rinconcito de Dios, paraiso de su deleite* (Burgos: Monte Carmelo, 1998), 209.

9. Teresa's mother, Doña Beatriz de Ahumada, who died when Teresa was thirteen, may have also descended from Jewish converts. See Gareth Alban Davies, "St Teresa and the Jewish Question," in *Teresa de Jesus and Her World*, ed. Margaret A. Rees (Leeds, England: Trinity and All Saints' College, 1981), 54.

10. See Jodi Bilinkoff, *The Avila of Saint Teresa: Religious Reform in a Sixteenth-Century City* (Ithaca, N.Y.: Cornell University Press, 1989), 108–51.

11. Although the motif may be traced back to Plotinus (third century), the founder of Neoplatonism, the Christian Neoplatonist Pseudo-Dionysius was thought to be the "father" of emanation or processional language in Christian mystical texts; the Council of Trent (1545–63) awarded him impeccable doctrinal credentials. Six years after her death in 1582, the editor of the first complete edition of Teresa's works, Luis de León, affirmed her orthodoxy when he cited Teresa's influences: Bonaventura, Francisco de Osuña, Augustine, and Pseudo-Dionysius, all theologians who in different ways creatively manipulated the metaphor of procession to explain how an infinite God connects with a finite universe and how human beings may retrace the path connecting Creator to creation to enter into the divine presence.

12. Teresa de Jesús, *Moradas del castillo interior*, in *Obras completas*, ed. Efren de la Madre de Dios, O.C.D., and Otger Steggink, O. Carm. (Madrid: Biblioteca de Autores Cristianos, 1997), 470. What follows is my own translation.

13. Jane Ackerman, "Teresa and Her Sisters," in *The Mystical Gesture: Essays in Medieval and Early Modern Spiritual Culture in Honor of Mary E. Giles*, ed. Robert Boenig (Aldershot, England: Ashgate, 2000), 138.

14. See Teresa of Avila, *Interior Castle: St. Teresa of Avila*, trans. E. Allison Peers (New York: Image Doubleday, 1989), 46.

15. See Teresa de Jesús, "Fundaciones," 5:8, in *Obras completas*, 690. "Pues, ea!, hijas mías, no haya desconsuelo; cuando la obediencia os trajere empleadas en cosas exteriores, entended que, si es en la cocina, entre los pucheros anda el Señor, ayudándoos en lo interior y esterior."

16. See Barbara Newman's quotation from St. Jerome, who was well known among the monastics of Teresa's day, in *From Virile Woman to WomanChrist: Studies in Medieval Religion and Literature* (Philadelphia: University of Pennsylvania Press, 1995). "As long as a woman is for birth and children, she is different from man as body is from soul. But when she wishes to serve Christ more than the world then she will cease to be a woman, and will be called man" (4).

17. Teresa de Jesús, *Moradas*, 488.

18. Gillian T.W. Ahlgren, *Teresa of Avila and the Politics of Sanctity* (Ithaca, N.Y.: Cornell University Press, 1996), 110.

19. Teresa de Jesús, *Moradas*, 489.

20. Ibid., 500.

21. To continue speculating about how Teresa's generation depended on earlier technologies from different ethnic groups who had inhabited Spain, in this case, Muslim people who lived there for almost nine hundred years, see Thomas F. Glick, "Hydraulic Technology in Al-Andalus," in *The Legacy of Muslim Spain*, ed. Salma Khadra Jayyusi (Leiden, the Netherlands: E. J. Brill, 1994), 2:974–86.

22. Alison Weber, "Saint Teresa, Demonologist," in *Culture and Control in Counter-Reformation Spain*, ed. Anne J. Cruz and Mary Elizabeth Perry (Minneapolis: University of Minnesota Press, 1992), 171–95, says that Teresa's "principal aim" in the *Interior Castle* is to reassure her nuns against "fears of demonic possession," and that Teresa successfully "distanced herself and her nuns from a myth that increasingly held sway over her contemporaries' imaginations, which was the myth of a woman as the Devil's compliant sexual partner" (187). I would nuance this a bit. While some of Teresa's Spanish contemporaries believed this, others did not. Spain was one of the few countries in early modern Europe that did not seek out and persecute witches because Inquisition officials tended to consider such stories about women as superstitious nonsense. It is true that Alonso de la Fuente accused Teresa of having been under the influence of some "dark angel" as she wrote, since her work far surpasses the abilities of most women, as he argued. Indeed, that "dark presence" was the same entity that influenced Mahomet (Mohammad) and Luther as well, he will argue after her death in an attempt to prevent her work from being published as authentic Christian revelation.

23. For a history of women spiritual directors, Catholic, Orthodox, and Protestant, see Patricia Ranft, *A Woman's Way: The Forgotten History of Women Spiritual Directors* (New York: Palgrave, 2000). Ranft features Teresa's argument that women should choose their own spiritual directors, a conviction that influenced important women religious leaders in France such as Jane Frances de Chantal.

24. Teresa de Jesús, *Moradas*, 557.

25. The Catholic Church adopted the Gregorian calendar on the very date of Teresa's death, October 4, 1582, which changed that day to October 15. The Orthodox Church still follows the Julian calendar. Thanks to Fr. Gerard Sloyan for first bringing this fact to my attention.

26. In *Teresa of Avila and the Rhetoric of Femininity* (Princeton, N.J.: Princeton University Press, 1990), 98–122, Alison Weber describes such examples as composing Teresa's "rhetoric of obfuscation," which Weber describes as part of Teresa's ploy to portray her "avowed incompetence," a strategy used to avoid charges of mastery, which would make her work seem authoritative or worthy of male scrutiny.

27. See Elizabeth Ruth Obbard, *Land of Carmel: The Origins and Spirituality of the Carmelite Order* (Gloucester, England: MPG Books, 1999), for an excellent, condensed study of growth and change in the Carmelite Order from its medieval foundations in Israel to the community's transfer to Europe through early modern times. For the study of the primitive Rule of St. Albert, see pp. 36–47.

28. See Elizabeth A. Johnson, *She Who Is: The Mystery of God in Feminist Theological Discourse* (New York: Crossroad, 1993).

29. See Michael A. Sells's brilliant analysis in *Mystical Languages of Unsaying* (Chicago: University of Chicago Press, 1994) for his discussions of the difficulties

Marguerite Porete also encountered while attempting to express the experiences of mystical union. She was executed by the Inquisition in Paris.

30. See Patrick O'Neill, *Fictions of Discourse: Reading Narrative Theory* (Toronto: University of Toronto Press, 1994), 125; cf. O'Neill's definition of "poststructuralist" as open-endedness.

31. See Peter Rabinowitz's essay "Truth in Fiction: A Reexamination of Audiences," in *Narrative/Theory,* ed. David H. Richter (White Plains, N.Y. : Longman, 1996), 214.

32. Ibid.

33. See Paul Ricoeur, *Fallible Man,* trans. Charles A. Kelbley (New York: Fordham University Press, 1986), 95–96.

34. Weber, *Teresa of Avila,* 165.

2

RELIGIOUS RECONSTRUCTION
OF FEMININE SPIRITUALITY

Reading Past the Praise in *Salve Deus Rex Judaeorum*

SUE MATHESON

A contemporary of John Donne, Ben Jonson, and Andrew Marvell, Aemilia Lanyer published a collection of religious verses in 1611. A Londoner married to a court musician and one-time mistress of old Lord Hunsdon, Lanyer claims to have been inspired to write her book by a dream that delivered the title of the volume to her many years before she actually sat down with pen in hand. The finished product, *Salve Deus Rex Judaeorum*, is incredibly varied, consisting of ten dedicatory verses, all addressed to women; a short prose address to the long title poem; "Salve Deus Rex Judaeorum," a meditation written in ottava rima; and an appended poem, "The Description of Cookeham." As Barbara K. Lewalski points out in her excellent article "Seizing Discourses and Reinventing Genres," Lanyer's writing exhibits a good deal of sophistication incorporating a wide variety of genres—several kinds of dedicatory poems; a prose polemic; a meditative poem that contains an apologia, laments, and several encomia; and a country house poem. Technically versatile, Lanyer's voice changes in form but not in focus: 2,500 of the volume's 3,000 lines are written in praise of women.

Currently, Lanyer's praise of women is fueling an ongoing debate. To date, Lanyer's critics generally fall into one of two camps: those who investigate *Salve Deus Rex Judaeorum* as its author's bid for court patronage and those who read the work as a subversive proto/feminist text that interrogates and/or challenges male ideology. The exchange within and between these camps has resulted in a lively debate.[1] One group of critics, including A. L. Rowse, David Bevington, Pamela Joseph Benson, and Leeds Barroll, investigate *Salve Deus* in terms of Lanyer's bid for court patronage.[2] As Barroll notes in "Looking for Patrons," the phenomenon of Lanyer's life and work produces more questions than answers.[3] Living on the fringes of the Jacobean court, Lanyer, a converted, middle-class, Italian Jew, was at a disadvantage as a writer because of her gender, class, and race. She could not have chosen a more inopportune time to write and publish her work—shortly after the misogynist James I ascended the English throne. What could have prompted her to publish at such a time? How could Lanyer and the countess of Cumberland have met? There is little doubt that *Salve Deus Rex Judaeorum* was a serious bid on Lanyer's part for court patronage, but who, in Queen Anne's circle or the countess of Cumberland's menage, would champion such a radical manuscript in such a conservative climate?

The other critical group argues that *Salve Deus* is a carefully crafted, proto/feminist text that uses the conventions of praise to interrogate male ideology. Barbara K. Lewalski, Mary Ellen Lamb, Lisa Schnell, and Susanne Woods have all examined Lanyer's poems as subversive stylistic experiments that challenge many of her contemporaries' ideas about women and a woman's place in Jacobean society.[4] These readings are supported by critics, including Lynette McGrath, W. Gardner Campbell, Judith Scherer Herz, Jacqueline Pearson, Wendy Wall, Barbara Bowen, Brenda J. Powell, Janel Mueller, and Naomi J. Miller, who argue that *Salve Deus* interrogates and/or challenges male ideology by investigating other sociopolitical topics and tropes in Lanyer's work.[5]

In spite of the enthusiastic response to *Salve Deus*, Lanyer's choice of audience has created problems for her readers today. For example, Lanyer speaks from the margins of the court world, but she cannot be awarded the status of a feminist protest poet because, as Betty Travitsky points out in "The Lady Doth Protest: Protest in the Popular Writings of Renaissance Englishwomen," *Salve Deus* is aimed "at an elite audience."[6] Lanyer used *Salve Deus* to critique the sociopolitical institutions of her culture that discriminated against women, but she also attempted to use her work to align herself with individuals whose social status and power were derived from these institutions. Thus the tone of her praise often grates on the ear of the modern reader. In *The Paradise of Women: Writings by Englishwomen of the Renaissance*, for example, Travitsky agrees with Charlotte Kohler that *Salve*

Deus is "primarily sycophantic," "art for lucre's sake"—a text characterized by its "obsequiousness."[7]

During the Renaissance it was not unusual for writers like Edmund Spenser, Christopher Marlowe, and William Shakespeare to begin their works with flattering dedicatory prefaces, the purpose of which was to convince sponsors and potential patrons to support the author's future projects. It was unusual and ambitious for a woman to write, and even more unusual for that woman to step into the public arena and attempt to attract sponsors to support her work as an author. In early modern England, the matter of women's literacy was extremely controversial and the very act of writing by women considered highly suspect. Lanyer's entrance into the public arena with *Salve Deus* was a transgressive, arguably a subversive, act. It is not surprising, therefore, that she chose to begin *Salve Deus* with an apotheosis of Elizabeth I. By doing so, she not only aligned herself with the community of women whom she identified as literary patrons and writers, among them Queen Anne and Princess Elizabeth, who had established a court of their own separate from that of James I, but also reminded her readers of their recent, popular, and powerful precedent—a woman who used power and wielded authority. That Lanyer should identify with Elizabeth I is entirely appropriate when one considers that, born and raised during the reign of Good Queen Bess, she was temperamentally and intellectually an Elizabethan writing and publishing during the Jacobean period. Furthermore, as Barroll states, by vying for court patronage eight years after the death of Elizabeth I, Lanyer was competing "in a very tough arena, against accomplished male poets (already privileged because of their gender) with considerable political awareness and very powerful sponsors."[8]

Almost four hundred years later, the patronage issue, which arises when *Salve Deus* is read, still seems to be a matter of class and gender. Modern readers do not question the motives that lie behind the flattering verses found in male courtiers' poems: for instance, Spenser's dedications to Gloriana (Elizabeth I) at the beginning of *The Faerie Queene* have not elicited questions about the nature of his character and work. Unlike Lanyer, Spenser, a nobleman, is not considered a social opportunist in spite of his attempts to improve his position in court by flattering Elizabeth I with his verses. Lanyer's character and work, however, have been and continue to be affected by her use of the conventions of praise and blame and ceremonial oratory (also known as the epidiectic tradition). Like *The Faerie Queene*, Lanyer's long poem "Salve Deus Rex Judaeorum" (Hail God King of the

Jews) begins by acknowledging and extolling the virtues of a potential patron—Margaret, countess of Cumberland. When one studies Lanyer's bid for patronage in *Salve Deus* in the larger context of Renaissance writing, her use of praise seems merely to be part of the contemporary pattern in which writers functioned. Indeed, when compared to the Renaissance writer who attempted to attract patronage by inserting at least thirty different dedicatory epistles into the front of different issues of the same work, Lanyer's ten dedicatory epistles and praise of the countess of Cumberland seem to be moderate and even restrained. One wonders whether A. L. Rowse, in *The Poems of Shakespeare's Dark Lady*, would have been more sympathetic in his assessment of Lanyer's work and her bid for patronage had she, like the courtier Spenser, been exiled to Ireland and hoping to be able to return home when writing her poem.

According to Rowse, Lanyer was a heartless opportunist, the Dark Lady of Shakespeare's sonnets, and *Salve Deus Rex Judaeorum* nothing more than a piece of "rampant feminism" written in a fit of pique.[9] Rowse's allegations have been answered by critics engaged in defending and recovering Lanyer's work. David Bevington's "A. L. Rowse's Dark Lady," for example, does an admirable job of locating and investigating the flaws in Rowse's analysis of Lanyer's life, in particular that critic's reliance on the rather vitriolic Simon Forman, whom Lanyer consulted as an astrologer in 1597 and whose low opinion of Lanyer "as available for money may well be the result of his attraction to her and his ultimate frustration with their relationship."[10] As Judith Scherer Herz points out in "Aemilia Lanyer and The Pathos of Literary History," "few now take the Rowse narrative very seriously, but everyone takes it. That is, nearly all writing on Lanyer positions itself in relation to it, even to discount it, although for all we know it may be true."[11]

Although Rowse's allegations have, for the most part, been disallowed, Lanyer's ambitious use of praise in *Salve Deus Rex Judaeorum* continues to attract critical attention. Therefore I would like to suggest that Lanyer's use of praise is not only a strategy by which the poet hoped to win Margaret of Cumberland's future generosity and protection in particular and the sponsorship of Queen Anne's circle in general but also an imaginative reworking of a conventional subject, the worthiness of women, and its traditional metaphors. The volume's long title poem, "Salve Deus Rex Judaeorum," does not merely demonstrate women's worth by extolling the conventional values of beauty and virtue attributed to the countess of Cumberland. Rather, "Salve Deus" departs from the sociopolitical arena in which the *querelle des femmes* is generally situated and reconstructs the Judeo-Christian story.

In "Salve Deus," Lanyer daringly redefines human nature by reassign-ing the accepted and gendered notions of praise and blame generated by the Fall. It is my contention, therefore, that "Salve Deus Rex Judaeo-rum" should be read as a radical protest poem that demonstrates women's spiritual worth in two ways. First, Lanyer establishes the notion of women's worth by challenging the Pauline notion of marriage. Second, the poet posits a reasoned alternative to the popular view that women are by their very nature depraved creatures incapable of rational thought. In "Salve Deus," Lanyer argues that women, not men, are like Christ because they are capable of experiencing the "higher reason" of Wisdom. The result is a spiritual protest poem positing a theological framework that relocates Ja-cobean Englishwomen in their society *and* their religious tradition.

To appreciate the innovative nature of Lanyer's approach to her topic, one must turn from the arena of patronage to the larger historical context in which her argument about women's worth is grounded—the *querelle des femmes*. Also known as the woman controversy or the debate about women, the *querelle des femmes* began in the Middle Ages.[12] Its early partici-pants, among them Christine de Pisan, Bocaccio, and Geoffrey Chaucer, grounded their arguments about women's nature, its worth or lack thereof, in their readings of the Book of Genesis—especially the Eden narrative. Anti-woman writers used their readings of the story of the Fall to argue that it was the nature of all women to have depraved sexual and intellectual appetites because Eve's curiosity was responsible for Adam's lapse. Male and female writers generally countered the arguments of such tracts by producing Old and New Testament models of feminine virtue to refute illogical and often emotionally charged generalizations about the nature of the feminine.

Because the Fall resulted from the desire for knowledge, the general debate about the need for and the nature of women's education in the early Renaissance carried on by Vives, Thomas More, Thomas Elyot, and Roger Ascham may also be read as an argument inextricably connected with the issue of woman's worth. The popularity of Vives's *Instruction of a Christian Woman* (1529), for example, commissioned by Catherine of Aragon for her daughter, Mary, later Mary Tudor, and reprinted nine times by 1592, demon-strates the intense interest in the issue of women's education during the Renaissance. By the time Mary Tudor had taken the reins of power and a Catholic queen was sitting on the English throne, the issue of educating women had become very topical indeed.

By the 1550s the *querelle des femmes* had become heated in England. Carole Levin also attributes the increase in the *querelle*'s intensity to the presence of the Scottish Regent, Mary of Guise, and Mary I of England. David Lindsay, Thomas Becon, Christopher Goodman, and, especially, John Knox presented hostile arguments against women ruling that were grounded in the Aristotelian definition of woman as an irrational, imperfect man.[13] Invariably these arguments returned to what Ian Maclean identifies as one of the strongest barriers to conceptual changes concerning the status of women during this period—marriage.[14] Indeed, the Pauline definition of marriage, based on the assumption that Reason must rule Nature, became one of the misogynists' strongest rationales for the exclusion of women from men's social and political functions.

John Knox, for example, entered the *querelle* in 1558 with the publication of *The First Blast of the Trumpet against the Monstrous Regiment of Women*—God's word on the "unnatural" practice of women reigning over men. According to Knox, "to promote a woman head over men is repugnant to nature and a thing most contrarious to that order which God hath approved in that commonwealth which he did institute and rule by his word."[15] Although Elizabeth I's reign effectively silenced Knox's voice in England, James I's succession to the English throne helped to reestablish and reinforce the notion that women were inferior to men. As Joan Kelly notes, not even Knox could surpass James's revulsion to female power. Like Knox, James based his idea of the proper relationship between men and women on Paul's Letter to the Ephesians—"his advice to his eldest son on his marriage was: 'Ye are the head, she is the body. It is your office to command, hers to obey.'"[16]

When one considers the astonishing number of women who held power in Britain during this period, it is not surprising that the question of female power was an issue of paramount importance to men and women alike. In Scotland, the Regent, Mary of Guise, and later her daughter Mary Stuart, Queen of Scots and James I's mother, ruled independently. In England, Mary Tudor or Bloody Mary, Lady Jane Grey, and Elizabeth I took control of the throne. Significantly, in spite of the number of women in power throughout the Renaissance, conduct books continued to use Paul's Letter to the Ephesians to encourage women to be obedient subjects to their husbands. Moreover, as Achsah Guibbory points out in "The Gospel According to Aemilia," the foundational verses from Ephesians were used not only to give religious sanction to the political hierarchy between man and wife in marriage but also to sanction established social and political order.[17] Thus, when James I took power in England in 1603, he used the symbol of authority found in Ephesians in his speech to his first English parliament.

Defining the relationship between a monarch and his subjects as a marriage, he said, "I am the Husband, and the whole Isle my lawful Wife. I am the head, and it is my Body."[18]

Of the women who did publish their writing during the Renaissance and the Jacobean periods, a substantial number participated in the *querelle des femmes*. Pamphleteering became the medium in which the woman controversy was most energetically conducted. One of the first women to enter the debate in pamphlets was one Jane Anger. Her book, *Jane Anger, her Protection for Women To defend them against the Scandalous Reports of a Late Surfeiting Lover* (1589), was written in response to an antiwoman pamphlet that has been lost. Nonetheless there is little doubt that the *querelle* ensured a brisk business for book publishers, the men who slung mud at the nature of women in general, and their respondents. One of the most well known of the *querelle* pamphlets, *The Arraignment of Lewd, idle, forward and unconstant women or the vanity of them*, by Joseph Swetnam, was published in 1615, reprinted six more times before 1691, and then reprinted several times more in the eighteenth century.[19] The notorious *Arraignment* elicited many responses from women, among them, Esther Sowernam's *Esther hath hanged Haman; or, an Answer to a lewd Pamphlet* and Constantia Munda's pamphlet *The Worming of a mad Dog*. In "(M)other Tongues: Maternity and Subjectivity," Naomi J. Miller locates Lanyer in the vanguard of those who defended women's worthiness by pointing out that her prose polemic "To the Vertuous Reader" anticipates Munda's attack on Joseph Swetnam.[20]

As both Mueller and Miller note, Lanyer enters the *querelle* with "To the Vertuous Reader," and as Lewalski argues in "Of God and Good Women: The Poems of Aemilia Lanyer," "To the Vertuous Reader" is "a remarkable contribution" to the *querelle*.[21] Lanyer begins her preface to the title poem by explaining that she has written her "small volume, or little booke" because she has heard that it is " the property of some women, not only to emulate the virtues and perfections of the rest, but also by all their powers of ill speaking, to ecclipse the brightness of their deserved fame."[22] By praising women in "Salve Deus," she hopes that her examples of women's worth will be "sufficient to inforce all good Christians and honourable minded men to speake reuerently of our sexe, and especially of all virtuous and good women" (77).

As Lewalski notes, Lanyer contributes to the *querelle* by first lecturing those women who "speake unadvisedly against the rest of their sexe" and denouncing the men who have forgotten that they owe their existence to women before providing biblical evidence to support her claim that God

himself has affirmed women's moral and spiritual equality to men and list-
ing the honors accorded to women by Christ.[23] Here it should be noted
that while women's writing was viewed with suspicion, women often participated in the public debate about women's worth. As Lewalski suggests,
by identifying herself as a *querelle* writer, Lanyer validated her use of praise
because she aligned herself with a tradition of writing about women in
which women had participated since the Middle Ages.[24]

From whatever period of the *querelle* the debaters spoke, medieval,
Tudor, Elizabethan, or Jacobean, the sociopolitical arguments put forward for or against women's worth were firmly grounded in religious and
philosophical ideas. Given the Pauline undertones of Knox's argument and
James I's advice, Lanyer's was a shrewd decision to move the *querelle* out of
the political forum to the religious arena in order to address the problem
of women's worth. In doing so, she effectively won the debate in "Salve
Deus" by undercutting the premises of her opponents' arguments. Using the
misogynists' own sources to demonstrate women's worth rather than the
lack of it, Lanyer's unconventional rereading of the Bible posited a radical
redefinition of human nature in which her use of praise and blame in the
epidiectic manner was clearly an opening gambit.

As Elaine Beilin has noted, Aemelia Lanyer was the first woman to
write serious epidiectic poetry, poetry of praise, about women.[25] In "Salve
Deus," Lanyer's rehabilitation of the feminine begins in the traditional
manner of the epidiectic poem. She identifies virtue as the proper object of
praise and her subject as an ideal type—Margaret, countess of Cumberland, is a "faire example" who lives "without compare."[26] Lanyer, however,
quickly modifies the Petrarchan posture that exalts women's beauty. In the
countess's case, Lanyer posits, physical beauty is not important. Traditionally, the Petrarchan lover worships the unattainable object of his affections
from a distance—meditating at length and in great detail on the beauty of
his beloved and thereby enslaving his heart and causing himself joy and
despair. Discounting the importance of her lady's physical beauty, Lanyer
says, "That outward Beautie which the world commends / Is not the subject I will write upon" (79). Only the beauty of the countess's spirituality,
which "enrich'd with Vertue shines more bright," inspires Lanyer, the devoted and humble servant, to worship the countess from afar (85).

At the beginning of the poem, Lanyer justifies her choice of subject by
examining its worldly counterpart. Worldly beauty, she explains, is clearly a
limited and perverse use of the flesh for the sake of pride and glory. For those
who "glory most in it," she says, "most their danger lies" (85). Citing histori-

cal and legendary examples, women like Helen, Lucrece, and Cleopatra, Lanyer demonstrates that those who define their lives in terms of their conventional beauty find only "blood, dishonour, infamie, and shame" (86). The countess of Cumberland's beauty, however, is neither corrupt nor corrupting because her "Grace doth all imperfect thoughts controule" (78).

Having presented a feminine model of virtue, the poet turns her attention to the nature of men, and it quickly becomes apparent that her defense of the feminine rests on the recognition that women have been unjustly blamed for man's folly, which Lanyer attributes to man's nature. According to Lanyer, man's nature is to blame woman for the Fall, and in the epidiectic tradition of presenting models, she proceeds to make her case. The masculine model is not one of virtue. Rather, it reveals itself to have always been vice. Her examination of the disciples' behavior in the Garden of Gethsemane, which emphasizes their "great weakness in the flesh," begins with a sarcastic reference to Peter's faith: "Saint Peter thought his faith could never fall," she says, "no mote could happen in so cleare a sight" (89). Portrayed as a spiritual opportunist who "thought above them all, by Faith to clime," Peter is "most to blame" for Christ's sufferings (90). Lanyer uses the flesh itself to link the disciples through guilt by association with Christ's tormentors. Like the Romans and Jews, "wretched Worldlings made of dust and earth," the disciples are "the Scorpions bred in Adam's mud" (91). Peter and the disciples "were the cause thou [Christ] must endure these blowes" (91).

Lanyer's unapologetic use of language is Christ's—open, direct, and without pretense. Her rather harsh treatment of Peter and the disciples not only is the result of her straightforward style but also is grounded in her understanding of the Fall. Because Eve was not forewarned when she ate the fatal apple, the poet argues, Adam, rather than Eve, "was most to blame" for the lapse in the garden (103). Unlike Eve, who erred "for knowledge sake," Adam was the "ground" of all "Evill" (104). Adam, a creature of the flesh, was attracted to the apple's worldly beauty. He ate the fruit because it was "faire" (104).

Although Adam's imperfections are obvious to the speaker, and by now, to her virtuous readers, these faults, according to Lanyer, have not been perceived by men in general. If anything, Adam's behavior seems to have been used as a blueprint by his heirs. Believing themselves morally superior to women, Lanyer says, men have not recognized their own imperfections and have become tyrants. In her version of Christ's passion, she argues that man, not woman, fell a second time, when Pilate condemned Christ to death. Responsible for the Fall and the crucifixion, men seem to have little control over the weakness of their flesh. In "Salve Deus," men are proud, unruly, self-absorbed, disobedient, and fickle.

As Mueller has pointed out, possible antecedents for Lanyer's argument in Eve's defense make a fascinating if inconclusive subject. From 1451 to 1453 a public dispute took place between Ludovico Fosccarini, a Venetian doctor of canon law, civil law, and medicine, and a learned Veronese noblewoman, Isotta Nogarola, on the subject *Of the Equal or Unequal Sin of Adam and Eve*. Like Nogarola, Lanyer argues that Eve's sin was unequal in being less than Adam's because Eve sinned through ignorance, Adam was responsible for restraining Eve, and Eve was given a lesser punishment than Adam—she would bear children, but Adam was condemned to labor and to death.[27]

Even though she is writing in the spirit of a polemic, Lanyer is not merely engaged in redistributing misogynistic stereotypes. Instead, her treatment of Gethsemane and the Fall begins by examining the significant irony of men's "boast of knowledge which he [Adam] tooke / From Eves fair hand as from a booke" (76). According to Lanyer, the Fall is not the result of eating the forbidden fruit of knowledge. Rather, man's imperfect nature is the result of his own depravity. Forewarned when he fell, Adam succumbed to depravity when he decided to eat the apple. As a result, man cannot be considered "wise." Thus Caesar's "friend" Pilate is a "faultie Judge" (108). Ignoring his "worthy" wife's message to open his eyes and see "the truth" of Christ's divinity, he sentences his prisoner out of political self-interest to please "sinful people" (102, 105). Clearly, like Caiphas's "Owly eies," male justice is blind (101).

As Lewalski notes in "Of God and Good Women: The Poems of Aemilia Lanyer," "all the guilt of the Fall" belongs to Adam, who was undeceived, and any faults that women may have inherited from Eve are "far outweighed by the guilt and malice of men."[28] Moreover, according to Lanyer, man may have lost his knowledge of divine things in the Fall, but woman did not. Like Nogarola, Lanyer bases her argument on the premise of Eve's ignorance in Eden. Lanyer's account of the Fall, however, is far more daring in its scope and more radical than Nogarola's. As Mueller contends, Lanyer's portrayal of Pilate's wife prefigures by several years other women authors' analyses of the Fall of Adam and Eve, when the English controversy about women entered its early-seventeenth-century phase.[29] Since Eve ate the apple only for the sake of knowledge and was motivated to share it by "too much love," Lanyer claims that the first woman did not share Adam's guilt (104). In "Salve Deus," the consequences of Eve's innocence are profound. Because of Eve's innocence, a connatural sympathy exists between Christ and the Daughters of Jerusalem. Christ will not answer Pilate or Herod, but "these pore women" "bid move their Lord, their Lover, and their King / To take compassion, turne about, and speake / To them" (109). Because of this connaturality, Pilate's wife also is able to recognize Christ.

Lanyer explains the affinity between women and Christ in her treatment of the countess. Because she is a virtuous woman, the countess also participates in the image of God that was thought to have been lost in the Fall. Not only does she recognize the face of God, which is reflected in the natural world at the Cookeham estate, but she also lives in a state of indeterminate being that exists in neither God nor man. The countess is what Frank Manley terms "a figure of perfect contemplation, the mind freed from the trammels of corporeal existence":[30] she is drawn from "caring what this world may yield" by her "meditation of this monarch's love" (84). In short, like attracts like. Christ attracts the countess because "Spirits affect where they doe sympathize" and "Wisdom desires Wisdom to embrace" (129). Married to "her God," Lanyer's "Pure-thoughted" lady becomes a Wisdom figure—the female consort, some believe the female counterpart, of Jehovah found in the Old Testament (87).

Married to her God, the countess is engaged in theocentric contemplation. According to Joseph B. Collins, in its simplest form, theocentric contemplation is the ascent of the mind to God by means of nature, the contemplation of its creatures and the order, symmetry, and beauty of the universe. Since the mind can rise in successive steps to God by contemplating beauty, material and spiritual, the framework of theocentric contemplation is Platonic; indeed, after its adoption by St. Anselm, it came to be called in medieval philosophy the method of "Platonic induction."[31] In such a framework, the profane, natural world is a "shadow" or reflection of the sacred world or the world of the ideal. As physical manifestations of spiritual reality, nature and the universe necessarily are images, albeit imperfect ones, of God. By meditating on the order, symmetry and beauty of nature and the universe, the contemplative can recognize the face of God or the Ideal encoded in the natural world.

At the beginning of "Salve Deus," the countess's Neoplatonic admiration of goodness induces the image of God in nature. In *The Dignity of Man*, Pico's "eagles of heaven endure bravely the very brightness of the sun at noon."[32] Like Pico's eagles, the countess's "Eagle eyes behold the glorious Sunne / Of th'all-creating Providence," which directs "All worldly creatures their due course to run" (80). Her "Eagle eyes" permit her to see what her human eyes do not discern—not only the "Sunne" but also the "Son" of

God. Moreover, she is able to induce the image of the divine in the profane world. "[I]n these his creatures," she "behold[s] his [God's] face" (80). The English countryside reveals "Paradice" to the lady's "sweet sight" (79). Like St. Teresa, the countess sees "traces of the Creator" in nature itself.[33]

In theocentric mysticism, the journey of the soul rests on the formula of man-nature-God. Accordingly, nature in "Salve Deus" acts as the mediator between the individual and the divine. In this poem, Lanyer playfully adapts the theocentric formula to be read as woman-nature-Christ. Lanyer's treatment of nature as mediator is far more subtle than her praises of her patroness or her detraction of the disciples. Modeled on a pattern of gardens that point toward and ultimately express the union with the ineffable, "Salve Deus" moves from Cookeham to Gethsemane to Eden to Solomon's arbor and may be read in terms of a series of variations on the metaphor of the earthly paradise that establish thematic connections between the feminine and nature and, finally, the feminine and Christ.

Drawing on what Manley terms the universal tendency in the Renaissance to regard woman in general as Eden,[34] summarizing in herself the land of the heart's desire, Lanyer carefully links nature with feminine qualities. "Sweet Gethsemaine," for example, "that blessed Garden," embodies the quality of passivity (90). "Hallowed by his [Christ's] presence," Gethsemane "yet could make no defense / Against those Vipers, objects of disgrace / Which sought that pure eternall love to quench" (90). Ironically, Peter's reaction when seeing Christ at "the very brinke / Of grisly Death" in the garden aligns him with Christ's tormentors (97). Moreover, as Lanyer indicates, Peter's show of force paradoxically illustrates the fallen nature of his consciousness. "To draw thy sword in such a helpless cause," she says, "Offends thy Lord and is against the Lawes " (97).

Because nature is a mediatrix, it is hardly surprising that Lanyer's treatment of the garden metaphor includes the Mater Dolorosa and presents the image of the garden as a thinly disguised womb. Lanyer, it should be noted, as Beilin remarks, is no proponent of Mariology.[35] She does not promote devotion to or the worship of the Virgin Mary. Nowhere in the poem does the feminine appear in the Virgin Mary's role of intercessor. Indeed, the poet specifically points out in her preface that the divine aspect of maternity is not limited to the Mother of God. "[A]ll good Christians and honorable minded men" should "speak reverently of our sexe," she says (78). Thus Lanyer includes the Virgin Mary in the garden metaphor because she is a woman—not because she is the mother of Christ. Significantly, in "Salve Deus," the countess, "from whose faire seeds of Virtue spring these plants," is also included in this metaphor (124). Moreover, Lanyer uses the garden metaphor to strengthen women's affinity with Christ. "Borne of woman," Christ is described as "the Jessie floure and bud" (121). Because physical reality in this image expresses its spiritual counterpart, the Virgin's "Faultless fruit" embodies a "wisedome" that "strikes the wisest person mute" (111): significantly, all nature responds to Christ's present: "No Creature having sence though ne'r so brute, / But joyes and trembles when they heare his voice" (124).

The "natural" metaphor culminates when Lanyer yokes physical regeneration with spiritual rebirth. The resurrected Christ, himself reborn, becomes a garden. A "Bridegroome that appeares so faire," Christ has "lips like Lillies" that drop "down pure mirrhe" and cheeks like "beds of spices, flowers sweet" (120). Lanyer's source for this description of Christ is clearly the *Song of Solomon*, in which the Bridegroom's "cheeks are like beds of spice or chests full of perfumes" and whose "Lips are lilies, and drop liquid myrrh."[36]

An ecstatic vision in which the garden expresses the image of God, Lanyer's Christ-Solomon is a variation of the Edenic paradise that redeems the physical world and its attendant mortality, suggested by the myrrh dripping from Christ's lips. Furthermore, Christ-Solomon also provides an important counterpoint to the earlier treatment of the countess by uniting heaven and earth. Again modifying the Petrarchan convention of detailing the beloved's physical perfections—always expressed as snowy white skin, red cheeks and lips, and golden hair—for their own sake, Lanyer induces Godhead in the beautiful figure of the Bridegroom. The figure's physical beauty clearly expresses his spiritual goodness.

Keeping in mind that Adam chose the apple for its attractiveness and Pilate accepted the notion that Christ wanted to be a *deus rex judaeorum* on earth, this refiguring of Christ's beauty is yet another way of rejecting appearances that are merely literal. Christ the Bridegroom recontextualizes the sensuous appearance of the conventional Petrarchan lady. Like Petrarch's Laura, Christ's face is white "unto snowe," his cheeks are "like scarlet," and his lips are "scarlet threds"; even his head is likened to the "finest gold" (120). Christ's physical "perfection" encodes the spiritual Ideal. Like the Bridegroom in the *Itinerarium Mentius in Deum*, Christ-Solomon takes on "the feminine character of Mercy or Wisedom."[37] Lanyer's description of Christ-Solomon could be hardly more Neoplatonic, for his "feminine" beauty reflects the "Wisedom" contained within him. Bride and Groom are truly wed in a hermaphroditic image. Indeed, the poet's conflation of the Bible and Plato concludes her metaphor by re-envisioning the resurrected Christ as a paradisal Man—a hermaphroditic Adam.

Having reconciled the opposites of man and woman, male and female, in a symbol of wholeness, Lanyer completes the "taske of Beauty" that she "tooke in hand" (120). She then redefines the nature of marriage. Using the archetypal union of groom and bride, Solomon and Sheba, she revises Paul's concept of wedlock in which reason rules nature, man rules woman. In Lanyer's vision of marriage, there is no need for reason to rule nature because nature embodies the "higher reason" of Wisdom—God's image. Thus, when Solomon and Sheba marry, "Wisdom to Wisdom yielded true content, / One Beauty did another Beauty greet, / Bounty to Bounty never could repent, / Here all distaste is trodden under feet" (128). At the conclusion of the metaphor, the poet again identifies the problem of reclaiming paradise with the problems attending men and women on earth. Because Solomon and Sheba's equal partnership is an imperfect version of the ideal marriage (Solomon, albeit the "wisest," is still fallen man), Sheba, "this great Majestick Queen[,] comes short" of the countess because Margaret of Cumberland has "a greater . . . sought and found / Than Salomon in all his royalties" (132).

Keeping the imperfect nature of the profane world in mind, the poem appropriately concludes with a list of exempla illustrating the path that postlapsarian men and women must travel to reach Christ. Lanyer introduces the Christocentric model of mysticism, which posits the Christ figure as mediator, as the next stage of the soul's journey. Decked in red and white clothing, the countess herself desires to tread the "worthy steps" of the martyrs (136) because the "Pilgrimes travels" must imitate "the Shepheards cares" (136, 133).

Again, the method by which the individual encounters the divine that Lanyer proposes is inductive. One must imitate the model set forward by the martyrs who, in turn, modeled their journeys on Christ's to experience Godhead. Significantly, the traditional Christocentric formula of man-Christ-God has been adapted to be read as woman-martyr/Christ-God. Her contemplative marriage with Christ therefore seems to be only the first step of her journey to God: like Christ, the Fruit of Wisdom that has become the Bread of Eternal Life, the countess must undergo yet another, final transformation to achieve union with the divine.

In the final analysis, "Salve Deus Rex Judaeorum" belongs to what Barbara K. Lewalski terms a vanguard in the poetry of compliment. As Lewalski points out in "Imagining Female Community: Aemilia Lanyer's Poems," *Salve Deus Rex Judaeorum* defends and celebrates a community of worthy women that begins with Eve and ends with Lanyer's contempories.[38] Published "at a time when English Protestants were making a serious, self-conscious, and not unsuccessful attempt to develop a distinctly Protestant meditative theory and literature," like Donne's *Anniversaries*, "Salve Deus," the volume's title poem, arrives at a profound spiritual truth through the praises of an individual.[39] Lanyer's study of Margaret, countess of Cumberland, celebrates women's spirituality by demonstrating that virtuous women, made in the image of God, possess an affinity with the divine. Her argument in the long title poem is supported by exempla drawn from the Old and New Testaments, while the poem's contemplative model "naturally" unifies her extended rehabilitation of the feminine.

Because "Salve Deus" is rooted in the *querelle des femmes*, Lanyer's proposition that women should be awarded a privileged but not a superior position in society is this text's most remarkable aspect. Writing for both men and women, Lanyer, unlike Thomas Elyot in his *Defense of Good Women*,[40] promotes the spiritual equality of the sexes rather than the elevation of one at the political expense of the other. Moreover, unlike women writers like Rachel Speght, Lanyer does not urge men to live up to a godlike ideal. On reflection, however, this may not be remarkable at all. After all, Christ himself repudiated political power. If she had elevated women at the expense of men or encouraged men to elevate themselves over women, Lanyer herself would not have been following Christ's example. Instead, she would have been engaged in "the folly" that she attributes in her preface to "evill disposed men, who forgetting they were borne of women, nourished of women, and if it were not by the means of women, they would be quite extinguished out of the world . . . do like Vipers deface the wombs wherein they were bred, onely to give way and utterance to their want of discretion and goodnesse" (77).

NOTES

This essay is dedicated to the memory of Dr. Helen Molitor.

1. For a comprehensive list of books and articles about Lanyer's work and life, see Karen L. Nelson's "Annotated Bibliography: Texts and Criticism of Aemilia Bassano Lanyer," in *Aemilia Lanyer: Gender, Genre, and the Canon*, ed. Marshal Grossman (Lexington: University Press of Kentucky, 1998), 235–54.
2. A. L. Rowse, *The Poems of Shakespeare's Dark Lady: Salve Deus Rex Judaeorum by Emilia Lanier* (New York: Clarkson N. Potter, 1978); David Bevington,

"A. L. Rowse's Dark Lady," in Grossman, Aemilia Lanyer, 10–28; Pamela Joseph Benson, "To Play the Man: Aemilia Lanyer and the Acquisition of Patronage," in Opening the Borders: Inclusivity in Early Modern Studies, ed. Peter C. Herman and Edward W. Taylor (Newark: University of Delaware Press, 1999), 243–64; Leeds Barroll, "Looking for Patrons," in Grossman, Aemilia Lanyer, 29–48.

3. Barroll, "Looking for Patrons," 45.

4. Barbara J. Lewalski, "Seizing Discourses and Reinventing Genres," in Grossman, Aemilia Lanyer, 49–59; Mary Ellen Lamb, "Patronage and Class in Aemilia Lanyer's Salve Deus Rex Judaeorum," in Women Writing and the Reproduction of Culture in Tudor and Stuart Britain, ed. M. E. Burke et al. (Syracuse, N.Y.: Syracuse University Press, 2000), 38–57; Lisa Schnell, "Breaking 'the Rule of Cortezia': Aemilia Lanyer's Dedications to Salve Deus Rex Judaeorum," Journal of Medieval and Renaissance Studies 27, no. 1 (1997): 77–101; Susanne Woods, "Aemilia Lanyer and Ben Johnson: Patronage, Authority, and Gender," Ben Jonson Journal: Literary Contexts in the Age of Elizabeth, James and Charles 1 (1994): 15–30, "Vocation and Authority: Born to Write," in Grossman, Aemilia Lanyer, 83–98, and "Women at the Margins in Spenser and Lanyer," in Worldmaking Spenser: Exploration in the Early Modern Age, ed. Patrick Gerard Cheney and Lauren Silberman (Lexington: University Press of Kentucky, 2000).

5. Lynette McGrath, " 'Let Us Have Our Libertie Againe': Amelia Lanier's 17th Century Feminist Voice," Women's Studies 20 (1992): 331–38, and "Metaphoric Subversions: Feasts and Mirrors in Amelia Lanier's Salve Deus Rex Judaeorum," Literature Interpretation Theory 3 (1991): 101–13; W. Gardner Campbell, "The Figure of Pilate's Wife in Aemilia Lanyer's Salve Deus Rex Judaeorum," Renaissance Papers, 1995, 1–13; Judith Scherer Herz, "Aemilia Lanyer and the Pathos of Literary History," in Representing Women in Renaissance England, ed. Claude J. Summers and Ted-Larry Rebworth (Columbia: University of Missouri Press, 1997), 121–35; Jacqueline Pearson, "Women Writers and Women Readers: The Case of Aemilia Lanier," in Summers and Rebworth, Representing Women in Renaissance England, 45–54; Wendy Wall, "Our Bodies/Our Texts? Renaissance Women and the Trials of Authorship," in Anxious Power: Reading, Writing, and Ambivalence in Narrative by Women, ed. Carol J. Singley and Susan Elizabeth Sweeney (Albany: State University of New York Press, 1993), 51–71; Barbara Bowen, "Aemilia Lanyer and the Invention of White Womanhood," in Maids and Mistresses, Cousins and Queens: Women's Alliances in Early Modern England, ed. Susan Frye, Karen Robertson, and Jean E. Howard (New York: Oxford University Press, 1999), 274–303; Brenda J. Powell, " 'Witness Thy Wife (O Pilate) Speakes for All': Aemilia Lanyer's Strategic Self-Positioning," Christianity and Literature 46, no. 1 (1996): 5–23; Janel Mueller, "The Feminist Poetics of 'Salve Deus Rex Judaeorum,'" in Grossman, Aemilia Lanyer, 99–127; Naomi J. Miller, "(M)other Tongues: Maternity and Subjectivity," in Grossman, Aemilia Lanyer, 143–66.

6. Betty Travitsky, "The Lady Doth Protest: Protest in the Popular Writings of Renaissance Englishwomen," English Literary Renaissance 14, no. 3 (1984): 256.

7. Betty Travitsky, The Paradise of Women: Writings by Englishwomen of the Renaissance (Westport, Conn.: Greenwood Press, 1981), 29, 29, 92.

8. Barroll, "Looking for Patrons," 42.

9. Rowse, *Poems of Shakespeare's Dark Lady,* 20.

10. Bevington, "A. L. Rowse's Dark Lady," 20.

11. Herz, "Aemilia Lanyer," 126.

12. For more information about the *querelle des femmes,* see Natalie Zemon Davis and Arlette Farge, eds., *A History of Women in the West,* vol. 3, *Renaissance and Enlightenment Paradoxes* (Cambridge, Mass.: Harvard University Press, 2000); Linda Woodbridge, *Women and the English Renaissance: Literature and the Nature of Womankind, 1540–1620* (Urbana: University of Illinois Press, 1987); and Katherine Usher Henderson and Barbara F. McManus, eds., *Half Humankind: Contexts and Texts of the Controversy about Women in England, 1540–1640* (Urbana: University of Illinois Press, 1985).

13. Carole Levin, "John Fox and the Responsibilities of Queenship," in *Women in the Middle Ages and the Renaissance; Literary and Historical Perspectives,* ed. Mary Beth Rose (Syracuse, N.Y.: Syracuse University Press, 1986), 116.

14. Ian Maclean, *The Renaissance Notion of Woman: A Study in the Fortunes of Scholasticism and Medical Science in European Intellectual Life* (New York: Cambridge University Press, 1980), 66.

15. John Knox, *The Political Writings of John Knox: The First Blast of the Trumpet against the Monstrous Regiment of Women and Other Selected Works,* ed. Marvin A. Breslow (Cranbury, N.J.: Associated University Presses, 1985), 62.

16. Joan Kelly, *Women, History and Theory* (Chicago: University of Chicago Press, 1984), 89.

17. Achsah Guibbory, "The Gospel According to Aemilia," in Grossman, *Aemilia Lanyer,* 204.

18. Quoted in ibid.

19. See Mia Cabbibo and Sarah Davis's excellent introduction to "Excerpt, Joseph Swetman's *The Arraignment of Lewd, Idle, Froward, and Unconstant Women,*" retrieved October 27, 2003, from the Early Modern Texts Project Web site: www.valpo.edu/english/emtexts/sweetnam1.html.

20. Miller, "(M)other Tongues," 157.

21. Mueller, "The Feminist Poetics"; Miller, "(M)other Tongues"; Barbara K. Lewalski, "Of God and Good Women: The Poems of Aemilia Lanyer," in *Silent but for the Word: Tudor Women as Patrons, Translators, and Writers of Religious Word,* ed. Margaret Patterson Hannay (Kent, Ohio: Kent State University Press, 1985), 212.

22. Aemilia Lanyer, "To the Vertuous Reader," in Rowse, *Poems of Shakespeare's Dark Lady,* 76. Subsequent page citations to this work will be given parenthetically in the text.

23. Lewalski, "Of God and Good Women," 211–13.

24. Ibid., 212.

25. Elaine Beilin, *Redeeming Eve: Women Writers of the English Renaissance* (Princeton, N.J.: Princeton University Press, 1987), 177.

26. Aemilia Lanyer, "Salve Deus Rex Judaeorum," in Rowse, *Poems of Shakespeare's Dark Lady,* 84. Subsequent page citations to this work will be given parenthetically in the text.

27. Mueller, "The Feminist Poetics," 120.

28. Lewalski, "Of God and Good Women," 217.

29. Mueller, "The Feminist Poetics," 121.

30. Frank Manley, *The Anniversaries* (Baltimore: Johns Hopkins Press, 1963), 22.

31. Joseph B. Collins, *Christian Mysticism in the Elizabethan Age with Its Background in Mystical Methodology* (Folcroft, Pa.: Folcroft Press, 1969), 45.

32. Giovanni Pico della Mirandola, *The Very Elegant Speech on the Dignity of Man*, trans. Charles Glenn Wallis (Annapolis, Md.: St. John's College Press, 1949), 12.

33. Collins, *Christian Mysticism*, 48.

34. Manley, *The Anniversaries*, 113.

35. Beilin, *Redeeming Eve*, 190.

36. Song of Sol. 5.13, King James Bible.

37. Collins, *Christian Mysticism*, 226.

38. Barbara K. Lewalski, "Imagining Female Community: Aemilia Lanyer's Poems," in *Writing Women in Jacobean England* (Cambridge, Mass.: Harvard University Press, 1993), 213.

39. Lewalski, "Of God and Good Women," 79.

40. Thomas Elyot, *The Defense of Good Women* (1545), SCT 7658, in *Early English Books: 1475–1600* (Ann Arbor, Mich.: University Microforms, 1938–), microform.

3

"SHE IS BUT ENCHANTED"

Christianity and the Occult in
Lady Mary Wroth's *Urania*

SHEILA T. CAVANAGH

Lady Mary Sidney Wroth (1587?–1653?), niece to Sir
Philip Sidney and the countess of Pembroke, was a member of England's
most prominent Elizabethan literary family. It is not surprising, therefore,
that she is noteworthy for her own writing. As the first known English
woman to compose a sonnet sequence, a prose romance, and a play, Wroth
rightly claims a significant place in the history of early modern English literature.[1] Wroth occupied a privileged position as a highly educated, well-
connected woman able to write an extensive fictive narrative. The *Urania*,
therefore, provides an opportunity to view an early modern woman's imaginative realm in an unusually extensive form.[2] Her voluminous romance
The Countesse of Montgomery's Urania is remarkable in many ways, but
for the purposes of this essay I will focus upon Wroth's intriguing spiritual
investigations in this text.[3] Throughout her romance, Wroth presents a
Christian world while simultaneously portraying a wide array of characters
and experiences from occult domains. Although her literary spiritual explorations intersect with those crafted by other early modern romance
writers, the boundaries she depicts between conventional religion and hermetic domains remain more elastic than those portrayed in most contemporary narratives.[4] In this essay, I will discuss Wroth's relatively seamless
incorporation of the supernatural into a fictive environment that becomes
increasingly Christianized as the narrative progresses. Wroth demonstrates

considerable interest in the dominant intellectual issues of the day, including those related to spirituality, and her romance illustrates a keen engagement with the problems and fascinations associated with both the occult and Christian realms.

The *Urania* consists of two parts, totaling approximately six hundred thousand words. Part One was published in 1621 and provoked an enormous outcry due to its controversial portrayal of numerous contemporary figures.[5] This part of the romance was not reprinted until 1995, when Josephine Roberts's masterful edition made the *Urania* widely available for the first time. Until recently, the manuscript continuation of the narrative existed in a single holograph copy, housed in Chicago's Newberry Library.[6] It was published in 2000, however, so that readers finally have access to the complete work, which centrally considers the interwoven stories of the royal offspring of Morea, Naples, and Romania. Over the course of the romance, these groups of cousins engage in innumerable romantic and political adventures, ascend to their respective thrones, and marry partners chosen in concert with the powers of destiny. The political and romantic adventures of Pamphilia and Amphilanthus lie at the heart of the narrative. Pamphilia, a character based in part on Wroth herself, rules over the eastern kingdom of Pamphilia, a post she inherits through the bequest of her uncle. Amphilanthus, with whom Pamphilia engages in a lengthy, emotionally painful courtship, begins the romance as younger son to the king of Naples. He later inherits that throne, then becomes king of the Romans and is elected Holy Roman Emperor.[7] Throughout the narrative, the stories of these characters' romantic, political, and spiritual adventures facilitate Wroth's literary exploration of a kinetic universe that displays her fascination with contemporary philosophy, literature, science, and politics.[8]

Wroth's concurrent interests in both scientific and hermetic explications of the universe derived from a wide range of sources. Her family's libraries were renowned for their substantial and eclectic collections, the countess of Pembroke was known for her encouragement of scientific inquiry,[9] and the Sidney family had long supported the work of John Dee and other occult practitioners. Through her family's political involvement, Wroth also had ready access to news on related topics from the Continent.[10] As a result, her romance reflects her awareness of related, yet disparate spiritual dialogues, such as James I's encouragement of the pan-Christian movement,[11] the interconnected universe espoused by hermeticists such as Robert Fludd,[12] and romance writers' traditional reliance on enchantments to further their narrative agendas. The *Urania*, therefore, draws together an impressive array of source materials to explore a host of spiritual possibilities.

Wroth's examination of Christianity centers on the public lives and responsibilities of her characters. Since the central figures in the romance are predominantly monarchs or close affiliates to the ruling powers of a cluster of western European countries, this emphasis upon efforts to extend the reach of Christianity generally approximates seventeenth-century historical reality. The *Urania* is striking, however, for its advocacy of Christian unity. Wroth's apparent support for King James's idea of a pan-Christian world manifests itself in her erasure of the kinds of divisions between Protestants and Catholics that contributed to the Thirty Years War.[13] Thus, although she situates her narrative in the countries most affected by this conflict and creates fictive counterparts to key participants, such as the king of Bohemia and the Holy Roman Emperor, Wroth suppresses the divisiveness that characterized Protestant-Catholic relations during this period.[14] Instead, she crafts a portrait of allied Christian rulers united against non-Christian forces as they work to spread Christianity around the globe.

One of the most unusual key players in this representation of a cooperative and generally triumphant Christian alliance is Rodomandro, the dark-skinned king of Tartaria who marries Pamphilia in the manuscript *Urania*.[15] An enormous territory that stretched across Asia, Tartaria during this time was a noted Moslem power. Although pockets of Christianity could be found in certain parts of the region, the historic "Great Cham" was never the Christian general portrayed by Rodomandro. In fact, the Great Cham, whose line stretched from Genghis Khan and Kublai Khan for several generations before reaching Pamphilia's husband, was often considered a god himself and was said to have extrahuman powers. The historic "Great Cham," therefore, would never have fulfilled a role comparable to that represented through Rodomandro. Wroth, however, capitalizes upon Tartaria's geographic breadth to create a figure who could facilitate Christian circumnavigation and conversion of the globe. Since Rodomandro's territories conceivably stretched as far as China and India, this king's affiliation with Pamphilia and his close working relationship with Amphilanthus, the Holy Roman Emperor, support Wroth's speculations about this prospect. While this ambitious vision is never achieved definitively during the romance, the repeated successes of Amphilanthus, Rodomandro, and their allies present a promising portrait that contrasts sharply with seventeenth-century reality. Although numerous interpretive problems surround Rodomandro's portrayal in the narrative, therefore, his religious utility remains unquestioned.

Notably, however, the text never provides much substantive information about the kind of Christianity that is being upheld. Wroth's uncharacteristic silence could be designed to strengthen the suppression of Protestant-Catholic tensions through a lack of specific doctrinal or ceremonial references.[16] Since the various Christian countries and armies in the story need to be united to overcome their enemies, the absence of controversial traits or practices obviates the need to address the significant differences that obstructed such alliances historically. To be "Christian" in the *Urania*, therefore, predominantly means that one operates according to approved behavioral guidelines, with adherence to few identifiable spiritual tenets.

Behaviorally, however, the distinctions between Christian and non-Christian become increasingly clear as the romance progresses. Possibly in response to the contemporary threat of Christians being attracted toward the Moslem faith,[17] Wroth crafts an unequivocal representation of Christian gentility in contrast to the unseemly demeanor of those who live outside the structures of Christianity. Christianity, therefore, becomes the marker that determines how people should be treated and how they can be expected to act, with civility being exclusively a trait of Christian characters. This pattern manifests itself most strikingly in the manuscript *Urania*, where characters regularly link Christianity with demands for particular behaviors.[18] When the besieged "true Sophy of Persia" engages Pamphilia's brother Rosindy to intervene on her behalf, for example, both parties place Rosindy's cooperation within a Christian context. Accordingly, Lindafillia, the Sophy, exhorts Rosindy in this manner: "[C]onsider if I have nott most just cause to demaund ayde of all Christian princes (I beeing a Christian my self) to assist mee and deliver mee out of the hands of such wickednes and treacherie" (2:170). In response to this plea, Rosindy offers a parallel observation: "[T]hink noe thing of a Pagan enniimy when you have the Christians on your side" (2:171). As this brief exchange suggests, both figures recognize an implied obligation for Christians to help each other, particularly in the face of "Pagan" opposition.[19]

This assumed requirement for Christians to behave civilly toward one another and to help each other in times of duress recurs frequently. Thus, when Urania's husband, Steriamus, the king of Albania, encounters the beset Lady of Robolly, she offers embarrassed apologies for the rudeness of her Christian servants: "[S]he cowld noe way help, the nature of the people and ther breeding, beeing wholy rusticall and savage, '-allthough,' sayd she, 'they are Christians" (2:148). Although Steriamus accepts her request that he not be too harsh with her staff, he notes their apparent unworthiness to claim Christianity: "'Itt is little seene,' sayd the King, 'and more unfitt that such creatures should beare that hapy and glorious body of Christianitie, who have nott morall sivilitie nor due respect to you'" (2:148). As this interlude indicates, rude behavior is least tolerated among those whose Christianity purportedly reserves them for better things.

Christians holding inferior positions do not always behave inappropriately, however. When Pamphilia's brother Parselius becomes a pilgrim and encounters the wicked Drudeldoro, for instance, the evil giant's servants unsuccessfully entreat their master to respect Parselius's holy status: "[S]ome perswaded with him, telling him this wowld bee an abominable staine to all Christians if poore Pillgrims for keeping their Vowes showld bee soe curstly intreated" (2:345). When the giant disregards their pleas, the servants immediately turn their allegiance to Parselius, who handily defeats and kills the servants' unruly master. Although it later becomes clear that Parselius's commitment to his life as a pilgrim is shaky at best (2:396), the behavior of the servants in this episode makes it clear that a Christian affiliation is meant to signal civility, regardless of an individual's social standing.

Although many malicious characters take paths resembling Drudeldoro's and reject the perceived benefits of Christianity, evildoers occasionally reform and convert. In one instance, moreover, a penitent Lydian wants to be christened but is told that he cannot be sanctified because he has been a Christian previously. When he learns, however, that he can "bee reconsiled to the Christian Church" (2:362), he is overcome with emotion: "And hee with infinite (indeed the greatest) expressions of joye that ever man cowld showe receaved itt, and with as much dutifull reverence parformed his part" (2:362). Thus, at the same time that characters regularly profess astonishment that anyone could willingly abandon or live outside Christianity, the text leaves room for both conversion and reconciliation.[20]

Although this brief overview of Lady Mary Wroth's representation of Christianity in her romance includes some private encounters, it also illustrates her tendency to highlight the importance of Christianity in civic and international affairs and to locate most of her references to Christianity within fairly official environments. At the same time that the *Urania* promotes the expansion of Christian influences around the world, therefore, it most commonly separates this realm from the highly personal stories that it also considers in detail.[21] It is rare, in fact, for characters to refer to Christianity in their private conversations, although the religious affiliation of these figures is never called into question. Still, the Christianity that is most frequently invoked in the narrative appears to designate worthiness and to accompany civility rather than illuminate personal devotional practices.

This division between public and private spirituality in the *Urania* supports Wroth's extensive examination of the occult in her text. While mystical experiences are conventional in romance, Wroth's insistence upon the Christianity of the world she fashions could easily impede her exploration of some of the occult persons and experiences that she chronicles in her narrative. The innumerable supernatural events fit easily within the structure of the romance, however, and any conflicts between the occult and Christian doctrine remain unspoken. Like Marsilio Ficino and other influential hermetic and Neoplatonic writers, therefore, Wroth appears to be experimenting with a model of Christianity that can accommodate other spiritual configurations.[22]

Although the various occult encounters are not always beneficent or benign, the primary representative of these mysterious domains is the wise and virtuous seer Melissea. This strong, yet kindly woman intervenes regularly in the lives of the main characters. Her power apparently emanating from her books (2:397), Melissea involves Pamphilia and her cohort in an array of unworldly events, including enchantments, pilgrimages, and restorative leaps into treacherous waters. A familiar character type from the world of romance, Melissea's presence could offer a continual challenge to the Christian framework of the narrative, but the absence of specific Christian details seems to work in her favor.[23] Since the *Urania*'s Christianity does not present a clear doctrine that would denounce her activities, and because she operates only on behalf of a royal group openly identified as Christian, Melissea is able to guide, exhort, chastise, and protect numerous figures in the narrative without apparent opposition from Christian leaders or practitioners.

By creating this environment where Christianity and the hermetic arts can coexist peacefully, therefore, Wroth provides herself with an extended opportunity to explore spiritual realms and practices that would not normally be found in a world so insistently defined as Christian. Although she stops short of venturing very far into the territories associated with black magic,[24] she makes magic a central part of her characters' regular experiences. These enchantments and other mystical events become so ordinary, in fact, that Rosindy is heard to utter the dismissive comment that provides my title: "'[W]hy waile you thus,' said Rosindy, 'since shee is but inchaunted?'" (1:411). Thus, despite the *Urania*'s portrayal of the quest to Christianize the world, the royal characters often have recourse to the occult to resolve the confusions and difficulties of their love lives.

At the same time that civic events are linked to Christianity, therefore, the occult helps organize, complicate, and resolve the multitude of romantic confusions that permeate the narrative. Since a significant number of the *Urania*'s characters fall in love with inappropriate persons, Melissea and her assistants spend a considerable proportion of the romance providing solace and salvation to a host of lovelorn figures. With rare exceptions, such as Pamphilia's and Parselius's abrupt decisions to become religious persons (1:583; 2:323), these incidents rarely involve Christianity. Instead, Wroth draws upon the hermetic arts and the romance tradition to help these characters find their destined mates, at the same time that she takes the opportunity to consider what the world might be like if such magical endeavors could coincide with more conventional religious practices.

Although many occult interventions occur privately, they occasionally involve fairly public spectacles. This openness may reflect an understanding that even the most personal aspects of these royal characters' lives can have important implications for their kingdoms. Since marital alliances frequently unite countries, for example, or determine who will rule, the romantic escapades of these royal cohorts have far-reaching consequences. Fortunately, Melissea, the prime instigator of these events, remains benevolent and trustworthy, with a special affinity for the Morean royal family (2:61). The mystical events that she orchestrates, therefore, always benefit both the lovesick individuals and their countries.

One of the most noteworthy incidents of this kind in the published text involves many of the main characters, most of whom spend the early part of the romance in love with the "wrong" member of their party. Urania, who eventually marries Steriamus, is heartsick over Parselius, who abandoned her to marry Dalinea. Steriamus is pursuing Pamphilia, but she remains captivated by Amphilanthus, a character known for his continually changing affections. In this episode, Amphilanthus takes his sister to St. Maura, at the behest of Melissea. Told that he must fling Urania into the water, Amphilanthus sorrowfully tells her that "Heaven appoints it so" (1:230). Not willing to let Urania perish alone, Amphilanthus then resolves to "ende with her" by entering the water with his sister in his arms. The faithless Parselius comes to a similar conclusion, announcing that "Parselius will never outlive Urania" before also jumping off the rock (1:230). Eventually, everyone in the party survives the dunking and emerges with new goals and feelings: "Now was Steriamus released of his unfortunate love, esteeming Pamphilia wholly for her worth, not with passion thinking of her. Urania's desires were no other then to goe into Italy to see her father: and Dolorindus to accompany his friends whither they would goe. Thus happily were all delivered of the most burdenous tormenting affliction that soules can know, Love; and love was pleased, because now he might have new worke in new kinds" (1:231). Although the narrative refrains from addressing the effect of the water upon the perpetually amorous Amphilanthus, other than noting that he "was so overcome with comfort and joy, discerning this fortunate and blessed issue of the adventures" (1:231), the rest of the characters leave the scene ready to embrace their new lives without any residual romantic feelings toward their former beloveds.

While the text makes it clear that the characters risk death when, as Sappho was purported to do, they leap from a high rock (1:230),[25] their willingness to trust in Melissea and in "fate" manifests itself often. In this instance, for example, when the seer first instructs Amphilanthus to take Urania to St. Maura, he interrupts her attempts to reassure him that this course of action is prudent: " 'Nay, say no more,' cryd he, 'this is enough and let me this enjoy, Ile feare no ills that Prophecies can tell" (1:190). Urania has a similar response when Amphilanthus tells her that "Heaven appoints it" (1:230), although she seems fairly convinced that death is imminent: "You wrong me much to thinke that I feare death. . . . [F]ulfill your command" (1:230). Although "Heaven" is never identified with more specificity, readers can ascertain that it is somehow linked with powers of fate or destiny that do not obviously coincide with more clearly "Christian" spirituality.[26] As noted, Wroth appears to be experimenting with spiritual models that tie Christianity to circumstances of state while other forces attend to affairs of the heart.

This kind of divide between disparate spiritual influences arises even when mystical events keep the rulers separated from their countries for lengthy periods. Accordingly, many of the central rulers disappear from the worlds of court and battlefield into enchantments at times when their love is being tested. Although the narrative acknowledges that the rulers' absences may not be wise politically, and although kings occasionally stay home because of pressing obligations, enchantments imprison most of the main characters and many of their children at regular intervals. Once again, the spiritual powers in charge of these enclosures are never identified, although the participation of Melissea and her family and the kind of events that occur suggest that Wroth is drawing simultaneously from her hermetic knowledge and her spiritual imagination in these scenes.

The two major enchantments in the published *Urania* occur at the "Throne of Love" and the "Enchanted Theater."[27] Each episode makes it clear that whatever magic is invoked in these unnatural spaces, it is not strong enough to resolve the complicated relationship between Pamphilia and Amphilanthus. The enchantment at the Throne of Love is sought actively by the characters, including Pamphilia, who has obtained her subjects' permission before undertaking the challenge, as she explains to Amphilanthus: "(. . . [W]ith the consent of my people, leaving the government for this time with the Councell) we came to adventure for the Throne of Love" (1:168). Although Amphilanthus is involved in a romantic dalliance with Antissia during this period, he joins with Pamphilia to try their luck at the enchantment, which has already imprisoned the six couples who preceded them (1:168). After pausing to knight Antissia's nephew, the king of Romania, Amphilanthus leads Pamphilia into the enchantment, where the pair successfully pass through the gates of "desire," "constancy," and "love" before freeing the lovers who have failed to complete the enchantment. At the moment of their triumph, a mysterious voice awards the pair their victory: "Loyallest, and therefore most incomparable Pamphilia, release the Ladies, who must to your worth, with all other of your sexe, yeeld right preheminence: and thou Amphilanthus, the valliantest and worthiest of thy sexe, give freedome to the Knights, who with all other, must confesse thee matchlesse; and thus is *Love* by love and worth released" (1:170–71). Thus, although the adventure began with Pamphilia quizzing Amphilanthus over his relationship with Antissia, the duo proves triumphant, even as "the Pallace and all vanished" (1:170).

This mysterious, disembodied voice parallels many other unexplained phenomena in the *Urania*. In the manuscript, for example, Urania and Steriamus encounter an equally inexplicable appearance of a disembodied hand during an ordinary conversation at their home. In the midst of their concern about the absent Pamphilia's state of mind, they receive an unusual message: "Placing them selves by the fountaine againe, discoursing as beefor, appeerd out of the water a delicate, faire, white hand, which held a scrole in itt. Steriamus reached att itt, butt Urania must have itt. She taking itt, read itt. The subject was that Pamphilia was nott soe happy as she might bee if with her, soe desiring she showld bee sent for" (2:306). Neither Steriamus nor Urania evinces any concern over this unconventional event. Instead, Urania decides immediately to invite Pamphilia for a visit after calmly offering an explanation for the unexpected vision: "This is certainly som devine spiritt, pittiing her ill fortunes, which provokes us to move for her presence heer. Wee must send by any meanes" (2:306). As soon as the invitation is settled upon, no further discussion of the unusual messenger follows, even though it makes another dramatic, brief appearance when the summoned Pamphilia is sitting near the fountain with Urania: "They had nott longe satt in this discourse, butt the same hand came up againe, holding a little booke of golde, and an other, but a farr largger scrole. Pamphilia tooke them bothe, read the scrole, opened the booke, read itt, blusht till teares came in her eyes, then closed them both, putt them up, sighed, and so they satt downe together again" (2:307). As soon as Pamphilia composes herself, the pair resumes their conversation without any discussion of the scroll, the book, or the hand. Once again, therefore, this remarkable occurrence is accepted with equanimity.

Immediately after the second interaction with the mysterious hand, moreover, Pamphilia encounters Leutissia, a water nymph whose life was saved, though changed, by similarly unexplained circumstances. In this instance, however, one member of the queen's party indicates that not all the characters in the narrative remain calm when confronted with the supernatural. Upon hearing Leutissia's unexpected voice, "The Merry Marquise" fearfully attempts to hide herself from the occult domain, going "into her chamber wher she shutt up her self, bolting and closing the doores so faste as iff she had the art to shutt even spiritts from her" (2:309). Pamphilia dismisses her friend's concern, however, and apologizes to Leutissia for the Marquise's abrupt departure: "Most beeloved and honored Nimph (and amongst the watry powers certainly Sacred, Godhead beelonging to you), lett nott the mistake of a merry minded lady bee offencive, who (I dare answere for) did nott any thing with intent of offending" (2:309). As Pamphilia's conciliatory words suggest, the queen presumes that the nymph is "sacred," not a figure to be feared. Despite the Marquise's skittishness, therefore, the water nymph receives a warm welcome into Pamphilia's community.

In addition, Leutissia's ensuing story enables Wroth to provide a supernatural solution to a kind of problem she describes in other parts of her romance—namely, a woman's sexual vulnerability to powerful men. In this instance, Leutissia describes becoming embroiled in a struggle precipitated by the unlawful desires of her lover's father. The aptly named Demonarus lusts after his daughter Lydia and seeks his wife's assistance in facilitating Lydia's rape. When his wife refuses, Demonarus flies into a rage, eventually killing Lydia, her mother, and Leutissia's lover Amarintus. Surviving the bloodbath, Leutissia flees. Although she claims not to fear death, the terrified woman is afraid that she will be raped. Accordingly, she literally throws herself at the mercy of the spiritual world: "[S]uch shame as I sawe prepared for mee, made mee fly, and Cry with all fervencie for help to the Silvaine or watry Godheads, and soe I hapined hapily in their powers. For having with happy speed attain'd the brimm of this Sweet fountaine, I lept into itt, criing to Diana ore the water nimphs to save mee, who both heard and commiserated my distress, imbraced mee, and sweetly held mee up a little to see some comfort in (though blooddy) yett Just revenge" (2:312). Thus, miraculously saved from certain death or ravishment, Leutissia watches the evildoer die, then spends the rest of her life as a nymph. Although such an event would be familiar in the works of Wroth's literary predecessors, it is unusual within the *Urania* for a character to cross from the human to the supernatural realm. Nevertheless, this transformation further illustrates the narrative's ability to accommodate a range of spiritual beings and influences.

At the same time, the narrative's failure to specify the origins of "the voice" or "the hand" discussed or to offer much explanation about Leutissia's transformation exemplifies Wroth's consistent reluctance to identify the sources for such otherworldly happenings. These events serve as two of the many instances where the narrative details an occult incident, then refuses to provide any explanation for its existence or for its ready accommodation into a Christian world. Although it would be easy to discount this pattern by accepting that "these kinds of things happen in romance," such an easy dismissal would obscure an important aspect of Wroth's spiritual explorations. By incorporating such unfathomable entities and events into her text, Wroth extends her examination of the possibility of a "unified universe." Just as eliminating differences between Protestants and Catholics enables a vision of a united Christianity encircling the globe, effacing disjunctures between Christianity and the occult creates the space for a world where a wide range of previously competing spiritual forces can operate without undue friction. Since she is writing in an intellectual environment that does not yet definitively distinguish between scientific and hermetic fields such as astrology and astronomy, Wroth appears to be imagining a universe that is unconstrained by conflicting spiritual powers. In this way, she demonstrates her fascination and familiarity with contemporary religious and philosophical discourse, as well as her broad reading in English and Continental romance.

The *Urania* is not designed as utopian fiction, however, and Wroth does not craft a world where the kind of harmony she often envisions can always flourish without opposition. Instead, her keen sense of reality regularly intrudes into her narrative, reminding readers that even characters in romance fall prey to conflicting responsibilities. Amphilanthus, for instance, finds himself unable to respond immediately when he and his comrades receive "the heavy tidings of the losse of the whole worlds beauty" at the Enchanted Theater (1:374). Moreover, his friend Steriamus's reaction to the news underscores both the seriousness of the situation and the fleeting nature of experiences crafted by spirits: "Steriamus fell into such passion, as none thought he would have enjoyed the Kingdome, longer then one doth their love in a vision" (1:374). Similar to the adventure at the Throne of Love, the episode at the Enchanted Theater portrays a captured Pamphilia, Urania, and a group of their female friends, thus leaving this royal community bereft of its most prominent female members.

In response, all of the central kings and princes set out on a rescue mission, but Amphilanthus soon discovers that his official duties cannot be discarded so quickly. Although the party decides to let this king take the most expeditious marine route "as if the businesse most concerned him" (1:374), Amphilanthus is stopped before he can leave, with the news that "Italy was all on fire" (1:375). Reluctantly, he turns back to "his poore Countrie," (1:375), while the narrator bemoans Pamphilia's loss: "Alas, unfortunate Lady, what will become of you? this is the last time for some moneths, hee shall come so neare, but yeares before his affection bee so much" (1:375). But however urgent Pamphilia's plight may appear to be, Amphilanthus's responsibility toward his country takes precedence over his obligations to her.[28]

This kind of intermingling of spiritual events, political occurrences, and romantic entanglements facilitates more than the machinations of a complicated prose romance. As noted, Wroth remains interested in the possibilities and problems of a unified universe. Although this conflict between Amphilanthus's heart and his official duties certainly reflects the ongoing struggles that impede his relationship with Pamphilia, therefore, it also illustrates one of the many points of tension that recur between the different facets of this interconnected world. None of the individual elements of this environment can triumph consistently over the others. Hence, Melissea's powers are limited (2:182), political successes cannot be guaranteed, natural forces can direct but not determine characters' fates, and love remains far from omnipotent. At the same time, however, each of these realms interacts with the others, as the romance continually demonstrates to its audience that spirituality, physicality, love, and politics can never be separated completely.[29]

This coalescence becomes even more striking in the manuscript continuation of the *Urania*, where Wroth expands the range of hermetic activities experienced by her characters. Possibly because the author knew that publication was improbable for this portion of the narrative, the second half of the romance ventures farther into the world of the occult, even though the battles become increasingly Christianized. In particular, the next generation of knights and rulers faces extended enchantments, bears prophetic birthmarks, and encounters mystical beings and occurrences with more regularity than their predecessors experienced. While the world portrayed in Part One often included extraordinary creatures or events, in the second part of the *Urania* these emissaries from the occult appear to predominate.

One of the most prominent changes involves the nature of the enchantments that ensnare the characters. As the journeys to the Throne of Love exemplify above, enchantments in the printed text are often eagerly sought by the main characters. In fact, the anticipation and voluntary participation associated with such adventures (1:411–12) indicate that they represent sources of advancement and entertainment as often as they provoke concern. Characters thus seek out enchantments because they provide opportunities for chivalric and romantic renown. Rosindy's disparagement of these events, therefore, seems appropriate.[30] These kind of mystical encounters often seem less benign in the manuscript, however, because they involve the royal families' children.[31] Although the bereft parents occasionally receive word that their offspring are well, though inaccessible, the loss of these children causes tremendous grief (2:145). The amusement often associated with enchantments, therefore, diminishes when those involved are children.

Yet although this group of enchantments prompts significant sorrow, it also reflects the complexity of most aspects of the *Urania*'s vision of the universe. The enchantments in the manuscript *Urania* frequently either encourage appropriate behavior, punish transgressions, or help alter established hierarchies in the romance. The loss of the children, for example, prompts significant behavioral changes on the part of both established figures and new members of the chivalric and royal communities. It also keeps the young characters safe until they are mature enough to inherit their rightful places in society. Although the specific details of these particular enchantments receive little elaboration, therefore, this mystical fostering of the royal offspring leads to widespread consequences for all of the families involved.[32]

When the children vanish, for example, their disappearance instigates a series of events that significantly changes the composition of the chivalric world. Many of the elder knights, including Parselius and Rosindy, have withdrawn from active knightly participation by the time their children become the object of major searches. This crisis draws these men out of retirement (2:166), but it concurrently drains the military resources of the countries involved by keeping these older soldiers engaged in quests to rescue their children. Accordingly, numerous positions of authority become available to ambitious youths who might otherwise not have risen to prominence so readily. While the veteran knights venture off to retrieve their children, the growing political turbulence that they leave behind demands attention. As the absence of seasoned military leaders becomes increasingly problematic, therefore, a host of natural sons and other untested young men step forward to fill the void.[33]

This dearth of experienced knights enables Wroth to explore a world where legitimacy is not a prerequisite to renown.[34] In fact, the new knight who seems destined to be the hero of the "new age" being introduced comes from completely unknown parentage, although it seems likely that he is son to Amphilanthus.[35] The ultimate challenge, therefore, the saving of the "true Sophy" (2:355), appears to be reserved for this "Knight of the Faire Designe," a young man whose name is hidden even from himself and whose title represents his ambiguous identity. While the romance stops before this final enchantment is resolved, there is ample evidence to suggest that the successful completion of this enchantment will lead to some kind of resounding triumph for both Christian and occult forces in the narrative. The apparent "savior" of the Urania's world—the "glory of the earths glory" (2:366)—is thus chosen from outside the standard patrilineal structures that traditional laws and churches would have supported. Apparently, the "new age" about to dawn operates under substantially different guidelines than the old.

Although the loosening of conventional responses to legitimacy might suggest that the manuscript Urania espouses more liberal interpretations of behavioral standards in romantic relationships, many of the other occult interventions into characters' love lives would indicate otherwise. In contrast to the primary characters in the first part of the narrative, who generally made their own romantic decisions,[36] members of the subsequent generation are granted less discretion in this realm. Like the Knight of the Faire Designe, who bears graphic evidence of his future, many of the enchanted children carry distinctive birthmarks that will help establish their identity and will ensure that they marry their destined partners.[37] Unlike their parents, therefore, who often fell in love with persons who were intended for others, this new generation receives supernatural assistance in their quest for marital happiness. Although the birthmarks do not always provide unequivocal guidance,[38] they still tend to keep those who carry them focused on searches for particular people rather than embroiled in the kinds of romantic tangles that often frustrated their parents.

These birthmarks further demonstrate the widespread acceptance of the occult within this Christian world. None of the characters ever question the origin or veracity of these marks, just as they never doubt the reliability of other messages provided through supernatural means. While this easy acceptance is part of the generic expectations for a text of this kind, the multiplication of such hermetic influences also indicates that Wroth feels increasingly confident in the occult expansion of her fictive world. This rising level of comfort does not, however, imply that the hermetic realm becomes more comfortable for the characters in the *Urania*. As Wroth expands her forays into these domains, she begins to use her characters' encounters with mystical beings and events as a way to show that individuals' actions provoke consequences. Thus, although some characters, such as Amphilanthus, often seem impervious to serious repercussions for their selfish or misguided decisions, less privileged characters offer cautionary tales to remind readers that the influence of supernatural powers can be considerable and can last a long time.

Pamphilia's brother Selarinus, for instance, falls prey to a lascivious spirit early in the manuscript *Urania*. Weaving what appears to be a fabricated tale linking her with the ruling families of Tartaria and Frigia, this persistent succubus does not initially stay with Selarinus long enough to do much harm, although she sets the stage for his later enslavement (2:7–9). When she reappears, however, she immediately lures him into a sexual relationship that will keep him captivated for many years (2:303–5). While the extent of Selarinus's volitional participation remains uncertain, particularly toward the end of his captivity, he initially appears to be engaging in consensual intercourse that eventually results in two children, who are put into the foster care of a benevolent woman (2:401). Despite Selarinus's social prominence, therefore, he is unable to escape supernatural sexual bondage or its problematic progeny.

This episode serves several functions in Wroth's exploration of spiritual realms. As many of the examples considered thus far suggest, the *Urania* contains innumerable supernatural forces that are generally benevolent or benign. But although Wroth spends the most narrative time on such helpful occult practitioners, she does not omit recognition of the kinds of darker powers that can emanate from other worlds. By including a member of a central family in this episode, Wroth is acknowledging that involvement with spiritual powers can have considerable societal ramifications. She also displays a noteworthy level of narrative courage in her willingness to introduce fairy children into the romance. Many of her predecessors, including Shakespeare and Spenser, flirt with related topics, but it remains uncommon for a writer of her era to incorporate supernatural children into a royal family. Her boldness, however, enables her to further consider the concept of a unified universe by breaking down conventional boundaries between human and supernatural beings. In conjunction with the erasure of common impediments associated with illegitimacy, this apparent inclusion of nonhuman children into the royal lineage of Epirus and Morea facilitates her early conceptualization of a universe where such boundaries between humans and other beings no longer carry significance. Although Wroth does not explore such a possibility in detail, she brings the question into open consideration.

Although Selarinus's circumstances are unusual, he is not the only member of Pamphilia's family to learn hard lessons through supernatural sources. Parselius is also confronted with significant consequences for the choices he made during his life. As readers of the complete text know, Parselius has a checkered history, particularly where his amorous entanglements are involved. Early in the narrative, Parselius becomes romantically involved with Urania. When they are apart, however, the faithless knight meets, marries, and impregnates the virtuous Dalinea. Subsequently, after being overwhelmed by grief during a dream, Parselius fabricates an excuse to abandon his wife, returns to his home, and attempts to deny everything when Dalinea presents her story and her baby to Parselius's astonished family (1:241–42). Soon realizing that his protestations are unlikely to be believed, Parselius acknowledges his wife and child and returns with them to their home in Achaya.

Hundreds of pages later, after producing additional children and participating in innumerable adventures, Parselius receives his punishment for this early mistreatment of his family. The supernatural facets of this episode are once again overseen and interpreted by Melissea. The narrator also provides explanatory commentary, moreover, because the incident defies credulity. She assures her audience, however, that the scene should be accepted, no matter how improbable it may appear to be (2:318). She then provides a description of Dalinea's posthumous enchantment that further stretches the imaginative bounds of hermeticism's influence on the text: "A mighty number of lights appeered in the sky; a strange-formed and built Castle appeering in the middest of thos lights, and in the Castle a most stately Tombe. This was seene apparantly, and truly beeheld by all eyes. Itt came att the first, extreame high; when neerer the Citty, itt stroped the lights of that brightnes and glory, as itt was impossible to discribe the extreame luster of them; then came lower, and so by degrees desended" (2:318). When Melissea interprets these mysterious images, she tells Parselius that his youthful indiscretions have altered the succession in Achaya (2:321–22). She further instructs him to become a pilgrim and to leave Dalinea's body, which will rest in this space for several years. In this world of monarchs, Parselius's "punishment" is quite severe, but he accepts it readily. Although he wavers in his commitment to life as a pilgrim (2:396), he does not question the justice of this supernatural response to his early mistakes. At the same time, the text further signals its vision of an interconnected spiritual domain by using mystical experiences and Melissea's instructions to send Parselius on the path of a Christian pilgrim. The romance gives no indication that anyone finds this correspondence strange or unusual; instead, both narrator and characters respond as though this correlation demands no special response.

As these few examples from the complete *Urania* suggest, Lady Mary Wroth devotes much of her lengthy romance to spiritual investigations. Drawing from contemporary intellectual discussions and historical circumstances as well as from the traditions of romance literature, Wroth creates a fictive universe characterized by active spiritual interventions in human lives. Since Wroth appears to have written most, if not all, of the *Urania* for private circulation, she allows herself considerable freedom in the kinds of spiritual events she constructs. Although the abrupt ending of her narrative, which stops in midsentence (2:418), and the profusion of characters, details, and events undermines any efforts to portray a unified universe in the *Urania*, Wroth nonetheless creates a world wherein the realms of spirituality, physicality, history, topography, and romance influence each other through striking, innovative interactions. Now that the complete *Urania* is in print, therefore, we have access to one early modern woman's detailed exploration of the multifaceted roles of spirituality in human existence.

NOTES

1. Wroth's play is called *Love's Victorie*. Her sonnet sequence, which appears to be related to the *Urania*, is entitled "Pamphilia to Amphilanthus." See Mary Wroth, "Love's Victory," in *Renaissance Drama by Women: Texts and Documents*, ed. S. P. Carasano and Marion Wynne-Davies (London: Routledge, 1996), 91–126.

2. The *Urania* often presents its stories from a female perspective, so that the author's sex remains evident throughout the text. Her spiritual investigations are less overtly "female" in nature, although she diverges considerably from the bulk of women's spiritual writing from this era. The combined influences of Wroth's status, personality, and creativity lead to a text that is often unusually forthright in its spiritual conceptualizations. For an overview of the role of women as authors, readers, and characters in early modern fiction, see Helen Hackett, *Women and Romance Fiction in the English Renaissance* (New York: Cambridge University Press, 2000).

3. Most extant spiritual writings by women from this period fall into more traditional religious genres, such as poetry.

4. Wroth's text makes it clear that she was well read in both the English and the Continental romance tradition. Although spiritual concerns appear in these other texts, Wroth is distinctive in depicting a realm with strong, regular interplay between Christian and hermetic forces.

5. For an account of the controversy, see Josephine Roberts, ed., *The Poems of Lady Mary Wroth* (Baton Rouge: Louisiana State University Press, 1983).

6. The sole extant copy of the manuscript *Urania* was purchased by the Newberry Library in 1936 (Case MSfY 1565, W95, n.d.). See Josephine A. Roberts, Suzanne Gossett, and Janel Mueller, introduction to *The Second Part of the Countess of Montgomery's Urania*, by Mary Wroth, ed. Josephine A. Roberts, Suzanne Gossett, and Janel Mueller (Tempe: Arizona Center for Medieval and Renaissance Studies, 2000), xxiii. Josephine Roberts was in the midst of preparing this text for publication when she tragically died in a car accident in 1996. Thanks to the generosity of her family and the gracious erudition of Suzanne Gossett and Janel Mueller, this major editing project was completed and the second volume of the manuscript published in 2000. Throughout this essay, page citations to the *Urania* will come from the two modern published editions. Citations from Part One (*The First Part of the Countess of Montgomery's Urania*, by Mary Wroth, ed. Josephine A. Roberts [Tempe: Arizona Center for Medieval and Renaissance Studies, 1995]) will be listed "1:x" and those from Part Two will be listed as "2:x."

7. The character of Amphilanthus appears to be based on Wroth's cousin, William Herbert, with whom she had an extended relationship. Although they never married each other, Wroth bore Herbert two children.

8. I discuss this aspect of the *Urania* in detail in Sheila T. Cavanagh, *Cherished Torment: The Emotional Geography of Lady Mary Wroth's Urania* (Pittsburgh, Pa.: Duquesne University Press, 2001).

9. For a discussion of the countess of Pembroke's scientific activity, see Margaret P. Hannay, "'How I These Studies Prize': The Countess of Pembroke and Elizabethan Science," in *Women, Science, and Medicine 1500–1700: Mothers and*

Sisters of the Royal Society, ed. Lynette Hunter and Sarah Hutton (Gloucestershire, England: Sutton Publishing, 1997), 108–22.

10. Wroth's father and cousin each held official posts that included considerable travel.

11. For an extensive account of James I's interest in the pan-Christian movement, see W. B. Patterson, *King James VI and I and the Reunion of Christendom* (New York: Cambridge University Press, 1997). The monarch's support of this controversial endeavor was noteworthy in an era so characterized by strife between various Christian denominations. Wroth's support of this concept demonstrates her willingness to embrace unpopular ideas.

12. Although there is no solid evidence that Wroth read Fludd's works, her text represents the kind of interconnected, kinetic universe that Fludd explores. See Robert Fludd, *The Origin and Structure of the Cosmos,* trans. Patricia Tahill (Edinburgh: Magnum Opus Hermetic Sourceworks, 1982). It appears likely, though not definite, therefore, that she had knowledge of Fludd's controversial writings.

13. C. V. Wedgwood, *The Thirty Years War* (New Haven, Conn.: Yale University Press, 1939), provides a valuable history of the Thirty Years War.

14. This erasure of tensions between Protestants and Catholics is particularly noteworthy, since William Herbert was noted for his anti-Catholicism. See John Richard Briley, "A Biography of William Herbert, Third Earl of Pembroke, 1580–1630" (Ph.D. diss., University of Birmingham, 1961), 534.

15. For contemporary accounts of Tartaria and the Great Cham, see my "The Great Cham: East Meets West in Lady Mary Wroth's *Urania,*" *Meridian* 18, no. 2 (2000): 87–103. I also discuss the historic position of Tartaria at length in Cavanagh, *Cherished Torment.*

16. Roberts et al.'s introduction to their edition of the manuscript *Urania* makes a related suggestion: "Although Wroth renders all but invisible the confessional differences among the Christian characters of Part Two, as she had in Part One, there is a newly virulent strain of revulsion towards Islam that threads itself through Part Two" (2:xxxiii).

17. See Nabil Matar, *Islam in Britain: 1558–1685* (New York: Cambridge University Press, 1998), for an informative account of Islam's impact on British society during the early modern period. Robert Cawley's books offer considerable detail about the many places that concerns and judgments about the Islamic world enter early modern literature. See Robert Rawston Cawley, *Unpathed Waters: Studies in the Influence of the Voyagers on Elizabethan Literature* (Princeton, N.J.: Princeton University Press, 1940), and *The Voyagers and Elizabethan Drama* (Boston: D. C. Heath, 1938).

18. As Roberts et al. point out, however, the behavior of the Christians becomes less civil in the manuscript (2:xxxiii).

19. Despite the invocation of Christianity, the occult plays a crucial role in this scene, with the besieged woman announcing that she knows Rosindy "through divination" (2:169). A magician had given her specific knowledge of Rosindy's eventual appearance in her life.

20. In a similar episode, Amphilanthus christens the penitent wife of Lamurandus (2:190).

21. There are exceptions to this pattern, however. Parselius, for instance, is reminded of his Christianity when he succumbs to grief over Dalinea's passing (2:321), and Amphilanthus struggles with his Christianity while in despair over mistreating Pamphilia (2:383).

22. See Ernst Cassirer, *The Individual and the Cosmos in Renaissance Philosophy* (New York: Barnes and Noble, 1964), 186, for one discussion of Ficino's efforts to reconcile the occult with Christianity. Wroth's spiritual investigations often coincide with Ficino's studies and with prominent philosophical examinations by authors such as Henry Cornelius Agrippa, Pico della Mirandola, Ramon Lull, and the writer known as Hermes Trismegistus. Each of these writers published works that were enormously influential in the intellectual life of the early modern period. Broadly identified as hermetic or Neoplatonic writers, these authors examined different aspects of the interplay between the physical and spiritual worlds known to them. See Marsilio Ficino, *Three Books on Life*, ed. Carol V. Kaske and John R. Clark (Binghamton: Center for Medieval and Early Renaissance Studies, State University of New York, 1989).

23. Figures like Melissea appear regularly in early modern romance. While it is not uncommon for such characters to interact with Christians, Wroth makes this seer a more intimate member of this Christian cohort than one would typically expect in this kind of narrative.

24. Although she makes rare mention of some black arts such as necromancy (2:329), she does not expand upon these topics.

25. In this episode, Wroth's characters emulate Sappho's famous leap off the precipice.

26. Despite this apparent affinity between Christianity and the occult, Amphilanthus briefly struggles with his split affiliation between the two realms (2:383).

27. These episodes both allude to similar scenes in Edmund Spenser's *Faerie Queene* (1596), although the situations faced by Spenser's characters are quite different.

28. The narrator's lament for Pamphilia soon proves to have merit, moreover. Almost as soon as Amphilanthus arrives in Italy, he is presented with a request that he marry the king of Dalmatia's daughter. Although he declines, he does not refuse, instead claiming that he wants to know "what was become of his Sister and Cosin" (1:375) before pursuing the possibility of this marriage.

29. This configuration of love, politics, and spirituality also reflects Wroth's understanding of related concerns in works such as Spenser's *Faerie Queene*.

30. Not everyone agrees with Rosindy's assessment, however. Selarinus is dismayed by this nonchalant attitude because his beloved is trapped at the enchantment (1:411).

31. Missing, lost, and stolen children are a commonplace of early modern romance that Shakespeare, Spenser, and Sidney, among others, often re-create.

32. The children are lost when they are traveling to see the queen of Naples. Different stories are included about their fate, which might have been altered or consolidated if the manuscript had ever been revised.

33. When encountering some of these knights for the first time, Amphilanthus notes their extreme youth: "The Emperour, looking much upon them, thought

hee showld know ther faces, ore att least the structures of them, for ther youth made him assured they had nott binn in his time abroad, butt as if new out of the shell" (2:145).

34. This sympathy toward illegitimate children presumably was related, at least partially, to the status of Wroth's own children.

35. Mary Ellen Lamb, for instance, in *Gender and Authorship in the Sidney Circle* (Madison: University of Wisconsin Press, 1990), argues that Amphilanthus and Pamphilia are the young man's probable parents (145, 148).

36. Although there are countless stories of forced marriages in the *Urania*, most of the central characters avoid these.

37. Distinctive birthmarks appear frequently in the romance tradition.

38. The story of Floristello, Lindavera, and Candiana is particularly confus- ing, for instance. The Roberts et al. introduction credits Micheline White with sorting through the ambiguous details of this episode (2:xxx).

REFLECTIONS ON THE SACRED

The Mystical Diaries of Jane Lead and Ann Bathurst

AVRA KOUFFMAN

In the late seventeenth century, the mystic Jane Lead(e) (1623/4–1704) and her disciple Ann(e) Bathurst[1] wrote extraordinary journals detailing their spiritual visions. The act of journal keeping was not, in itself, unusual; by the mid-1600s, it was fairly common for literate Protestant Englishwomen to keep religious diaries. Apart from Lead and Bathurst, however, few Stuart women diarists ventured into mystical territory. On occasion, they used passionate language to convey fervent religious feeling. The Restoration diarist Mary Rich, countess of Warwick, wrote, "God was pleased exsidingly to ravish my soule with deasires" (July 30, 1666). Even flickering moments of ecstasy are not entirely unknown. When the Puritan Anne Venn found her heart "very dead, and dull to any spiritual service," God suddenly appeared "abundantly above even my expectation, in some sense riding triumphantly and gloriously."[2] Venn, however, described her plight using a familiar Puritan[3] trope—that of the "dead" heart at prayer. She and her diarist peers usually evoked longings for God in sanctioned sentences authorized by the clerical establishment. By contrast, Jane Lead and Ann Bathurst celebrated a joyful, lyrical journey of spiritual discovery in poetic, imaginative, unusual prose. Although asserting female spiritual agency and authority could and often did prove dangerous for women in Stuart England, they chose to partake in a mystic tradition whereby they depicted themselves as members of a spiritual elite— Christians who had experienced union with God.

Further, although at least thirty-five female Stuart Englishwomen left diaries and commonplace books filled with religious observations and meditations,[4] these women did not attempt to publish their journals, since the self-exposure incurred by releasing private diaries would have been regarded as unwomanly and unseemly. Occasionally, a diarist received posthumous publication in a Christian edition edited by her cleric. Normally, the cleric responsible for this task selected the diarist's most self-effacing entries and published them as evidence of the deceased's Christian virtue. Lead was uniquely radical as the only Stuart woman to authorize the publication of her spiritual diaries in her lifetime, freely describing her surreal experiences in order to initiate her audience into her mystical worldview.

Although she suffered from financial difficulties and dependencies for much of her life, Lead writes as an initiate of the divine and conveys an air of calm authority and expertise in religious matters. Accordingly, her narrative persona is that of a woman who does not seek or require outside authorization for her beliefs and experiences. The self-confidence Lead exudes in her journals is apparently inspired by contact with a divine inner light, and she privileges a self-designated, inner-derived source of power.

Lead's strong sense of herself as a woman and a spiritual leader is clear from the start of her text, entitled *A Fountain of Gardens* (1697–1701). Although Lead implies, in traditional fashion, that her primary reason for publishing is to spread God's glory, she is not falsely modest about her role of author. In the preface to the first volume of her spiritual diary,[5] Lead records mystic visions dating from 1670. Even before receiving these revelations, she writes, she "lived in som good Degree of an Illuminated Knowledge" (1:6), and she offers readers a "mystical dispensation" (1:13). Her instructions to her readers are to "seriously apply your self to this Way and Method of God's Immediate Teaching: Which then you shall find to open the Center of your own soul" (1:7). Whereas Stuart-era authors in the throes of religious fervor often plead with, or warn, readers to adopt a particular doctrine or stance, Lead neither beseeches nor cajoles. Instead, her narrative persona suggests she has valuable information and will share it if requested to do so. Rather than mourning her unworthiness to write or apologizing for her gender, she immediately states that the purpose of her book is to enlighten her readers: "for the Universal, Enlightening, Leading and Refreshing, for the Dove Flocks belonging to the Great Shepherd, to whom such Pastures lie open to be freely fed upon; I think my self obliged to Publish for these Ends, what can be recovered of the Process and Diary of my Life, since I have been under revelations from the Spirit of my Lord" (1:4).

As for those who are not prepared to embark sincerely on a mystical journey, Lead curtly suggests that they "forbear Rash and Censorious Judgment upon those Things that are at present above their Reach" (1:14). She puts a practical spin on the Christian virtue of self-abasement, briskly telling other seekers to "keep very Low, entring into a Self-Annhiliation, So as a Nothing to be, with reference to the Creaturely Being, that the All-Deifick Unction may arise as an overflowing Tide" (1:14–15). She does not suggest that women are creatures unworthy of receiving the Lord's blessing, nor does she imply, in a Calvinist manner, that only predestined believers are fit to receive God. Lead merely says, in the mystic tradition, that men and women alike must quiet the mind and disassociate from the ego to merge with a higher consciousness.

Lead's guiding narrative principle is ingenious. She presents her explication of esoteric concepts in the form of a personal journal and testimony. After briefly admonishing her audience to follow specific practices and instructions in her preface, she quickly switches tactics by relaying her story as a personal, spiritual quest in the body of her text. Readers are lured in, if only to find out what happens next. Lead successfully uses the rhetorical strategy of testimonial, so prevalent in the seventeenth century, to put forth her mystical ideas.

To prepare readers for her surreal forays into the mystical, Lead forewarns of the need to read her text metaphorically. She mentions "the Similitudes and Visions which are published here, God many times coming down to unfold himself in this Figurative and Parabolical" (1:8). Lead thus teaches her readers how her text should be read—that is, figuratively and parabolically. Readers should expect the bizarre. Within the text, Lead announces, one will find "such Mysterious Things as haply may rarely be found elsewhere" (1:15). Her editor cautions that Lead's subject matters are "of the greatest Consequence, though they be couche for the most part under certain Parable, Similitudes, and Visional Idea" (2:A2). Her writing abounds with visions and parables, which are often effective conduits for the ideas she wishes to convey. Lead's texts are rife with imaginative stylings and creative rendering of spiritual concepts.

Lead's strength as a stylist is, in part, attendant on her use of brief but memorable parables. These parables, replete with vivid imagery and characterization, illustrate religious precepts. One, for instance, recounts: "In the night there was presented to me, two Forms very displeasing to my Eye, being Cloathed with a Hairy Goats-Skin, where spots and blotches did appear so unlovely, as I was much disgusted at the sight of them. [Then they] . . . rent this outward Deformity in twain. . . . And I beheld two sweet amiable children came forth" (January 12, 1677/8, 2:9). Here, rather than state that sin is ugly, Lead describes monstrous, sinful creatures. Her striking use of imagery allows the reader to grasp, viscerally, that sin itself is a deformity. Later, Lead reveals that the "innocent and all-beautiful Babes" of her parable who come forth from the ugly goat-skin are human beings who have cast off "that thick and cloudy smothering Body of Sin" that previously disfigured them (3:10). In time, Lead feels, all humans will enjoy "the shining face of a transmuted Body" (2:27).[6] But until this transformation occurs, patience is necessary. As Spirit explains, "[T]he Holy thing, which is rising out of the Center, must have time to work through all that dark matter, which doth lie in the vale of Flesh" (2:516). Matter, like sin, is disdained as undesirable but ultimately illusory and transcendable; Lead's imaginative and gripping use of parable underscores this idea.

Not all of Lead's writing is stylistically laudable. Lead was extremely prolific in her chronicling of spiritual visions, and some parts of her texts are marred by awkward repetition of tropes and ideas. Her lengthier entries can be difficult to follow, since events rarely follow each other in a clear linear progression. Her own (unnamed) editor is not overflattering about her literary technique; he calls her style of prose "mind-chatter" and concedes that many readers will find nothing in her text but "an Enthusiastick Jargon of Words" (2:A2). Lead herself acknowledges her editor's comments and does not seem offended by them, although scattered among the scores of words and entries are beautiful, ecstatic visions, described in memorable prose. She writes, "I felt the Deity to arise, to a *Molten Sea* of Transparency. This was a God-over-running with a glowing Stream. Indeed Voices and Seraphims; Sounds and Lightnings; Tastings, Feelings, and Spicy Scents broke in all at once" (4:233–34). Other passages are far less heightened.

Throughout Lead's texts, her writing veers dramatically from the poetic and lyrical to the repetitive and impenetrable. Perhaps her writing is of such variable quality because she was not the primary editor and arranger of her miscellaneous papers for publication. Lead's editor proposes a few commonplace reasons as to why Lead's texts are jumbled or incomplete: "There is indeed a great Part lost of what She had Written in loose Shreds of Paper, for the sake of her own Memory, and for monitions and Encouragements to some few Particular Friends; not thinking of their Publication in the least: As also a Book Written in her own Hand, which was sent to an Honourable and Pious Lady. . . . The Death of her Intimate Friend, who diligently transcribed all her Spiritual Papers, has prevented us from seeing many Things, that would Doubtless have been preserved by him" (4: unpaginated advertisement). Despite the standard assertion that Lead did not expect publication of all her papers, she clearly allowed for the publication of her diaries. Her entries first appear in her 1694 text, *The Enochian Walks with God*. The multivolume *Fountain of Gardens* is composed almost entirely of her journal entries. However, if she did not edit her scattered papers into their final published form, Lead may not be responsible for the repetition and confusion that sometimes mars the flow of her passages and obscures the links between them.

Whereas Lead's extensive use of allegory, symbol, and mystic tropes sets her apart from her diarist peers, these stylistic devices usefully enable readers to situate her within a broad Christian framework and tradition. Lead relies strongly on the trope of vision, recurrent in Christian literature since Christ transfigured himself before Peter, James, and John and since Paul saw through a glass darkly. In her visions, everything is made apparent. Normally, she suggests, humans do not acknowledge how ignoble they are: "[W]e have seen our selves in a flattering Glass, and have been thereby deceived" (3:177). As her spiritual education progresses, Lead learns to see God's literal "inspiration"—his breath. Jesus himself teaches her to see this in a vision. She tells us, "The Eye of my Spirit saw it thin as the Mist, only as the coulour of the Sun-Beams. Then said the Word in me, What dost thou now see but the Spirit and Breath!" (1:346). As truth is revealed, the Divine Essence and its emanation become visible. Several of Lead's conceits and imagery, such as her depiction of the Divine as luminous, or her configuration of the body as the prison of the soul, can be traced back to Platonic thought.

To be more specific, Lead participates in, and is influenced by, a theosophic school of thought based on the work of the German mystic Jacob Boehme (1575–1624). Both Lead and Reverend John Pordage, her close colleague, were adherents of Boehme, also known as Behemists. Arthur Versluis credits Boehme with helping to popularize a strand of seventeenth-century Protestanism in which practitioners focused on Sophia, the figure of divine wisdom; insisted upon "direct spiritual experience"; and shunned sectarianism.[7] Boudewijn Koole describes Boehme's Sophia in both spiritual and sexual terms: "Sophia, the Wisdom of God, is the personification of God's growing Self- consciousness, pregnant with the models of the world to be created: yet nevertheless herself chaste, and spiritual."[8] Even today, Boehme remains well known for the dignity with which he treated the female aspects of the Divine.

Like Boehme, Jane Lead draws on the figure of Sophia to concentrate on the female aspect of divinity. Sophia appoints herself as Lead's teacher, and thereby the reader's guide, through numerous mystic lessons. Sophia tells Lead, "Behold I am God's Eternal Virgin-Wisdom, whom thou hast been enquiring after; I am to unseal the Treasures of God's deep Wisdom unto thee" (1:18). Sophia then suggests that Lead regard her as a mother. Lead agrees, saying, "For if I would apply myself to her doctrine, and draw my Life's Food from no other breast, I should know the recovery of a lost Kingdom" (1:25–26). Manifest here is the eroticizing of the maternal and of Lead's attraction to Sophia, "the Figure of a Woman, most richly adorned with transparent Gold, her Hair hanging down" (1:19). Later, Lead's descriptions become more suggestive, as Wisdom becomes the "fair, wise, rich, and noble bride" whom Lead hotly pursues (1:118): "Celestial Dignity and Throne-Powres therby confered to make this Bride all-desirable, from which lustrous Presentation of her perfect Comeliness and Beauty into one Spirit I was all inflamed, making complaint, bemoaning ourselves how we might possibly compass the obtaining this matchless Virgin-Dove for our Spouse and Bride, who with her piercing fiery Arrow of Love, had us wounded so deep, as no Cure throughout the Circumference of this lower sphere could be found" (1:119). Lead's writing is quite florid, if not lurid, and she manages to convey strongly the eroticized sense of yearning after God that characterizes the religious writing of her era. But whereas other Stuart women diarists uniformly sigh after Jesus, Lead casts her beloved deity as a female—the Virgin-Wisdom.

Sophia begins by teaching Lead the first principle of mysticism, that there are realms beyond the bodily and tangible. Each human has a physical body that must be transcended before one can experience the soul. Sophia tells Lead to "Sequester and draw out of thy Animal Sensitive Life; that is too gross: I cannot appear til that disappear. There must be Spirit with Spirit, Light with Light" (1:25). One must first be "departed out of all Animal Sense, which is gross, heavy and ponderous," to experience the finer, more ethereal realms (1:86). Spirit explains that mortals who have gained acquaintance of their Transparent Body "shall have the ability to put off and on their Etherial Body, as occasion requires. For thus Christ did after his Resurrection, or else his Disciples would have been terrified of his presence" (3:17–18). Lead likewise suggests Moses "could never have consisted in his Elementary Body 40 days together to hear, & see, & receive the Law from God's own mouth" and that for this reason Moses' corporeal form was "sublimated into a Spiritual Glory, which was not altogether withdrawn, when he came down . . . for such a shine was still left, as the People could not bear to behold Him without a veil" (3:19). Lead repeatedly indicates that the incandescent light of naked Spirit is too bright to be borne by the physical eye; accordingly, access to exalted realms of spirit requires a dis-association from the physical body.

Regardless of the state of one's outward physical form, the soul is im-mortal and part of the divine. To sense the soul while in the body, one must concentrate on love, "for we live, move, and have our Eternal Spiri-tual Being from it" (4:244). Lead is told by Spirit, "Remember you are but transiently in this World to be: Your Home is with me, appearing and dis-appearing in the Body Corporeal" (4:297).

Lead's goal is to experience a "Mystick Union" of her soul with God (4:369). This merging or union is depicted as a blissful quietude wherein the soul has "clear Sight, and true Enjoyment of God" (4:370). Lead pres-ents Christ as one who urges souls to return to their "exalted State" of unification with him: "On Christ: He thus, and after this manner, speaks to a Soul: Would you be what I am? And where I am? And return unto your Ancient exalted State? Then so love Me, and your True Eternal Self in union with me" (4:257). In this exalted union, the Soul knows and ex-periences everything. Lead depicts this "Mystic Union" as deriving from a merging of the soul "into the Superessential Being" (4:369). Then follows a cessation of movement and effort where the Soul "rests from Labour . . . quietly possessing the immense Goodness. . . . Oh how little of this did I know, before I came to sink away from the outward Bodily Array . . . or be-fore I could find my self to be a Particle of God, as Light in his Light" (4:369–70). After she experiences her soul's eternal nature as an element of God's being, Lead attempts to lessen her identification with her ego-defined self and body and henceforth attempts to focus exclusively on her soul's identity as a "Particle of God" (4:370).

Lead stresses that, to experience one's spiritual glory, both the physical and mental self must be mastered. She endorses the conceit that the nature of our thoughts determines our reality: "[B]y Counsel of thoughts, the Gov-ernment of the inward Kingdom of the mind [is] swayed" (3:80). Lead notes that "whatever is resolved upon interiourly is executed accordingly, as op-portunity presents," thus anticipating, by several centuries, New Age tenets, the concept of creative visualization and the premise of modern hypno-therapy (3:81). For Lead, thoughts are "continually at the Kings Counsel-Table making Laws, and determining matters, concerning the Kingdom within" (3:81). These thoughts are "magical essences" (3:81), and "according to the Nature of them, whether Spiritual and Weighty, or Earthly, Drossy, and Light, so accordingly ideas were opened in the understanding, and the Wil framed to a consent thereunto, whether evil or good" (3:80). Since thoughts powerfully influence one's state of mind and inner landscape, Lead feels, it is wise to direct and control them.

Yet paradoxically, to achieve God-realization, it is necessary to cease thinking altogether, albeit temporarily. Lead strongly advocates cessation of thought, although she knows it is highly difficult to achieve this goal. She writes, "Now the great Query is, *How possibly can the Earthly thoughts be suspended? During the time of their bodily life, they will act their part for self-preservation*" (3:268). In the mystic tradition, Lead acknowledges the ego as unlikely to wish to annihilate itself or to cede supremacy over the creature, yet argues that the mind and its ability to reason can ultimately only hinder one's experience of the Divine. As Lead explains, "[N]ever could I hear, feel, see, or tast the Powers and Joys of the Light Kingdom, till I was passed out of the Cloudy Pillar of mine own benighted Reason" (1:85). She cautions readers that those who reside "in the Region of Traditional and Literal Knowledge, according to the Rational Wisdom of Man . . . through the Innundation of the Spirit must all be drowned" (1:4). For Lead, reasoning one's way to enlightenment is impossible.

Indeed, in Lead's mystic schema, wisdom and reason are oppositional. To achieve the former, one must sacrifice the latter. But since humans can rarely bear to relinquish their capacity to reason, Sophia, the personification of wisdom, is bored. The great mass of humanity has not refined itself enough to interest her. Sophia complains that "a pure Crystalline Mind is so rarely to be found, and in no other will God appear" (1:27). Purity of mind for Sophia and Lead does not seem to connote clarity of thought. Instead, this purity is found in the emptiness, quietness, and stillness of a silenced mind, a mind or ego that has escaped dependence on thought and its attendant mind-chatter.

Language, like rational thought, is thus not privileged but debased. Lead prefers to celebrate experiences considered nonlinguistic. Those who manage to transcend the ego-mind and its noisy thoughts are promised the bliss of the "enclosed Deep, where the Law of Silence" reigns. In this "*Eternal Nothingness*," what Lead calls "Vocal speakings" are abandoned (3:256). She writes of her visits to silent realms of Spirit: "I was uncloathed of all Similitudes, Figures, and Images; no Words or Cogitations could be admitted" (4:262). Nevertheless, she is forced to communicate her experiences to readers in words, and a "Voice" tells her of silent spiritual beings, saying, "their language thou must come to know in thy riper Age" (4:208–9). Although not every language is verbal or aural, Spirit here communicates to Lead through a "Voice," rather than by visual or tactile means. Lead's text illustrates the familiar paradox of the writer who attempts to communicate nonlinguistic experiences through words, although Lead does not acknowledge or address this problem directly.

Experiential learning, which is portrayed as independent of human writing or speech, is continually held up as the paradigm, and goal, of Lead's spiritual journey. Students progress by learning and heeding "the Rules that are taught in Wisdom's school" (3:333). In her journals, Lead is a student; by publishing them, she becomes a teacher. A strict taskmistress, Lead expects dedication and single-mindedness from her own students: "For this school is not for any such, as stand divided and wavering in their Minds, betwixt two Worlds. There must be a Resolution taken to stick to One only study. Then entred we may be, as Newborn in this High and Celestial University" (3:335). Experiential study, undertaken to gain wisdom, is the paradigm used to describe Lead's spiritual pilgrimage throughout her texts.

Although her writings are predominantly concerned with the intangible, Lead also acknowledges corporeal concerns. She implies that she would like to forsake the cares and concerns of the flesh but finds it difficult to do so when physical pain plagues her. She complains, "I felt such bitter Agonies in my outward Man" (1:451) and laments that the "Spirit of the Mind" is housed in a body that can be "depressed by Sickness" (1:351). Lead's body is twice a source of difficulty, both because it often ails her and because it must be protected from external ills and dangers. Despite her spiritual prowess, Lead is physically dependent on male allies to protect, shelter, and secure her from hazards like homelessness, hunger, and— although she does not say so directly—sexual attack.

The need to house and feed her physical form encroaches on Lead's ability to prioritize her spirituality. As a widow, Lead felt a need for protection and shelter that ultimately led her to move in with the maverick ex-minister John Pordage and his wife, against the wishes of Lead's scandalized brother. In her journals, Lead acknowledges the necessity of securing her physical safety in order to have the freedom to concentrate on her inner life. She writes, "Provision has been made for me, as disappointments happen for my outer support; my great fear and concern being left the necessity of my Corporeal Life, should distress and prevent the rising up of my Spiritual Life, which hath been my only care to keep up" (February 5, 1678/9, 3:61). Luckily, Lead prospered in Pordage's household. Together, the pair studied the works of Jacob Boehme and led a congregation.[9] After Pordage's death, Lead "assumed leadership of their congregation and immediately began publishing her own works."[10] Nonetheless, despite Pordage's support, Lead became destitute and lived, for a time, in a house of charity.

In her published diaries, Lead does not dwell extensively on her financial burdens or attribute her economic woes to gender iniquities. Instead, in the spirit of her allegorical text, she transmutes her social critique into spiritual metaphor. In *The Tree of Life* (1699), she uses a trope of marital property practices, cleverly positioning Christ as a perfect bridegroom who offers his wife love and justice in the form of financial equity between partners: "Believe that Christ will settle upon this espoused Bride all that is his: that she shall have a mutual Interest with him, in what the Father hath put into his Hand. . . . [H]erein she will be put into a Joint-possession, with the Lord her bridegroom, as her Propriety."[11] God, the divine and wished-for Father, bestows his blessings on Christ, who will share all with his bride in a "mutual Interest" and "Joint-possession." If God and Christ approve this practice, who can dare to oppose it? Like countless Stuart rhetoricians, Lead casts God as supportive of her cause. By taking an accepted trope—the Bride of Christ—and altering it to reflect a vision of a heavenly union where the bride receives parity with the groom, Lead uses Christian iconography to argue for a female agenda.

Lead's concern with female economic parity probably stems, in part, from her own experience. Born Jane Ward to a large, albeit landed, family, she experienced mystic visions as a teenager and wished to devote herself to God rather than wed. But she acceded to parental prompting and married a relation, William Lead(e). The couple had four daughters, three of whom predeceased their mother. Lead lived with her husband from 1644 until his death in 1670. At this time, Jane Lead, now in her mid-forties, became impoverished due to the misdeeds of bankers and her husband's lack of a written will. The widow Lead was, in her own words, "left in dire and extreme want, which forced me even more to place my assets into Heaven."[12]

It took more than two decades after her husband's death for Lead to gain renown and the attendant financial support of wealthy followers. In the 1690s, a patron, Baron Kniphausen, discovered her texts and paid for them to be translated into German. The translations sparked Continental interest in Lead's teaching. As she entered her seventies, a spiritual group called the Philadelphian Society formed around her and carried on after her death in 1704. Ironically, Lead cautions seekers against idolizing gurus and "Personalities, which will nothing avail him to know, and probably may do . . . great Hurt," particularly when one may more profitably "retire into the inward Depth of his own Heart" (2:529). Yet even if Lead had wanted to shrug off her hard-won respect as the leader of the Philadelphian Society, it would have been impractical for her to do so. As Grace Jantzen points out, medieval mystics used status derived from their purported direct experience of God to win respect and privileged treatment from their contemporaries.[13] In the Stuart era, Lead followed suit.

Lead's eventual role as the female leader of a spiritual community was, like the publication of her diaries in her lifetime, significant. Paula Mc-Dowell argues that Lead's position—"as the respected leader of a nonconformist sect, with two learned male scribes, a congregation of some 100 followers, and a continental, as well as local, audience—was itself a challenge to traditional modes of order."[14] Lead relinquished the prototypical role of Stuart Protestant woman as sermon-goer, anxiously scribbling down notes on a male cleric's sermon. Instead, Lead herself became the oracle of divine knowledge and, in a reversal of tradition, had male disciples to hang on her words and do the busywork of orchestrating the publication of her texts.

However, even at her most successful, Lead remained dependent on men to furnish her with financial security. Without access to an inheritance or a lucrative profession, her economic status depended on the male protection extended to or withdrawn from her at various points in her life and career. With such patriarchal constraints to overcome, it is little wonder that Lead turned inward to learn from Sophia, the female personification of Wisdom. As Smith points out, "Wisdom is for Jane Lead a coherent mental and emotional understanding of paradoxical reality in which a feminine ideal might be bride of Christ while a female person might be essentially powerless."[15] One lure of Lead's inner journeys is that her spiritual adventures are undertaken in what is ultimately a safe haven; no one in Lead's spirit world wants to hurt her. If Lead is not precisely in charge in the spirit realm, at least those in authority, like God and Sophia, wish to protect and encourage her. Herein lies part of spirituality's appeal for Stuart women: it is a domain where they can create for themselves the vivid experiences and acquire the sense of self-importance that society is loath to grant.

Lead's depiction of her dramatic experiences and her self-presentation as a spiritual authority were emulated by her disciple and fellow diarist Ann Bathurst. Bathurst's work has received little analysis, since her manuscripts are lengthy,[16] mainly unpublished, and housed in Oxford's Bodleian Library.[17] Details of her life are also difficult to come by, although Phyllis Mack describes her as a "respectable, middle-aged widow" and a member of

Lead's Philadelphian society.[18] Since Lead and Bathurst record similar mystical visions in the late 1670s, it is possible that the two women were already working together at this time.

Even a cursory glance at Bathurst's work reveals traces of Lead's influence. Bathurst's extant manuscript journals cover the years 1679–96. A very early Bathurst entry echoes Lead's journals in both vocabulary and content. Bathurst discusses an "Aerial Body" and a "Spiritual Eye" before arriving at the same conclusion as Lead; namely, that certain mystic states cannot support what Bathurst describes as "a weighty body of flesh." Rather, Bathurst explains, the spiritual seeker must be ensconced in an "Aerial Body" for mystical experiences to occur (June 11, 1679). Just as, for Lead, Christ after his Resurrection had to put off his "Etherial Body" so that his disciples would not be terrified of his presence (3:17–18), and Moses, after encountering God, became so luminous that "the People could not bear to behold Him without a veil" (3:19), Bathurst draws on a common representation of the Beatific Vision to describe a "Glorious sun" too bright for her eyes to look upon—"I could not behold it": "[I]f I did look towards it, it began to appear; as if it did declare that nothing hindred its ariseing, but my weakness, yt could not bear it; and thereby shews his tenderness to compaysienate our weakness being in bodys of thick clay" (June 11, 1679). In Bathurst's vision, God's *sun* cannot appear in full brightness; in Lead's text, God's *son* cannot appear. Bathurst, like Lead, describes spiritually exalted states as too luminous to be endured by those who dwell in less incandescent realms.

Bathurst's work is notable for the intricate, fantastic, and far-flung nature of her visions. Theorists who incline toward the psychological will appreciate her entries, which are based on a series of surreal visions or dreams. In her journal entry for July 12, 1680, Bathurst alludes to a symbolic "golden Girdle." Two years earlier, in an entry for July 10, 1678, Jane Lead writes about the "Girdle of the Trinity," also referred to as the "*Girdle of Unity*, clasped on by the Buckle of Faith" (212–13). In Bathurst's dream-vision, the size and nakedness of her body become the metaphors by which she measures her spiritual and physical fitness. At the start of this vision, Bathurst writes, "An angel came with a pair of compasses to measure my bigness" (July 12, 1680). Bathurst hopes to attain equal size with a mysteriously titled "M. F.,"[19] who has been made various promises, "some years agoe, that should be fulfilled when one came to be of equall weight & measure with Her." Since Bathurst does not yet equal M. F. in size and stature, Bathurst's Angel points toward the compasses, "as if there were something wanting." The scales are then moved to a more spiritual setting. Bathurst notes, "[M]y friends Angel was all in pure white in one scale." Two members of the "Unity of Love" clothe Bathurst in golden garments like their own and place her on the other scale, where, she recalls, "then I seem'd to be of exact height, bigness and weight." Now that Bathurst has reached proper dimensions, she must be properly arrayed: "Thereafter I was taken to the B. B.[20] and became like one naked." After Bathurst is returned to her natural, naked state, she is again clothed, this time in shining garments. The Apostle Peter, Bathurst writes, "cast a thin white Garment over me." In the presence of Moses and Aaron, Bathurst is "adorned with such garments as they had of very rich gold . . . and girt about wth a golden Girdle." Now that Bathurst is properly attired, she can be initiated into a society of God's closest companions: "[A]ll the Patriarchs & Apostles stood on each side of me as I was coming forth, and all spoke with great love & kindness to me as I went along by them, being so richly adorned for the glory of ye father & the Son. After this, a word came to me in this manner, did not I say to Thee, I would come & dwell wth thee? Now I am come by the breathing & flowings of Life in you" (July 12, 1680). Bathurst's celestial companions admire her garments, since they understand she wears them to celebrate the Son and Father's glory. Indeed, God promises to live with Bathurst and grant her desire "to be filled with Love & patience, this my virtue flowing in you" (July 12, 1680). Although the identity of M. F. is never disclosed, the bizarre and mysterious vision ends happily, with Bathurst safe in the presence of Spirit.

As this vision illustrates, Bathurst's writing is ripe, and rife, with body imagery. In various visions, she depicts the female body as clothed, naked, transcendent, and impregnated. I read these images as primarily positive and affirming. Diane Purkiss, by contrast, argues that "fasting, food imagery, and the metaphors of bodily dissolution and female reproduction" enable Stuart women prophets to "explore the contradictory possibilities of a female body autonomy and an autonomy outside the gendered body." She feels the earthly female body "must be disavowed in order to construct the female body as an acceptable sign" and argues that the strength and plenitude of Jane Lead's imagery relies "on the female body's metaphoricity. . . [a]s a trope for a spiritual state." Ultimately, "increased elevation to a spiritual plane . . . brings about the bodily dissolution desired."[21] My own contextualization of Bathurst and Lead's work in the canon of Christian mystical writing suggests these two authors echo and affirm the mystic idea that the need to transcend the flesh applies to all humans, male and female. Just

as Puritans and Dissenters of both genders are expected to abase themselves before God, mystics must transcend whichever corporeal body—
male or female—their spirit inhabits. As Bathurst learns, union with God
also requires the discipline to transcend one's own will: "I was taught yt
That *Nothingness* I saw my self in, in ye Unity of Love was the *No-will* that
I must come to. . . . I must have no will, no desire . . . but be still in God's
will. . . . And I saw this *Nothing-will* . . . as a sacrifice He was well pleased
with. . . . When we have no own-will but his will, the Kingdome of Glory;
is not the Glory of it the Harmony of it? all to move in the Center of ye
Divine will, as they receive from Him: and so far as we are acted from the
Influences of heaven, and move in the Divine will, so far there is harmony
betwixt us & glory" (May 16, 1680). Images of union with God and nega-
tion of self commingle in Bathurst's work, as they do in the writings of con-
temporaneous male spiritual seekers. So when Purkiss contends that Stuart
women mystics "foreground their souls" in order to "narratively discard
their subject bodies," this assertion strikes me as simultaneously true and
false.[22] It seems to me that Lead and Bathurst foreground their bodies even
as they call attention to their attempts to transcend them. The women's
bodies are simultaneously celebrated and discarded as the site where this
transcendence occurs.

Certainly, maternity figures prominently in Bathurst's work. In one vision, she calls forth her deceased children to visit her. She also locates spiritual power in her womb: "I had a light that shined from my stomach like a
sun. . . . This was the first time I received, or knew I had, the flame" (July 26,
1679). Soon afterwards, she is visited by Christ and God the Father: "[T]hey
opened up my stomach . . . and went into my stomach, and closed it up
again. . . . O the joy! that I had gotten my God, my saviour and redeemer,
sitting in me, as on a throne of refiner's fire" (September 10, 1679). Bathurst rejoices in a maternity that is at once spiritual and sexual.

Bathurst's maternal rhetoric remains celebratory throughout decades
of journal writing. By the mid-1680s, she becomes a healer and receives re-
quests to pray for the dead children of various friends. In the 1690s, she
praises the "fulness & plentitude" of milk-giving breasts, as does Lead, and
incorporates them into religious allegories of passion and spiritual yearning: "I am as pent milk in the breast, ready to be poured forth & dilated into
Thee, from whom my fulness flows with such fulnes & plentitude: & pleas'd
when eas'd" (June 30, 1693).

Male and female elements combine in a sexual-spiritual union in Bathurst's visions. Although God the Father is ever-present, Bathurst always

includes a female religious element in her work. The womb, impregnated with a spiritual flame, gains power as God sits within. The "pent milk in the breast, ready to be poured forth & dilated into Thee" reverses the traditional imagery of the male gushing forth into the female.

What is most notable about Bathurst's work is the joyousness that pervades her writing. Seventeenth-century spiritual diarists span a broad spectrum. They range from Hell-fearing, self-castigating Calvinists to members of more optimistic sects focused on inner light, the love of Christ, and divine forgiveness. Bathurst is of the latter cast. She chronicles the "depths of endless love" experienced in "the depth of the love of God" (June 30, 1693). Her ecstatic rants may well be culled, in part, from the Bible or other religious texts:

> Having had many considerations of the depth of the love of God . . . the soul breaks forth, O thou bottomless love! . . . I cry out, Jubilee of praise, when shalt thou be sung in our streets, and we as a well-tun'd Instrument of praise sing thee forth! . . . O Thou offspring of David & the Jews, how the virgins love thee! . . . All hallowed sweetness be given unto thee thou Song of Love & Divine Jubilee. The word DIVINE has such an emphasis In it, I could stop at it & go no further. . . . As to love add DIVINE, what may it amount to! . . . [T]his word Divine is too great for me to think on. (June 30, 1693)

Bathurst exuberantly proclaims, "O, Love has taken away my heart, Love divine, which shines through every part," and she finds herself awash in a "Sea of redeeming love" (June 30, 1693). Her blissful language and experience contrast strongly with the ominous prophecies of hellfire and damnation so commonplace among Dissenting diarists earlier in the century.

Oddly, Bathurst wrote at a time when a strong animosity existed toward religious fanaticism and "enthusiasm," which was often blamed for prompting the mid-century's Civil War. Partly to avoid this hostility, later diarists became, in the main, markedly more secular. Yet Bathurst's 1693 entry reminds us that certain segments of English society did not abandon a mystical religious discourse, nor did they eschew a rhetoric that was passionate, even ecstatic, in its intensity.

It is ironic that Cromwell's Dissenters fought so ferociously for a spirituality in which inner light, personal conversion, and the intimate relation of the individual to God matter most. The irony lies in the realization that, though its proponents were willing to suffer and die for the freedom to practice their beliefs openly, Stuart Protestantism was the sort of religion that could easily go underground, so to speak, to circumvent societal criticism. Lead and Bathurst, like mystics before them, concentrated on the glories of the inner landscape; cultural politics came a poor second. Yet by asserting female mystical power and by praising the glory of the spiritual feminine, Lead and Bathurst did make a political contribution. Their texts are not entirely ethereal: Lead and Bathurst touch on motherhood, female poverty, and unfair gender practices. But they choose to filter their social commentary through a mystic lens and privilege mystical experiences as the focus of their journals. Their imaginative and lavish exploration of this sacred territory, largely uncharted by women life-writers in seventeenth-century England, makes for some of the most fascinating reading of the late Stuart era.

NOTES

1. Jane Ward Lead's last name has variously been recorded as Lead or Leade, while Bathurst's first name has been recorded as Ann or Anne.

2. Mary Rich, *Memoir of Lady Warwick, also her diary from a.d. 1666–1672*, ed. Antony Walker (London: Religious Tract Society, 1847), and Anne Venn, *A Wise Virgin's Lamp Burning: The experiences of Mrs. Anne Venn (Daughter to Col. John Venn & member of the Church of Christ at Fulham): written by her own hand, and found in her closet after her death* (London: E. Cole, 1658), 125. I will use dates for diary entries instead of page numbers wherever possible. Most manuscript diaries and some published diaries list entries by date; occasionally, the headings are more ambiguous.

3. In the Stuart era, religious diary keeping was primarily a Protestant activity that came into being as a substitute for the Catholic ritual of confession. Protestant diaries fell into two broad categories: Anglican and non-Anglican. Diarists of the latter persuasion are variously referred to as Puritan, Dissenter, or nonconformist. Their journals are generally more God-fearing and self-negating than Anglican diaries of the same period. Since Lead and Bathurst were nonconformists, the celebratory, life-affirming tone of their journals is all the more notable.

4. My doctoral dissertation (Avra Kouffman, "The Cultural Work of Stuart Women's Diaries" [Ph.D. diss., University of Arizona, 2000]) examines extant manuscripts and published texts by thirty-five female diarists. My access to Stuart women's manuscript diaries was far from comprehensive, since it was limited to manuscripts preserved in libraries and archives located in or near London and Oxford, England. Also, many Stuart women's diaries have been lost or destroyed in the centuries since they were written.

5. See Jane Lead, *A Fountain of Gardens: or, A Spiritual Diary of the Wonderful Experiences of a Christian Soul under the Conduct of Heavenly Wisdom* (London,

1697–1701). Lead published these diaries in a four-volume set. I refer here to the first of three published volumes. The entries in vol. 1 cover the years 1670–76; vol. 2 covers 1677; the two-part vol. 3 covers 1678–86. Vol. 3, pt. 2, was printed separately in 1701; in her preface to it, Lead calls it "the Fourth and Last Volume" (A3), so I will refer to it as vol. 4. Volume and page citations to this work will be given parenthetically in the text.

6. Here and elsewhere, Lead participates in a literary tradition that depicts religious transcendence and illumination as conjoined.

7. Arthur Versluis, *Wisdom's Book: The Sophia Anthology* (St. Paul, Minn.: Paragon House, 2000), 11.

8. Boudewijn Koole, *Man en vrouw zijn een: De androgynie in het Christendom in het bijzonder bij Jacob Boehme* (Utretcht: HES Publishers, 1986), 2:3.

9. Catherine Smith, "Jane Lead's Wisdom: Wisdom and Prophecy in Seventeenth-Century England," in *Poetic Prophecy in Western Literature,* ed. Jan Wojcik and Raymond-Jean Frontain (Cranbury, N.J.: Associated University Presses, 1984), 60. Smith was one of the first literary critics to attend to Lead's writing; see also Catherine Smith, "Jane Lead: The Feminist Mind and Art of a Seventeenth-Century Protestant Mystic," in *Women of Spirit: Female Leadership in the Jewish and Christian Traditions,* ed. Rosemary Ruether and Eleanor McLaughlin (New York: Simon and Schuster, 1979), and "Jane Lead: Mysticism and the Woman Cloathed with the Sun," in *Shakespeare's Sisters: Feminist Essays on Women Poets,* ed. Sandra Gilbert and Susan Gubar (Bloomington: Indiana University Press, 1979).

10. Paula McDowell, *The Women of Grub Street: Press, Politics and Gender in the London Literary Marketplace 1638–1730* (Oxford: Clarendon Press, 1998).

11. Jane Lead, *The Tree of Faith, or the Tree of Life* (London: J. Bradford, 1696), 24–25, quoted in Smith, "Jane Lead's Wisdom," 58.

12. This is Catherine Smith's translation of a quotation culled from the German-language "Life of the Author," which was attached to six of Lead's tracts published between 1694 and 1696. Smith, "Jane Lead's Wisdom," 59.

13. Grace Jantzen, *Power, Gender, and Christian Mysticism* (New York: Cambridge University Press, 1995).

14. McDowell, *Women of Grub Street,* 178.

15. Smith, "Jane Lead's Wisdom," 62.

16. The Bodleian MS Rawl. D. 1262—the first volume of Bathurst's manuscript journal—spans the years 1679–93 and covers 607 large pages. The Bodleian MS Rawl. D. 1263—the second volume of the manuscript journal—continues where the first volume left off, in 1693, and ends in the year 1696. This latter [transcribed] volume is ninety-nine pages of quite small handwriting.

17. I would have liked to have studied Bathurst's work in detail for this project, but limited time at the Bodleian Library prevented me from transcribing more than a few long entries. I am grateful to Phyllis Mack for including selected passages from Bathurst's journals in *Visionary Women: Ecstatic Prophecy in Seventeenth-Century England* (Berkeley: University of California Press, 1992), and where necessary, I quote from Mack's transcriptions. I identify passages by date.

18. Ibid., 8.

19. One reader suggested that "M. F." may stand for the initials of the well-known Quaker pamphleteer, Margaret Fell, who often signed her pamphlets "M. F."

20. Bathurst does not clarify whom she means by "M. F." or "B. B."

21. Diane Purkiss, "Producing the Voice, Consuming the Body: Women Prophets of the Seventeenth Century," in *Women, Writing, History: 1640–1740*, ed. Isobel Grundy and Susan Wiseman (London: B. T. Batsford, 1992), 158, 152, 151.

22. Ibid., 151.

5 RITUAL AND PERFORMANCE IN CHRISTINA ROSSETTI'S "GOBLIN MARKET"

DEBRA CUMBERLAND

Christina Rossetti's poem "Goblin Market," composed in 1859 and published in her 1862 volume, *Goblin Market and Other Poems*, has received more critical response than any of her other works. The poem recounts the tale of two young sisters, apparently living alone, who are tempted by evil goblin merchant men. Laura gives in, nearly dies as a result, and is saved by her sister Lizzie. William Michael Rossetti claimed that his sister did not mean anything profound by the poem,[1] while the critic Mrs. Charles Eliot Norton referred to "Goblin Market" as "one of the works which are said to defy criticism."[2] Despite these assertions, critics have discussed "Goblin Market" as (among other things) a diatribe against capitalism, a celebration of lesbian love, an early analysis of anorexia nervosa, and a "commentary on the shaping of Christina Rossetti within the Victorian literary marketplace."[3] The richness of the poem, however, accommodates yet another interpretation, one that emphasizes the performative nature of "Goblin Market": a poem intended to be felt and enacted as an embodiment of the construction of a faith rather than to transcribe a straightforward religious message.

The study of Laura and Lizzie's religious performances — in other words, the enactment of their faith — is important to understand women's religious sensibility in nineteenth-century England. Despite prohibitions against

engaging in theological debate (described by John Ruskin as the "dangerous science for women"), women nonetheless often looked to transform
biblical exegesis by reappropriating sacred imagery. Lizzie's enactment of
Christ's passion and her Eucharistic offering of herself to Laura is experienced primarily through her physical being rather than through language.
Her faith is acted out and interpreted through the body, much in the manner
of mystics such as Julian of Norwich, who depicted Christ as a nurturing
mother, "in whome we be endlesly borne."[4] Mysticism appealed to women
such as Rossetti since it offered an alternative vocabulary that needed no
interpretation from a higher authority. "Goblin Market" thus explores the
role of Christian ritual as a means of empowerment to women. The religious performances in the poem become the catalyst for creative and personal autonomy.

By rejecting the patriarchal, commercial values of the goblins with their
gold-plated dishes, Rossetti instead reclaims the power of sacred myth and
ritual for Laura and Lizzie, and hence for all women, when they take on the
ancient roles themselves and retell the stories on their own terms. When
the sisters gather later in life to recount their experiences to their little
ones, their husbands are mentioned but not seen, and the sisters do not
mention God; instead of asking their little girls to look to Christ for help,
they ask them to look to each other, for "there is no friend like a sister."[5]
God-given power is found in a narrative celebrating women's outwardly
directed sacred powers, much as Christ's passion would be narrated and
performed within the Christian Church.

Ritual is an important aspect of "Goblin Market," for it is through ritual
that Laura and Lizzie gain power and understanding of themselves and learn
to interpret their world. According to Mircea Eliade, "Rituals are symbols in
actual reality; they function to make concrete and experiential the mythic
values of a society, and they can therefore provide clues to the mythic values themselves. Hence rituals *act*, they perform, modulate, transform. . . .
[S]ymbolic items and places in rituals are transformations of the ordinary
into the extraordinary."[6] As Eliade implies, there is a strong connection between performance, theater, and ritual, meaning that ultimately every religious worship service and ritualistic action has performative dimensions.
This is especially clear in the context of medieval mysticism, where the performance of one's religion was often a means of gaining power and authenticity for women.[7] The term *performance*, of course, covers a wide range
of meanings and activities, including dance, music, sport, and work, all
of which have their own rituals. As Richard Schechner and Willa Appel

suggest, performance offers "transformation of being and/or consciousness" whereby the performers and the spectators are often transformed, either "permanently, as in initiation rites, or temporarily as in aesthetic theatre."[8] When an audience weeps through a play, or a family participates in a community ritual, they are, for a brief moment, transported into another reality and subtly shaped and changed through their leap of faith into another realm and time. By telling family stories that have been handed down through the generations and participating in community ceremonies, we gain strength and insight through connectedness with each other and through our attempt to recapture (as Eliade notes) a past sacred moment in the present.

Barred from participating in theological discourse, women needed to seek out other means of interpreting Scripture.[9] Thus Christina Rossetti presents her readership with a narrative that embodies and reenacts Christ's passion rather than engaging in discussion and analysis. In short, she chooses to embody faith. As a result, Rossetti not only reclaims Christian ritual for women through Lizzie's own reenactment of Christ's sufferings but potentially offers the same transformative experience for her audience. John Keble, Victorian sermon writer and author of the popular The Christian Year, also believed in the sacramental power of poetry, whereby words could enact a change within the reader, much as God's word enacts change.[10] Readers therefore have the opportunity to share Laura and Lizzie's experience of the sacred through the body—auditory and oral (the experience of reading aloud/listening) as well as emotional (the transformative potential of reading as incantatory a piece as "Goblin Market").

As Jan Marsh notes, "Goblin Market" "demands that it be read aloud," for "half the pleasure of the verse is lost if read silently."[11] D. M. R. Bentley hypothesizes that "Goblin Market" was written to be read aloud to an audience of fallen women and Anglican Sisters at the St. Mary Magdalene Home for Fallen Women at Highgate Hill, where Christina Rossetti worked as an associate sister before the publication of Goblin Market and Other Poems in 1862.[12] The performative power of the piece also was evident to Rossetti's contemporaries. Alexander Macmillan, Rossetti's publisher, read the poem out loud to his wife and family to see if they liked it as much as he did. Macmillan wrote to Dante Gabriel Rossetti that he had read it to a "number of people belonging to a small working-man's society here [Cambridge.] They seemed at first to wonder whether I was making fun of them; by degrees they got still as death, and when I finished there was a tremendous burst of applause. I wish Miss Rossetti could have heard it."[13]

Christina also refers to a reading in a letter to her brother Dante Gabriel: "Have you heard about the Goblin Market reading? It comes off tomorrow at the Queen's Concert Rooms," to which, she notes, "Mama and Maria intend to go."[14] These stories indicate that Rossetti's work relies heavily upon a communal, ritualistic understanding of performance and the reading act as a shared experience, much as the hearing of the spoken word of God in a church service would have the effect of transforming the listener/reader. As a result, her work often defies logical analysis, since it relies largely upon a more emotional and embodied understanding of faith. Critics looking for linear, rational plots have, as a result, often been confused.

In 1881, when Rossetti published *A Pageant and Other Poems*, featuring *The Months: A Pageant*, as a drawing room piece, some critics responded by seeking rational explanations for the plot. D. M. Stuart notes in her biography, *Christina Rossetti*, that *The Pageant* was "written at the request of Maria Francesca's sisterhood."[15] *The Months: A Pageant* was performed at the Albert Hall "and elsewhere," though Stuart notes that "the only defect is one of monotony" and states with relief that no other plays sprang from her pen, since *The Pageant* reads as if the "characters come on and announce themselves like the tyrants and patriarchs of a medieval drama."[16] Rossetti's dramatic sensibilities lay in the direction of the medieval: the miracle play, for instance, with which *The Months: A Pageant* has dramatic affinities. In fact, the same complaint Stuart wields against *The Pageant* is often heard in regard to "Goblin Market": that there is no logical explanation for why things happen. Rossetti's interest was not really in creating a plot-oriented narrative but in dramatically re-creating key aspects of Christianity: temptation, Eucharist, redemption. She attempted to make the experience as vivid to her readers as if they were experiencing it for themselves firsthand by creating a mythic landscape strong in ritualistic, performative language.

Much of Rossetti's poetry is, in fact, set up as opposing characters having a conversation. This conversational colloquy lies at the heart of the meditative exercise. Many of her poems, such as "The Hour and the Ghost," "Christian and Jew: A Dialogue," and "The Three Enemies," are written in dialogue form. As Louis Martz notes, the meditative poem is "a work that creates an interior drama of the mind; this dramatic action is usually . . . created by some form of self-address, in which the mind grasps firmly a problem or situation deliberately evoked by the memory, brings it forward toward the full light of consciousness, and concludes with a moment of illumination, where the speaker's self has, for a time, found an answer to its conflicts."[17] As Martz explains, the poetry of meditation was given form in the spiritual exercises of St. Ignatius and was adopted by British poets Southwell, Donne, Crashaw, and Herbert, all of whom Rossetti read as a young woman and copied into her own verse-books.[18]

This meditative mode of poetry for Rossetti has a powerful, dramatic, and transformative capacity, for meditation has the ability to re-create spiritual events within the self and thus transform the self. Martz explains that "meditation . . . brings together the senses, the emotions, and the intellectual faculty of man: brings them together in a moment of dramatic, creative experience."[19] Rossetti's most meditative poems reenact Christ's passion as if she were a participant. As a result, they have the capacity through the dramatic reenactment within the poem to inscribe the passion and Christ's suffering onto the reader's own psyche, most notably through questions in the poem that demand answers. In "Behold the Man!" Rossetti asks, in re-creating the crucifixion, "Can Christ hang on the cross, and we not look?"—demanding that the reader too place him- or herself dramatically and imaginatively back at the moment of Christ's suffering. In "The Descent from the Cross," Rossetti likewise asks the reader to re-envision Christ's moment of death: "Is this the Face without a flaw, / The Face that is the Face of Love?" (3–4). Rossetti's imposition of the sacred experience, written from an "if I were there" perspective, effectively inscribes the experience upon the reader's heart and mind.

"Goblin Market" borrows from these performative qualities inherent in the meditative mode, both in its dramatic reenactment of sacred events and in its transformative qualities. Part of the transformative power of "Goblin Market" springs from its free-form rhythm and structure, so expressive of an individual self. No less a critic than John Ruskin was unnerved by the absence of order in Rossetti's verse. Rossetti was fond of a more free-form verse, while Ruskin favored a tidier line. He objected to the irregular metrical freedom in Christina's verse and to its distinctive musicality. When Dante Gabriel sent "Goblin Market" to Ruskin for his opinion, Ruskin responded,

> I sate up till late last night reading poems. They are full of beauty and power. But no publisher—I am deeply grieved to know this— would take them, so full are they of quaintnesses and offenses. Irregular measure (introduced to my great regret in its chief willfulness by Coleridge) is the calamity of modern poetry. The *Iliad*, the *Divina Commedia*, the *Aeniad*, the whole of Spenser, Milton, Keats, are writ-

ten without taking a single license or violating the commonplace for metre: your sister should exercise herself in the severest commonplace of metre until she can write as the public like.[20]

Ruskin here associates regularity and conformity with order, control, and economic success (writing as the public liked and expected), while Rossetti, in practicing an irregular rhythmic style, chose a path celebrating an independence of spirit that valorized the feminine, the rhythmic, and the sensual. Ruskin's criticism thus sets up the essential dilemma enacted in "Goblin Market": the commercial values of the spirit, embodied in the goblins, as opposed to Lizzie, who follows the path she finds the least corrupting, no matter what the lure.

Rossetti's independent spirit, captured both in her form and in her celebration of female spirituality, intrigued, baffled, and occasionally alarmed reviewers. Most reviews were complimentary, with the most unequivocal praise coming from Mrs. Charles Eliot Norton. Norton praised Rossetti as a "mystic" in her 1863 review of "Goblin Market," citing Rossetti's ability to link the everyday world with the supernatural, rendering a "vivid and wonderful power" akin to "The Rime of the Ancient Mariner."[21] Other reviews, more guarded, were in keeping with the *Saturday Review's* anonymous critic, who maintained that " 'Goblin Market' " was a "story of too flimsy and insubstantial character to justify or to bear the elaborate detail with which it is worked out."[22] This "flimsy character," however, is a part of its ritualistic element, for the point of the poem is not the character of Laura and Lizzie but their enactment of a faith, the "mysticism" that Mrs. Norton praised. As in "The Rime of the Ancient Mariner," to which Norton compared "Goblin Market," the characters reenact a sacred event and capture its meaning through ritualistic storytelling at the end of the poem.

The ritualism of "Goblin Market" is first expressed through the incantatory sound of its language and the manner in which it is performed. Lizzie's enactment and embodiment of Christ, as she offers herself Eucharistically to Laura, valorizes the feminine, performative dimension of mysticism over the goblins' rational, corrupt materialism. Rossetti accomplishes this first through an exploration of the spoken word. As in church ritual, such as a priest/minister's performance of a communion, marriage, or baptism, Rossetti is interested in drawing attention not so much to what is *said* as to what is *reenacted* as a result of what is being said: in other words, the performative element of language. She draws attention to sound in terms of how people speak and how people react to what is spoken. For instance, the goblins "sound like doves," only the sound is deceptive. However, when Laura and Lizzie leave their safe home and head out to do their errands, Laura is fooled by the goblins' cries and refuses to listen to Lizzie's warnings.

Laura's capacity for temptation says as much about her spirituality as it does about the goblins' deceptive nature. Rossetti herself notes in her spiritual tract *Letter and Spirit* that one of the first injunctions in the commandments is to "Hear O Israel; The Lord our God is one Lord."[23] As Rossetti comments, Eve's problem is that by being, through birth, "gracious and accessible, she lends an ear to all petitions from all petitioners."[24] Laura is unable to discriminate and interpret accurately what she hears. Like Eve, she lacks the capacity for proper interpretation through these senses, and this leads to her transgression.

Attentive critical interpretation is especially important in "Goblin Market" because the seductive rhythmic quality of the verse is intentionally calculated to confuse both Laura and Lizzie, as well as the reader.[25] "Goblin Market" begins by confronting the issue of interpretation as performance. How does an audience interpret and understand what it sees and hears? How do we accurately name and understand what we are presented with in the world around us, whether on a stage, on a page, or within our own home? Rossetti casts her audience in the same situation as the two girls: the audience must listen to the long, lush, musical rendering of twenty-nine recited orchard fruits, "All ripe together / In summer weather" (15–16), and decide how to interpret what they hear. As Rossetti's poems, such as "The Descent from the Cross," place the reader at the moment of crucifixion, so here Rossetti places the reader at the moment of temptation and seduces them alongside Laura and Lizzie. Part of "Goblin Market" thus becomes a reclaiming and cleansing of the senses in order to force the reader to be aware and hear, see, and accurately learn how to interpret the sacred.

The incantatory quality of Rossetti's verse obscures that the girls—and the poem's readers—are outside a normal understanding of space and time. Her lush language seduces, causing Laura (and by implication the poem's readers) to believe that it is possible for pears, plump greengages, apples, oranges, and "plump unpecked cherries" to be "all ripe together in summer weather." The mythic quality of the world in "Goblin Market" is further elaborated by Lizzie's urgent question, "Who knows upon what soil they fed their hungry, thirsty roots?" (44–45). By heightening the mystery of origins, the poem leads the reader to realize that the world of "Goblin Market" belongs to the mysterious, the unnatural—even the mythic. This collapse of the ordinary rules of time is another example of how sound seduces in "Goblin Market," enticing Laura to forget that contemplating the origins of things—the soil upon which the goblins feed—is key to understanding spiritual truths.

Not initially seeing the fruit, Laura and Lizzie first hear the fruit described by the goblins: "Morning and evening / Maids heard the goblins cry / Come buy our orchard fruits, / Come buy / Come buy" (1–4). The warm, open vowel sounds, the long litany of repeated fruit, urge the reader to linger alongside Laura and feast over the words: "Apples and quinces, / Lemons and oranges, / Plump unpecked cherries" (5–7). The doubleness of the sounds makes it difficult to distinguish one fruit from another, just as it becomes increasingly difficult for Laura to distinguish right from wrong. As the goblins insinuate, the fruits are "Sweet to tongue and sound to eye" (30). They sound good, they taste good, but their fundamental nature is, in fact, anything but good.

Laura is transformed as she *listens* to the goblins; crouching in the rushes, she hears them, "pricking up her golden head" (41). Transformation is the effect that hearing the word of Christ is supposed to have upon the listener, of course, as is easily noted in much Christian ritual, where the singing of hymns or the spoken and written word of God transforms the errant soul and leads him or her back to the fold. Laura's transformation is not of this nature, for only Christ can truly transform. Lizzie's "veiled . . . blushes" (35) indicate that she is attracted by the goblins' seductive, musical cry, but Laura responds in a manner more appropriate to answering the call of Christ: she bows her head in prayerlike submission. Laura, however, submits to the goblins, not to God. The goblins seduce her through their proper ritualistic props, imitative of Christian ritual: one goblin "weaves a crown" (99), and one "heaved the golden weight of dish and fruit" (102–3), in parody of communion. While Laura lingers, Lizzie, knowing that their "offers should not charm us," responds by thrusting "a dimpled finger / In each ear, shut eyes and ran" (67–68), blocking herself off from the goblins' sensory assault that is slowly transforming her sister.

In setting up this dichotomy between the girls and the goblins (the pure love of Christ as opposed to the feast the goblins offer), Rossetti contrasts the rational and commercial world of the goblins, lugging their dishes and their plates, with the prerational, feminine world that she celebrates. The Oxford Movement, with its burgeoning interest in ritual, mysticism, and the medieval, valorized mysticism for its feminine qualities. John Keble's Tract 89, "On the Mysticism Attributed to the Early Fathers of the Church," celebrates the mystical and irrational, as opposed to the "common sense and practical utility" that Keble calls "the very idols of this age," an age he describes as full of "hurry and business."[26] The Oxford Movement's celebration of more feminine, mystical elements in Christianity alarmed some, such as Charles Kingsley, who found the movement effeminate and as a result called for a more "muscular Christianity." By contrast, the Oxford Movement did in fact find a place for women in the Anglican sisterhoods, which, despite their limitations, fostered feminine communities, female friendships, and women's right to choose—although the choices were still limited. Rossetti herself valorized the role of the contemplative above the role of the wife, for "Her maker is her Husband, endowing her with a name better than of sons and of daughters."[27] Rossetti contrasts a female meditative approach to spirituality with the goblins' crass commercialization of Christian ritual with their shrill cries of "come buy, come buy" and their appropriation of Christian symbols (dishes and plates) for commercial uses.

Rossetti makes this distinction clear by her emphasis upon the goblins as "merchant men" (474) and by their commodification of Laura's body.[28] Laura gives in to the goblins after they "clipped a golden lock" (126) from her head in exchange for the money that she does not have. She eagerly sucks "their fruit globes fair or red: / Sweeter than honey from the rock, / Stronger than man-rejoicing wine, / Clearer than water flowed that juice: / She never tasted such before" (128–32). However, as with Eve's new-found knowledge when she tastes the fruit, Laura finds that her knowledge comes with a price. The next day, heading to the bank, Laura discovers that although she listens, she cannot catch "the customary cry," with its "iterated jingle / Of sugar-baited words" (230–34). Lizzie, however, can hear the goblins' fruit-call, but she "dare not look" (243). When Laura realizes that she can no longer hear the cry of the goblin fruit merchants, she turns "cold as stone" and fears that she has "gone deaf and blind" (259). The goblins' seduction has rendered her powerless by cutting her off from the sensory world. Laura peers through the "dimness, nought discerning" (262), and loses the capacity to perform her daily household tasks: "She no more swept the house, / Tended the fowls or cows, / Fetched honey, kneaded cakes of wheat / Brought water from the brook: / But sat down listless in the chimney-nook / And would not eat" (293–98). She grows gray, her tree of life "withering at the root," and becomes incapable of performing her domestic tasks with Lizzie. Her seduction has stripped her of her creative, interpretative self, leaving her as good as dead to her world.

Laura's illness is significant, for the housework that Laura and Lizzie perform is celebrated through Rossetti's heightened language as a sacred and consecrated act, performed in a particular manner, and part of the rhythmic pattern of the sisters' lives.[29] The tasks are part of the ordinary makeup of their lives as well as an act ordering and consecrating their household. The domestic rituals of milking, kneading, fetching water, and airing out the house sustain, purify, and structure their world and serve to reflect the quality of that natural order. They do not stay out past twilight, a time significant in that it separates night from day, or the world of the goblins from the world of the girls. As they sleep, they are depicted not simply as two sisters curled up for rest but as images that conjoin purity and power: "two blossoms on one stem, / Like two flakes of new-fall'n snow, / Like two wands of ivory / Tipped with gold for awful kings" (188–91). Nature guards and smiles upon them benevolently, the wind sings a lullaby, the moon and stars gaze down at them, and owls and bats flap discreetly so that they sleep peacefully.

The contrast Rossetti draws between the girls and the goblins reflects the two modes of being Eliade identifies in the world: those of the sacred and the profane. The girls' world, belonging to the domestic, harmonious with nature, wholly distinct and other from that of the goblins, evokes the divine, the sacred, while the goblins' world, associated with the secular world of the commercial, evokes the profane. The sacred, however, exists not only within the domestic space inhabited by Laura and Lizzie, but also within the sisters themselves: the sacred is housed within them. Laura dwindles because her "fire" has been burned away by her contaminating encounter with the goblins. As Rossetti writes, "But when the moon waxed bright / Her hair grew thin and gray; / She dwindled, as the fair full moon doth turn / To swift decay and burn / Her fire away" (276–80). Rossetti uses "fire" elsewhere in her writings to refer to Christ as a "fire of love," emblematic of the mystic's passion for union with the divine. Laura's inability to think and feel has plunged her into a "dark night of the soul"; she loses her ability to hear and see ("gone deaf and blind" [259]) and, as a result, her ability to perform her household rituals, effectively cutting her off from the sacred. Her symbolic loss of virginity at the hands of the goblins also reflects the religious notion of virginity as a key to the contemplative life, an inner "spiritual state," as Elizabeth Petroff notes, "that makes visions possible"[30] in the contemplative's union with the divine. Thus the goblins not only lull Laura in through their false, melodic cries but gain their ultimate control over her by making her incapable of hearing and interpreting.

Unlike the sisters, Jeanie dwindled and died through an encounter with the goblin men. She died because she, like Laura, read the wrong meaning into the goblins and thus "took their gifts both choice and many" (159). As a result, she "who should have been a bride; / But who for joys brides hope to have / Fell sick and died" (313–15). The key word for Rossetti here may be *gift*. Unlike the goblin merchants, Lizzie offers herself to her sister with the right attitude, freely and out of love, with no expectation in return. Her fruit therefore heals instead of harms. The goblin fruit only serves to commodify and corrupt human and divine relationships.[31] Its transformative powers lead to a slow withering away, as opposed to the fruit of Christ, which has the power to transform and heal.

The erotic element in Laura and Lizzie's relationship is further evidence of their spirituality, much like the sublimated erotic relationship between the worshipper and the divine, a longing for the Godhead that often manifested itself in highly sexualized language and imagery. One example would be of St. John the Divine, who described his communion with God as laying "his head on his lover's breast," the lover being Christ, just as Laura and Lizzie lie "cheek to cheek and breast to breast / Locked together in one nest" (197–98). The sisters' differentiation springs from how they interpret the world, for physically they are practically identical.[32] Some critics, such as Germaine Greer, interpret this "doubleness" as suggesting a lesbian identity.[33] Rossetti quotes extensively from the erotic, mystical Bride/Bridegroom imagery of the Song of Songs in all of her devotional texts, and *Letter and Spirit* uses similar language in its description of the mystic seeking divine love: "Her spiritual eyes behold the king in his beauty; wherefore, she forgets, by comparison, her own people and her father's house. . . . She loves Him with all her heart and soul and mind and strength; she is jealous that she cannot love him more; her desire to love Him outruns her possibility, yet by outrunning it enlarges it."[34] The sublimated eroticism in this passage is similar to the relationship that Laura and Lizzie have to each other, where their personalities are so fused that they are described as "locked together in one nest."

The fruit listed at the beginning of the poem is an emblem of erotic love as well as sin and hence also has this double quality, which becomes differentiated through interpretation. Temptation through fruit, of course, recalls Eve and sin, but the apple can also be connected to Christ, as in the Song of Songs, which in its most traditional interpretation (certainly common in the nineteenth century) was an allegory of the church's longing for God. In the Song of Songs, the lover sits beneath the shade of the apple tree, which is compared to Christ. The anonymous eighteenth-century hymn, called "Jesus Christ the Apple Tree," arranged by Elizabeth Poston, depicts Christ in similar language: "The tree of life my soul hath seen / Laden with fruit and always green. / . . . / The trees of nature fruitless be / compared with Christ the apple tree." Christ here is connected to the apple, which brings life and health, not sin. As the hymn reads, the fruit of the apple tree provides restoration, as opposed to the goblins' fruit, which causes Jeanie to die and Laura to waste away, for "This fruit doth make my soul to thrive / It keeps my dying faith alive."[35] Laura, while hungering for more, grows thin and wastes away, but Lizzie, who does not "open her mouth lest the goblins should cram a mouthful in," thrives. The key difference between the two, however, is not that Laura ate and ate till she could eat no more and that Lizzie kept her lips shut but that they have different interpretations of what the fruit signifies. The fruit thus is the fruit of sin as well as the fruit of Christ. The apple and the rest of the fruits are neither good nor evil but both, because each element in the poem has the capacity to be both. Laura's capacity for misinterpretation (her inability to read accurately the signs of grace in the natural world, as the Tractarians remind us) can be mimicked by the audience, calling attention to the precarious, unstable quality of salvation. The story could, and often does, turn out quite differently, depending upon the power of interpretation that the reader/audience brings to the experience.

Like Laura and Lizzie, the reader must also learn to accurately interpret the goblins. Just as the fruit symbolizes both the fruit of sin and the fruit of Christ, Laura and Lizzie learn that the goblins may sound like "doves" (77) as well as sounding "shrill" (89). The goblins in fact are constantly shifting; they do not seem to have a stable identity. When they spy Lizzie, the goblins come toward her, "Flying, running, leaping, / Puffing and blowing / Chuckling, clapping, crowing, / Clucking and gobbling, / Mopping and mowing, / Full of airs and graces, / Pulling wry faces, / Demure grimaces, / Cat-like and Rat-like / Ratel and wombat-like / Snail-paced in a hurry" (331–44). Many of these descriptions are contradictory, and many involve both masculine and feminine characteristics. "Demure" certainly sounds stereotypically feminine, as does "pulling airs and graces." Others, particularly the words connected to animals, such as "rats" and "wombats," remind us of the Pre-Raphaelite Brotherhood, the circle of artists surrounding Christina Rossetti and her brothers, Dante Gabriel and William Michael Rossetti. Wombats were, of course, Dante Gabriel Rossetti's favorite animal; the entire menagerie might be found at his home, Cheyne Walk, another speculation that critics cite to compare the goblins to the Pre-Raphaelite Brotherhood.[36]

Who or what the goblins represent is not as important as their means of wielding power over the two girls through the use of masks. Rossetti clearly indicates that the goblins are intentionally altering their features for an intended effect: "pulling wry faces" and "demure grimaces" and moving "catlike" and "ratlike" in an attempt to simulate a foreign identity. Ronald Grimes defines masking broadly enough to include any "body transforming device concerned with the head area . . . for masking is the making of a second face, often used for concealing identity and wielding power."[37] The goblins wield such power over Laura. The use of masks, Grimes notes, increases the power of performance; the goblins' myriad facial expressions and gestures can be interpreted as springing from the desire to conceal identity and wield control by appearing as something Other. This Otherness lends them the element of mystery, of seduction, perhaps even of the transcendent. Lizzie, through her ability to accurately read the goblins as evil ("We must not look at goblin men / We must not buy their fruits" [42–43]), gains power over the goblins through this ability to identify and name them, which in turn gives her the strength to resist their assault.

Lizzie's ability to accurately read the goblins' true nature grants her God-like powers: an ability to transform herself and the world around her. Salvation in "Goblin Market" comes through Lizzie's reenactment of Christian ritual: taking on and performing the role of Christ.[38] Such a reenactment of Christian ritual, described by Eliade, seeks a "reactualization of the same mythical events," and with "each reactualization" humanity "has the opportunity to transfigure" human existence in the present.[39] While Lizzie does not literally nail herself to a cross, her gesture is equivalent in female terms: she leaves herself vulnerable by placing her body in danger at the goblins' hands. She allows herself to be assaulted in order to take back the restorative fruit. The goblins "[k]icked and knocked her" (428), "mauled and mocked her" (429), "scratched her" (427), and "pinched her black as ink" (427) as they turn to violence in an attempt to make her eat. However, Lizzie's affliction (an attempted rape rather than Laura's seduction), willingly undergone for another, is depicted as the source of her strength, for as she crosses the bank, on her pilgrimage, she sees and hears in a new way: "for the first time in her life / [She] began to listen and look" (328–29), Rossetti writes.

Lizzie's heightened awareness and performance as Christ transform her physical being and move her into the realm of the sacred. She is no longer described in relation to her sister, in terms of twos, "like two blossoms" (188) or "two flakes of new-fall'n snow" (189), but in language linking her to Christ. She is "white and gold" (408), the colors of purity; like a lily (409), a flower linking her to Easter and Christ; and "like a rock" (410), the phrase Christ used to describe Simon Peter, as the rock upon whom he would build his church. Lizzie is also described as a "beacon left alone / In a hoary roaring sea" (412–13), another link to Christ, who is described as the light of the world. Lizzie recognizes her power, for she, even under the goblins' assault, "Would not open lip from lip / Lest they should cram a mouthful in: / But laughed in heart to feel the drip / Of juice that syrupped all her face" (431–34). Lizzie's sacrificial gesture is one not of passivity but of choice; her silence is not powerlessness but strength.

As "Goblin Market" makes clear, Lizzie's new-found strength overwhelms the goblins; defeated by her resistance, they vanish: "Some writhed into the ground, / Some dived into the brook / With ring and ripple, / Some scudded on the gale without a sound, / Some vanished in the distance" (442–46). Lizzie's defeat of the goblins has caused some critics to compare "Goblin Market" to fairy tales,[40] where, after the heroine performs her task, the harsh conditions she endured mysteriously vanish, and happiness is restored, usually through the betrothal of the prince and the princess. Rossetti, however, revises this form by emphasizing that the strength Lizzie gains through self-knowledge leads to spiritual enlightenment. The trials both sisters endure are similar to the tasks enacted in the Bible as a part of a trial or test of spirituality, a honing of the will and the mind: Christ's sojourn in the wilderness for forty days and forty nights, Abraham's trial on Mt. Moriah with his son Isaac. Lizzie's task is to bridge the two worlds of the sacred and profane and offer, like Christ, nothing less than herself. What she brings to the world is her knowledge. Lizzie also offers herself to Laura in an echo of Christ's words: "She cried 'Laura,' up the garden, / 'Did you miss me? / Come and kiss me. / Never mind my bruises, / Hug me, kiss me, suck my juices / Squeezed from goblin fruit for you'" (464–69). Lizzie's ritual reenactment of the Eucharist in this scene is not simply a proffering of the body and blood of Christ but an offering of herself as the Eucharistic food, gained through her strength, self-sacrifice, and love.[41]

Lizzie's offering of her body as a Eucharistic feast is in the medieval tradition; C. W. Bynum has observed the medieval association of Christ's body with female bodies, both giving nourishment.[42] The Eucharist is, of course, as Grimes notes, the most sacred and ritualistic of gestures in the Christian tradition. Christians who "eat the ritual body and drink the symbolic blood ingest power which resides in the elements as a result of the primal sacrifice and the subsequent priestly consecration of the elements."[43]

In return for the power consumed, devotees are to make their lives a "living sacrifice," as Lizzie does with Laura. Laura recognizes the quality of this ritualistic sacrifice, for when she hears Lizzie's words, she starts "from her chair, / Flung her arms up in the air, / Clutched her hair: / "Lizzie, Lizzie, have you tasted / for my sake the fruit forbidden?" (475–79). This exchange between Laura and Lizzie contrasts with the goblins' feast, which brings death instead of life. In *The Face of the Deep*, Rossetti speaks of the word of God as a nourishing substance, telling of a young woman who, when dying, "fed on the Word of Life, being evidently fed with food convenient for her."[44] Elsewhere, she asks that all might receive "the sincere milk of thy word"[45] and pleads, "O Christ our God, remember Thy strong and weak ones, great and small, men and women for good. Remember the nursing Fathers and nursing Mothers of Holy Church."[46] Rossetti thus looks to Christ's maternal behavior for an understanding of the sacred.

As Elizabeth Petroff notes, "[T]he process of visions taught women not to sacrifice their desire but to transform it" so that their ultimate desire would be directed toward a divine union.[47] Rossetti contrasts this pure, healthy eroticism, celebrated through Lizzie's offering of herself, to the carnal knowledge gleaned at the hands of the goblins. Communion is celebrated as a gift; we receive Christ's offering and, in return, freely offer up our own lives. Laura, at Lizzie's bidding, "kissed and kissed and kissed her with a hungry mouth" (492) until "Swift fire spread through her veins, knocked at her heart, / Met the fire smouldering there" (507–8), and she falls down at last, "Pleasure past and anguish past" (522), her sister's gift curing her. The passionate ecstasy Laura experiences in "Goblin Market" is evoked elsewhere in Rossetti's spiritual writings, where she speaks of consuming the body and the blood of Christ as part of a loving relationship leading to divine union. As Rossetti asks in one prayer, "[G]ive us grace, I implore Thee, to discern Thee spiritually in the most Blessed Sacrament of Thy Body and Blood; to receive Thee into souls prostrate in adoration, to entertain Thee with our utmost love."[48] Christ's sacrifice is thus reenacted in "Goblin Market" through Lizzie and Laura's loving relationship.

Christ's sacrifice is also understood through enactment of his suffering and physical pain. Lizzie's illness likewise attests to Rossetti's emphasis upon affliction as a process toward spiritual growth. Public displays of such suffering become one means of validating and authorizing spiritual experience. Lizzie's and Laura's afflictions gain meaning and authenticity because the girls witness them and interpret their meaning for each other. Rossetti understood the significance of suffering and public witness and instructed her readers to suffer, in her spiritual tract *Time Flies*. Referring to Christ, Rossetti wrote: "His natural and His spiritual life began one with privation, the other with suffering. Let us not be too eager to lie soft and warm, or too chary of undergoing pain."[49] Suffering and the desire to suffer properly for God were connected with the saint's spiritual journey and path to saintly power. Victorian sermon writers such as Thomas Keble also referred to the necessity of affliction along the path to spiritual growth: "[C]omprehending as one may almost say the dying words of the Savior, the not merely benefit, but the absolute *necessity* of affliction in some shape or other, to wean our hearts from worldly affections, and to turn them to God, is most energetically set forth."[50] That growth, however, comes at great physical and mental cost. In Laura's case, she must suffer a near-death experience to understand her sister's sacrifice; in Lizzie's, her spiritual power is validated through her abuse at the hands of the goblins, which gives her the authority and power to heal her sister. In so doing, Lizzie embodies the Victorian feminized Christ, who was often depicted as a compassionate healer, the "great physician," "characterized by 'feminine' attributes of compassion, pity and sympathy."[51]

Such an emphasis upon affliction, suffering, and abuse as steps toward spiritual growth reveals a seemingly contradictory flight into the body, as well as a desire to escape traditional expressions of female sexuality without shame, a plight apparent to Christina Rossetti through her work as an associate sister at Highgate Hill. By "performing" as Christ, women are able to evade the fate of heterosexual sex and motherhood. While Laura and Lizzie do have children in "Goblin Market," they seem to appear minus any fathers, which recalls the invisible father of the Incarnation and the Immaculate Conception. Salvation occurs through the intimate relationship with another woman, rather than a man, and a communal sense of shared experience, not through any doctrine or representative of the institutional church.

At the end of the poem, Laura and Lizzie function, it seems, much like an Anglican sisterhood. The Anglican sisterhoods also celebrated women's shared experience and women's narratives. Rossetti's work as a volunteer at the St. Mary Magdalene Penitentiary in Highgate Hill, a home for fallen women, gave her "access to a uniquely feminocentric view of women's sexuality and simultaneously opened her eyes to its problematic position in Victorian culture."[52] The women joining Anglican sisterhoods were engaging in a radical act, for they chose to "reject the law of the father" by choosing a heavenly bridegroom rather than an earthly one and by living in a community of women forgoing marriage and childbirth. Christina Rossetti's own sister, Maria, was a member of an Anglican sisterhood, and

Rossetti throughout much of her life lived in a household composed of women: her mother, her sister (until she moved into the Anglican convent), and her aunts.

Sisterhoods were also deviant in terms that "Goblin Market" celebrates: through their rejection of the patriarchy and their celebration of empowering female narratives. Stories of female martyrs could give women a sense of potential in their own lives and a sense of their own autonomy. Like the sisterhoods, Laura and Lizzie create their own community. When Laura and Lizzie's girls' "little hands" (560) are joined together, to form a circle at the end of the story, their handholding becomes a ritualistic celebration of female power in community. The creation of a circle forms sacred space and conjoined power. In forming the circle, and telling the story, time once again takes on the mythic proportions experienced in what Rossetti calls that "long gone" time. The insights gained when touched by what Richard Schechner calls the "Transcendent Other" must now be applied to "real time." Laura alludes to this, for when "little hands" are joined together at the end, in preparation for her story, she speaks of herself and her sister Lizzie and cautions the little ones to look to them, their mothers, and to each other for salvation—she makes no mention of any heavenly father or the patriarchal church.

The offering of salvation in "Goblin Market" occurs through the two women and their loving relationship, evoked through their capacity to inscribe meaning on their lives through their ritualistic narrative powers and reenactment of Christian ritual. Storytelling in "Goblin Market," taking place at the domestic hearth, becomes a way to reinterpret God and spirituality in terms of a female epistemology that defines the divine in domestic terms, the creation of an intentional community, and the dedication and fostering of women's spiritual development. The gift Lizzie significantly gives to Laura through her Christ-like gesture is not simply the gift of life but the gift of language as well.

NOTES

1. William Michael Rossetti, ed., *Poetical Works of Christina Georgina Rossetti, with Memoir and Notes* (London: Macmillan, 1906), 459.

2. Mrs. Charles Eliot Norton, "'The Angel in the House' and 'The Goblin Market,'" *Macmillan's Magazine*, September 1863, 401.

3. For an outline of criticism on "Goblin Market," consult Jane Addison, "Christina Rossetti Studies, 1974–1991: A Checklist and Synthesis," *Bulletin of Bibliography* 2 (March 1995): 73–93. For an analysis of "Goblin Market" within the context of the Victorian literary marketplace, see Alison Chapman's "The Afterlife of Poetry: 'Goblin Market,'" in *The Afterlife of Christina Rossetti* (New York: St. Martin's Press, 2000), 131–56.

4. Julian of Norwich, *A Book of Showings: Long Text*, ed. Edmund Colledge and James Walsh (Toronto: Pontifical Institute of Medieval Studies, 1978), 580. My understanding of the term *mysticism* is derived from Evelyn Underhill's definition of it as "the expression of the innate tendency of the human spirit towards complete harmony with the transcendental order" that "dominates [one's] life and, in the experience called 'mystic union,' attains its end" (xxi). For a detailed analysis of mysticism, see Underhill's *Mysticism: The Preeminent Study in the Nature and Development of Spiritual Consciousness* (New York: Doubleday, 1990).

5. Christina G. Rossetti, "Goblin Market," in *The Complete Poems of Christina Rossetti*, 3 vols., ed. R. W. Crump (Baton Rouge: Louisiana State University Press, 1979–90), 562. Subsequent line numbers will be cited parenthetically in the text.

6. Mircea Eliade, *Myths Rites, Symbols: A Mircea Eliade Reader*, ed. Wendell C. Beane and William G. Doty (New York: Harper and Row, 1975), 1:164.

7. See Caroline Walker Bynum's classic study *Jesus as Mother: Studies in the Spirituality of the High Middle Ages* (Berkeley: University of California Press, 1982) for a discussion of medieval women's embodiment of their faith. Bynum explores how women's efforts to imitate Christ involved becoming the crucified, fusing with the body on the cross, rather than simply patterning themselves after him.

8. Richard Schechner and Willa Appel, *By Means of Performance: Intercultural Studies of Theatre and Ritual* (New York: Cambridge University Press, 1990), 4. For an introduction to performance theory, see Richard Schechner, *Essays on Performance Theory, 1970–1976* (New York: Drama Book Specialists, 1977).

9. See Joel Westerholm, "'I Magnify Mine Office': Christina Rossetti's Authoritative Voice in Her Devotional Prose," *Victorian Newsletter* 84 (1992): 11–17.

10. John Keble, "Tract No. 89: On the Mysticism Attributed to the Early Church Fathers," in *The Evangelical and Oxford Movements*, ed. Elisabeth Jay (New York: Cambridge University Press, 1983), 149.

11. Jan Marsh, *Christina Rossetti: A Writer's Life* (New York: Viking, 1994), 235.

12. D. M. R. Bentley, "The Metricious and the Meritorious in 'Goblin Market': A Conjecture and Analysis," in *The Achievement of Christina Rossetti*, ed. David Kent (Ithaca, N.Y.: Cornell University Press, 1987), 58.

13. Dante Gabriel Rossetti, Christina Rossetti, and William Michael Rossetti, *The Rossetti-Macmillan Letters: Some 133 Unpublished Letters Written to Alexander Macmillan, F. S. Ellis, and Others, by Dante Gabriel, Christina, and William Michael Rossetti, 1861–1869*, ed. Lona Mosk Packer (Berkeley: University of California Press, 1963), 7.

14. Christina Rossetti, *The Letters of Christina Rossetti*, vol. 1, *1843–1873*, ed. Antony Harrison (Charlottesville: University Press of Virginia, 1997), 294.

15. D. M. Stuart, *Christina Rossetti* (London: Macmillan, 1930), 109.

16. Ibid., 109.

17. Louis L. Martz, *The Poetry of Meditation: A Study in English Religious Literature of the Seventeenth-Century* (1954; rev. ed., New Haven, Conn.: Yale University Press, 1962), 330.

18. Marsh, *Christina Rossetti*, 46.

19. Martz, *The Poetry of Meditation*, 1.

20. William Michael Rossetti, ed., *Ruskin: Rossetti: Pre-Raphaelitism. Papers 1854 to 1862* (New York: Dodd, Mead, 1899), 258–59.

21. Norton, "The Angel in the House," 404.

22. "Review of *Goblin Market and Other Poems*," *Saturday Review*, May 24, 1862, 595–96.

23. Christina Rossetti, *Letter and Spirit* (London: Society for Promoting Christian Knowledge, 1883), 7.

24. Ibid., 17.

25. Mary Arseneau, "Incarnation and Interpretation: Christina Rossetti, the Oxford Movement, and 'Goblin Market,'" *Victorian Poetry* 31 (Spring 1993): 79–93, also discusses Rossetti's emphasis upon interpretation as a moral act. Katherine J. Mayberry notes the importance of a "moral interpretive system" to "Goblin Market" in *Christina Rossetti and the Poetry of Discovery* (Baton Rouge: Louisiana State University Press, 1989). Chapman's "The Afterlife of Poetry" explores the poem as a "paradigm for reading its own reception history" and ends with a "consideration of Jeanie as a figure for reading and the reading effect" (131).

26. Keble, "Tract No. 89," 133.

27. Rossetti, *Letter and Spirit*, 91–92.

28. For a Marxist discussion of "Goblin Market," see Terrence Holt, "'Men Sell Not Such in Any Town': Exchange in 'Goblin Market,'" *Victorian Poetry* 28 (Spring 1990): 51–67. Also see Elizabeth Campbell, "Of Mothers and Merchants: Female Economics in Christina Rossetti's 'Goblin Market,'" *Victorian Studies* 33 (Spring 1990): 393–410, for an argument exploring the commodification of women in the marketplace.

29. See Kathryn Allen Rabuzzi's *The Sacred and the Feminine: Toward a Theology of Housework* (New York: Seabury Press, 1982) for a discussion of housework as a sacred, ritualistic activity.

30. Elizabeth Alvida Petroff, *Medieval Women's Visionary Literature* (New York: Oxford University Press, 1986), 34.

31. See Richard Menke's article "The Political Economy of Fruit" for a discussion on imperialism and "Goblin Market" in *The Culture of Christina Rossetti: Female Poetics and Victorian Contexts*, ed. Mary Arseneau, Antony H. Harrison, and Lorraine Janzen Kooistra (Athens: Ohio University Press, 1999), 105–35.

32. A large number of critics have written on sisterhood in "Goblin Market." Among them are Helena Michie, "'There Is No Friend Like a Sister': Sisterhood as Sexual Difference," *ELH* 56 (Summer 1989): 401–21, as well as Dorothy Mermin, "Heroic Sisterhood in 'Goblin Market,'" *Victorian Poetry* 21 (Spring 1983): 107–18, and Janet Calligani Casey, "The Potential of Sisterhood: Christina Rossetti's 'Goblin Market,'" *Victorian Poetry* 29 (1991): 63–78. An earlier study of sister-

hood is Winston Weathers's "Christina Rossetti: The Sisterhood of Self," *Victorian Poetry* 3 (Spring 1965): 81–89.

33. Germaine Greer, introduction to *Goblin Market,* by Christina Rossetti (New York: Stonehill, 1975), xxxv.

34. Rossetti, *Letter and Spirit,* 91–92.

35. See Sir David Willcocks and John Rutter, eds., *100 Carols for Choirs* (New York: Oxford University Press, 1988), 330.

36. For a discussion of visual representations of the goblins, see Lorraine Janzen Kooistra, "The Representation of Violence/The Violence of Representation: Housman's Illustrations to Rossetti's 'Goblin Market,'" *English Studies in Canada* 19 (September 1993): 305–28.

37. Ronald Grimes, *Beginnings in Ritual Studies* (Washington, D.C.: University Press of America, 1982), 76.

38. Lizzie's role as a female savior is discussed by Marian Shalkhauser, "The Feminine Christ," *Victorian Newsletter* 10 (Autumn 1956): 19–20, among others.

39. Mircea Eliade, *The Sacred and the Profane: The Nature of Religion,* trans. Willard R. Trask (New York: Harper and Row, 1959), 106–7.

40. See Maureen Duffy, *The Erotic World of Faery* (London: Hodder and Stoughton, 1972), for a discussion of "Goblin Market" in relation to fairytales.

41. See Lynda Palazzo, *Christina Rossetti's Feminist Theology* (New York: Palgrave Press, 2002), for a discussion of Lizzie's spiritual authority as representative of both Christ and wisdom figures.

42. See Caroline Walker Bynum, *Holy Feast and Holy Fast: The Religious Significance of Food to Medieval Women* (Berkeley: University of California Press, 1987), for an exploration of food and food-related practices in the piety of medieval women.

43. Grimes, *Beginnings in Ritual Studies,* 41.

44. Christina Rossetti, *The Face of the Deep: A Devotional Commentary on the Apocalypse* (London: Society for Promoting Christian Knowledge, 1892), 534.

45. Christina Rossetti, *Annus Domini: A Prayer for Each Day of the Year, Founded on a Text of Holy Scripture* (Oxford, England: James Parker, 1874), 7.

46. Rossetti, *The Face of the Deep,* 434–35.

47. Petroff, *Medieval Women's Visionary Literature,* 18.

48. Rossetti, *Annus Domini,* 133.

49. Christina Rossetti, *Time Flies: A Reading Diary* (London: Society for Promoting Christian Knowledge, 1885), 1.

50. Keble's sermon is given as an appendix ("A Sermon of Thomas Keble's") in Isaac Williams, B.D., *The Autobiography of Isaac Williams,* ed. Sir George Prevost (London: Longmans, Green, 1892), 182.

51. Catherine Judd, *Bedside Seductions: Nursing and the Victorian Imagination* (New York: St. Martin's Press, 1998), 161.

52. Mary Carpenter, "'Eat Me, Drink Me, Love Me': The Consumable Female Body in Christina Rossetti's 'Goblin Market,'" *Victorian Poetry* 29 (Winter 1991): 417.

THE MIRRORING OF
HEAVEN AND EARTH

Female Spirituality in Elizabeth Prentiss's
Stepping Heavenward and Elizabeth Stuart
Phelps's *The Gates Ajar*

RORY DICKER

In "Our Thanksgiving," a short story that appeared in
Harper's New Monthly Magazine in December 1865, Elizabeth Stuart Phelps
depicts a mother who has been unable to reconcile herself to the loss of
her son Willie, a soldier killed during the Civil War. Although she lives
with her husband and four children, Mary virtually ignores them, preferring
instead to wallow in her grief and to cherish—even idolize—the memory
of the first-born son who died months earlier. Mary's focus on her dead son
causes her both to neglect her family and to fall out of temper with them:
even as her children grow excited about the next day's Thanksgiving feast,
Mary is "almost vexed with their thoughtless joy."[1] To Mary, Thanksgiving
represents the anniversary of the last time she ever saw Willie alive. Mary
smarts under the pain of this loss and feels that the holiday is nothing but
a mockery: "Thanksgiving!" she exclaims to herself. "I could have laughed
at the word. Should I give thanks? For this desolated fireside, for that vacant
chair and silent voice, for the vanished smile and touch and household
blessing, for those few dimmed letters, and the heart-ache of that lock of
clinging hair, and the grave beneath the early snows—should I give thanks
for *these?*" (83). In describing the emptiness caused by Willie's death, Mary

concentrates on what she does not have in her life, rather than on those blessings that remain with her.

A dream she has the night before Thanksgiving helps Mary to shed her self-pity. In her dream, Mary imagines that it is Thanksgiving and she is both unable to greet her children and unwilling to perform a task that was "Willie's fancy" (84). At the dinner table, which she has set with an extra place for the absent Willie, she turns and sees her lost son: "I looked deep, deep into his eyes. I saw the old, rare smile; I touched his own bright curls upon his forehead; I spoke to him; he spoke to me" (84). One can almost sense Mary's glee as she realizes that no one else has seen or heard Willie, that her interchange with him is private; she feels special because "I alone was chosen" (84). However, Mary has been "chosen" not simply out of regard for her relationship to Willie but rather because of the bad behavior for which he is about to reprimand her. Willie gives Mary "a certain sad, reproachful look, that I had caught on his face once, years ago, when I accused him with injustice of some trifling childish fault—a look that had haunted me in many a still hour since" (84). At this moment, parent and child reverse roles as Willie silently reproaches his mother for her self-indulgent grief. Willie's reproof becomes more explicit as he says, "*I* want them to be happy. *I* want you to enjoy the day. Did you think *I* should not be with you, mother?" (84). Willie's final query indicates his disappointment in Mary, who, like a latter-day Doubting Thomas, has needed physical proof of his immortality.[2]

Mary's dream about Willie effects much change in her behavior. When she awakens, upset because Willie has gone, Mary describes her dream to her husband John. John suggests the possibility that Willie was more than an apparition in her mind's eye, that "perhaps the boy *has* been to you" (85). To John and Mary, Willie's brief return from the dead—whether actual or imagined—offers reassurance of his eternal life; when the clock strikes twelve moments later, John insists that they offer up a special Thanksgiving prayer. Mary's willingness to pray with her husband at this point in the story indicates that her attitude has shifted: whereas she initially questioned what she had to be thankful for, seeing Willie in her dream enables her to understand that he will always remain a part of her life. Willie's presence also permits her to resume her duties as the mother she "used to was," a woman who throws herself into "the very making of my pudding" (85). Mary's domestic life reverts to its former happy state; she can love her children as she formerly did and make a joyful home for them and her husband. In addition, Mary begins to participate in the life of her community; at church on Thanksgiving morning she remarks that "somehow the service stole way down into my heart" (85). This comment indicates that Mary does more than merely attend church in body; touched to the center of her being, Mary feels a part of a religious community. Mary's repaired heart makes her a functioning member of society once again.

By setting her story against the backdrop of the Thanksgiving holiday, a day with both personal and political implications, Phelps dramatizes the symbiotic relationship between private and public spirituality. First celebrated by the Massachusetts Bay colonists in the seventeenth century, Thanksgiving became an annual national holiday only—and seemingly ironically—during the Civil War.[3] Understood in terms of the newly created national holiday, a day with a complex and intertwined religious-political significance, Phelps's story links private and public dimensions of spirituality. In titling her story "Our Thanksgiving," Phelps suggests the possibility of multiple sites of religious experience. On the one hand, since the story demonstrates the way in which, by accepting her son's death, Mary returns to her family, *our* refers to the private, domestic thanksgiving shared by Mary and her loved ones. However, because Mary's healed heart enables her to join in the church's celebration of the day, the word *our* also has a larger, more public significance. While Phelps's story does not directly address a national thanksgiving, in showing a repaired heart, family, and community, it offers a way of healing the entire nation by starting at the individual level. This pattern of reconstituted faith suggests that public religion is subordinate to private feeling, that religious healing on the national level cannot occur until mending begins, not merely at the domestic level, but inside the individual heart.

This essay argues that during the 1860s, as Americans struggled to make sense of the enormous losses that they and their nation had experienced as a result of the Civil War, religion became a more private, personal, and individual experience; Americans needed to discover ways to repair themselves, their homes, and their communities, and they found that they had to begin at the individual, rather than the corporate, level. Although historian Seymour M. Lipset has asserted that, beginning in the early nineteenth century, American religion was "predominantly activist, moralistic, and social rather than contemplative, theological, or innerly spiritual,"[4] the 1860s are significant because they mark a shift during which religion became more "contemplative" and "innerly spiritual." Whereas the war intensified the "activist" and "social" approach to religion by emphasizing the commitment people could make to their nation through engaged, public spirituality and organized benevolence, the war's aftermath—and the healing so inevitably a part of this time—insisted on private examinations of the self. Solitary contemplation certainly was not an innovation of the 1860s: the earliest Puritan settlers based their religious practice on private scrutiny of their thoughts and behaviors, and such self-examination continued during the eighteenth century. However, starting in the early nineteenth century, the revivalism of the Second Great Awakening disrupted the traditional Puritan emphasis on self-examination and replaced it with a focus on public displays of conversion.[5] By 1861, when Horace Bushnell completed his landmark treatise *Christian Nurture*, people had begun to grow dissatisfied with the excesses of revivalism.[6] In disputing the idea that one could become a Christian only by undergoing a conversion experience and instead positing that children, with the benefit of good parental influences, could gradually develop into Christians, Bushnell situated religious experience in the private realm of the home and suggested that the domestic scene was the site for spiritual nurture.

As Christian nurture became associated with the home, women—the guardians of the hearth—assumed primary responsibility for the religious training of all members of the family. Various historians have described this connection of women and religion. Nancy Cott has explained how, by the early nineteenth century, New England ministers assumed that women were "happily formed for religion" because of such "natural endowments" as "sensibility, delicacy, imagination, and sympathy."[7] In "The Feminization of American Religion: 1800–1860," Barbara Welter explains that, "in the period following the American Revolution, political and economic activities were critically important and therefore more 'masculine,' that is, more competitive, more aggressive, more responsive to shows of force and strength," whereas religion, "along with family and popular taste, was not very important, and so became the property of the ladies."[8] Religion itself assumed traits stereotypically associated with women, since it became "more domesticated, more emotional, more soft and accommodating—in a word, more 'feminine.'"[9] In her influential, if frequently disputed, study *The Feminization of American Culture* (1977), Ann Douglas discusses the way in which a liberalized Protestantism led to a feminized or emasculated American culture, one in which the rigorous and severe Calvinism of the Puritans was replaced by maudlin sentimentality; female literature supplanted male theology as the way to communicate religious values.[10]

Although historians such as Cott, Welter, and Douglas, in their discussions of the feminization of religion, have ostensibly privatized religion by associating it both with women and with the home, they do not address the kind of private religion that I am interested in, one that is contemplative, individual, and female centered. Indeed, fiction of the later part of the 1860s illustrates how religion became privatized and individualistic as women attempted to monitor themselves and their spiritual progress. In particular, novels by Elizabeth Prentiss and Elizabeth Stuart Phelps reveal both how organized religion grew less important than the development of a personal relationship with God and how Christian nurture gained primacy over the conversion experience.[11] What is striking about Prentiss's and Phelps's novels is that they depict female religious experience as a way for women to gain autonomy, self-worth, and self-determination. Their novels reveal that women's role as the spiritual guardians of others is subordinate to their involvement in the search for spiritual meaning for themselves. In demonstrating that religious experience was more interior and private than a domestic conceptualization of religion would suggest, I do not wish to imply that spirituality was entirely cordoned off from either domestic or communal spaces. Indeed, in contesting the notion that religious space can be conflated with either the public or the private sphere, I argue for a dynamic interchange between private spiritual experience and external sites of spirituality; this essay works from the premise that multiple sites of religious experience exist outside the paradigm of public and private spheres. The main innovation of Prentiss and Phelps, however, is their insistence that women's spirituality is important to women's development as individuals, and not just to their moral guardianship over their families.

Prentiss's *Stepping Heavenward* (1869) and Phelps's *The Gates Ajar* (1868) belong to the tradition of domestic fiction, a form of nineteenth-century fiction written mainly by women that celebrated women's power as moral guardians of their children and husbands. Domesticity can be viewed as an ideology whose power came from limiting the roles that were available to women; the cult of true womanhood, as formulated by historian Barbara Welter, prescribed that the nineteenth-century woman be pious, pure, domestic, and submissive. Mandating that women have these attributes would certainly seem to outlaw any behaviors that fell outside these parameters. Yet, as Lora Romero states in her discussion of Nancy Cott's *Bonds of Womanhood*, domesticity sought to return to women and the home at least "some of the social status that they lost to declining household production and the related isolation of women and children."[12]

That is, if women were no longer producers of goods within the household, then they could at least produce good within the members of their household. As Sarah Josepha Hale, the editor of *Godey's Lady's Book* and a proponent of the domestic ideal, asserted: "The strength of man's character is in his physical properties—the strength of woman lies in her moral sentiments."[13] According to this logic, women had the power to influence their husbands and male children to do good.

Particularly when it is compared to the aristocratic system it challenged, one can see the ways in which domesticity offered women freedom. It is important to remember that the domestic ideal arose as a response to the objectification and "exchange of women within an aristocratic patriarchal system," particularly in England and France.[14] Instead of valuing women for their beauty and attractiveness, as did aristocratic patriarchy, domesticity posited both that women had selves that needed to be educated and that women needed this education to be good wives and mothers. In *Strictures on the Modern System of Female Education* (1799), the British educator Hannah More insisted that women should be valued for such internal qualities as good judgment, domestic knowledge, and morality.[15] Although from the perspective of the twenty-first century domesticity may seem retrograde, since it celebrates women's placement in a seemingly confined social space, in the context of the nineteenth century, it offered women a great deal. Domesticity valued women for their interior lives—both the domestic worlds they created and maintained and the moral qualities their minds and souls promoted. The domestic ideal also gave women power to effect social change: because virtually everybody had a home in which women were dominant, women had the potential to exert a wide influence; domestic values had the potential to dominate the world.[16]

Although both Prentiss's and Phelps's novels certainly espouse the values of domesticity, they are less concerned with women's moral guardianship over others than with women's personal spiritual development. As a result, the treatment of spiritual growth in Prentiss's and Phelps's novels differs from its treatment in earlier domestic novels.[17] Domestic fiction, also known as "sentimental fiction" or "woman's fiction," was popular in the United States in the mid–nineteenth century. Purchased and read mainly by women, domestic novels relied on a common plot that told the story of a young girl, often an orphan, who must make her way in a world that seems to thwart her at every turn. In *Woman's Fiction*, Nina Baym describes the "overplot" of the domestic novel, explaining that when she meets with hostility from the world, the heroine realizes that she possesses inner resources:

"[T]he failure of the world to satisfy either reasonable or unreasonable expectations awakens the heroine to inner possibilities. By the novel's end she
has developed a strong conviction of her own worth as a result of which she
does ask much of herself."[18] The domestic heroine learns to make use of
her "inner possibilities," sometimes relying on the help of a mentor or religious teacher. In fact, the mentor figure often shows the heroine how to control her own desires and feelings—her unhappiness, disappointment, rage—
by sublimating them in prayer and other religious practices. As a fiction
that charts female self-development, domestic fiction also dramatizes the
heroine's mastery of the feminine skills that are required of her as an adult
woman. In particular, domestic novels show their readers how to submit
both to God's will and to a more immediate patriarchal authority: husbands.
Domestic novels usually end with the heroine's marriage: after discovering
her own capacities and how she needs to control her own feelings, the heroine locates her strengthened and repaired psyche in the safe world of marriage and home, submitting herself to the direction of her husband.

Whereas earlier domestic fiction tends to demonstrate how young
women follow various external rules to achieve piety, in Prentiss's and
Phelps's novels, such rules become internalized as the heroine struggles
to live up to self-imposed guidelines rather than externally derived ones.[19]
While fictional depictions of spirituality in both the 1850s and 1860s de-
emphasize the significance of religious institutions, domestic fiction of the
1850s still tends to show the heroine in contact with spiritual guides and ad-
visers, especially male ministers.[20] Thus, in Susan Warner's *The Wide, Wide
World* (1850), Ellen Montgomery gains religious knowledge from both her
friend Alice Humphreys and John Humphreys, a minister-in-training. Most
important, in the 1850s, "religious faith permits the heroine to carry off the
victory in many complex social games for which she is radically handi-
capped."[21] For instance, in *The Wide, Wide World*, when Alice teaches Ellen
to respond to Aunt Fortune's cruelty with gentleness, meekness, and obedience, Ellen's aunt leaves her alone, thereby giving the girl a good deal of
freedom. In this situation, Christian behavior—turning the other cheek—
becomes a "social strategy" that enables Ellen, the weaker party, to emerge
victorious over her aunt.[22] In contrast, Prentiss's and Phelps's novels show
that heroines gain more individual self-sufficiency than social rewards as a
result of their spiritual learning. That is, these novels suggest that personal
nurture—divorced from duties to others—is at the center of female spirituality. Just as important, while fiction of the 1850s seeks to make the hero-

ine fit for a domestic role, Prentiss's and Phelps's novels show women attempting to ready themselves for the afterlife.

Although little read today and known mainly to specialists of nineteenth-century women's literature, both Prentiss's and Phelps's novels were
incredibly popular in the late nineteenth century. Reported to be the second best-selling book by a woman during the nineteenth century, second
only to Harriet Beecher Stowe's *Uncle Tom's Cabin*, *The Gates Ajar* sold
more than one hundred thousand copies in the first few years of publication and continued to be read at least until the turn of the twentieth century.[23] *The Gates Ajar* not only jump-started Phelps's career but also made
her a good deal of money; shortly after the publication of the novel, her
publisher James T. Fields sent her a royalty check for $600 and informed
her that the novel had already sold four thousand copies. Nearly thirty
years later, Phelps wrote in her memoir that this was the "largest sum on
which I had ever set my startled eyes."[24] Although its sales were not as high
as those of *Gates*, Elizabeth Prentiss's *Stepping Heavenward* went through
many editions in the United States, was read widely in Britain, Canada,
and Australia, and was translated into French and German.[25] One of the
reasons for the popularity of these two books was the way they touched
women personally and offered them specific instructions on how to ease
their private pain and suffering.

The diary format of *Stepping Heavenward* and *The Gates Ajar* indicates
that readers used these texts to gain step-by-step instruction on self-reform
and self-improvement. Ann Douglas has referred to Elizabeth Prentiss's
Stepping Heavenward as a "prayer manual,"[26] and, according to one of Prentiss's eulogists, the novel "was taken by tired hands into secret places,
pored over by eyes dim with tears and its lesson prayed out at many a Jab-
bok. It was one of those books which sorrowing, Mary-like women read to
each other, and which lured many a bustling Martha from the fretting of
her care-cumbered life to ponder the new lesson of rest in toil."[27] In a similar fashion, Elizabeth Stuart Phelps, who has been called a "self-appointed
preacher," wrote a slim volume that she hoped would console a generation of women and teach them about heaven.[28] In its depiction of Mary
Cabot's concomitant loss of her brother and her faith—what Barton Levi
St. Armand calls a "double bereavement"—Phelps's *The Gates Ajar* both
addressed itself to and mirrored the confused spiritual state of its readers.[29] Yet at the same time, in showing Mary's developing understanding of
death and the afterlife, the novel also aimed to restore such a state of belief

in its readers, who found Mary's return to faith reassuring and appealing.[30] Prentiss's and Phelps's novels about spirituality offered them a chance to write texts that would be the basis of readers' meditations. Often, these novels acted, at least in a sense, as a "substitute for the church."[31] That is, just as these women wrote prayer manuals and behaved like preachers, the religious experiences of readers mirrored those of the characters about whom they read: their spiritual lives grew private and individual and, if only indirectly, contested the primacy and authority of the conventional, orthodox religious sphere.

As the Civil War came to an end, authors tended to treat religion as a more private concern, depicting characters who looked inward and tried to understand and improve their spiritual selves. Elizabeth Prentiss's *Stepping Heavenward* (1869) reveals a seemingly paradoxical combination of both self-denial and self-absorption. That is, even as Prentiss's novel describes moments in which characters need to subordinate their own wishes to those of others, it also tends to depict as more important these characters' attempts both to know themselves and to build up their inner spiritual resources. Prentiss's text emphasizes the importance of self-monitoring rather than living up to externally derived rules.

In her novel *Stepping Heavenward*, Elizabeth Prentiss creates a character who, if not self-sufficient in her effort to become a better, more "heavenly" person on earth, relies more on a relationship with God than on one with another person. In Prentiss's novel, the main character's relationship with Christ is the most crucial relationship in the novel, and it is a relationship continually in the process of developing. Writing to a friend in 1869, Prentiss stated that she read Elizabeth Stuart Phelps's *The Gates Ajar* "with real pain": "I do not think you will be so shocked at it as I am, but hope you don't like it. It is full of talent, but has next to no Christ in it, and my heaven is full of Him."[32] Although the opinion that *The Gates Ajar* "has next to no Christ in it" is debatable, since Christ is the "*best* friend"[33] of Winifred Forceythe, one of the main characters, Prentiss's comment reveals how important such a relationship was to her; in her novel, Prentiss demonstrates how her main character goes from trying to force herself to love God to experiencing the fullness of a "personal love" of Christ.[34]

While Elizabeth Prentiss claimed that her heaven was "full" of Christ, her novel does not spend much time describing what that heaven looks like. Instead, *Stepping Heavenward* is more concerned with providing a "blueprint for personal holiness"; as a result, it follows the pattern of what Barbara Welter has called the spiritual "how-to" book.[35] Rather than spending much time imagining and describing heaven, *Stepping Heavenward* charts the self-examinations of its main character, Katy Mortimer Elliott, a woman who cares more about living a "heavenly" life on earth than about what will be the content of the life to come. If, in Louisa May Alcott's *Little Women* (1868), Marmee teaches her daughters the importance of self-scrutiny by giving them copies of John Bunyan's *Pilgrim's Progress*, Prentiss actually depicts the process of self-examination in a more detailed fashion because the diary format allows her to directly present Katy's efforts to better herself. By paring away plot and the development of characters other than Katy, Prentiss reveals the importance of self-formation.

Stepping Heavenward presents Katy's struggle to become a Christian. Initially published serially in the *Chicago Advance*, Prentiss's novel appeared in October 1869. Written in journal form, the novel describes the life of Katy Elliott over a twenty-seven-year period as she matures from a selfish, frivolous teenager into a responsible, though still passionate, wife and mother whose cares and tragedies are frequently difficult for her to bear.[36] Ann Douglas has written that the novel's power "comes from Prentiss' clear perception that the housewife's work is never finished, and hence never fully successful, satisfying—or rewarded. Katy Elliott masters one practical or familial problem only to have another crop up; the static moment of achievement, the well-earned narcissistic pause for applause is by definition impossible."[37] Although I would not assert that Prentiss found women's work either unsuccessful or unsatisfying, Douglas rightly identifies the sense of process that informs the novel's worldview: just as housework is never finished, neither is the struggle to become a Christian. In spiritual development, as in housework, there is no one "static moment of achievement," since new problems consistently appear; no "pause for applause" occurs, for the rewards Prentiss proffers are heavenly and not to be felt on earth.

Katy repeatedly describes the course of her spiritual progress as difficult and, as a result, nonlinear. Just like the course of true love, the process of stepping heavenward does not run smooth; indeed, as Katy remarks, "[O]ur course heavenward is like the plan of the zealous pilgrims of old, who for every three steps forward, took one backward" (108). The novel opens on Katy's sixteenth birthday, and the Katy we meet on this day is temperamental and skittish. Although she has determined to keep a journal, since she has already "begun half a dozen, and gotten tired of them after a while" (13), we see not just her short attention span but also her unwillingness to do the kind of soul searching and self-examination journal writing would require. Indeed, Katy does not seem particularly interested in inspecting her thoughts and actions very deeply or carefully. This quality is emphasized when Katy writes that she "can't make good prayers" because she "can't think of anything to say" (15). Katy complains: "I do not love to pray. I am always eager to get it over with and out of the way so as to have leisure to enjoy myself" (21). Like many young people, Katy seems more interested in fun than in the difficult work of spiritual searching.

Early in the novel, the unexpected death of her father and the painful and humiliating breakup of a romance force Katy to begin to mature. She attempts to reform her life but becomes frustrated by her own limitations; she tells Dr. Cabot, her minister, that she is "angry with myself, and angry with everybody, and angry with God. I can't be good two minutes at a time. I do everything I do not want to do, and do nothing I try and pray to do" (65). Dr. Cabot informs her that, even if all she says is true, "God loves you," and this information makes Katy feel "quieted," "sorrowful," and "satisfied" (66). Learning that God loves her is a turning point in the development of Katy's faith; she feels comforted and at peace. Yet, in spite of this new knowledge, she continues to struggle with her faith; she explains that, although she is "pretty good" on Sundays, "on week-days I am drawn along with those about me" (82). She gets caught up in "innocent" but worldly pleasures, such as "going to concerts, driving out, singing, making little visits"; these distractions all "make religious duties irksome" (82–83). Katy summarizes her frustration by stating that "[t]he truth is the journey heavenward is all up hill. I have to *force* myself to keep on" (83). Katy tells her problems to Dr. Cabot, who writes her a letter that sparks the second turning point in Katy's spiritual development. This letter, which is inserted into the novel's text, teaches Katy that she needs to be willing to "go to Christ Himself, not to one of His servants" (96). Dr. Cabot tells Katy that, to show gratitude for God's pardon, she must consecrate herself "entirely to Him, body, soul, and spirit" (97). Although she "cannot will to possess the spirit of Christ; that must come as His gift," Katy "can choose to study His life, and to imitate it" (100). Dr. Cabot's letter inspires Katy to "see that I have no right to live for myself, and that I *must* live for Him" (101). Katy's happiness centers not on "getting to heaven at last," which was formerly her main preoccupation, but on understanding God's love and redemption (101).

Although Katy's faith has shifted quite radically even by the time she is in her early twenties, she still suffers setbacks; reading the Bible and praying make her aware of her ignorance and imperfection, and awareness of this ignorance makes her feel discouraged. Writes Katy: "And the more earnestly I desire holiness, the more utterly unholy I see myself to be. But I have pledged myself to the Lord, and I must pay my vows, cost what it may" (102). At one point, Katy becomes utterly dejected; she states that "[a] stone has more feeling than I. I don't love to pray. I am sick and tired of this dreadful struggle after holiness; good books are all alike, flat and meaningless" (104). In spite of these moments of discouragement, Katy manages to persevere.

The majority of the novel chronicles this perseverance, showing how various significant experiences influence Katy's spiritual growth. As an exemplary nineteenth-century woman, Katy's life revolves around the domestic world, which is where most of her challenges occur. When she is twenty-two, she marries Ernest Elliott, a reserved but loving doctor, and one of Katy's most enduring struggles has to do with his aloofness; his undemonstrative nature clashes with her passionate and expressive one. Katy would like Ernest to be demonstrative and romantic; instead, his medical practice often keeps him away from home, and when he is with her, Ernest does not express his feelings but instead assumes that Katy knows how much he cares for her. Katy feels especially unhappy when Ernest's father and sister Martha come to live with them shortly after their marriage. Katy wishes that Ernest had told her of his intention to invite his relatives to live with them; she feels that, in extending this invitation, he has not taken her feelings and desires into account. Katy feels oppressed by Ernest's grave father and dour sister, both of whom seem to object to her effusive, excitable personality. Over time, Katy grows to accept the presence of her in-laws; she begins to understand that, as a Christian wife, she must develop "self-forgetfulness," an ability both to ignore her own wishes and desires and to accept God's will.

In the first years of her marriage, Katy meets Mrs. Campbell, an old woman whose loving nature Katy greatly admires. Katy tells Mrs. Campbell that she is "in a disheartened mood, weary of going round and round in circles, committing the same sins, uttering the same confessions, and making no advance" (194). Even though Katy feels that she is not advancing, people around her notice a change in her; in a letter inserted into the novel, Katy's aunt writes to Katy's mother that Katy's "Christian character is developing in a way that amazes me" (197). At least some of this spiritual progress, it would seem, is due to what Katy learns from Mrs. Campbell, who reads to her from Thomas à Kempis's *Imitation of Christ*. Through this text, Katy discovers that only Christ can give her sanctification; she must "learn Christ" through prayer (194) and turn over her spiritual life to

Him, even though doing so makes her feel that she is not being active enough. The discovery that she cannot work for her sanctification is crucial to Katy; she gains more faith in Christ's power as a result. Although Katy makes this important discovery, she continues to be tested throughout her life: she nearly dies from a serious, though unnamed, illness, and she experiences the loss of one of her children. Throughout these trials, Katy's dependence on prayer grows, as does her love of God, even when she is critical of her failings as a person.

Katy's greater confidence in her understanding of spirituality becomes evident in her relationship with Mr. Elliott, her father-in-law. Katy's belief in a loving God indicates a progressive stance at odds with traditional Calvinist doctrine. Indeed, Prentiss underscores this liberal view both through her gentle critique of the gloomy faith of Mr. Elliott and through her depiction of the softening of Mr. Elliott's harsh religious views, mainly as a result of Katy's influence. Katy believes in a God of love, not a God of punishment. Prentiss dramatizes the conflict between traditional Calvinist and more liberal Congregational perspectives through her depiction of Mr. Elliott, a severe old man who feels that Katy's "mirthfulness" is inconsistent with any "real earnestness" of religious feeling (173). Mr. Elliott's version of religion is pessimistic: he laments that "God has cast him off forever, and that his sins are like the sands of the sea for number" (179). He chastises Katy for making an idol of her newborn baby: "The Almighty is a great and terrible Being," he warns. "He cannot bear a rival; He will have the whole heart or none of it. When I see a young woman so absorbed in a created being as you are in that infant, and in your other friends, I tremble for you, I tremble for you!" (200). Mr. Elliott "trembles" because his God is a jealous God, one who would punish Katy for idolatry. When he catches her reading Shakespeare, Mr. Elliott states that "Christians do not need amusement; they find rest, refreshment, all they want, in God" (216). Katy explains that reading "profane" books on occasion can only do good: "if you would indulge yourself in a little harmless mirth now and then," she tells him, "your mind would get rested and you would return to divine things with fresh zeal. Why should not the mind have its season of rest as well as the body?" (216). Katy's version of Christianity is more relaxed than Mr. Elliott's; she recognizes that "harmless mirth" will serve to refresh her and enable her to devote herself to her religious life "with fresh zeal."

Although she does not explicitly state her adherence to such a philosophy, it seems likely that Katy advocates Christian nurture. Unlike traditional Calvinists, who believed in man's total depravity and damnation,

Katy feels that families—and not just conversion experiences—could provide means of grace, thereby enabling the development of Christian believers simply by virtue of their being raised in a nurturing, loving environment. Katy realizes that, even though she is an adult, she herself is still in need of Christian nurture; to teach her children proper behavior, she must constantly work to correct her own character. She writes: "[W]hat I want them to become I must become myself" (236). Katy's belief in the importance of nurture teaches her "to carry religion into everything" (313); because she realizes that she acts as an example for her children, Katy understands that "religion is a vital part of one's self, not a cloak put on to go to church in and hang up out of the way again until next Sunday" (314). Prentiss borrows from the French mystic Francis Fenelon the idea, expressed by Katy's husband Ernest, that "[i]nstead of fancying that our ordinary daily work [is] one thing and our religion quite another thing, we would transform our acts of drudgery into acts of worship" (351). In so doing, Katy can influence those around her by a prayerful attitude that is daily and normative. Katy's belief in a loving and nurturing God becomes most evident when her father-in-law wants her to teach Ernest, her four-year-old son, that "he is a sinner, and that he is in a state of condemnation" (243). Although Katy recognizes that she is responsible for her child's soul, she feels that Ernest "will learn that he is a sinner only too soon, and before that dreadful day arrives I want to fortify his soul with the only antidote against the misery that knowledge will give him. I want him to see his Redeemer in all His love, and all His beauty, and to love Him with all his heart and soul, and mind and strength" (243–44). Katy counters Mr. Elliott's stern picture of an unforgiving God who condemns all sinners with a picture of a loving, beautiful "Redeemer" who inspires her child to love him in return. Katy wants her child to learn of God's love instead of his judgment.

Prentiss's novel offers its most sensitive theory of spirituality not just through its liberal attitude toward God's love but in its perspective on the individuality and privacy of faith. Belief, the novel argues, is something unseen that exists inside oneself. When Katy's father-in-law questions her "state before God," she realizes that he does not perceive the depth of her faith (180). "It is true he sees my faults; anybody can, who looks," she reflects, but "he does not see my prayers, or my tears of shame and sorrow; he does not know how many hasty words I repress; how earnestly I am aiming, all the day long, to do right in all the little details of life. He does not know that it costs my meticulous nature an appeal to God every time I kiss his poor old face, and that what would be an act of worship in him, is an act of self-denial in me. How could he know? The Christian life is a hidden life, known only by the eye that sees in secret. And I do believe this life is mine" (180). Katy does not suggest that all faith is invisible; she knows, for instance, that her father-in-law recognizes acts that he can see, such as her good works toward the sick. Indeed, it is Katy's visible goodness to him and to others that ultimately makes Mr. Elliott come to love and admire Katy. But those elements of her faith that are internal—her prayers, tears, repressed thoughts—remain concealed, and these elements, Katy suggests, more accurately reflect her personal faith than do her good works. As a result, Mr. Elliott has no idea of her doubts, struggles, and questions, those parts of her faith that continually renew and reinvigorate her spirituality. Late in the novel, Katy states: "My faith in prayer, my resort to it, becomes more and more the foundation of my life, and I believe, with one wiser and better than myself, that nothing but prayer stands between my soul and the best gifts of God" (333). One's personal relationship with God, a relationship developed through the invisible activity of prayer, counts for more than any external show of faith.

Just as faith is internal and private, it is also individual and different for each person. When her husband defends Katy to his father, he explains that "people are individual in their piety as in other things, and cannot all be run in one mold" (221). Ernest wants his father to see that no two Christians are alike, that those traits that seem suspicious to the older man actually reveal Katy's piety. As individuals with diverse traits, people naturally experience and manifest faith in different ways. Although throughout her life Katy has various spiritual mentors—chief among whom are her minister and her mother—she comes to recognize that "the Christian life must be individual, as the natural character is" (291). This statement is important because it shows that faith depends on the uniqueness of the individual, whose particular "character" causes a unique development of spirituality. Just as important, though, the use of the word *individual* and her admission of the limited usefulness of her mentor figures signal that faith is a private and solitary matter that concerns the personal relationship of the individual and God. Katy's stance bears an eerie resemblance to the position about the solitary nature of the individual soul articulated many years later by Elizabeth Cady Stanton in "The Solitude of Self" (1892). This similarity to a sentiment expressed by the much more radical Stanton—a woman whose *Woman's Bible* divided her from mainstream women's rights activists in the late nineteenth century—is significant. On the surface, Prentiss's novel argues for the self-schooling of the proper Christian woman, a woman who will make the Christian nurture of her children the highest priority in her life and whose life is contained by domestic codes and rituals. Yet beneath the surface Prentiss suggests that most crucial to the existence of such a giving and nurturing woman is the recognition of the individual and solitary nature of her soul, a soul whose faith is highly personal and unique. Only by nurturing the solitary soul can a woman have anything substantive to offer others by way of Christian nurture.

Like *Stepping Heavenward*, Elizabeth Stuart Phelps's *The Gates Ajar* depicts a woman's journey from spiritual despair to spiritual satisfaction. For Mary Cabot, the main character of Phelps's novel, this spiritual happiness is based on a highly individual understanding of Christian doctrine and a personally developed concept of the relation of heaven and earth. In her memoir *Chapters from a Life* (1896), Elizabeth Stuart Phelps describes the experience of writing *The Gates Ajar* at her father's house in Andover, Massachusetts, where he was a professor of Sacred Rhetoric and Homiletics at the Andover Theological Seminary. One day, after escaping her unheated room in search of a warmer place to write, she went to the dining room, which, to her dismay, was "neatly laid out in the form of a church congregation, to which a certain proportion of brothers were enthusiastically performing the duties of an active pastor and parish."[38] Phelps sardonically notes that, as she hoped to write about "the nature of amusements in the life to come," seeing her brothers "play church" provided "a definite check to inspiration."[39] Phelps's negative assessment of the church's ability to inspire her makes sense in light of Katy Elliott's discovery that true faith is internal and individual and not mediated through institutions. For Phelps, because she hoped to discuss the way in which the individual could regain faith, seeing such an obvious reminder of the external space that she viewed as a failed inspiration would naturally prompt derision.[40] Because it offers a negative commentary on ministers, Phelps's *The Gates Ajar* presents a harsher critique of the established, conservative Calvinist Church than does *Stepping Heavenward*, which mainly faults the rigid faith of Katy's father-in-law. In her novel, Phelps proposes alternative religious spaces to the church; although she insists on the importance of a personal and private faith, as does Prentiss, she focuses on the way in which an external site of religious devotion—whether heaven or nature—interacts with the private self.

Elizabeth Stuart Phelps wrote *The Gates Ajar* to comfort "the helpless, outnumbering, unconsulted women; they whom war trampled down, without a choice or protest; the patient, limited, domestic women, who thought little, but loved much, and, loving, had lost all."[41] Phelps understood such grief firsthand: Samuel Hopkins Thompson, a young man to whom she was deeply attached, died at the battle of Antietam in October 1862.[42] Although Phelps and Thompson were not engaged, his death enabled her to sympathize with the countless women "whose misery crowded the land" during the 1860s.[43] Phelps's own grief and her empathic understanding of others' grief prompted her to write *The Gates Ajar*, a novel that became phenomenally popular and spawned two sequels in the 1880s, *Beyond the Gates* (1883) and *The Gates Between* (1887).

Told in the form of a journal, *The Gates Ajar* describes the immense grief of twenty-four-year-old Mary Cabot, whose only brother Royal, a soldier in the Union army, is killed in the last months of the war. Mary's despair at Roy's death causes her to withdraw into herself: she resents "that most exquisite of inquisitions, the condolence system" (8), as well as the unsympathetic attitude of the Congregationalist deacon, who intimates that Roy may not be in heaven since he "never made a profession of religion" (15). Although she is "a member of an Evangelical church, in good and regular standing," Mary begins to question her faith and to imagine God as "dreadful" (10). Only the arrival of her aunt Winifred Forceythe and Faith, her aptly named niece, brings Mary out of her depression. Widowed for three years, Winifred teaches Mary both that God loves her even more than Roy does and that heaven is not an abstract realm where disembodied souls reside but is instead a domestic paradise, a "home" where Roy "will meet you at the door . . . and lead you into the light and the warmth" (38). Winifred teaches Mary a new kind of faith, one that is Christ centered, rather than God centered. That is, Winifred teaches Mary about a God who sacrificed his only son out of love for humankind. This lesson bears a striking resemblance to the kinds of lessons Katy Elliott tries to impart to her father-in-law in *Stepping Heavenward*. In discussions with Mr. Elliott, Katy explains that "God is really so near, really loves us so; is so sorry for us" (216). In defending her love for her son to Mr. Elliott, who feels that such love is a sign of idolatry, Katy says: "[T]he more Christ-like I become the more I shall be filled with love for every living thing" (200). Katy's discussions and example make an impression on Mr. Elliott, who, by the end of his life, has abandoned some of his rigidity; Katy even notices "how much more he reads the New Testament than he used to do, and that the fourteenth chapter of St. John almost opens to him of itself" (266).

The idea of a welcoming and loving God makes an impression on Mary Cabot, just as it does on Mr. Elliott.

One of Phelps's goals in *The Gates Ajar* is to contest and critique orthodox Calvinism's depiction of heaven and to offer in its place an alternative, female vision of bliss.[44] Phelps faults the orthodox church both for its lack of sympathy to the bereaved and for its abstract explanation of the afterlife. In *Chapters from a Life*, Phelps asserts that "even the best and kindest forms of our prevailing beliefs had nothing to say to an afflicted woman that could help her much. Creeds and commentaries and sermons were made by men. What tenderest of men knows how to comfort his own daughter when her heart is broken? What can the doctrines do for the desolated by death? They were chains of rusty iron, eating into raw hearts."[45] Phelps sees the masculine attitude of Calvinism as preventing the consolation of grieving women; even the most "tender" men rely on doctrines and creeds that, because they are written and understood by men, constitute a language that, as it does not grapple with grief, disconnects them from the grief of the "afflicted." In *The Gates Ajar*, Deacon Quirk's reliance on doctrine enables him only to "confer" with Mary on her "spiritooal condition" instead of offering any sincere consolatory gestures (13). He can only remind her that "[a]fflictions come from God, and, however afflictin' or however crushin' they may be, it is our duty to submit to them. Glory in triboolation, St. Paul says, glory in triboolation" (14). Like a chain of "rusty iron," the deacon's doctrinal message of the necessity of resignation and his pat refrain of "glory in triboolation" eat into Mary's "raw heart."

Phelps also criticizes the inaccessibility of the afterlife described by orthodox Calvinism. In *The Gates Ajar*, Mary objects to both the vagueness and the impersonality of her minister's depiction of heaven. Mary characterizes her reaction to her minister's sermon on heaven as follows: "I wanted something actual, something pleasant, about this place into which Roy has gone. He gave me glittering generalities, cold commonplace, vagueness, unreality, a God and a future at which I sat and shivered" (51). Mary feels disheartened by Dr. Bland's unreal, general picture of the afterlife; as Nancy Schnog has asserted, the inadequacy of the minister's approach has less to do with "doctrine per se" than it does with "biblical interpretation through the eyes of the male minister."[46] In other words, the interpretation of the Book of Revelation offered by Mary's minister relies on vague generalities and abstractions; true to his name, Dr. Bland can articulate only bland, nonspecific descriptions of heaven. According to Dr. Bland, heaven is an eternal state of holiness and happiness, where "[w]e shall study the character of God" (48–49). People in heaven also spend a great deal of time "glorifying" God, writes Mary as she recalls the minister's sermon: "There was something about adoration, and the harpers harping with their harps, and the sea of glass, and crying, Worthy the Lamb! and a great deal more that bewildered and disheartened me so that I could scarcely listen to it" (49). Particularly discouraging to Mary is Dr. Bland's assertion that, although "we shall recognize our friends in heaven, . . . there would be no special selfish affections there" (49). This concept upsets Mary, who views heaven as a chance to reunite with Roy and to recapture her "special" relationship with him. Just as "special affections" will not exist in heaven, neither will individuality, according to Dr. Bland, since the soul "will have no interests to conceal, *no thoughts to disguise*. A window will be opened in every breast, to show to every eye the rich and beautiful furniture within!" (50). A lack of individuality in heaven reinforces the idea that people love all souls equally and do not retain the "special affections" they experienced on earth.

In the place of Dr. Bland's "glittering generalities," Mary's Aunt Winifred substitutes a concrete vision of heaven. Because Winifred's heaven resembles the "something actual, something pleasant" that Mary craves, many critics have called it a place of wish fulfillment, a place where unfulfilled earthly dreams can come true.[47] Indeed, heaven, as Winifred describes it, is like earth, only better: reunited with long deceased loved ones, people need never worry about eternal separation. People will "talk and laugh and joke and play," and "there will be no troubles nor sins, nor anxieties nor cares, . . . no ugly shades of cross words or little quarrels to be made up; no fearful looking-for of separation" (56). Winifred imagines that heaven will have mountains, trees, flowers, books, and, above all, houses. In fact, Phelps's afterlife is domestic; heaven bears a striking resemblance to home.[48] Having houses in heaven seems natural to Winifred, who asks Mary to picture "what a homeless, desolate sort of sensation it gives one to think of people wandering over the 'sweet fields beyond the flood' without a local habitation and a name" (94). Just as heaven holds the promise of tangible "pretty things"—which, for Winifred's daughter Faith means the prospect of pink blocks to play with and gingersnaps to eat—the people in heaven will be concrete and embodied. Rather than "wandering about in a misty condition," people "have some sort of body" in heaven (77).

Winifred's heaven appeals to Mary not only because of its resemblance to earth but also because of the opportunities for loving contact that it offers. Whereas the afterlife of orthodoxy promises that friends will feel no special affection for each other, in Winifred's afterlife, people bear strong feelings for their loved ones. Before she meets her aunt, Mary laments that her brother, "away in that dreadful Heaven, can have no thought of me, cannot remember how I loved him, how he left me all alone" (17). When Winifred first tells Mary that she will see Roy in heaven "as you saw him here" (38), Mary envisions this meeting as a kind of repossession: "Roy my own again,—not only to look at standing up among the singers,—but close to me; somehow or other to be as near as—to be nearer than—he was here, *really* mine again! I shall never let this go" (39). Just as reassuring to Mary as the promise of such future contact with Roy is the fact that, because he continues to love her, Roy is always nearby. Winifred assures Mary that "our absent dead are very present with us" (60) and manifests this belief in her own private conversations with her dead husband John. When they go to visit Roy's grave, Winifred tells her niece that Roy is "close beside you . . . , trying to speak to you through the blessed sunshine and flowers, trying to help you and sure to love you,—right here, dear" (66).

Although Winifred's heaven holds out the promise of tangible "pretty things" and reunions with loved ones, because it depends upon thinking about the future or life to come, this vision complicates characters' relationship to their present domestic situations. More specifically, in imagining the afterlife, Mary, like her aunt, projects her past into the future because heaven depends on "pleasant remembering" of the past (91). In heaven, Winifred "expect[s] to have my beautiful home, and my husband, and Faith, as I had them here" (95). While she concedes that Faith, since "she can't always be a baby," may go off "into a home of her own" (95), Winifred resolutely incorporates into her heavenly vision the happiest elements of her earthly past, hoping to "build me a beautiful home in Kansas,—I mean in what was Kansas,—among the happy people and the familiar, transfigured spots where John and I worked for God so long together" (148). Like her aunt, Mary wants to transplant happy moments from the past into the future; she wants to re-create her relationship with Roy in the life to come. Heaven also offers the chance to correct the past's imperfections or inadequacies. For instance, Winifred tells Clo Bentley, a Sunday-school pupil who has "an absorbing passion for music, which she has always been too poor to gratify," that in heaven she will have a piano and "play just as much as you care to" (98). Similarly, Winifred explains to Deacon Quirk's gawky son Abinadab that he will be "much fairer" in heaven than he is on earth (119). In Winifred's heaven, earthly imperfections and problems disappear, and earthly successes can be relived.

Yet, in creating a heavenly future that depends upon the reliving or correcting of the past, Winifred appears to leave out a crucial part of the equation: the present. Indeed, when Winifred first arrives, Mary's present domestic situation has fallen far short of the heavenly perfection of Katy Elliott, whose home, at least at certain points, resembles the heavenly realm. Roy's death has disrupted Mary's interest in domestic duties; Mary states that "I have fallen quite out of the way of active housekeeping, and have almost forgotten how to entertain a friend" (30). Physically alone because Roy has been at war for most of the last four years and psychologically solitary as a result of his death, Mary has not concerned herself with domestic affairs, and as a result, her home is uncomfortable and far from heavenlike. Furthermore, although the advent of her guests causes Mary to correct some of her domestic oversights so that Winifred and Faith will not be literally "homesick," or made sick by her home (30), Mary's continual interest in "go[ing] to heaven awhile" (129) and discussing the afterlife with her aunt would seem to mean that her home would grow less comfortable as her interest in her future, heavenly home—as opposed to the present earthly one—increases.

In spite of the seemingly problematic equation between future and past that omits much consideration of present domestic life, Mary's earthly life does not deteriorate but, in fact, rejuvenates. This improvement occurs because, although an interest in the future might seem to distract one from the importance of the present, in fact, the concept of heavenly domesticity reminds one of the possibility of a heavenly earth. As the "platonic ideal" of domestic life,[49] heaven offers a model on which earthly residents can base their efforts to revise their woefully inadequate homes so that they measure up to their past and future.[50] As Paul Carter has stated, "The kinds of heavens men hope for can be taken as unconscious commentary on what they cherish or regret in this world."[51] Taken a bit further, the perfection that Mary notices and admires in heaven not only reveals her unhappiness about "this world" but also indicates a goal for which she can strive. Thus the possible self-absorption that would seem to be an inevitable by-product of Mary's excessive interest in heavenly affairs disappears because of her desire to improve her present world. As always, Aunt Winifred provides the inspiration for such behavior; instead of interesting herself exclusively in dreaming of the time to come when she will reunite with her husband, Winifred teaches a Sunday-school class and cares for the poor. Mary describes her aunt as "a thoroughly busy Christian, with a certain 'week-day holiness' that is strong and refreshing, like a west wind. Church-going, and conversations on heaven, by no means exhaust her vitality" (98). Like Katy Elliott, who carries her religion into everything she does, Winifred is not just a "Sunday" Christian but has a "week-day holiness." Mary also teaches Sunday-school and, more important, grows interested in other people. She learns to work in "small and insignificant" ways, doing things "so pitifully trivial sometimes, that I do not even like to write them down here" (127). She learns "to be pleasant" to her servant, "charitable" to a nosy neighbor, and "faithful" to her pupils; as a result, she discovers that "one's self becomes of less importance" (127).

More and more, the novel hints, Mary's present will have to do with Faith, Winifred's daughter; Mary's selfish interests become subordinate to the needs of Faith, who becomes Mary's responsibility when Winifred dies at the end of the novel. One day, Mary sews a dress for Faith and discovers that it "seemed to do me good to do something for somebody after all this lonely and—I suspect—selfish idleness" (85). Late in the novel, when Winifred secretly goes to the doctor, Mary and Faith spend the afternoon together, climbing trees and playing make-believe. In reflecting on the day's activities before bed, Mary is surprised "that I should have spent the afternoon like a baby and almost as happily, laughing out with the child, past and future forgotten, the tremendous risks of 'I spy' absorbing all my present; while what was happening was happening, and what was to come was coming" (149–50). Although Mary concentrates on the contrast between her innocent frolicking with Faith and the ominousness of Winifred's illness, what is actually most interesting about Mary's description is that it both reveals heaven in the present and demonstrates the way in which the Platonic ideal of domestic bliss modeled in the afterlife becomes visible and possible in the everyday world. To live a successful, heavenlike life on earth, the passage seems to argue, one need only act "like a baby": by spending the day "laughing" and playing "happily," Mary forgets the "past and future" and lives only in the present. Thus the novel does not suggest that the focus on the afterlife damages one's ability to live in the present, domestic, earthly realm; rather, discovering the prospect of a heavenly realm enables one to perfect the present by living in it and caring for others.

Although Mary's final role as Faith's guardian would seem to bring her closer to an other-centered spirituality, a spirituality that Katy Elliott cares deeply about but also seems to move beyond by the end of *Stepping Heavenward,* neither novel aims to divorce women from their homes or communities. In Prentiss's novel, Katy continues to be a wife, mother, and community member even as she gains knowledge about the independence, autonomy, and individuality of her spiritual self. By the end of *The Gates Ajar,* Mary has become linked to another human life and cannot wallow in the selfish misery she reveals at the novel's start. Yet, in spite of her newly established family, Mary has gained a highly individual understanding of her personal faith; with the help of Winifred, she nurtures herself into a position of happiness and security from which she is able to successfully guide the Christian nurture of Faith. Both novels, then, argue for female self-determination as a way to transform not just one's own soul and spirit but also the spirits of one's family and community. The transformations experienced by Katy Elliott and Mary Cabot echo the change experienced by Mary, the protagonist of Phelps's earlier short story, "Our Thanksgiving," with which I began this essay. Like Mary, whose healed heart permits her to return to her family and community, Katy and Mary, with their reinvigorated spiritual centers, can work to better themselves and others. As a result, *Stepping Heavenward* and *The Gates Ajar,* like Phelps's earlier short story, reveal the interconnectedness of the projects of personal and public spiritual rejuvenation.

NOTES

1. Elizabeth Stuart Phelps, "Our Thanksgiving," *Harper's New Monthly Magazine* 32 (December 1865): 82. Subsequent page citations to this story will be given parenthetically in the text.

2. Ann Douglas has noted that "[c]onsolation literature of all forms between 1820 and 1875 became preoccupied not just with the last scenes and earthly resting places of the dead but with their celestial destinations and doings." Ann Douglas, *The Feminization of American Culture* (New York: Anchor, 1988), 214. Although Douglas's point is well taken and certainly proven by texts such as *The Gates Ajar,* which I will discuss later, consolation literature also focused on the dead's presence on earth as they watch over and interact with the loved ones they have left behind.

3. Hale did not invent the idea of a national Thanksgiving; as early as 1789, George Washington set aside the last Thursday in November as a day of thanksgiving, but this celebration was a one-time event, not an annual one. For more in-

formation on Hale's connection to the creation of Thanksgiving as a national holiday, see Sherbrooke Rogers, *Sarah Josepha Hale: A New England Pioneer, 1788–1879* (Grantham, N.H.: Tompson and Rutter, 1985), 96.

4. Quoted in Robert N. Bellah, "Civil Religion in America," *Daedalus* 96 (1967): 12.

5. Maxine Van de Wetering, "The Popular Concept of 'Home' in Nineteenth-Century America," *Journal of American Studies* 18 (1984): 10–11.

6. Although he published two "Discourses on Christian Nurture" in 1847, Bushnell rewrote and enlarged these texts in 1861, when *Christian Nurture* appeared. In addition to these first discourses, the 1861 edition contains a second part, which provides practical information about Christian nurture and child development. The 1861 edition is thus the complete edition and "final re-writing of the book." Luther Weigle, introduction to *Christian Nurture*, by Horace Bushnell (New Haven, Conn.: Yale University Press, 1967), xxxv.

7. Nancy F. Cott, *The Bonds of Womanhood: "Woman's Sphere" in New England, 1870–1835* (New Haven, Conn.: Yale University Press, 1977), 128, 129.

8. Barbara Welter, "The Feminization of American Religion: 1800–1860," in *Clio's Consciousness Raised: New Perspectives on the History of Women*, ed. Mary S. Hartman and Lois Banner (New York: Harper, 1974), 138.

9. Ibid., 138.

10. See Colleen McDannell's discussion of Douglas in *The Christian Home in Victorian America, 1840–1900* (Bloomington: Indiana University Press, 1986), 18. Mark Twain commented on this association of women writers and sentimentalized religion; in *The Galaxy* in 1871, he asserted that religion had come to be transmitted "*through the despised novel and Christmas story . . .* and NOT from the drowsy pulpit!" Quoted in David S. Reynolds, *Faith in Fiction: The Emergence of Religious Literature in America* (Cambridge, Mass.: Harvard University Press, 1981), 1.

11. In his analysis of southern women and the Civil War, George Rable makes a similar point: just as "congregations steadily shrank during the war," religion itself grew less institutional and more private after the war. George C. Rable, *Civil Wars: Women and the Crisis of Southern Nationalism* (Urbana: University of Illinois Press, 1989), 225–26. For a good discussion of southern women and religion, see chap. 8 of Drew Gilpin Faust, *Mothers of Invention: Women of the Slaveholding South in the American Civil War* (Chapel Hill: University of North Carolina Press, 1996).

12. Lora Romero, *Home Fronts: Domesticity and Its Critics in the Antebellum United States* (Durham, N.C.: Duke University Press, 1997), 24.

13. Quoted in ibid., 15.

14. Ibid., 20.

15. Quoted in ibid., 21.

16. Nina Baym, *Woman's Fiction: A Guide to Novels by and about Women in America, 1820–70* (Ithaca, N.Y.: Cornell University Press, 1978), xxvii.

17. Donna M. Campbell compares Jo March to Ellen Montgomery to show how the two young women undergo similar spiritual difficulties. See Donna M. Campbell, "Sentimental Conventions and Self-Protection: *Little Women* and *The Wide, Wide World*," *Legacy* 11, no. 2 (1994): 118–29.

18. Baym, *Woman's Fiction*, 19. For a succinct summary of the domestic novel, see Donna M. Campbell, "Domestic or Sentimental Fiction, 1830–1860." *Literary Movements*, October 5, 2002. Retrieved October 30, 2002, from www.gonzaga.edu/faculty/campbell/enl311/domestic.htm.

19. Campbell, "Sentimental Conventions and Self-Protection," 121; Steven Mailloux, "Cultural Rhetorical Studies: Eating Books in Nineteenth-Century America," in *Reconceptualizing American Literary/Cultural Studies: Rhetoric, History, and Politics in the Humanities*, ed. William E. Cain (New York: Garland, 1996), 27.

20. Baym, *Woman's Fiction*, 44.

21. Ibid., 44.

22. Ibid., 43.

23. Christine Stansell, "Elizabeth Stuart Phelps: A Study in Female Rebellion," *Massachusetts Review* 13 (1972): 239.

24. Elizabeth Stuart Phelps, *Chapters from a Life* (Boston: Houghton, Mifflin, 1896), 109.

25. George L. Prentiss, *The Life and Letters of Elizabeth Prentiss* (New York: Anson D. F. Randolph, 1882), 3.

26. Douglas, *Feminization of American Culture*, 216.

27. Quoted in Prentiss, *Life and Letters*, 281.

28. Lori Duin Kelly, *The Life and Works of Elizabeth Stuart Phelps, Victorian Feminist Writer* (Troy, N.Y.: Whitson Publishing, 1983), 31.

29. Barton Levi St. Armand, "Paradise Deferred: The Image of Heaven in the Work of Emily Dickinson and Elizabeth Stuart Phelps," *American Quarterly* 29 (1977): 57.

30. Lori Duin Kelly makes a similar point, asserting that "[t]he enormous sales of *The Gates Ajar* suggest that it met the spiritual needs of a generation of believers who were devastated by the effects of the Civil War." Kelly, *Life and Works*, 11. Mary Angela Bennett explains the success of *Gates* as follows: "It was a time when religious speculation was popular and timely. Many had let go their faith in the certainties of orthodoxy and had not yet found consolation in a more liberal theology. To such *The Gates Ajar* came as an answer to their perplexities. It gave them, moreover, the sort of answer they most wished for. They found in it the result of the wishful thinking of one very much like themselves." Mary Angela Bennett, *Elizabeth Stuart Phelps* (Philadelphia: University of Pennsylvania Press, 1939), 45.

31. James D. Hart, "Platitudes of Piety: Religion and the Popular Modern Novel," *American Quarterly* 6 (1954): 321.

32. Prentiss, *Life and Letters*, 266.

33. Elizabeth Stuart Phelps, *The Gates Ajar* (1868; reprint, Cambridge, Mass.: Belknap, 1964), 155. Subsequent page citations to this novel will be given parenthetically in the text.

34. Elizabeth Prentiss, *Stepping Heavenward* (1869; reprint, Amityville, N.Y.: Calvary Press, 1998), 384–85. Subsequent page citations to this novel will be cited parenthetically in the text.

35. Barbara Welter, *Dimity Convictions: The American Woman in the Nineteenth Century* (Athens: Ohio University Press, 1976), 105.

36. Willard Thorp has stated that, while Katy's spiritual journey is more "eventful" than that of *The Wide, Wide World*'s Ellen Montgomery, "her piety is—eventually—greater, probably because, once she gets going, she works at it every hour of the day." Willard Thorp, "The Religious Novel as Best Seller in America," in *Religious Perspectives in American Culture* (Princeton, N.J.: Princeton University Press, 1961), 2:211.

37. Douglas, *Feminization of American Culture*, 216.

38. Phelps, *Chapters from a Life*, 102.

39. Ibid., 102.

40. When Phelps wrote *Gates*, Andover was a bastion of Calvinism; as such, its theologians asserted a belief in the infallibility of the Bible, the sovereignty of God, predestination, and the depravity of man, views that Phelps would contest during the course of her life. For more information on Phelps's biography, see Kelly, *Life and Works*.

41. Phelps, *Chapters from a Life*, 98.

42. Bennett, *Elizabeth Stuart Phelps*, 43.

43. Phelps, *Chapters from a Life*, 97. Although Carol Farley Kessler has suggested that the act of writing *The Gates Ajar* offered Phelps a therapeutic opportunity to heal herself, I would argue that Phelps is more concerned with helping others than with consoling herself. Carol Farley Kessler, *Elizabeth Stuart Phelps* (Boston: Twayne, 1982), 30.

44. In *Elizabeth Stuart Phelps*, Carol Farley Kessler points out the incipient feminism of Phelps in *Gates*: Winifred's heaven offers a "haven in which women might realize their potential" (21). Indeed, Kessler posits that the novel is not just consolation literature but social criticism, since it hints at ways in which people—and women in particular—suffer on earth (32).

45. Phelps, *Chapters from a Life*, 98.

46. Nancy Schnog, "'The Comfort of My Fancying': Loss and Recuperation in *The Gates Ajar*," *Arizona Quarterly* 49 (1993): 141.

47. St. Armand, for instance, states in "Paradise Deferred" that heaven "becomes not simply a home but a private kind of Paradise, furnished with concrete and material wish-fulfillments" (61).

48. Many critics have discussed the way in which nineteenth-century authors domesticated the heavenly realm; Phillip Shaw Paludan, in *"A People's Contest": The Union and Civil War, 1861–1865*, 2d ed. (Lawrence: University Press of Kansas, 1996), notes the era's interest in "domesticating death, robbing it of its terrors, sentimentalizing it" (367). In particular, though, critics have pointed out the way in which Phelps's heaven resembles the domestic realm. Ann Douglas calls this heaven "a continuation and glorification of the domestic sphere." Ann Douglas, "Heaven Our Home: Consolation Literature in the Northern United States, 1830–1880," *American Quarterly* 26 (1974): 502.

49. Baym, *Woman's Fiction*, 297.

50. Nina Baym makes a similar point in *Woman's Fiction*: "Critics have noted that this book was an attempt to save the idea of heaven for a troubled constituency. It was just as much an attempt to save the domestic, rural, middle-class

earth by locating its platonic ideal in heaven. This fading earth was the earth woman was supposed to rule by her influence; if it was lost, so was she" (297). Whereas Baym emphasizes the need to recuperate the earth so that women would remain powerful, I am more interested in exploring the way in which heaven itself becomes a model for earthly life. Welter, in *Dimity Convictions*, similarly posits that the "sexual democracy of heaven" can offer a model for the earth: such democracy "is seen not as a substitute for the imperfect society on earth but as a paradigm of those Heavenly Cities which forward-thinking and progressive nineteenth-century Americans should be constructing" (113).

51. Paul Carter, "'If a Man Die, Shall He Live Again?'" in *Passing: The Vision of Death in America*, ed. Charles O. Jackson (Westport, Conn.: Greenwood, 1977), 114.

7

"WHO HAS NOT FOUND THE HEAVEN — BELOW — / WILL FAIL OF IT ABOVE — "

Emily Dickinson's Spirituality

ROXANNE HARDE

On her deathbed in the spring of 1886, as Emily Dickinson prepared to push open "the Rumor's Gate," she returned twice to a theme that she had set in a poem some thirty years before, the story of Jacob and the angel. In this poem, written near the beginning of her poetic career in 1859, Dickinson tells and quotes from the story in Genesis 32:25, in which Jacob wrestles and bests an angel, then tells him, "I will not let thee go, except thou bless me."[1] However, writing at the end of a life lived fully in the absolutes of love and faith, Dickinson revises the story according to her own theological conclusions. She argues that she has earned the prize; she has more blessings to give than to receive. She declares in a note of March 1886, "How ecstatic! How infinite! Says the blissful voice, not yet a voice, but a vision, 'I will not let thee go, except I bless thee.'"[2] Then to Thomas W. Higginson she writes, "Audacity of Bliss, said Jacob to the Angel 'I will not let thee go except I bless thee'—Pugilist and Poet, Jacob was correct—."[3] Dickinson's revision of Genesis 32 makes clear her connection between the secular world and her spiritual state, and it provides insight into the process by which she gained understanding of her own spirituality. Rather than asking the divine for blessings, as does Jacob, Dickinson begins both revisions declaring herself as blessed, having gained a joy from living that is "ecstatic," "infinite," an "audacity of bliss." She aligns herself with Jacob as both "Pugilist and Poet," then confers her blessing with "the blissful voice."

Clearly, Dickinson's spirituality is not a typically Christian concern to integrate prayer, life, and thought, although she does rely upon the language of the church. Rather than engaging in a spiritual quest that would see herself in loving union with God, or separating herself from the world in order to become one with her self, Dickinson's spirituality, her concern with the state of her spirit, aims for a sense of unity with the world that enables understanding of the Absolute. I posit that Dickinson centers her quest for spirituality within the Christian context of faith and doubt and that she expresses understanding of her spirit alongside her theological and eschatological preoccupations. Dickinson simultaneously wishes for and denies the possibility of knowledge of God through divine self-disclosure, even as she finds the presence of divinity in nature. Additionally, she works to reconcile notions of the kingdom of God with her present spiritual condition, to shape understanding of final destiny through lived experience. I use the terms of Ursula King to suggest that Dickinson's spirituality was "a process of transformation and growth," not set apart from or added onto her life.[4] King finds spirituality too often associated with a religious stance separate from the secular world, although spirituality "has to do with the age-old human quest to seek fulfilment, liberation and pointers towards transcendence amidst the welter of human experience."[5] I argue that Dickinson fought throughout her life to tie religious faith firmly to her material reality, that she struggled to understand the transcendent through her lived experience, and that ultimately, "Pugilist and Poet," Dickinson was correct; she used her awareness of spiritual experience to hold her readers and to bless them with her vision and her voice.

Dickinson spent her life interrogating the dichotomies of belief and doubt with a language firmly tied to the discourse, doctrine, and rites of the Christian Church in which she was raised.[6] Within this framework, her epistolary and poetic examination results in her movement from doubt and rejection of her church to a faith that is the acceptance of both belief and doubt. I believe it is possible—through reading her letters and poems as a woman's life-writing and as highly metaphorical, cryptic, imaginative writing—to illuminate Dickinson's movement to faith as one woman's spiritual journey.[7] This essay takes as its points of reference the work of feminist theologians and literary critics to analyze Dickinson's poetic articulation of her spiritual experience. Through her rejection of the patriarchal church, and through her ties to her community and the domestic sphere, her absolute love of life and the world, and her connection to the physical as well as the spiritual, Dickinson lived the transformative powers of feminist spirituality. I argue that in the intensity with which she asks "Is Immortality true?", in her understanding of faith as "Not precisely Knowing / And not precisely Knowing not," in her dare to "see a Soul *at the white heat?*"—in all of this, Dickinson uses poetry to express an intensely spiritual life.[8] To that end, I will investigate first Dickinson's examination of faith and doubt as a critical practice, then her view of friendship as a theological construct, and finally methods of connecting spirit and body to understand fully her spiritual state.

"FAITH SLIPS—AND LAUGHS, AND RALLIES—": FAITH AND DOUBT AS CRITICAL PRACTICE

From the nineteenth-century minister Calvin Colton to the contemporary religious historian Wilfred Cantwell Smith and the psychoanalyst Julia Kristeva, theorists look to the etymology of *faith* and find that all ancient forms of the word define it as the resting of one's heart.[9] Thus, from its earliest form, faith has encompassed more than the realm of the soul or the body. The heart, in this case, means the center of one's being rather than the emotive or romantic impulse. The intentional resting of one's heart indicates the choice to engage with faith in all its aspects: intellectual, devotional, and spiritual. Belief is merely the holding of certain ideas, but faith is an accord with a vision of transcendent value and power, the divine in the world, and a preoccupation with ultimate concern, the final experience of body and soul.[10] Smith writes that faith is more personal than belief, that "it is an orientation of response; a way of seeing whatever one sees and of handling whatever one handles; a capacity to live at a more than mundane level; to see, to feel, to act in terms of a transcendent dimension."[11] Faith, then, is a quality of human living, a person's evolved and evolving method of constructing and experiencing self, others, and world, of shaping life's purposes, meanings, and loyalties, in light of one's chosen understanding of transcendence. The opposite of faith is not doubt but the nihilistic inability to imagine any transcendent environment or meaning, even negative meaning.

Dickinson's examination of doubt is intrinsic to her canon: immediate, pervasive, and urgent, its import is magnified by its place within the structures of her religion.[12] Just as her Calvinist Congregational Church invites her preoccupation with negative meaning, her ability to doubt fuels her imagination and empowers her poetry. If she is concerned with writing her living self, she is equally concerned with writing her dead self, a self that her church and her culture continually invited her to envision and rehearse. The dead bodies that fascinate Dickinson throughout her work are only one of her methods of expressing doubt, but they are powerful and pervasive. That the restrictive structures and doctrines of her church cause much of the tension in Dickinson's life and work is obvious, but this structure contributes equally to her power, which Carolyn Heilbrun defines as "the ability to take one's place in whatever discourse is essential to action and the right to have one's part matter."[13] Dickinson appropriates religious discourse to criticize but also to confirm, to express her doubt but also her faith, and thus to understand her spiritual state. Because she took her place in the dominant discourse of her Calvinist Church and insisted on her own theorizing about God, her part does matter.

Dickinson chose religion as the place of her spirituality and her faith; Christianity provides the structures for her thought and her work. Susan Dowell and Linda Hurcombe write that their work in feminist spirituality "reinforces a conviction that a yearning for spiritual dimension is as powerful amongst those who have rejected the church as those who remain."[14] Dickinson turned away from the gathered church, not her religion. Beth Maclay Doriani's study of Dickinson's prophetic voice comes out of the realization that, "despite the patriarchal biases of American Protestant Christianity," American women "do not totally reject their religious heritage, despite the tensions they experience with it . . . that religious tradition and the Bible itself offer vehicles through which female writers, thinkers, and potential speakers can be affirmed and even empowered in their practice."[15] Dickinson is empowered by more than the symbolic and semiotic structures given her by Christianity. She is, first of all, "profoundly influenced by the old Calvinist idea that all of life is religion."[16] In addition, Dickinson's Protestant tradition, in arguing for the dignity of the individual, the primacy of individual conscience, and the imperative of impassioned protest against injustice, also authorizes, even requires, a critique of itself.

Through her critique of Calvinism, Dickinson defines her spiritual state and the shape of her faith. She exemplifies feminist theology's tenets of community and mutuality when she criticizes the Bible as "a word / Which bears a sword."[17] And while she knew her Bible well, and drew from it to explain her spiritual state, she did not hesitate to call it "an antique Volume— / Written by faded Men" in her poetic critique of Calvinism and predestination.[18] In fact, the Calvinist Congregational Church of her childhood draws her harshest criticisms. Calvinism, revivals, and patriarchal Amherst formed the arena in which Dickinson developed her sense of self and answered the call to poetry. Karl Keller looks at the Awakening's antirational and introspective frenzy resulting from the sensationalist ideology of New England's early Calvinists, a frenzy of revivals reaching its peak in Dickinson's time and place. He points out that "horror stories can be told about the revivalist life of the Valley when Emily Dickinson was growing up."[19] But if there was horror, there was also inspiration; Calvinism provided her with drama and stimulated a search, and Keller argues that "of the many factors that made her a poet and made her the poet she was, the conversion tactics of hope, heat, and guilt appear to have exerted the greatest influence."[20] While the tactics of the Second Awakening and the tenets and rituals of Calvinism may have shaped Dickinson's poetry, she removes those influences from the sanctuary and incorporates them into the domestic.

In so doing, Dickinson uses the language of Calvinism to criticize Calvinism, even as she reshapes that language into the means of articulating her spiritual state.[21] For example, in Poem 301, Dickinson undermines, with his own explanations, Calvin's exhortation to distrust lapsed reason and trust divine plan. She writes, "I reason, Earth is short— / And Anguish— absolute— / And many hurt, / But, what of that." This topic is the one that preoccupies and vexes Dickinson throughout her letters and poems, but the speaker here is pragmatic to the point of indifference as she dismisses Calvin's reason to deny human reason. There is a scientific objectivity that not only rebuts Calvin's ideas about reason and predestination but also goes on to confirm analytically a heaven that operates under its own terms, not Calvin's: "I reason, that in Heaven— / Somehow, it will be even— / Some new Equation, given— / But, what of that?" In this poem, the restraint and self-scrutiny engendered by Calvinism itself allow her to control intense emotion even as she criticizes Calvin's tenets and refuses to engage in an established theology. Where Anne Bradstreet seems elevated as woman and poet by her Calvinist faith and self-sufficient responsibility for her soul, Dickinson seems forced by Calvinism into substantiality, into an embrace of her material reality that pervades her poetry.[22] The Congregational Church provided an unacceptable forum for Dickinson's faith, and in each calculated "But what of that?" lies her movement to her own spirituality. I argue that throughout her work she rejects the heavenly "Equation" offered by predestination and substitutes instead a spirituality based on love.

Eventually, Dickinson accepts a permeable and intangible bond between the world she loves and the heaven she has always dreaded, to embrace doubt as intrinsic to faith. She writes in early 1871, "[T]o be remembered is next to being loved, and to be loved is Heaven, and is this quite Earth? I have never found it so."[23] She states clearly that the transformative power of spirituality must begin with love and faith, which are both physical and intangible: "[E]ach of us gives or takes heaven in corporeal person, for each of us has the skill of life."[24] Thus Dickinson's attention to faith and doubt as critical practice allows her to understand her spirituality as "a horizon of transcendence in the midst of life."[25] Her consideration of faith in Poem 501 juxtaposes her move away from the pat answers offered by Calvinism and education against her new willingness to imagine the transcendent and the immanent. "This World is not Conclusion" begins with a flat assertion of faith, and one of the few end-stopped lines in her poetry: there is something after death. The poem speculates about what that something may be and calls the unknown a "species," implying that it lives and fits into a known category. The speaker points out that in the face of eternity the wise are as fools and that "Men" have suffered and still do not know. She moves from the difficulty of not knowing and the heavy absolute of pain in the crucifixion to the lightness and indeterminacy of faith:

> Faith slips—and laughs, and rallies—
> Blushes, if any see—
> Plucks at a twig of Evidence—
> And asks a Vane, the way—
> Much Gesture, from the Pulpit—
> Strong Hallelujahs roll—
> Narcotics cannot still the Tooth
> That nibbles at the soul—

Dickinson personifies "Faith" as a laughing girl, who wants to understand and follows the beckoning, baffling "species" that maintains its position "beyond," although it offers assurance in being "positive as Sound." Faith first acknowledges and dismisses evidence from a tree and the wind, then the evidence from the pulpit, which seems no more than another wind. The poem exemplifies a spiritual quest as the speaker struggles to bring doubt under the control of faith. The ultimate movement of this poem allows the possibility that part of life's wonder must remain unknown, and the poem trails off at the end as it points out that nothing will still the questioning, questing soul. The answers to the soul's questions, the solutions to its problems, come in the intangible, in faith, which will slip and laugh, then blush at its own elusiveness. However, faith also "rallies" in both meanings of the word, as a form of verbal banter and as a physical or emotional support; Dickinson's "Faith" may banter with the species beyond, but it will also support the life of that spirit.

"THE HUMAN HEART IS TOLD / OF NOTHING": LOVE AS SPIRITUAL EXPERIENCE

If examinations of her faith and doubt gave Dickinson the critical practice with which to understand her spiritual experience, her close and lifelong attachments to family and friends, especially to her sister-in-law, Susan Gilbert Dickinson, gave her the trust and mutuality necessary for a spiritual life.[26] As Wendy Martin notes, "[F]or Dickinson, intimacy, not conversion, was the sacred tie."[27] Mary E. Hunt finds in women's relationships "a useful theological construct. Friendship illuminates questions of ultimate meaning and value."[28] Hunt's starting point is a feminist theology that finds friendship to be a transformative political experience because it generates mutual responsibility, and she points out that the love of woman for woman is not narcissistic but transformative because it assumes women are important in their own right.[29] Similarly, Beverly Harrison views women's relationships as enabling a transformative worldview.[30] These theologians provide guides for understanding how Dickinson's participation in loving friendships with several other women empowers her poetic voice and helps her to theorize and express her faith. When Dickinson writes in Poem 491, "love is like Life—merely longer," she makes clear how friendship has shaped her eschatological conclusions.[31] When she declares in Letter 269 to Elizabeth Holland, "My business is to love. . . . My business is to *sing*," she explains that her spirituality is intrinsically linked to poetry.

Throughout her poetry, Dickinson links friendship and love to her spirituality, and she often sets them alongside her eschatological concerns. The meaning of immortality proves the most difficult for Dickinson to understand and control. Millicent Todd Bingham attributes Dickinson's preoccupation with death partly to the frequent loss of dear friends, her mother's anxieties about death, her own illnesses, and location, for "the Dickinson orchard adjoined the burying ground. . . . Every funeral procession must pass their house. The wonder is, not that Emily as a young girl thought and often wrote about death, but that any buoyancy of spirit remained."[32] Dickinson focuses early on her spirit and her concern for the afterlife in Poem 79, which begins by exclaiming, "Going to Heaven! / I don't know when— / Pray do not ask me how!" The speaker makes clear the point of her complaint, worry for "the two I lost," then envisions her own death with defiance and fear as she juxtaposes it against her love for the world and life. Dickinson first defiantly embraces the world and her own doubt:

> I'm glad I dont believe it
> For it w'd stop my breath—
> And I'd like to look a little more
> At such a curious Earth!

However, she then declares with equal certainty that those for whom she grieves are "going to Heaven":

> I am glad they did believe it,
> Whom I have never found
> Since the mighty Autumn afternoon
> I left them in the ground.

Dickinson thus writes for herself a theological revisionism that forms a hermeneutics of suspicion and desire. However, for those she loves, Dickinson sets forth a hermeneutics of hope as she purposefully shapes her vision of their deaths into a vision of grace, and her body of consolatory writing is vast and poignant. In the elegiac Letter 418, written immediately after the death of her father, Dickinson finds consolation in describing time spent with him, then expresses her love in an offer of self-sacrifice: "His Heart was pure and terrible and I think no other like it exists. I am glad there is Immortality—but would have tested it myself—before entrusting him." While she is trying to understand the afterlife, to control its meanings and implications, Dickinson prefers, for herself, faith that is dissected and examined through doubt. However, for her loved ones, Dickinson forgoes tight control and blurs the lines between that which can be known and the wonder that "is not precisely Knowing."[33]

Because understanding could not come to Dickinson in any meaningful way through the provisions of her church, she uses poetry to express love, console in the face of death, and thereby come to spiritual awareness and understanding. As Elisa New argues, Dickinson's methodologies show a confidence that spiritual experience is best described in terms other than religious doctrine, "because of religion's habit of concentrating power in a god who, as metaphor, shores up the power of other, material structures (the Patriarchy, the Law, the Truth)."[34] Dickinson concentrates her development of a spiritual life in her ability to love, and she explains it through poetry. When their father dies, Dickinson comforts her Norcross cousins but deliberately sidesteps the language of her church to make her own language more immediate and meaningful; she writes in Letter 278, "[L]et Emily sing for you because she cannot pray." Written at the height of the Civil War, Letter 298 describes to these cousins her vocation, in a way that conflates poetry with understanding the importance of simply living: "I remembered that I, myself, in my smaller way, sang off charnel steps. Every day life feels mightier, and what we have the power to be, more stupendous." Hunt writes that female friendship enables new, creative, and transformative methods of observing death and loss, of turning the observance into a celebration.[35] I argue that, in light of her close relationship with her cousins, Dickinson seeks to find the power of life in the face of mass carnage. Through the "smaller way" of her poetry, she uncovers spirituality as the dynamic force of life.

Furthermore, Dickinson suggests, as she moves past the strategies of Christian consolation, that real consolation is to be found in connection with others. Her attention to relationality allows Dickinson to conflate love and eternity in the assumption that the presence of love ensures the presence of heaven. This assumption enables her to move into the state of spiritual awareness from which she would later write in Letter 575, "By his intrusion, God is known— / It is the same with Life." In her consolatory writing prior to 1869, Dickinson comforted with standard reassurances. For someone whose revisioning of language was always powerful, her early consolations seem a mere echoing of pulpit phrases. Written in 1860, Letter 217 eulogizes their aunt: "I see nothing but her room, and angels bearing her into those great countries in the blue sky." Nine years later, from a perspective matured by love and faith, she comforts her cousin with a vision of death that speaks of her own search for understanding: "I know there is no pang like that for those we love, nor any leisure like the one they leave so closed behind them, but Dying is a wild Night and a new Road."[36] More telling is Letter 357, an epistle of comfort to her Norcross cousins, for in it Dickinson privileges pain as part of relationship: "[L]ove is that one perfect labor nought can supersede. I suppose the pain is still there, for pain that is worthy does not go so soon." She then pleads that they see this pain only as the residue of love: "[P]ut it out of your hearts

children. Faith is too fair to taint it so." Dickinson moves from loss to acknowledge love as immanence: "Love will not expire. There was never the
instant when it was lifeless in the world." She closes the letter with a poem
that begins, "God made no act without a cause / Nor heart without an
aim." I suggest that the rhetorical strategies of this letter first make clear
that mutuality and loss are conjoined: if there is love, there will be pain.
At the same time, love must supersede pain, and Dickinson gives it a life of
its own. The poem may begin with conventional Christian consolation,
but by resting the heart—the seat of faith and love—on connections with
others, she seems to argue that God made the heart specifically to love and
that love enables growth and transformation.

Dickinson uses the rhetoric of love to theorize religion, in particular
the love she shares with Susan, through which she finds the intangible made
real and permanent.[37] Beverly Harrison argues that what women know about
their spiritual states they have learned from each other and "have learned
by struggling to lay hold of the gift of life, to receive it, to live deeply into
it, to pass it on."[38] Harrison believes that together women "have always
been immersed in the struggle to create a flesh and blood community of
love and justice and that we know much more of the radical work of love
than does the dominant, otherworldly spirituality of Christianity."[39] When
Susan's sister dies, Dickinson writes in Letter 305, "Dear Sue—Unable are
the Loved—to die— / For Love is immortality— / Nay—it is Deity—."
They centered their friendship in Dickinson's lifelong literary project, which
seems to engender the expository nature of their relationship.[40] By en-
couraging her to delve deeply to hone her poetics, Susan also encouraged
Dickinson to express her self and the state of her spirit. Their love, while enriching Dickinson's life and art, proved that in the risk of one's self comes
the reward of spiritual understanding and enabled her to transform fear and
doubt into an assured faith and joy in life. Thus, when Susan's youngest
son died, Dickinson sent her an elegy that does not resort to the standard
rhetorical practices of the church that she rejected:

> The Vision of Immortal Life has been fulfilled—
> How simply at the last the Fathom comes! The Passenger and not the
>   Sea, we find surprises us—
> Gilbert rejoiced in Secrets—
> His Life was panting with them—With what menace of Light he cried
>   "Dont tell, Aunt Emily"! Now my ascended Playmate must instruct
>   *me.* Show us, prattling Preceptor, but the way to thee!

He knew no niggard moment—His Life was full of Boon—The
    Playthings of the Dervish were not so wild as his—
No crescent was this Creature—He traveled from the Full—
Such soar, but never set—
I see him in the Star, and meet his sweet velocity in everything that
    flies—His Life was like the Bugle, which winds itself away, his
    Elegy an echo—his Requiem ecstasy— . . .
Pass to thy Rendezvous of Light,
Pangless except for us—
Who slowly ford the Mystery
Which thou hast leaped across![41]

Dickinson begins with an assertion that places Gilbert in heaven, but rather than using "promise," she uses "vision" and introduces the idea of the corporeal. Heaven, for Dickinson, must allow the ability to see. The next phrase negates suffering and death; the child has gone peacefully to an assured sea. In life, Gilbert had been a young rascal, a trait his aunt found most endearing, and when she writes of his secrets, she conflates his love of play with his ascension. Gilbert's heaven will be exciting enough; his new life will suit him. Dickinson then turns to the grieving mother and, by equating the child with the sky and with light, she gives Susan a constant consolation. She constructs Gilbert's immortality and leaves night for herself and Susan. The ending verse acknowledges the pain of the mourners but assures for Gilbert the light, and the knowledge that they are all, eventually, making their way toward him.

For Dickinson, her love for Susan provides the ability to celebrate life in its complexity and to enable the spiritual understanding that because of love there is immortality. From this spiritual perspective, Dickinson becomes alive to paradox, to truth in contradiction, as she purposefully constructs for Gilbert a heaven of which she wants no part for herself. Hunt discusses the vision of female friendship as providing insight into living in a world defined by men while creating the world as women imagine it could be. She argues that women's friendships enable them to be religious agents, to name their experiences on their own terms, to make decisions on the basis of their experiences, and to live in relationships and form communities of accountability on the basis of those choices.[42] Dickinson expresses a theology based on love as the sign of immanence and the signifier for transcendence. After years of sharing emotional, familial, and poetic pursuits, Dickinson shares in Susan's suffering and follows her elegy with a note that offers comfort, constancy, and the transformative power of love: " The first section of Darkness is the densest, Dear—After that, Light trembles in—/ You asked would I remain? / Irrevocably, Susan—I know no other way—."[43] Dickinson wrenches into language certain almost unspeakable emotional states to articulate a spirituality that invokes the best of human possibility. Three years before her death, Dickinson sent Susan a gift with a poem that settles many of her own questions. Because of love, her heart already knows the transcendent power of spirituality, the invisible "nothing" that can transform the world:

By homely gift and hindered Words
The human heart is told
Of Nothing—
"Nothing" is the force
That renovates the World—[44]

"The Spirit lurks within the Flesh": Spirituality and Corporeality

Dickinson's concern with "the World" also finds expression in her many poems that juxtapose spirituality and corporeality. In line with Harrison's theories on the mediation of knowledge by the feminine body, I argue that Dickinson understands her spiritual state through its connections with earthly experience. Recent critical work has interpreted Dickinson's preoccupation with the corporeal, specifically with body parts and the dead body, as an epistemology of the self.[45] These readings engage in the movement toward seeing women's physical selves as intrinsic to women's spirituality and creativity. Dickinson may attend to fragmented or dead bodies in many of her poems, but she also focuses on the psyche—in its fullest definition as the combination of soul, spirit, and mind. Her poems that juxtapose body and soul push imagination into spiritual awareness and understanding, for they consider questions about immortality and find answers in physical and intellectual experience. In her body and soul poems, she finds self-knowledge through the paradox of knowing and not knowing, and in paradox she gives structure to the mysteries that most concern her.[46]

In her body and soul poems, Dickinson draws equally on both as imaginative ways of knowing her spiritual state, whether she juxtaposes them as paradoxical or complementary. In them she uncovers the theological, linguistic, and patriarchal ordering that has so long opposed and denied women. Naomi Goldenberg writes that separating the soul from the body is a well-established practice in Western thought and theology and that "whichever way the dichotomy is worded, body comes out as the thing valued less."[47] Goldenberg goes on to argue that the separation of mind and body is particularly damaging to women, who are linked to bodily nature, and she argues for "all future feminist theory to be firmly grounded in an understanding of the body's role in cognition."[48] The soul, always privileged over the body, is the great preoccupation of the church, and *logos* has been wrenched out of its place in classical rhetoric to become *Logos*, God's Word and his instrument in the redemption of the world. If *logos* is the ancient means of perceiving and apprehending life and creating a fuller understanding of the soul, thus spiritually enriching mortality, then for Dickinson *logos* is the means of understanding and *not* understanding both mortality and eternity. Indeterminacy of form, diction, narrator, and meaning is constant in her canon and operates as a steady, subtle metaphor for the unanswerable questions that most vex her, a metaphor that underpins the models of body and soul that she posits as the means to understanding spirituality.

Dickinson revises theology through poetry, revises the Word with her words, and redefines faith, not as a renunciation and submission to a conventional theology, but through a more encompassing theorizing about her spirituality. For example, Poem 1492, taken from a letter to a friend on the death of his daughter, begins with a quotation from Paul's Letters to the Corinthians and uses Paul to revision the body's place as concomitant with the soul. The poem seems certain of the chances for human soul and body through the body and soul of the passion, as the first stanza figures the soul as corporeal:

> "And with what body do they come?"—
> Then they do come—Rejoice!
> What Door—What Hour—Run—run—My Soul!
> Illuminate the House!

The poem goes on to figure "them" as real and give them primacy; Christ seems Paul's afterthought. I argue that in the presence of many in the one "Body," Dickinson changes the one Word into many, and the one form of grace into the possibility of many such forms:

"Body!" then real—a Face and Eyes—
To know that it is them!—
Paul knew the Man that knew the News—
He passed through Bethlehem—

While Dickinson struggled to accept personally Christ's intervention, her consolatory writing often commits fully the people she knew and their loved ones to Him. It is a source of wonder that Dickinson is able to comfort the bereaved with an assurance of something about which she was conflicted, and it is evidence of her ability to love. I believe that Dickinson's consolatory work is neither a pose nor a lapse into easy convention. She does not exhibit the search for empowered self-knowledge that Kristeva finds in patients grasping at organized religion for spirituality.[49] Rather, she understands Christ's love of this world; it mirrors her own and renders him possible. As Nancy Mairs writes, sometimes belief is a choice and a deliberate act of love.[50] Motivated by love, Dickinson chooses to reconcile faith and doubt, to combine her words into an assurance of the Word, to find the reason to "Rejoice." Thus her redefinition of the passion subverts prescribed linguistic modes and appropriates the terms of conventional Christian theology but revises that *logos* according to her own spiritual life.

In her revision, Dickinson articulates the body as often as she does the soul, but if Poem 1492 works to blur distinctions between the two as a means of understanding faith, her early poetry more traditionally subordinates body to soul. Throughout her canon, Dickinson's models articulate body and soul as separate, suffering, and mortal; as connected and uneasily facing death; as connected in a way that facilitates understanding of mortality and the possibility of eternity; and as connected in a rich spirituality that demands the unknown, "the Rumor's Gate." In the many poems in which Dickinson theorizes the afterlife and faith, she often includes the soul or spirit and some mention of the corporeal, if not the body outright. For spiritual health there must be a physical and a psychic life, connected and examined through a language that must, in turn, affirm and question the existence and nature of that life. Goldenberg suggests that women "seek our inspiration from theories and disciplines that see the body as the nexus of all human experience," and Adrienne Rich asks women to learn to "think through the body."[51] However, in her early poetry, Dickinson rarely thinks through her body. Rather, she often falls into the traditional privileging of the soul or models body and soul as dichotomous entities, joined unwillingly and remaining unallied. For example, in Poems 670 and 683, body and soul exist in an uneasy relationship, and one is given a voice openly critical and afraid of the other. In Poem 683, "The soul unto itself is an imperial friend," an autonomous entity "sovreign—of itself." This soul seems unlinked to anything, including the body, which might be the "Enemy" sending spies, a reading supported by the line that holds the soul "secure against its own." In Poem 670, the soul invades the body, but in both the soul is held superior, as Dickinson learned in church.[52] Poem 670 may characterize the soul as superior, but it is also a terrorist, and the speaker's sympathies clearly lie with the terrified body. The first stanza introduces the idea of a troubled interior: "One need not be a Chamber—to be Haunted." The middle stanzas describe the threat as internal, and each juxtaposes an external threat, which has progressively escalating degrees of danger, against the startling, and more dangerous interiority. Still, though the soul is interior, Dickinson knew the doctrine that evidences the soul as the Holy Spirit within each of us, and it is perhaps this connection that makes the very self suspect. In the fifth and final stanza an endless stand-off is reached as the body borrows a revolver and confronts its own soul, the "Superior spectre—/ More near."

Dickinson sets the uneasiness between body and soul in these poems in impersonal narratives. I argue that through modeling various personae, Dickinson facilitates the physical and spiritual combination necessary for constructing an understanding of the whole self. In Poem 1090, the speaker, her often present and nameless "I," becomes the self forced into possession of body and soul and unwilling to take responsibility for either; the speaker is ridden with unavoidable eschatological fears but begins the movement to a connected self simply by acknowledging ownership:

> I am afraid to own a Body—
> I am afraid to own a Soul—
> Profound—precarious Property—
> Possession, not optional—

Joanne Feit Diehl writes of this poem that "here the legacy of body and soul has become an agonizing condition; she feels unprepared and defenceless, not ready to face her God—the frontier of immortality that lies on the other side of the 'property' she has inherited."[53] However, although the speaker is afraid of taking responsibility for this precarious and unasked-for property, she still designates body and soul as profound, an adjective that indicates knowledge and cognition. In this poem, Dickinson turns away from privileging the soul and gives herself the disruptive "Double Estate."

Dickinson later shows the body and soul to be a balanced symbiotic relationship. By the age of fifty, Dickinson acknowledged the value and burden of both in Letter 643: "I am constantly more astonished that the Body contains the Spirit—Except for overmastering work it could not be borne—." Beverly Harrison discusses the human struggle to reconcile fear of death with the consolation of salvation, to balance the loss of the body against the gain for the soul. She writes that a "chief evidence of the grace of God—which always comes to us in, with, and through each other—is this power to struggle and to experience indignation. We should not make light of our power to rage against the dying of the light. It is the root of the power of love."[54] Dickinson's rejection of God stems from the cost of salvation, which she sees as a loss of the body and a subversion of a spirit whose weight can hardly be borne. In Poem 263 Dickinson posits the body, "a single Screw of Flesh," contesting the claim that the deity, "Some striding—Giant," lays upon the soul. Dickinson matches the bravado of this poem with angry accusation in Poem 315, where salvation becomes invasion and violation, first of the soul, and then of the body: "He fumbles at your Soul / As Players at the Keys." The movement from threatened soul to threatened body, "the brittle Nature," is made by degrees that build the poem to its climax. "Nature," supported by "Breath" and "Brain," introduces the corporeal body hunted by the supernatural hammer that finally "Deals—One—imperial—Thunderbolt— / That scalps your naked Soul." The Johnson variorum edition points out that Dickinson had proposed and rejected the variant "peels" for "scalps," a choice that emphasizes the violation of human body and soul and adds an American touch to the mixed and mythic metaphors. The anticlimax comes in a couplet that was left off the first time this poem was published: "When Winds take Forests in their Paws— / The Universe—is still—"; soul and body are held dead or too frightened to move, and the way to peace is blocked by the very assurance of grace.

As Dickinson integrates body and soul, she becomes suspicious of any move to separate them. For Dickinson, because it will separate body and soul, heaven will never be quite this life, and grace means only death. Feminist theologians insist that women need to appropriate and deepen the integration of the whole self, physical and spiritual, rational and relational. In Poems 384 and 1431, Dickinson's involuted phrasing allows the possibility of eternity for one and death for the other and never makes clear which is to have which. Poem 384 begins with a soul that will outlast the body: "My Soul—at liberty— / Behind this mortal Bone / There knits a bolder One—." The next stanza explains that soul and body have equal priority and laments the separation of the corporeal and spiritual bodies. This begs to be read against Poem 1431, where the soul "can farther fly" and in which "the body is a soul." As in Poem 315, Dickinson uses the idea of transformation; a body struck by cosmic energy is changed, and she fuses body and soul "for immortality." Poem 384 ends with the enigmatic "Captivity is Consciousness— / So's Liberty," a phrase that might seem to describe both life and death as fully realized human perception. However, Dickinson uses "consciousness" as part of her revision of *Logos,* and it is her idiom for death and for Christ, which therefore posits the oppositional readings that both body and soul face death or both are involved in the passion, as in my reading of Poem 1492 above.

The idea of not ever knowing with certainty engenders the idea of faith as a necessity for Dickinson; faith cannot work because of not knowing, and it must work for the same reason. Her ability to prevent the reification of language, to imagine and to express this wonder as "not precisely knowing / And not precisely Knowing not," allows her the means to reflect on her spiritual state in light of her theological concerns.[55] Toward the end of her life, she wrote variant poems that set forth the indeterminacy necessary for transcendence and center on "the Rumor's Gate," her idiom for heaven. Poems 1576, 1584, and 1588 share the final four lines; all are from letters; the first two are elegies outright, the last a musing on her own mortality. Poem 1576 begins with the quiet, regretful conviction that the soul will continue past the death of the body, "The Spirit lasts—but in what mode— / Below, the Body speaks, / But as the Spirit furnishes—." The speaker then describes music in the violin and tide in the sea as mysteries and juxtaposes those mysteries with that which sets the soul as the animating force in the body. The poem posits the soul's function in eternity and its possible reconciliation with the body. The ending, featured in the variants, first poses answers, then, finally, accepts that knowing is not possible in life:

> Does that know—now—or does it cease—
> That which to this is done,
> Resuming at a mutual date
> With every future one?
> Instinct pursues the Adamant,
> Exacting this Reply—
> Adversity if it may be, or
> Wild Prosperity,

> The Rumor's Gate was shut so tight
> Before my Mind was sown,
> Not even a Prognostic's Push
> Could make a Dent thereon—

The mystery of heaven is as constant as the mysteries of music or the tides or the spirit, but there is music and there are tides, and the transcendence of souls in bodies must be embraced as part of spiritual life.

Dickinson's poetic examination of the soul moves through a range of emotions, allows access to the body, and explores the possibility of salvation. Her models of body and soul set forth the free, questioning, and unique subjectivity that Kristeva both hopes for and expects from the combination of women's dissatisfaction and women's creativity.[56] Dickinson's insistent connection of body and soul allows her the unified individuality needed to stand as an autonomous subject and accept that there are many answers and no answer for the questions she must ask in her spiritual quest. Poem 1584 reaffirms the soul's immortality, and again the possible negative aspects of eternity and especially Deity are set forth, then strengthened by "the rumor's Gate":

> Expanse cannot be lost—
> Not Joy, but a Decree
> Is Deity—
> His Scene, Infinity—
> Whose rumor's Gate was shut so tight
> Before my Beam was sown,
> Not even a Prognostic's push
> Could make a dent thereon—

In another undated poem, Poem 1543, Dickinson writes, "'Twas Christ's own personal Expanse / That bore him from the Tomb—," but in Poem 1584 grace is not blessing but a decree. The opening lines are a terse description of predestination, and in this vision of heaven the mystery is foreboding. It is not unknown wonder or joy; it is only unknown.

Conversely, Poem 1588 brings the complete self to the rumor's gate, and the narrative is personal throughout, not just in the closing lines. This seems finally to give the speaker the role of the prognostic pushing at the gate. Dickinson's choice of this caller at heaven is particularly interesting, for in her time *prognostic* carried connotations of scientific examination

and the occult. Therefore, she tests eternity with both natural and supernatural inquiry and still must accept uncertainty:

> This Me—that walks and works—must die,
> Some fair or stormy Day,
> Adversity if it may be
> Or wild prosperity
> The Rumor's Gate was shut so tight
> Before my mind was born
> Not even a Prognostic's push
> Can make a Dent thereon—

In these three poems, Dickinson's faith proposes a revision of conventional
religion in its own language, an acceptance of dichotomies and of transience, and the importance of self-understanding. She finds that self centered in soul and body, both of which are necessary for full subjectivity and
creativity. Certainty, I think, when faced with the letters and those cryptic,
gnomic, intensely difficult poems, can be placed in Dickinson's movement
toward a faith that has little to do with formalized worship, a faith that
comes from accepting both the knowing and the not knowing inherent to
life. As Carolyn Heilbrun writes, "[W]omen have lived with too much clo-
sure"; we need to stop seeking in the definitive and look to the infinite.[57]

"For Angels rent the House next our's": Dickinson's Spirituality

In conclusion, I suggest that in Emily Dickinson's body of writing lies
clear evidence of the transformative powers of her spiritual experiences.
Cynthia Eller argues that "whatever works to make a woman stronger is
valid feminist spirituality," and Carol Ochs describes spirituality as the active, conscious, and deliberate process of coming into a relationship with
our experiences and reflections, a deliberate transformation of the self as
it is brought into a closer relationship with our reality.[58] In Dickinson's
obituary, Susan, the woman who knew her best, describes the poet's life as
a celebration, her spiritual state as transformative and redeemed: "To her
life was rich, and all aglow with God and immortality. With no creed,
nor formalized faith, hardly knowing the names of dogmas, she walked this
life with the gentleness and reverence of old saints, with the firm step of

martyrs who sing while they suffer."[59] Women's spirituality, Dickinson's spirituality, then, can be described as the process of transformation and growth
through full recognition and exploration of lived and felt experience. I
have argued that she experienced her life with a consciousness that was
acute and critical and that she found and wrote the spiritually powerful.
Dickinson chose to work and write in the discourse of her religion, to return to its symbols for the truths that she needed. She theorizes religion
into a spiritual quest that does not seek for one alternative among many;
her faith forms an integrative and transformative way of thinking. Her vocation and her ability to love allow Dickinson to imagine transcendence,
to envision the divine operating in the word. Therefore, when Dickinson
writes Susan in Letter 912, "Show me Eternity and I will show you Memory,"
she declares that, because of their long relationship, love is a certainty,
and memory is made corporeal. If the presence of love makes memory material, then eternity must also be a certainty. Dickinson's final act of love
was to comfort her cousins who would mourn her, as she writes the Nor-
crosses of her intention to join the God who made her; "Little Cousins,
Called back" is the text of her last letter.[60] Before this note, though, Dickinson sent a poem to her niece Martha in Letter 845. In it, she tells more
of faith than of belief, for she sets forth the absoluteness of her love of the
world and of life. It is an answer to the question "On what do you set your
heart?"; it fulfills Dickinson's commitment to life and to love, and it describes
her spirituality:

Who has not found the heaven—below—
Will fail of it above—
For Angels rent the House next our's,
Wherever we remove—

NOTES

1. Emily Dickinson, *The Poems of Emily Dickinson*, ed. Thomas H. Johnson
(Cambridge, Mass.: Belknap Harvard University Press, 1951), Poem 59. Because
Dickinson did not title her poems, I will refer to them by the numbers in the
Johnson variorum edition. Even with the new Franklin variorum and his manu-
script edition of the poems, Johnson's remains the standard scholarly tool for
Dickinson study.

2. Emily Dickinson, *The Letters of Emily Dickinson*, ed. Thomas H. Johnson and Theodora Ward (Cambridge, Mass.: Belknap Harvard University Press, 1958), Letter 1035. As with the poems, I will refer to the letters by the numbers given them by Johnson and Ward.

3. Ibid., Letter 1042.

4. Ursula King, *Women and Spirituality: Voices of Protest and Promise* (New York: New Amsterdam, 1989), 5. Like Mary E. Hunt, who argues in *Fierce Tenderness: A Feminist Theology of Friendship* (New York: Crossroad, 1991) that the term *spirituality* "has come to mean everything and therefore to mean nothing" (105), King finds most definitions too abstract but still useful. Therefore, when Hunt defines spirituality as "*making choices about the quality of life for oneself and for one's community*" (105), or Kristina K. Groover, in *The Wilderness Within: American Women Writers and Spiritual Quest* (Fayetteville: University of Arkansas Press, 1999), defines it as "positive transformative experience" (10), in King's view such definitions "highlight the understanding of spirituality as an integral, holistic and dynamic force in human life and affairs" (6). Further, King sets spirituality alongside feminism as a social movement *and* a category of critical thinking because it "dissects all areas of knowledge and culture to show their separateness, partiality and exclusiveness of women in order to seek a new way forward to a more integral and holistic way of thinking" (6).

5. King, *Women and Spirituality*, 5.

6. Linking Dickinson's form and language to her religion is a painstaking task, and several works focus on one aspect of the poetry in order to read Dickinson's religion. On biblical influence, see Peggy Anderson, "The Bride of the White Election: A New Look at Biblical Influence on Emily Dickinson," in *Nineteenth-Century Women Writers of the English-Speaking World*, ed. Rhoda B. Nathan (New York: Greenwood, 1986), 1–11; on Christology, see Dorothy Huff Oberhaus, "'Tender Pioneer': Emily Dickinson's Poems on the Life of Christ," in *Emily Dickinson: A Collection of Critical Essays*, ed. Judith Farr (Upper Saddle River, N.J.: Prentice Hall, 1996), 105–18; on hymnody, see Martha Winburn England, "Emily Dickinson and Isaac Watts: Puritan Hymnodists," in *Critical Essays on Emily Dickinson*, ed. Paul J. Ferlazzo (Boston: Hall, 1984), 123–31; on Calvinist theology, see Ronald Lanyi, "'My Faith That Dark Adores—': Calvinist Theology in the Poetry of Emily Dickinson," *Arizona Quarterly* 32 (1976): 264–76; on biblical grammar in Dickinson's poetry, see Christanne Miller, *Emily Dickinson: A Poet's Grammar* (Cambridge, Mass.: Harvard University Press, 1987); on Dickinson's use of Judeo-Christian prophetic tradition, see Beth Maclay Doriani, *Emily Dickinson: Daughter of Prophecy* (Amherst: University of Massachusetts Press, 1996). In addition, there are excellent formalist readings on Dickinson's hymnal rhymes by Judy Jo Small, *Positive as Sound: Emily Dickinson's Rhyme* (Athens: University of Georgia Press, 1990), and on Dickinson's hymnal tropes by Shira Wolosky, "Rhetoric or Not: Hymnal Tropes in Emily Dickinson and Isaac Watts," *New England Quarterly* 61 (1988): 214–32.

7. Critics like J. V. Cunningham, "Sorting Out: The Case of Dickinson," in *The Collected Essays of J. V. Cunningham* (Chicago: Swallow, 1976), caution against interpreting Dickinson through the biographical which would do disservice to the

woman and the poet. However, because her letters are part of her body of work and are as preoccupied with her spirituality as her poetry, there is justification in a contrapuntal reading that assumes an inherent biographical truth behind the issues of faith. I gloss these poems and letters as a method of spiritual examination, even as I read them as part of a poetic vocation preoccupied with faith. Ultimately, reading the poems and letters as fiction or as autobiography seems beside the point; under the hermeneutics of feminist theology, letters and poems may be brought to so rich an understanding of a woman's constructions of her self and her faith that it matters little if we draw the meanings of the writer's spirituality from biography or from fiction.

8. Dickinson, *Letters*, Letter 752a; *Poems*, Poem 1331; *Poems*, Poem 365.

9. See Calvin Colton, *History and Character of American Revivals of Religion* (London: Frederick Westley and A. H. Davis, 1832); Wilfrid Cantwell Smith, *Faith and Belief* (Princeton, N.J.: Princeton University Press, 1979); and Julia Kristeva, "Women's Time," in *The Kristeva Reader*, ed. Toril Moi (New York: Columbia University Press, 1986), 187–273, and *In the Beginning Was Love: Psychoanalysis and Faith* (New York: Columbia University Press, 1987). In "Women's Time," Kristeva discusses a radicalization of Christianity on the part of feminists. While she finds little of merit in religion and places her faith fully in psychoanalysis, she finds that the language of religion may provide the only discourse by which a subject may find full self-expression, and she approves of Christianity as an ideology that may avert humanity's self-sacrifice. In *In the Beginning Was Love*, she juxtaposes faith and psychoanalysis to point out that in the epistemological value and practical efficacy of both comes the assertion of autonomy, and that it is love that enables both successful analysis and faith. While she remains highly suspicious of religion, Kristeva recognizes that faith provides the energy needed for the art of living and that for many religious discourse is the only means of articulating faith.

10. I understand transcendence in the Christian sense, where the essential nature of God is epistemologically transcendent or incomprehensible to humans, but I am also guided by Emerson's view of transcendence as the divine operating as a guiding principle in humans. Therefore, the transcendent may not be known or understood, but it may be imagined and thus integrated into the operations of daily experience. Similarly, I understand immanence in its Christian meaning as God's omnipresence in the world, but I am also influenced by Dickinson's understanding of that presence as a tangible part of daily experience.

11. Smith, *Faith and Belief*, 12. My conclusions about faith are shaped in part by Smith and by minister and pastoral counselor James Fowler, whose *Stages of Faith: The Psychology of Human Development and the Quest for Meaning* (San Francisco: Harper and Row) theorizes the stages of Christian faith as a psychological process and understands faith as an enterprise that "shapes the ways we invest our deepest loves and our most costly loyalties" (5).

12. Critical attention to Dickinson's religion is plentiful and polarized. At certain points in their readings, Wolosky, "Rhetoric or Not," Anderson, "Bride of the White Election," and Cynthia Griffin Wolff, *Emily Dickinson* (Reading, Mass.: Addison-Wesley, 1988), find in Dickinson an assured belief I find unconvincing.

However, by reading Dickinson's poetry and letters as fiction and as forms of auto-biography, these critics have done foundational work in examining how Dickinson's religion has shaped her thought; so have Elisa New in *The Regenerate Lyric: Theology and Innovation in American Poetry* (New York: Cambridge University Press, 1995) and Doriani in *Emily Dickinson*.

13. Carolyn G. Heilbrun, *Writing a Woman's Life* (New York: Ballantine, 1988), 18.

14. Susan Dowell and Linda Hurcombe, *Dispossessed Daughters of Eve: Faith and Feminism* (London: SCM, 1981), 113.

15. Doriani, *Emily Dickinson*, ix.

16. Ibid., 186.

17. Dickinson, *Poems*, Poem 8.

18. Ibid., Poem 1545.

19. Karl Keller, *The Only Kangaroo among the Beauty: Emily Dickinson and America* (Baltimore: Johns Hopkins University Press, 1979), 49.

20. Ibid., 50.

21. Dickinson's spiritual self-reliance resembles, to a point, Emerson's and Whitman's. However, if their beliefs are part of their shared conception of a benevolent universe in which they are linked to all of nature and, for Whitman, to all of humanity, Dickinson's spiritual self-reliance is colored by her great awareness of death, pain, and loss. When she asks the Reverend Gladden, "Is immortality true?" (Letter 752a), she seems more concerned with answering the question herself or with indicating that the concept of an arbitrary deity is not enough to get at the whole truth.

22. For example, in her mother's legacy writing in "To My Dear Children," Bradstreet answers her litany of physical complaint by figuring each as a test from God, meant to remind her of the transience of this life and to prepare her soul for the next. Anne Bradstreet, *The Works of Anne Bradstreet*, ed. Jeannine Hensley (Cambridge, Mass.: Harvard University Press, 1967).

23. Dickinson, *Letters*, Letter 361.

24. Ibid., Letter 388.

25. King, *Women and Spirituality*, 222.

26. I argue in opposition to several critics—in particular David Porter, *Dickinson: The Modern Idiom* (Cambridge, Mass.: Harvard University Press, 1981)—who would have Dickinson an unsexed poet-commentator on a life that happened only in her imagination or to others.

27. Wendy Martin, *An American Triptych: Anne Bradstreet, Emily Dickinson, Adrienne Rich* (Chapel Hill: University of North Carolina Press, 1984), 86.

28. Hunt, *Fierce Tenderness*, 7–8. Taken from the Latin *ultimatus*, the ultimate tends to be used frequently in texts of theology and rarely defined. I understand the eschatological implications of the word to lie in its definitions as both the last and the fundamental. For example, the giving of grace is the final and best act of Jesus Christ, but it is also fundamental and largely unanalyzable. Thus, when Hunt discusses "ultimate meaning and value," I suggest that she writes of spiritual awareness of "last things" as an experience both profound and tacit.

29. Ibid., 52–53.

30. Beverly Wildung Harrison, "The Power of Anger in the Work of Love: Christian Ethics for Women and Other Strangers," in *Weaving the Visions: New Patterns in Feminist Spirituality*, ed. Judith Plaskow and Carol P. Christ (New York: HarperCollins, 1989), 218.

31. The variant to this poem substitutes "Faith" for each appearance of "Love." Both become the noun indicated by the "it" of the first verse; therefore, both are "like Life—merely longer . . . like Death, during the Grave," and both are "the Fellow of the Resurrection."

32. Millicent Todd Bingham, *Emily Dickinson's Home: Letters of Edward Dickinson and His Family* (New York: Harper, 1955), 180.

33. Dickinson, *Poems*, Poem 1331.

34. New, *The Regenerate Lyric*, 10.

35. Hunt, *Fierce Tenderness*, 121, 132.

36. Dickinson, *Letters*, 1332. Dickinson wrote this letter some seven years after "Wild Nights—Wild Nights" (Poem 249), which has been the subject of much critical attention. Her comment that dying is a wild night opens up other possible ways to read the passion in this poem.

37. I have elected to refer to Susan Huntington Gilbert Dickinson as Susan. To Dickinson, she was Susie, then Sue or Susan. Johnson refers to her as Sue throughout, while he gives Mabel Loomis Todd the title of Mrs. Todd, but in all of Susan's names, there is no combination that does not also refer to someone else, hence my use of "Susan."

38. Harrison, "The Power of Anger," 214.

39. Ibid.

40. There are several readings of the Dickinson-Susan relationship as a collaborative friendship. Martha Nell Smith examines the collaborative nature of their correspondence and finds "the written products of a biographical situation—Dickinson's decades-long relationship with the woman who shared so many of her literary and cultural interests, who resided literally a stone's throw away for virtually all of Dickinson's adulthood, and whom the poet loved intensely." Martha Nell Smith, *Rowing in Eden: Rereading Emily Dickinson* (Austin: University of Texas Press, 1992), 158. Where Margaret Homans, in "'Oh, Vision of Language!': Dickinson's Poems of Love and Death," in *Feminist Critics Read Emily Dickinson*, ed. Suzanne Juhasz (Bloomington: Indiana University Press, 1983), 121, argues that Dickinson's relationship with Susan is not lesbian, and indeed that their sameness engenders stasis, Smith, in *Rowing in Eden*, argues that "whether harmonious, conflicted, inspiring, or frustrating, Dickinson's intense involvement with Sue was . . . her most fertile poetic plain" (140). Similarly, Suzanne Juhasz argues that "her relationship with Sue has importance for Dickinson far beyond the help it provides her in practising her craft." Suzanne Juhasz, "Reading Emily Dickinson's Letters," *ESQ: Journal of the American Renaissance* 30 (1984): 179.

41. Dickinson, *Letters*, Letter 868.

42. Hunt, *Fierce Tenderness*, 16–17.

43. Dickinson, *Letters*, Letter 874.

44. Dickinson, *Poems*, Poem 1563.

45. For example, Camille Paglia, in *Sexual Personae* (New York: Vintage, 1990), catalogues Dickinson's use and mutilation of body parts, categorizes such poetic acts as alienation from the female body and self, and finds in Dickinson the persona of "Amherst's Madame de Sade" (640). In a much different reading, Cynthia Griffin Wolff looks at Dickinson's use of body parts and dead bodies as a Romantic grotesque construction of the female author and self. Cynthia Griffin Wolff, "[Im]pertinent Constructions of Body and Self: Dickinson's Use of the Romantic Grotesque," in *Emily Dickinson: A Collection of Critical Essays*, ed. Judith Farr (Upper Saddle River, N.J.: Prentice Hall, 1996), 129.

46. Douglas Novich Leonard, in "Emily Dickinson's Religion: An Ablative Estate," *Christian Scholar's Review* 13 (1984): 333–48, gives a very fine reading of the paradox in religion as Dickinson's means to self-definition. Leonard's reading informs my discussion only peripherally, but it is interesting for its use of Kierkegaard to examine Dickinson's existentialism and for its reading of a fascicle as a unit eight years before Sharon Cameron published *Choosing Not Choosing: Dickinson's Fascicles* (Chicago: University of Chicago Press, 1992).

47. Naomi Goldenberg, "Archetypal Theory and the Separation of Mind and Body: Reason Enough to Turn to Freud?" in Plaskow and Christ, *Weaving the Visions*, 246. Goldenberg acknowledges the gendered argument that privileges soul over body, which comes first from the ancient credo of logos, which was in turn appropriated by the Western Christian tradition.

48. Ibid., 247.

49. Kristeva, *In the Beginning Was Love*, 9–11.

50. Nancy Mairs, *Ordinary Time: Cycles in Marriage, Faith, and Renewal* (Boston: Beacon Press, 1993), 21.

51. Goldenberg, "Archetypal Theory," 249; Adrienne Rich, *Of Woman Born: Motherhood as Experience and Institution* (New York: Bantam, 1976), 290. In her early poetry, Dickinson privileges the soul or portrays soul and body as suspicious of each other. She writes to Joseph Lyman of her chief concerns, sometime in the early 1860s: "I conclude that space & time are things of the body & have little or nothing to do with our selves." Richard Sewall, *The Lyman Letters: New Light on Emily Dickinson and Her Family* (Amherst: University of Massachusetts Press, 1965), 71.

52. Margaret Thickstun argues that this patriarchal attitude came directly from the Pauline epistles: "Paul's subordination of women within marriage and the church because of their physical nature authorizes this devaluation of women and codifies it as an integral part of his gospel. While men have the flexibility to be both spiritual and physical . . . women become ontologically and essentially identified with 'body.'" Margaret Olofson Thickstun, *Fictions of the Feminine: Puritan Doctrine and the Representation of Women* (Ithaca, N.Y.: Cornell University Press, 1988), 7. Thickstun points out that although Paul is not contemptuous of the body in its gracious state, the way that a body becomes gracious is by subordinating itself to a head (7).

53. Joanne Feit Diehl, *Dickinson and the Romantic Imagination* (Princeton, N.J.: Princeton University Press, 1981), 25.

54. Beverly Wildung Harrison, *Making the Connection: Essays in Feminist Social Ethics* (Boston: Beacon Press, 1985), 20.

55. Dickinson, *Poems,* Poem 1331.

56. Julia Kristeva, *New Maladies of the Soul* (New York: Columbia University Press, 1995), 224.

57. Heilbrun, *Writing a Woman's Life,* 130.

58. Cynthia Eller, *Living in the Lap of the Goddess: The Feminist Spirituality Movement in America* (New York: Crossroad, 1993), 3; Carol Ochs, *Women and Spirituality* (Totowa, N.J.: Rowman and Allanheld, 1983), 9–10.

59. Susan Huntington Gilbert, "Obituary," *Springfield Republican,* May 18, 1886.

60. Dickinson, *Letters,* Letter 1046.

"NOTHING BUT SPIRITUAL DEVELOPMENT"

Mary Butts's *Ashe of Rings* and *Scenes from the Life of Cleopatra*

ROSLYN RESO FOY

From the time Mary Butts (1890–1937) was a young girl growing up in her family home in Dorset, England, she knew and felt the force of the spiritual within. Believing herself to be a *seer*, even as a young girl, Mary Butts knew that there was something in the natural world, in which she immersed herself, that would sustain and preserve her in the face of all difficulties. With the early influence of the Romantic poets, especially William Blake, William Wordsworth, and Percy Bysshe Shelley, she fortified herself with the knowledge that there was something sacred in nature that offered insight into a region beyond the world of physical reality. From this sacred world, Mary Butts discovered a source of spiritual strength and power that was paramount to her life and her work. She was an intellectual child of nature in the tradition of Wordsworth and the nature mystics, she educated herself in the anthropological work of Sir James Frazer and Jane Ellen Harrison and the Cambridge Ritualists,[1] she studied ancient and classical mythology, and she later wrote pamphlets on the decline of faith in early-twentieth-century society and on society's encroaching destruction of the natural environment.[2] Immersion in natural and primitive worlds led her later to the source of this strength in the pattern of ritual, myth, and mysticism.

Seeing herself as an authentic initiate and heir to the spiritual past of her family's land at Salterns, Butts ritualistically joined with the mythical and primitive origins of nature itself. This respect for the natural world places Butts in the contemporary company of "spiritual feminists, ecofeminists, ecologists, antinuclear activists and others."[3] Carol P. Christ, a pioneer in the recent women's spirituality movement, who identifies herself as a "feminist thea-ologist," claims that "the crisis that threatens the destruction of the earth is not only social, political, economic, and technological, but is at root spiritual. We have lost the sense that this earth is our true home, and we fail to recognize our profound connection with all beings in the web of life."[4] Mary Butts would have agreed wholeheartedly with Christ and the ecologists because she knew even as a very young girl that nature not only offered a way into a theological understanding of life but also presented an opportunity to join with a world that lies beyond the ostensible natural world. Butts felt the connection with what Carol P. Christ calls the "web of life," and she knew intuitively and prophetically that preservation of the past and the natural energies of that past (found in nature) would assist in interpreting, understanding, and healing the chaos and confusion of the present.

Writing in her diary in Paris on May 2, 1927, Butts clarifies these longings that had been with her since childhood: "What apart from the specific work of writing is what interests me? Nothing but spiritual development, the soul living at its fullest capacity. That is the lever, the new synthesis, or vision or faith. I have not got it yet, but I am beginning to know what is wrong with the times. And many of the things we do are not wrong, it is our way of doing them. They are good things—pederasty and jazz and opium."[5] In her search for the spiritual, Mary Butts ignored any limits or constraints. She experimented with drugs (opium, hashish, cocaine, heroin, and alcohol) as one means to induce the mystic state, and her life and work were part of the journey toward a mystic union with an ultimate reality, a force beyond the physical and the source of all knowledge.[6] Her writing became the one outlet for her quest to lift what she called the "black curtain" that hung across her way to discover what she termed "a perception of the nature of the universe as yet unknown to man."[7]

Part of that "black curtain" was a spiritual crisis in Butts's world that had been created by Darwinism in the second half of the nineteenth century. This crisis eventually generated a renewed interest in replacing what had been lost. For example, the spiritualism and occult practices of Madame Blavatsky, the Theosophical Society, Rosicrucianism, and the Hermetic Order of the Golden Dawn provided some with a way to satisfy the spiritual cravings, and the concern for and interest in spirituality found a fol-lowing among the modernists of the twentieth century. Like W. B. Yeats and Hilda Doolittle (H. D.), Butts dabbled in the occult; like T. S. Eliot, she intertwined her knowledge of classical mythology with contemporary issues. Butts's spiritual quest in some ways mirrored that of D. H. Lawrence and his interest in primitive religions and nature mysticism. Her inquiries into the occult and magic clearly resembled those of W. B. Yeats and his probe for the renewal of a spiritual center to help redefine and order the chaos of early-twentieth-century society. In tune with T. S. Eliot's obser-vation in "*Ulysses*, Order and Myth" (1923) that myth was "a way of con-trolling, of ordering, of giving, a shape and a significance to the immense panorama of futility and anarchy which is contemporary history,"[8] Butts knew that a refiguring of her mythical past was one step toward healing a wounded society, as well as individual souls. Her friendship with H. D. showed similar concerns about feminist revisionist mythmaking, even if their approaches to such issues proved to be very different.

Yet Butts's spirituality is idiosyncratic, distinct in its sense that her blending of Christian and pagan topoi informed the search for an authentic divine heritage that she believed lived within her own English blood. Her female characters draw from a primal goddess source uniting Judeo-Christian spirituality with a matrilineally pagan one. What mattered for Butts, how-ever, was not the label of the spiritual revelation or connection. Rather, she drew from all sources to combat the spiritual failure of the world she inhab-ited. In a letter to her friend Hugh Ross Williamson, she wrote that the mystical experience is "the one way of finding out what things are,"[9] and her life and her writing are a testament to this search. Salterns, her family's home and its surrounding countryside, served to initiate her into its sacred realm; it offered her the primal experience of autochthony, what Mircea Eliade defines as "the feeling of *belonging to a place*."[10]

This primal instinct, however, did not place Butts in the realm of what one might label a traditional mystic. Evelyn Underhill's customary stages of the Mystic Way (awakening of the Self to consciousness of Di-vine Reality, Purgation, Illumination, Dark Night of the Soul, Union: the true goal of the mystic quest)[11] do not quite elucidate the spiritual path of Mary Butts. Butts best defines her own idea of mysticism in her 1933 review on *The Later Life of Wordsworth*, in which her description of Wordsworth's mysticism gives insight into her own: "[I]n his mysticism Paganism and Christianity met and were fused at that white heat which alone puts an an-tithetic good into men's possession."[12] The blending of the pagan and the

Christian in her work allows her to discover a source of power that is also the origin of the female divine. From a goddess/priestess source, combined with a sense of a living presence permeating all life, the majority of Mary Butts's work attests to a longing for spiritual union and consciousness, a desire to heal her own confusion about the world and to relieve the chaos of early-twentieth-century society. Through such an approach, Mary Butts imbues her work with the state that she identifies as "living in two worlds at once." Her first novel, *Ashe of Rings* (1925), and one of her last novels, *Scenes from the Life of Cleopatra* (1935), illustrate how Butts's identification with her own natural landscape and her spiritual ancestors in the form of "the female principle of life" influenced her work in general and offered her a way into an ancient spiritual realm. For Butts, these sources of creative energy opened a journey into a past that could provide solace and answers to a soul searching for a way to heal what Butts called the "dis-ease" of the modern world and, at the same time, offered aid in handling her own emotional demons.

As the great-granddaughter of Thomas Butts, patron and friend of the Romantic mystic and poet William Blake, Mary Butts knew early in her life that spiritual forces were alive both in nature and within her. At Salterns, her family home, Butts grew up surrounded by forty-two of Blake's original works. Combined with a Wordsworthian sense of the sacredness of the natural environment, these paintings helped form the mind of an intelligent, independent, and extraordinary young girl aware of her own consanguinity with nature and the spiritual world. In *The Crystal Cabinet*, her autobiography of childhood, Butts identifies herself, her ancestors, and the natural world at Salterns with "a secret common to our blood. A secret concerned with time and very little with death, with what perhaps medieval philosophers called *aevum*, the link between time and eternity. With which goes an ability to live in two worlds at once, or in time and out of it."[13] From her early novels and short stories to her essays and pamphlets on the twentieth century's loss of belief, Mary Butts examined and, most importantly, desired a way to join with the spiritual source that she encountered in her early childhood as "seeings."

The Crystal Cabinet, though written retrospectively from 1935 to 1937, the year of her death, investigates the origins of the spiritual in the formation of Butts the artist. Having a close, and what she considered a sacred, relationship with the natural world, Butts first encountered her "seeings" in the elements of nature that helped to nurture her spiritual beliefs and that also became a source of strength. In her identification of the feminine with the divine, Butts established the credential of goddess/priestess that became essential to her fiction. One of Butts's journal entries indicates the intensity of her belief: "There is more divine life in me than in any man I have known. I wish to formulate a theory—a perception of the universe as yet unknown to man."[14] In *Rebirth of the Goddess*, Carol P. Christ recognizes the Goddess as "the power of intelligent embodied love that is the ground of all being. The earth is the body of the Goddess. All beings are interdependent in the web of life. Nature is intelligent, alive, and aware."[15] Butts, perhaps not totally aware as a young child of her own feminist roots with such a goddess source, certainly grew to understand the significance of her "seeings" and their connection to the natural world as a foundation of female power.

Such power could be conjured only by those whose authentic immersion in nature's primal origins helped identify it as a living being. In *The Crystal Cabinet* Butts writes, when observing a storm surging across Poole Harbour, "I could not think of it as anything else but a live thing, as visible as it seemed to Wordsworth that it might be . . . a true daimon, as the young of each race first see power" (10–11). The intelligence of the natural world then embeds itself as a kind of consciousness that offers its initiates a way to tap into the potency of this "living" essence; in fact, it is a character that plays a genuine role in her life and her work. Like Carol P. Christ's Goddess, the "female principle of life" for Butts inspires hope for the future and infuses power into her life. Christ claims that "[t]he return of the Goddess inspires us to hope that we can heal the deep rifts between women and men, between 'man' and nature, and between 'God' and the world, that have shaped our western view of reality for too long."[16] Although Christ is commenting on late-twentieth-century society, Mary Butts also recognized a need to resurrect the Goddess, along with her healing rituals. Only through connections with primal origins can humanity find a route toward mending a society whose spiritual underpinnings have been ripped from it by war or by science and technology. Looking to the future by glancing backwards toward her sacred past, Butts knew that she would have to struggle to find common ground for her intellect and her spirituality in a newly evolving world.

It is perhaps not possible to overstate Mary Butts's connection to the spiritual and mystical. Having been raised and educated by her father until his death when she was fourteen, Butts was a precocious and fiercely intelligent child who did not take any experience lightly. She was a questing soul even as a child, and her education in the classics led her clearly to an identification with the elements of nature and her own goddess/initiate origins as a source of potency for a young woman whose world was traditionally patriarchal. She reacted keenly to her mother's sense of the role that women were supposed to play in late Victorian and early Edwardian England. In fact, from her readings and early education, Butts rejected her mother's admonition that "men did not like women who 'knew things'" (122). Butts's education also included interest in the anthropological investigations of Sir James Frazer and Jane Ellen Harrison into the role of ritual and myth in primitive societies. The work of Harrison, a leading Hellenist of her day and a woman writing in a field of male scholars, primarily from 1900 to 1915, contributed to Mary Butts's artistic vision. Indeed, Jane Ellen Harrison and the Cambridge Ritualists helped form Butts's notions of the potential of ritual to prevent disaster, and she drew on their work as sources to enrich her own. Their writings also facilitated her idea of *mana*, an elemental force that individuals try to acquire from a totem or god. Immersion in such theories led her toward a definition of her "seeings" as *"Amor Intellectualis Dei,"* what she defines in *The Crystal Cabinet* as a "perception of a hierarchized universe, awakened by every order in the external world" (258).

Because she was an intelligent and well-read young girl, she understood the role of knowledge, rejected the female role defined by her mother, and struggled to define her own identity through her readings, the natural world, her art, and eventually drugs and the occult. Nature's spiritual mysteries offered her a way to connect with a higher energy and contributed to her mystical longings. In her search for a nonorthodox connection with the source of such power, she records another seeing in *The Crystal Cabinet* while kneeling on her window sill and looking out beyond the trees to the stars: "I knew what they were called, I knew they were there, but for the first time I saw them as the host of heaven. . . . I adored. And have managed to keep the same eyes that saw them that night—the eyes of the same child. Understanding, without the least difficulty, that this was the answer to my worry about God, establishing in my mind where God was to be looked for, and how things could be called 'like' God" (10). Sensing that she herself was a chosen initiate of ancient rituals, Mary Butts knew that her writing would have to explore the role of the spiritual in the lives of her characters. In fact, like primitive humans that Butts was examining in her readings, she sensed in the sacredness of her own natural world that she was a chosen initiate of its past. Or as Carol P. Christ observes, "While images and metaphors inspire the rebirth of the Goddess, rituals bring her power into our lives."[17] Butts knew from her study of Jane Ellen

Harrison that ritual was a powerful force from which to draw strength and to help bring order and power into one's life; returning to a goddess origin through initiation and ritual clearly created power in Butts's own life. Once again in *The Crystal Cabinet*, Butts recounts an experience at Badbury Rings (a series of prehistoric mounded circles several miles northwest of Poole Harbour):

> That afternoon, I was received. Like any candidate for ancient initiations, accepted. Then in essence, but a process that time after time would be perfected in me. Rituals whose objects were knitting up and setting out, and the makings of correspondence, a translation which should be ever valid, between the seen and the unseen. . . . Like any purified, I was put through certain paces; through certain objects, united to do their work, made from the roots of my nature to such refinements of sense-perceptions as I did not know that I possessed, made aware of those correspondences. (266)

As a result of her youthful seeings and her mother's rejection of female authority, Butts, and her fictional female characters, possessed an awareness of a primal, spiritual past. Her readings and her seeings led her toward "a theophany, a shining out of a God" (186) whose authority and power she ultimately joined with her own.

The conflation of Mary Butts with her female characters appears most clearly in her first novel, *Ashe of Rings,* and in her later work *Scenes from the Life of Cleopatra.* In *Ashe of Rings* the life of Vanna Elizabeth Ashe mirrors Butts's own life and spiritual concerns. Vanna, like most of Butts's female characters, must call upon her primal goddess/priestess origins in her struggle against the evils of World War I, embodied in the character of Judy Marston. In the knowledge of her spiritual strength, Vanna invokes her divine powers (white magic) to combat the witchcraft and black magic of Judy—a metaphor for war and all it encompasses. The struggle between dark and light forces takes place on the sanctified grounds of Rings Hill, the Ashe family's land that offers both good and evil power. Yet, as an authentic heir to its heritage, Vanna knows that her power for good will eventually prevail.

In Butts's 1933 afterword to the London edition of *Ashe of Rings,* she characterizes this novel as a "War-fairy-tale," a sort of wish fulfillment of the way she hoped things could end.[18] She recognized that they could only end this way in fiction; yet such idealization of the efficacy of positive spiritual

energies finds expression precisely in fiction. Patrick Wright's Marxist chapter on Butts has called her work "a writing full of panic at the realization
that the world it craves can, for very good reasons, no longer exist any-
where *but* in texts; and in bizarrely Gothic, cranky and hallucinatory texts
at that."[19] The panic of Wright's assessment is precisely what makes this
first novel a significant accounting, not only of Butts's personal concerns
but also of the anxieties of an entire nation that longed for an end to the
devastation caused by World War I. If her heroine is elitist in her pursuit of
and desire for a return to an idealized past, so are the English whose way of
life has been turned completely upside down. Fiction offered Butts a creative avenue to address such longings.

In *Ashe of Rings*, Butts examines the life of Vanna Elizabeth Ashe,
daughter of an aging patriarch whose marriage to a woman thirty years his
junior has produced Vanna and her brother Valentine. From the beginning
of the marriage, the concept of authenticity and racial inheritance plays
an important role in the text and prepares the way for the spiritual journey
of Vanna, the true and natural heir to Rings, its magic and its mystery.
After Vanna explores the ritualistic protective devices of the Ashe family's
pagan past and the violation of the sacred Rings Hill ("a precinct like Ele-
usis") by Vanna's mother, she departs to London, "the year before the end of
the war, when there was very little to eat; and along with the strengthless
food and the noises at night, friendship had lost its generosity and passion
turned *à rebours*."[20] The emphasis on Vanna's spiritual heritage then becomes the major focus of the plot. Exiled from her ancestral and sacred
home by her mother, Vanna shares a flat in London with Judy Marston.
Judy is evil. She thrives on the destruction and chaos brought on by war,
and along with Vanna she struggles over the soul of Serge, a white Russian
émigré and artist who, like Vanna, is alienated from his past. Vanna resolves to rescue Serge's soul from the depraved Judy Marston. To do so, she
must conjure up the heritage of her primal past and its spiritual powers.
Leaving the city, another symbol of chaos and destruction, Vanna returns
with Serge to the sacred and healing forces of her family's Rings Hill, reminiscent of Butts's own Badbury Rings.

Through the agency of birth and race, Vanna realizes that the only
way to combat the dark powers of Judy (femme fatale, witch) is to reclaim
what is rightfully hers—the power of Rings and its pagan past. Vanna
must comprehend her source of strength by recognizing her own legitimacy and her connection to the awesome spiritual powers of nature. Only
an authentic heir, an initiate of the sacred past and its mysteries, can com-

bat the evil forces of the present—be they war, metaphors for war, threats to one's past, or destruction of one's racial heritage. In her study of spirituality in American women writers' texts, Kristina K. Groover notes that "the characters in these texts repudiate the scripts of conventional religion, substituting the stories of their own lives as sources of truth."[21] Similarly, Butts's female characters dismiss conventional beliefs and find in their own past a source of truth, an "alternative paradigm"[22] that allows them to locate the divine in a retold or refound primal faith.

For Vanna Ashe, returning to her home offers her a connection with the primitive forces of the natural world and makes her intensely aware of her power, her source of magic, and her supernatural heritage. Once back at Rings Hill, she assumes her sacred role of pagan adept, priestess, and goddess, and through this medium of spiritual authenticity, she invokes her primal past and its origins. In response to an attempted rape, choreographed by Judy and her new lover Peter Amburton, Vanna undresses, melds her body with the sacred stone on Rings Hill, and prays to her ancestors and their own magical strength, "Florian and Ursula, my father and mother in Ashe" (181). Vanna becomes the embodiment of an ancient priestess who practices the ritual and magic bequeathed to her by her ancestors, and at the same time fuses with the animism of the land—all sources of genuine spiritual authority. Vanna's spiritual reality, like that of her ancestors, is polytheistic, multiple, and infinite. She fights, not only to survive, but also to maintain a tradition, a sense of place and of self that is vital to her existence. Butts thus establishes the role of the female in a position of authority, both literally and spiritually.

As a true heir, Vanna prefigures and affirms the independent spirit of the modern woman, a woman who rejoins with her spiritual goddess past and reconfirms the force of that past within herself and in her relationship with others. The Butts female protagonist finds herself between two worlds, or as Butts herself wrote in her afterword, dated Spring 1933, fourteen years after the original publication of *Ashe of Rings:* "Some very curious things went on, in London and elsewhere, at that time; a tension of life and a sense of living in at least two worlds at once. . . that other women . . . remembered their antique priesthood of life" (232). Through her spiritual joining with the primitive, Vanna offers a way to heal the chaos and terror of the present. As Carol P. Christ, Kristina K. Groover, Carol Ochs, and others have suggested, this healing is offered both individually and communally. Vanna understands that she is the rightfully established and proven head of the Ashe family, in full possession and knowledge

of her control. Yet her spiritual strength is exactly what she offers as healing power to her own family and to the confusion of a society torn by war
and spiritual bankruptcy. In *Ashe of Rings* one of the characters comments
that "I think we are spectators of a situation which is the mask for another
situation, that existed perhaps [in] some remote age, or in a world that is
outside of time" (44). This world "outside of time" is Vanna's spiritual center. She learns to draw strength from that center and asserts herself as a natural inheritor of a world where involvement with the supernatural blurs the
line between human and divine.

Mary Butts does not locate spiritual force only in positive, healing
ways. The character of Judy Marston as the alter ego to Vanna illustrates
another root of spiritual strength. Judy is a formidable opponent to Vanna;
her black magic conjures forces that are equally real to those of Vanna's
white magic. During a sexual escapade with Serge, Judy dances before a
mirror with a small sickle knife when she thinks Serge is not looking. She
conjures her demons, symbolically castrates Serge, and holds him in her
thrall. In another episode when Judy ends her affair with Serge, she springs
at him and bites his wrist. When he leaves, she is lying on the floor sucking
his blood from her sleeve. This drawing of blood acts as an initiation into
her wicked cult and anticipates her intentions to call up the infernal spirits when she arrives at Rings Hill with Vanna's cousin Peter Amburton.
With an assurance that these spirits are real and living, Peter recognizes
the power of the elemental forces that he and Judy have summoned earlier.
In response to Judy's prodding, Peter sacrifices his dog in order to desecrate
the place of enchantment and to call up the chthonic forces alive on
Rings Hill. In fear he tells her: "I won't touch that stone. It's alive—we
woke it up earlier. I remember. The dog's blood turning into a white poison
and moving the stone. Oh, God!" (189). Such dark forces are equally a
part of female spirituality. In spite of the power of these infernal demons,
Butts makes it clear that Judy's dark forces are indeed formidable but ultimately inferior to those of Vanna's authentic heritage. Judy fails because she
seeks control through evil; her consciousness connects with the dark elements of the past. Judy lives on death, both physical and spiritual: "People
like Judy live on the fact of it [war], and get spirit-nourishing food out of
the ruin of so much life" (149). Vanna's spirituality is not more real; it is
simply more positive and life affirming.

Although Vanna struggles to combat the dark forces of Judy and manages to assert her own authority, Serge is finally caught in Judy's spell. He
is both attracted to and repulsed by her actions in the way that humans are

attracted to and repulsed by war and wickedness. The mix of desire and revulsion not only explains the horror of war and its spiritual destruction in society but also examines the ancient history of humankind and its drive toward death and annihilation. Vanna's spiritual prowess, Butts finally concedes, is no match for the evil in others. Serge enjoys his suffering and believes that "life has turned evil" (225); Judy's erotic evil is more real than the goodness Vanna represents. Goodness seems merely an illusion, while pain and suffering are real and true, reflecting the actuality of Serge's Russian heritage and the war-ravaged society that has lost its spiritual center.

Vanna, however, draws strength from her goddess/priestess origins. She is the adept whose healing must come through the magic of Rings, which has crowned her its heir and which helps make the veil between the visible and the invisible world occasionally transparent. At the end of the novel, Vanna has reclaimed her position as heir to the Ashe family and its heritage. Because Valentine's paternity is in question, he is subsumed by her power and the clear understanding that she, the female spiritual initiate, is the valid Ashe of Rings. Through acceptance and immersion in her own spiritual past, through the redefining of the paradigm of the spiritual quest, Vanna offers a clear sense of position for women, not as innocents needing protection, but as rightly acclaimed heirs to the past and its spiritual richness.

By the time Mary Butts was writing *Scenes from the Life of Cleopatra* (1934, published 1935), her flamboyant lifestyle and her art had become calmer. Alienated from her family over issues of money and her bohemianism, Butts found that her lifestyle afforded her the freedom she sought as an independent woman. Moving within the circle of the high modernists throughout most of her early life, Butts never clearly identified with any single group. Instead, she remained an independent, idiosyncratic bohemian defining her own style and beliefs.

The last years of Mary Butts's bold and bizarre life, as well as her art, were a continued attempt to reconnect with that ancestral past, specifically with her goddess/priestess origins, and she used whatever method might work to this end. In January 1932, Mary Butts was living in Sennen Cove near Land's End, Cornwall, with her second husband Gabriel Aitken, an alcoholic and a homosexual. Yet she was once again close to the natural world of her youth and its spiritual energies. Her life had led her through her desertion of John Rodker (her first husband) and her only child Camilla, to an affair with Cecil Maitland, a Scottish artist and Joyce critic, to immersion in drugs and the occult and alienation from her own family, and finally to her marriage with Aitken and their retreat from the madness of the world in Cornwall. Butts was at this time still addicted to opium, but she found a sort of peace in Cornwall that she had not felt since her child-hood at Salterns. By 1934, Aitken left her. Mary Butts spent the remainder of her brief life immersed in the natural world, became an Anglo-Catholic, formed a friendship with the local vicar, and fought to save the church at Sennen Cove. While in Cornwall, she published her two historical nov-els (*The Macedonian* and *Scenes from the Life of Cleopatra*), poetry, several ar-ticles on magic and supernatural fiction, and numerous reviews. At this time she also began a third historical novel, *Julian the Apostate,* and com-pleted her autobiography of childhood, *The Crystal Cabinet.* Still addicted to opium and drinking Champagne Wine Nerve Tonic, Butts had nevertheless abandoned the flamboyant lifestyle of the twenties and thirties. She died on March 5, 1937, after an operation for a gastric ulcer. She was forty-six.

During the years 1932–37, before her death at Sennen Cove, however, Mary Butts decided to put her knowledge of ancient history to work in fic-tion. After the successful publication of her book on Alexander the Great, *The Macedonian,* in 1933, she continued work on her second historical novel, *Scenes from the Life of Cleopatra,* and completed it by the end of March 1934. It appeared in 1935 to a great deal of attention. In Cleopatra, Butts discovered a woman who embodied frustrations, misunderstandings, and authentic spiritual forces similar to her own. In 1971 Oswell Blakeston remembered some admirers of Butts's work remarking on its publication, "Oh, I never realized Cleopatra was so like Mary Butts."[23] In fact, Butts felt a keen sense of identity with Cleopatra and shared with her a confusion and frustration of family history that "justified the lifestyle chosen by each woman to survive."[24] In 1933, two days before publication of *The Mace-donian,* Butts writes in her diary: "Can I now write the life of Cleopatra I have so often told myself. Yes—if this is the key—(were my family ruined to show me this?)—that she could no longer stand the degradation of the Lagidae? If that is the key to it all. . . *if I'm right,* I can do it. . . . I feel as though all the pieces of a puzzle were falling into place. It explains Caesar, her ridding herself of her kin, her cultivation of herself."[25] Cleopatra be-comes for Butts not only a historical sovereign but also a woman, a goddess, an avatar of Isis, and a source of power that Butts had fought to identify in women and in herself throughout her life. By examining Cleopatra as an inheritor of the sacred from her ancestors, Butts fuses the energy of *mana,* what Jane Ellen Harrison describes as an "unseen power lying behind the visible universe,"[26] with the primal force of the female divine. As a woman, a queen, and a legitimate goddess, Cleopatra confirms an authority for women who delve into their mystical origins and who inherently sense their source of power. As Carol Ochs has observed in *Women and Spirituality*, "The spiritual life is not forced, contorted, agonized, or rare—it is ordinary, readily available, and it surrounds us all."[27] In *Scenes from the Life of Cleopatra* Mary Butts not only offers historic possibilities from which to draw but also embeds the spiritual quest in a "readily available" past.

In *The Macedonian* Butts prepares the way for the interpretation of Cleopatra's heritage as one of sanctity and authenticity. When Alexander visits Siwa and the temple of the god Amen-Ra, he is welcomed by the local high priest as the son of Amen-Ra, accepts the proclamation of his divinity, and senses his own connection with the divine as the son of god. In Greek and Macedonian tradition a hero might be the son of a god and yet human. Alexander discovers that he contains a spiritual energy that "was not a person. It was something that shaped equally the Universe and an acorn, and It called him friend."[28] As a descendant of Ptolemy I, ruler of Egypt from 323 to 285 B.C., the reputed son of Lagus, a Macedonian of common birth and friend of Alexander of Macedon, Cleopatra assumes her place on the Egyptian throne, balancing both Greek and Egyptian power and connection with divinity. By opening *Scenes from the Life of Cleopatra* with a brief summary and reference to Alexander's history, Butts conjoins the two origins of power with her interpretation of Cleopatra and establishes her position in Egypt as royalty and goddess, the last of the Lagidae.

What is most interesting perhaps about Butts's portrayal of Cleopatra is that Cleopatra's voice only filters through the narratives of others, in musings expressed in direct speech or in letters. What evolves, then, is a revised view of Cleopatra as a goddess who, like her Greek heritage, can be both human and divine. These "scenes" from her life are driven, as Ruth Hoberman has observed, "less by external events than by the workings of invisible forces. . . . But most significant (and underlying all these other parallels) is the role of mana in defining the great and shaping the course of human history—and in evading the dichotomies that work so much to Cleopatra's disadvantage."[29] In fact, in an appendix to the novel, Butts claims that she seeks to subvert the demonization of Cleopatra in history and literature. Taking Cleopatra's past biographers to task, Butts claims that to such male authorities, "the Queen is a wanton; and each baby she had an additional proof of it. Forgetting that men—historians or not—do not like to think, and so refuse to believe, in an active woman, alone, enjoying the use of power."[30] Once Octavian assumed power after the death of Cleopatra and Marc Antony, his malignant tales and legend fabricated after Cleopatra's death, Butts claims, tainted history's view of this queen and goddess. From Chaucer and Shakespeare to Bernard Shaw, Cleopatra, according to Butts, had never received a fair accounting, even though Shakespeare had something of a change of heart by the end of his play. Butts aimed to revisit history, and her novel should be understood, claims Hoberman, "in the context of women's efforts during this time to make room in Western culture for the very concept of a female maker of history."[31] Butts easily moves into the role of female maker and remaker of history.

Yet it is Cleopatra's difficulties with the male patriarchal system and its interpretation of her place in history that Butts feels must be addressed in her novel. Hoberman states, "Butts must have found a kindred spirit, one whose desire for knowledge and power had been mistaken (as had her own by her mother) for sexual insatiability. Butts's fascination with Cleopatra—and with Cleopatra's divine self Isis—grew out of that ambition and anger. Cleopatra-as-Isis offered her an alternative queen, one that brought together all the qualities her culture struggled to keep apart."[32] Once again the authenticity of spiritual/goddess origins offers Butts another avenue toward redefining the role of women in twentieth-century society, reaffirming her own quest for spiritual union and identification and reestablishing the source of power that was a part of our ancient past. Butts's view of Cleopatra offers such an alternative reading to that of past writers and respects the legitimacy of Cleopatra's reign and her divine connection, as well as her natural assumption of power.

Throughout the historical narrative, Butts uses a variety of voices. Not only does she use a narrator who smoothly allows musings from numerous players to intersect the narrator's own voice, but she also presents scenes of the history through the eyes of Caesar, Antony, and Iras and Charmian (Cleopatra's two attendants). The voice of Cleopatra herself remains filtered, almost otherworldly, so that she seems like the mana that lies beneath the surface of all life. The telling of the story itself is not new; it is Butts's attribution of and emphasis on natural divinity that permeates the role of Cleopatra and her effect on Western society that is novel. At one point when Cleopatra is moved to "speak like a divine woman," she tells Caesar:

> I was born to it, as you say, and all the time I was a child I was taught to do certain things. Public things; and to myself I put out my tongue at it, because of the people who believed it and the people who did not believe it. This for as long as I could. Then a time came when

they put me into the Sacred Robes and I stood before the people, holding the sistrum, when I did not think any longer, solemn or idle thoughts. It was then that I gave myself or was given to the air and the light and the earth, and to all those natures palpitating before me; and offered myself—or was offered—myself to myself. Then it is that I come out of myself, and Something—call it the Goddess— becomes me and I That. That which was August in time had departed; that which is eternally August entered. When it has done that, my body is as though it had been in a different state, as though it were impregnated with a life that is not the common run of the blood. I move, distinct, elated, but not with myself. I do not want— I am—power. I am filled to the lips though I do not speak. I have seen the things of which our actions are the translations. (220)

This lengthy quotation summarizes Butts's view of the assumption and the natural process of divinity. Cleopatra is born to it, just as Butts herself felt born to some primal connection with the sacred elements of the natural landscape of the English coast. It offers a bona fide, legitimate union with a realm beyond that of the external world.

The remainder of the narrative's associations of Cleopatra with her divine origins is subtle compared to Cleopatra's direct explanation. At Caesar's death she is "filled with the knowledge of the gods" (300), and at other points she becomes a "Goddess manifest" (336). Once she is married to Caesar and bearing Caesar's child, Caesarion, Charmian (Cleopatra's attendant) sees the union as a Hieros Gamos (Sacred Marriage). In one of her letters she states, "It is Isis and Osiris and Horus all over again, ready to happen to the world, if only the world will let it. If we can make people know. Only Caesar doesn't quite know what he is" (223). Cleopatra does, however, know her role, and in defining that role Butts revisits the historical narrative. Cleopatra is a woman, but she is a woman firmly and genuinely connected to her goddess past. Her assumption of that role is what allows her the power over her own destiny in spite of the fact that she falls in love. Yet human love cannot outweigh the superior role that offers power; it is the acquisition of spiritual power that permits Cleopatra to manipulate and control her own destiny. If her role to power is through her feminine sexuality and beauty, then this clever queen will assert such force as necessary. If, however, her source of power comes truly from her dual role of female and goddess, avatar of Isis, then her will can be reinforced, and Butts has found a way for the opposites to reside in one. This queen with knowledge and skill wields such power over the Roman and Egyptian world.

Elsewhere Mary Butts has written that "I have always had since I can remember an incomparable pleasure in finding someone psychically sick, and learning about it, and seeing if there is a way out. This feeling very much mixed up with sex—bed not necessary, but it makes things work better. That is any power I have seems to work better in that relation."[33] As with her interpretation of Cleopatra, Butts understands the conjoining of the human with the divine.

Similarly, Judy Marston (the dark side of Vanna) in *Ashe of Rings* attempts to control with her erotic power. Yet it is ultimately the authentic spiritual strength of Vanna's white magic that overcomes the purely erotic; both remain, however, essential elements of the spiritual journey. The spiritual offers a glimpse beyond the reality of the present while at the same time it proposes a way to live in this world. Carol Ochs, in defining spirituality, says, "The process of coming into relationship with reality is spirituality. . . . [S]pirituality is not merely a way of knowing, but also a way of being and doing. . . . The female developmental model focuses on relationship. Women's contribution to spirituality—the insight of their interconnectedness— is that full human maturity must entail coming into relationship with reality."[34] Both Vanna and Cleopatra come "into relationship with reality" and in their own individual ways use their spirituality and draw on their spiritual pasts in a movement toward Ochs's "full human maturity." Butts's spiritual quest is one that heals, seeks, and recognizes and learns from its brushes with the divine. Cleopatra and Butts are women first, but what Butts perceived as spiritual authenticity unites them to each other and to a way to have autonomy in a world with patriarchal boundaries. To identify with a divine past is in a sense a way to move above the fray and to reinvent or recall a world where women's spirituality removed barriers between the seen and the unseen worlds as well as between women and their external human worlds. It is a return, as Butts suggests in her pamphlet *Traps for Unbelievers*, not to any idealized or prescribed form but "to the raw thing" in "its most primitive form."[35]

Mary Butts and Cleopatra know that the origin of their strength is elemental to their roles as women in a world that has lost connection with its spiritual lineage. Both Vanna Ashe and Cleopatra draw from their spiritual heritage to affirm their rightful place in their individual societies and act upon such rights as women in control of their own destinies. Merlin Stone has observed that the "sexual and religious bias of many of the erudite scholars of the nineteenth and twentieth centuries" has influenced archeological texts that examine female religions that "flourished for years before the advent of Judaism, Christianity, and the Classical Age of Greece."[36] Stone explores the inaccuracies of these accounts in *When God Was a Woman* by asserting that the attitudes toward sexuality of the times when such works were written may have significantly influenced the interpretation of what they defined as "fertility cults." Instead, Stone argues that "archeological and mythological evidence of the veneration of the female deity as creator and lawmaker of the universe, prophetess, provider of human destinies, inventor, healer, hunter and valiant leader in battle suggests that the title 'fertility cult' may be a gross oversimplification of a complex theological structure."[37] Mary Butts resurrects such female deities and reinvents them as spiritual leaders, healers, and prophets of the twentieth century. Butts's Cleopatra and Vanna Ashe, like Carol Christ's Goddess, are the "power of intelligent embodied love that is the ground of all being."[38] By revisiting Cleopatra as an independent and self-defining woman, rather than as a manipulative, wanton femme fatale, and by identifying Vanna Ashe as a true heir to her sacred primal origins, Butts situates all women within their spiritual core so that they can take their rightful place alongside men as human beings with a powerful and nourishing spiritual past and present.

NOTES

1. The Cambridge Ritualists (Jane Ellen Harrison, Gilbert Murray, Francis M. Cornford, and, to a lesser degree, Arthur Bernard Cook) were a group of classical scholars who worked primarily from 1900 to 1915. For Harrison and Murray, ritual was an acting out to ensure fertility or to prevent disaster, and both stressed the primacy of ritual over mythology. Both were also leading Hellenists of their day, and Mary Butts drew from their writings and used much of their work to enhance her own. Like Harrison, Butts sought the origin of the religious impulse.

2. Mary Butts published one pamphlet dealing with the loss of faith in early-twentieth-century society, *Traps for Unbelievers* (1932), and another pamphlet that in a sense prefigured environmental concerns over the civilized world's intrusion on her sacred land, *Warning to Hikers* (1932).

3. Carol P. Christ, "Rethinking Theology and Nature," in *Weaving the Visions: New Patterns in Feminist Spirituality*, ed. Judith Plaskow and Carol P. Christ (San Francisco: Harper San Francisco, 1989), 314.

4. Ibid.

5. Quoted in Robert H. Byington and Glen E. Morgan, "Mary Butts," *Art and Literature*, 1965, 171.

6. Mary Butts was addicted to opium throughout her life. Her bohemian lifestyle in London, Paris, and Villefranche led her to other experiments with drugs and to a brief association with Aleister Crowley (The Great Beast) and his occult group in Cefalu, Italy. Within the madness of drugs, alcohol, decadence, and the occult, Butts longed for the visions she knew briefly throughout her life. In a journal entry recording her visit to Cefalu, Butts says that she talked to Crowley about astral journeys: "The idea is to find an authentic means of inducing the mystic state" (Byington and Morgan, "Mary Butts," 170). Drugs, decadence, writing—all were a part of Butts's search for that "authentic means."

7. Quoted in Nathalie Blondel, *Mary Butts: Scenes from the Life* (Kingston, N.Y.: McPherson, 1998), 100.

8. T. S. Eliot, "*Ulysses*, Order and Myth," in *Selected Prose of T. S. Eliot*, ed. Frank Kermode (New York: Harcourt Brace Jovanovich, 1975), 177–78.

9. Hugh Ross Williamson, "Three Letters," in *A Sacred Quest: The Life and Writings of Mary Butts*, ed. Christopher Wagstaff (Kingston, N.Y.: McPherson, 1995), 148.

10. Mircea Eliade, *The Sacred and the Profane: The Nature of Religion* (New York: Harcourt, Brace and World, 1959), 140.

11. Evelyn Underhill, *Mysticism: A Study in the Nature and Development of Man's Spiritual Consciousness* (New York: World Publishing, 1955), 205–6.

12. Mary Butts, "The Real Wordsworth," review of *The Later Life of Wordsworth*, by Edith Batho, *Time and Tide* 14 (December 2, 1933): 1448.

13. Mary Butts, *The Crystal Cabinet: My Childhood at Salterns* (London: Carcanet Press, 1988), 12. All subsequent page citations to this text will be given parenthetically in the text.

14. Quoted by Robert Byington, "The Writings and the World of Mary Butts," Tape 5, Proceedings of a Conference at the University of California, Davis, November 23–24, 1984.

15. Carol P. Christ, *Rebirth of the Goddess: Finding Meaning in Feminist Spirituality* (Reading, Mass.: Addison-Wesley Publishing, 1997), xv.

16. Ibid., xiii.

17. Ibid., 25.

18. Mary Butts, afterword to *Ashe of Rings*, by Mary Butts (London: Wishart, 1933).

19. Patrick Wright, *On Living in an Old Country: The National Past in Contemporary Britain* (London: Verso, 1985), 106.

20. Mary Butts, *Ashe of Rings and Other Writings* (Kingston, N.Y.: McPherson, 1998), 188. All subsequent page citations to this novel will be given parenthetically in the text.

21. Kristina Groover, *The Wilderness Within: American Women Writers and Spiritual Quest* (Fayetteville: University of Arkansas Press, 1999), 11.

22. Ibid.

23. Quoted in Blondel, *Mary Butts*, 382.

24. Roslyn Reso Foy, *Ritual, Myth, and Mysticism in the Work of Mary Butts: Between Feminism and Modernism* (Fayetteville: University of Arkansas Press, 2000), 123. In that book I examine the role of spirituality in all of Butts's work and its effect on her development as an artist.

25. Quoted in Blondel, *Mary Butts*, 335.

26. Jane Ellen Harrison, *Epilogomena to the Study of Greek Religion and Themis: A Study of Social Origins of Greek Religion* (New York: University Books, 1962), 68.

27. Carol Ochs, *Women and Spirituality* (Totowa, N.J.: Rowman and Allanheld, 1983), 14.

28. Mary Butts, *The Macedonian*, in *The Classical Novels: The Macedonian/Scenes from the Life of Cleopatra* (Kingston, N.Y.: McPherson, 1998), 39.

29. Ruth Hoberman, *Gendering Classicism: The Ancient World in Twentieth-Century Women's Historical Fiction* (Albany: State University of New York, 1997), 141.

30. Mary Butts, *Scenes from the Life of Cleopatra*, in Butts, *The Classical Novels*, 343. All subsequent page citations to this work will be given parenthetically in the text.

31. Hoberman, *Gendering Classicism*, 148.

32. Ibid., 140.

33. Quoted in Byington and Morgan, "Mary Butts," 171.

34. Ochs, *Women and Spirituality*, 10.

35. Mary Butts, *Traps for Unbelievers*, in Butts, *Ashe of Rings*, 326.

36. Merlin Stone, *When God Was a Woman* (New York: Harcourt Brace, 1976), xvi, xviii. Some ideas in Stone's work have subsequently been corrected by other scholars, but her work brought the history of the Goddess to critical attention.

37. Ibid., xix–xx.

38. Christ, *Rebirth of the Goddess*, xv.

MARVELOUS ARITHMETICS

Womanist Spirituality in the Poetry of Audre Lorde

SHARON BARNES

In Cancer
the most fertile of skysigns
I shall build a house
that will stand forever.

Audre Lorde, "Construction"

On December 28, 1977, less than two months before she delivered her brilliant essay "The Transformation of Silence into Language and Action"[1] as part of the "Lesbian and Literature" panel at the Modern Language Association's annual convention, Audre Lorde was informed by her doctors that she had a breast tumor with a roughly 60 to 80 percent chance of malignancy and would need to have surgery. In the essay, Lorde describes the painful three-week period between the time she received the news from her doctors and the surgery, during which she underwent an "involuntary reorganization" of her life and priorities. Part of the desperate self-analysis to which she subjected herself included an internal debate about whether she should attend the MLA convention and give a talk about lesbians and literature in the face of her changed life circumstances. Thinking about speaking at the convention and about how her medical situation affected her understanding of what was important to say coalesced in Lorde's mind with a larger feminist concern for speaking openly of her experience, regardless of how painful. She decided to deliver the paper and use the opportunity to urge her listeners to find their truths and speak them:

> I have come to believe over and over that what is most important to me must be spoken, made verbal and shared, even at the risk of having it bruised and misunderstood. That the speaking profits me, beyond any other effect. . . . I was going to die, if not sooner then later, whether or not I had ever spoken myself. My silences had not protected me. Your silence will not protect you. But for every real word spoken, for every attempt I had ever made to speak those truths for which I am still seeking, I had made contact with other women while we examined the words to fit a world in which we all believed, bridging our differences.[2]

The preoccupations Lorde affirms in this meditation are ones that appear consistently throughout her writing, before her diagnosis of breast cancer in 1978 and more urgently afterwards until her death in 1992.

The values articulated in "The Transformation of Silence into Language and Action" are elaborated into a more complete ethic in a later paper, "Uses of the Erotic: The Erotic as Power,"[3] which was delivered at Mount Holyoke College at the Fourth Berkshire Conference on the History of Women on August 25, 1978. Lorde's theory of the erotic as explained in "Uses of the Erotic" creates an ethic of speech, community, and activism that affirms key elements of Alice Walker's 1983 definition of womanism. Lorde's poems, especially her later poems about death, exemplify these values; interested in speaking the truth of her experience, in connecting with other women, and in contributing to the creation of a new and better world, Lorde's poetic work embodies these most basic and enduring elements of womanist spirituality, particularly as the poetry is an extension of Lorde's reinterpretation of the erotic.

Judith Plaskow and Carol P. Christ acknowledged Lorde's contribution to feminist spiritual thought when they solicited "Uses of the Erotic: The Erotic as Power" for their second collection of essays on feminist spirituality, *Weaving the Visions: New Patterns in Feminist Spirituality*, published in 1989. Placing Lorde's work alongside theologian Delores S. Williams's exploration of womanist theology in a section of the book entitled "Self in Relation," Plaskow and Christ correlated the work in this section with their observations of an emerging "immanental turn" in feminist spirituality. They asserted that the authors collected in the section, despite their differences, all agreed that "the self is essentially relational, inseparable from the limiting and enriching contexts of body, feeling, relationship, community, history and the web of life." Plaskow and Christ saw Lorde's reclaiming of the erotic as "a deeply spiritual power, because it puts us in touch with the creative energy of the life force" and as a concrete manifestation of the spiritual self in relation—requiring both personal transformation and a "rejection of those strands of both secular and religious culture that have defined the erotic as pornographic, the sexual power of women as source of sin, and all sexual feelings as lower, suspect."[4]

Lorde's exploration of the erotic, "that power which rises from our deepest and nonrational knowledge," explicitly asserts a spiritual element in contrast to what she calls Western culture's "pornographic" emphasis on "sensation without feeling."[5] Her claim is that the erotic is a resource inside all people that is "deeply female and spiritual" because it is anchored in deep feeling (53). Because Lorde's notion of the erotic focuses on feeling, unlimited to sex or sexuality, it offers women a source of psychic and emotional energy that is central to Lorde's understanding of the spiritual. Rather than this "plasticized" or "pornographic" notion of physical sensation, which is so often Western culture's definition of the erotic and which Lorde views as a source of women's oppression by men, Lorde's reclaimed erotic is "an internal requirement toward excellence. . . . [It] is not a question only of what we do; it is a question of how acutely and fully we can feel in the doing" (54). Lorde asserts that women should "be accountable" to the erotic, which means developing an understanding of one's deepest potential for joy and then holding that potential for joy as a standard for lived experience. This call to accountability is therefore a challenge to move beyond Western culture's conventional understanding of the erotic as sexual or physical sensation toward an understanding of the erotic as a deepened emotional response to all life experiences, which Lorde believes is essential to spiritual and political empowerment: "And that deep and irreplaceable knowledge of my capacity for joy comes to demand from all of my life that it be lived within the knowledge that such satisfaction is possible, and does not have to be called *marriage*, nor *god*, nor *an afterlife*" (57).

Lorde's understanding of the erotic as spiritual shares strong connections with Alice Walker's conception of womanism, including her focus on immanental divinity in the physical world. Both elide the urge "toward a more theocentric direction," as noted by Teresa L. Fry Brown, an urge felt by many women of color, who seem "to need a definite articulation of a living God consciousness."[6] Walker's god consciousness, well documented in *The Color Purple* and articulated by her in the introduction to the tenth anniversary edition, is a "journey from the religious back to the spiritual."[7] Walker writes in her essay "The Universe Responds" of "our inseparableness from the divine; and everything, especially the physical world, is divine."[8] Lorde's "Uses of the Erotic" emerges from a similar recognition. Though she eschews the term *divine*, Lorde makes a comparable journey in reclaiming the erotic from Western culture's emphasis on superficial sexual sensation to a womanist focus on deep feeling, including a connection to the political. In fact, Lorde claims that the political and the erotic have been split from the spiritual in a way that harms both. For her, the erotic, "those physical, emotional, and psychic expressions of what is deepest and strongest and richest within each of us, being shared: the passions of love in its deepest meanings," acts as an essential bridge between the spiritual and the political (56).

Also significant to an understanding of Lorde's notion of the erotic as spiritual is Walker's notion that the concept of womanism emerges from the folk description of someone who is "womanish," which Walker defines as a "black feminist," a woman engaged in "outrageous, audacious, courageous or *willful* behavior."[9] Lorde's redefined erotic and her poetry engage in this ethic through Lorde's fierce commitment to experience her life at a deeply conscious level and to share the truth of her experience with others. For Lorde, doing so is inherently grounded in feminism. In "Uses of the Erotic," she claims that being conscious of one's feelings and sharing them at this deeply spiritual level is essential to the feminist agenda; it "is female and self-affirming in the face of a racist, patriarchal, and anti-erotic society" (59). Layli Phillips and Barbara McCaskill, in their essay "Who's Schooling Who? Black Women and the Bringing of the Everyday into Academe, or Why We Started *The Womanist*," assert that "[p]erhaps the central organizing principle of womanism (if it can be said that there is one) is the absolute necessity of speaking from and about one's own experiential location and not to or about someone else's."[10] Lorde's assertion of the necessity of sharing one's self—including one's stories—in "Uses of the Erotic" relies on the absolute rule that one must do so without the "looking away" that she claims is part of Western culture's notion of the erotic experience as it relates to women. This commitment, articulated in Lorde's poetry and prose, shares Walker's commitment to womanism as a distinctly feminist endeavor.

Two other elements of Walker's definition, that a womanist loves other women and celebrates women's culture, yet fights for the "survival and wholeness of entire people, male and female,"[11] share aspects of Lorde's definition of the erotic: the emphasis on women's culture and the extension of the energy of that culture outward toward larger social change. Lorde notes in her conclusion of "Uses of the Erotic": "I find more and more women-identified women brave enough to risk sharing the erotic's electrical charge without having to look away, and without distorting the enormously powerful and creative nature of that exchange. Recognizing the power of the erotic within our lives can give us the energy to pursue genuine change within our world" (59). Focusing on Lorde's intention to *use* the erotic highlights how Lorde's redefined erotic is a womanist vision of both personal willfulness and community activism. At a personal level, the power of the erotic to transform one's life is that it instills in all of one's actions a pull toward an internal "sense of satisfaction and completeness" (54) and thereby empowers individuals to demand this satisfaction in more areas of their lives. It encompasses community activism because it also demands that women so empowered encourage others to do the same. Lorde's erotic involves "sharing deeply any pursuit with another person. The sharing of joy, whether physical, emotional, psychic, or intellectual, forms a bridge between the sharers which can be the basis for understanding much of what is not shared between them, and lessens the threat of their difference" (56). Of course, "women so empowered are dangerous" (55) because of their willingness to fight for a world in which all people are transformed through similar empowerment: "As women, we need to examine the ways in which our world can be truly different. I am speaking here of the necessity for reassessing the quality of all of the aspects of our lives and of our work, and of how we move toward and through them" (55).

A consequence of this internal sense of direction is a deeper connection with others who can join the fight for a more livable world. Lorde's erotic reclaimed emerges as a life philosophy that is akin to Walker's divinity in everything and to womanism's focus on self-expression and political activism, as articulated in groundbreaking womanist theological texts such as Katie Geneva Cannon's *Katie's Canon: Womanism and the Soul of the Black Community*.[12] The commitment to social justice, to freeing communities from "brutal cycles of misery and violence,"[13] is omnipresent in womanist spirituality, as is the emphasis on grounding such battles for freedom in the lived experience and moral wisdom of black women. In her analysis of the distinctions between the political agendas of black feminism and womanism, Ula Taylor concludes that both share "similar empowerment theories. Both avow grounding the activism of black women in their cultural heritage, . . . encourage black women to value and love self, . . . [and] recognize black women's serious, responsible commitment to creating a whole community devoid of dominance."[14] Such an agenda is the key to womanist spirituality as articulated in Lorde's poetry: as Lorde asserts in "Uses of the Erotic," it involves "willful" and "courageous" self-examination shared for use by others for political transformation:

> [W]hen we begin to live from within outward, in touch with the power of the erotic within ourselves, and allowing that power to inform and illuminate our actions upon the world around us, then we begin to be responsible to ourselves in the deepest sense. For as we begin to recognize our deepest feelings, we begin to give up, of necessity, being satisfied with suffering, with self-negation, and with the numbness which so often seems like their only alternative in our society. Our acts against oppression become integral with self, motivated and empowered from within. (58)

Sharing the erotic charge as Lorde redefines it expands on this womanist spiritual and political agenda; the shared deep feeling and political commitment that respects and loves the self also multiplies people's energy to work for change by expanding their consciousness of what is possible within themselves and in the world.

Finally, Walker's notion that a womanist "*Loves* the Spirit. Loves love and food and roundness. Loves struggle. . . . Loves herself. Regardless"[15] demonstrates another link between Lorde's redefined erotic and womanism: the emphasis on daily activity, or, as Phillips and McCaskill call it, "the everyday." For Lorde, deep participation with others "in all aspects of our existence" (57), including dancing, fighting, and writing and sharing poetry, is a precursor to political actions previously thought impossible. Lorde cites the erotic's root in the Greek word *eros,* which she defines as "the personification of love in all its aspects" (55). Lorde's use of the erotic thus takes the womanist emphasis on the everyday and empowers it through the "assertion of the lifeforce of women; of that creative energy empowered, the knowledge and use of which we are now reclaiming in our language, our history, our dancing, our loving, our work, our lives" (55). Through her "willful" and "serious" focus on the erotic as deep feeling—even about everyday matters—and her "courageous" speaking from the depths of her experience, through her intimate connections to other women, both sexual and nonsexual, and through her connections to community, whether the community of her immediate political surroundings or the more ethereal community of women warriors she counts herself among, Audre Lorde's writing manifests the basic traditions of Walker's notion of womanism.

Lorde's late, and arguably most powerful, poetry about death and dying in *The Marvelous Arithmetics of Distance*, her final book of poems published posthumously in 1993, enhances her spiritual vision of the erotic. The later poems demonstrate how Lorde's understanding of the erotic as deep feeling not only maintains its connections to speech, to conscious connection with others, and to political activism in the face of imminent death but is even strengthened by this awareness. The poems articulate Lorde's version of a womanist spiritual consciousness in their record of her perceptions of the dying process as a self- and other-empowering activity. Using not only her current experience but earlier moments of her life with her family, lovers, and the women (living and spirit) whose energy she relied on for physical and emotional support, Lorde's poetry creates a body of story and experience that she turns to repeatedly for strength in her journey. Lorde calls on her own past and on the history of women who have demonstrated, in myth or in life, this "well of deep feeling" for energy to face her death with her "eyes wide open" so that she and women who come after her can use her experience and her words for empowerment and transformation: "I mourn the women who limit their loss to the physical loss alone, who do not move into the whole terrible meaning of mortality as both weapon and power. After all, what could we possibly be afraid of after having admitted to ourselves that we had dealt face to face with death and not embraced it? For once we accept the actual existence of our dying, who can ever have power over us again?"[16] The "arithmetics of distance" is a powerful metaphor for this transformative consciousness. Lorde's late poetry broadens the themes that consumed her early work, giving her political activism in the areas of expanding the erotic, breaking silences, and building community an urgency and clarity that mark the power of her vision, what Alice Walker called "her cool stare back into the eyes of death."[17] Though as Lorde said, "I would never have chosen this path,"[18] the result of her open-eyed confrontation of death and dying, in both her poetry and her journals, is a record, a set of insights that offer her readers a blueprint for using the awareness of human mortality as a method for expanding consciousness of the spiritual, political, and personal meaning of living: "Living fully—how long is not the point. How and why take total precedence.[19]

Several of Lorde's late poems integrate her commitment to the erotic redefined through what Joy Bostic claims is the womanist imperative of speaking black women's multidimensional experiences.[20] In Lorde's late poems, this imperative is expressed through her focus on the significance, difficulty, and transformative potential of speaking in and to the face of death, combined with her expressed commitment to meeting experiences fully and the necessity of seeing her connection to women engaged in revolutionary transformation. Looking at the close of her life open-eyed, Lorde speaks what she sees and feels as a means of experiencing it, even the pain, more fully. Given Lorde's commitment, expressed in "Uses of the Erotic," to complete and "deep feeling in all aspects of our lives" (57), her extension of this eros even to her own death is not surprising. Under the guidance of her expanded notion of the erotic, exploring death is as much a part of her power and political responsibility as is her experience of great joy, both of which must be felt and expressed fully and honestly. She states this aim beautifully in the preface to her final poem, "Today Is Not the Day":

> I can't just sit here
> staring death in her face
> blinking and asking for a new name
> by which to greet her
>
> I am not afraid to say
> unembellished
> I am dying
> but I do not want to do it
> looking the other way.[21]

Lorde's self-examination in her poetic ruminations on death and her extension of this self-analysis to political transformation focus on how an intimate awareness of death influences her speech. Particularly moving in its awareness of her mortality and in its merciless investigation of her power to speak is the poem "Seasoning," which was originally published in 1978, just a year after Lorde's initial biopsy. She opens with the self-interrogating question, "What am I ready to lose in this advancing summer?" (259), which indicates both her growing awareness of the limitations of her time on earth and her knowledge that such awareness imposes decisions upon her about what is important and necessary in her life.

> As the days that seemed long
> grow shorter and shorter
> I want to chew up time
> until every moment expands
> in an emotional mathematic
> that includes the smell and texture
> of every similar instant since I was born.
> (259)

Her immediate response to the thought of her days trickling away is typical of Lorde's redefined erotic ethic in its personally demanding expectation of herself as political warrior-poet; she must "chew up time," enjoying every last moment, just as she must investigate how her experiences are influencing what she describes, in "The Transformation of Silence into Language and Action," as her attempts "to speak the truths for which I am still seeking."

Especially remarkable because it was written early after Lorde's initial diagnosis, so movingly documented in "The Transformation of Silence into Language and Action," "Seasoning" incorporates two themes that continued to dominate Lorde's thinking and that place her ethic of the erotic redefined squarely in the womanist spiritual community: the self-value necessary to fully and deeply experience all moments of her life and the difficulty, importance, and political necessity of sharing these experiences with others. In the opening lines she expresses her desire to consume the time she has left in an expansive way that allows her to taste, feel, and smell her own history, "every similar instant since I was born," at the same time. This "emotional mathematic" connects her past to the present so that each moment, lived and experienced to its fullest, brings her past to bear on her present and, ultimately, connects Lorde to a powerful and timeless wellspring of women's emotional experience. Thus Lorde rejects what she considers a Western powerlessness associated with illness and death in favor of a womanist celebration of the power that awareness of mortality brings, just as in "Uses of the Erotic" she rejects Western "pornographic" or superficial notions of the erotic that focus on physical sensation rather than on the depth of emotional experience that a more empowering womanist interpretation of that concept might offer.

Whereas later poems express more certainty about the value of speaking her experience, "Seasoning" continues, as perhaps is fitting of an earlier poem, to struggle with speech even as it affirms the creative arithmetic of time and distance. She asserts, "my mouth stumbles" because it is "crammed" with elements of her past. Time, friends, enemies, lovers, and different versions of herself are all factors in this "emotional equation" that combine into a vision, an image resting inside her own head, "the pot of gold" behind her eyes. In this earlier poem, spiritual certainty is still being negotiated. Anxiety about death and about the work that still remains to be done is expressed in an unwillingness to speak, even as Lorde knows that speaking her truth is the task she is most committed to, the one that her womanist ethic of the erotic insists she must do:

As the light wanes
I see
what I thought I was anxious to surrender
I am only willing to lend
and reluctance covers my face
as I glue my lips with the promise
of coming winter.

(259)

The complex equation of interactions—the "mathematics"—of past and present, including Lorde's past selves and the lives of her sister-warriors before her, remained a useful metaphor for Lorde until the end of her life. Marjorie Pryse, in her introduction to *Conjuring: Black Women, Fiction, and Literary Tradition*, discusses a similar element in the fiction of Alice Walker and Zora Neale Hurston that she calls "conjuring," a summoning of the ancestors that "gathers together all the creative force of her black and female forerunners." In Pryse's analysis of Walker, just as in Lorde's late poems, this pulling together includes collapsing chronological distance in order to acknowledge the "oath we all must take to continue the work of speaking with each other's tongues in our mouths, thereby illuminating women's lives."[22] The first poem in Lorde's final volume, *The Marvelous Arithmetics of Distance*, "Smelling the Wind," is a short love poem that directly addresses speech and uses "mathematics" as a metaphor for the spiritual journey associated with death in a manner that uses Pryse's notion of "conjuring." Whether or not Lorde was addressing a specific lover who sweetened a "season" of her life, the poem, written so close to the end of her life, asks readers to experience it as a metaphor for the upcoming spiritual journey. Lorde, toward the end of her days, is "rushing headlong" into a "new silence," the experience of death. She anticipates losing the face of her love on her "horizon" as she "cast[s] off / on another voyage" (423). Here, the silence seems neither crushing nor necessary to break but new, part of the complex, "marvelous" equation that the journey toward death evokes. She closes with:

> No reckoning allowed
> save the marvelous arithmetics
> of distance.
>
> (423)

Lorde seems expansive, hurtling out into the spiritual space off the "horizon" of mortality, forward into an experience where earthly "reckoning" is not "allowed" because it is irrelevant. The "marvelous arithmetics of distance" is reminiscent of both "Seasoning" and of conjuring's collapse of chronological distance in its expansive accounting of past, present, and future at once, a use of memory as an "enhance[ment of] what can and is to be."[23] As she prepares to leave this earthly sphere, where accounting is accomplished more often than not by clocks and bank accounts, Lorde affirms a spiritual realm in which the "only reckoning allowed" is the wonderfully inexplicable "arithmetics of distance" (423). "Smelling the Wind" evolves Lorde's goal, stated in "Seasoning," of expanding time in an "emotional mathematic" so that it includes her awareness of death as another level on which one can experience, enhance, and empower living. Lorde articulates this agenda in the later of two published volumes of journal entries and essays that detail her struggles with breast cancer: "I do not think about my death as being imminent, but I live my days against a background noise of mortality and constant uncertainty. Learning not to crumple before these uncertainties fuels my resolve to print myself upon the texture of each day fully rather than forever."[24] Struggling to reconfigure her understanding of death as a source of creative potential, Lorde returns to her erotic ethic of emotions fully explored, using it once again as a guide to her own spiritual power.

Later poems continue this struggle to articulate her understanding of death's empowering potential through a "conjured" collapse of past and present, as in "Never to Dream of Spiders," in which Lorde reconciles herself to the speed with which the remaining days are flying by. In the poem, Lorde notes that "one word" is made in the "breathless" silence, and yet it seems to take the weight of all of her words; similarly, the poem describes the days following a course of chemotherapy, but the descriptions also follow a larger "arithmetic" that is more about an assessment of her life than about days of chemotherapy. She opens with images of collapse, again relying on her past, resonating back to the conflation of past and future in "Seasoning":

> Time collapses between the lips of strangers
> my days collapse into a hollow tube
> soon implodes against now
> like an iron wall
> my eyes are blocked with rubble
> a smear of perspectives
> blurring each horizon
> in the breathless precision of silence
> one word is made.
>
> (414)

Despite her planning, despite the intensity with which she had been living and working since early in her diagnosis, the "death [that] heightens and sharpens my living,"[25] the death that is coming "soon," surprisingly "implodes against now / like an iron wall" (414). Lorde acknowledges that no amount of preparation can take away the sense of life being taken too quickly.

In "Never to Dream of Spiders," Lorde maintains her commitment to the womanist principle of self-value through telling one's story, despite the physical and mental fogginess imposed by chemotherapy. She attempts to accurately and concretely record her experience, but here she is beginning to turn her poet's eye toward her inward journey, where she once again creates a self connected—to herself and others, past and present. She feels "death . . . / a condemnation within my blood" (414), as she records the deathlike experience of chemotherapy. The final stanza incorporates surreal images of chemotherapy and the passage of time, marked as a sort of gateway through the "veiled door" of her fiftieth birthday. Leaving behind the material world marked in the poem by shredded paper, she is "never to dream of spiders" because she is entering the spiritual realm they represent in many traditional spiritual panoplies. The spider that Lorde asserts she no longer needs to dream of has connections in women's spirituality both to creation and to death.[26] Perhaps most revealingly, the spider in Aztec myth "represents the souls of warrior women from the pre-Aztec matriarchate, like the Amazonian Fate-spinners."[27] A student of women's spirituality, especially the Amazon myth, Lorde probably knew the connections between these histories and used them to understand her own entrance into the community of "souls of women warriors." The final image of "hoses" that "turned on" her, creating "the burst of light," articulates the physical holocaust brought on by chemotherapy even as it recalls an explanation she made in her journal about how the awareness of death sharpened her political commitment. In her final collection of prose, *A Burst of Light*, she explains the political vision behind the "burst of light":

> Sometimes we are blessed with being able to choose the time and the arena and the manner of our revolution, but more usually we must do battle wherever we are standing. . . . The real blessing is to be able to use whoever I am wherever I am, in concert with as many others as possible, or alone if needs be. This is . . . a time for the real work's urgencies. It is a time enhanced by an iron reclamation of what I call the burst of light—the inescapable knowledge, in the bone, of my own physical limitation. Metabolized and integrated into the fabric of my days, that knowledge makes the particulars of what is coming seem less important.[28]

Lorde's political commitment to speaking the truth, especially about death, in order "to rob it of some of its power over my consciousness" includes a commitment to "watch the death process . . . acutely" and write about it,[29] as is already evidenced by her attention to the physical experience of chemotherapy in "Never to Dream of Spiders." In the poem "Speechless" she attempts to turn the same careful consideration to the internal emotional/spiritual process. Once again addressing an individual beloved "you," Lorde first describes a wild, surrealistic scene, a "forest / strewn with breadcrumb fingers / sticky with loss," where "giddy trees" that are "stuffed with seductive chaotic songs" "wait   shaken" (463). Her connection to the earth religions through the goddess Seboulisa long since solidified,[30] Lorde combines familiar, personified forest imagery with an unsure, slightly ominous tone. The trees, stuffed with songs that are both "seductive" and "chaotic," are likened to "a goose bound for the oven" (463). Lorde is standing at the foot of steps leading into the forest, where the moon is seen hanging "like a spotlit breast" through "the wild arms of a twilit birch" (463). Preparing to remove from this sphere in which women have been so highlighted as mere body parts, Lorde is searching for a new way to both experience and express herself. She closes the vision by describing her own mouth and death's "distorting" effect on her voice:

> Death
> folds the corners of my mouth
> into a heart-shaped star
> sits on my tongue like a stone
> around which your name blossoms distorted.
>
> (463)

Always talking, always thinking about speech and power, Lorde hears her words differently under the stone-weight of death. In *A Litany for Survival*, the film that Michelle Parkerson and Ada Gay Griffin rushed to complete as Lorde neared the end of her life, Lorde says, her voice softened and cracked by illness: "I always counted on my voice, being able to read my poetry back, being able to hear it in a certain way and the hearing would connect inside of me with the feeling, and that's part of the structure and technique. And I don't have that because I hear differently now."[31]

Lorde's imperative to write of her experience shares the womanist concern for how her message affects other parts of her life and other people. A journal entry from 1986 reveals Lorde's singular ability to integrate her priorities, including the need for communion with women—both her past selves and women-warriors she has never met—with the necessity for love, art, spiritual connection, and with the political necessity of understanding all of these issues as potentially transformative for herself and others. She writes of sitting in a meeting with a "sharp" black woman, as they planned an article for a black women's magazine. They were discussing whether it should focus on Lorde's particular struggles with cancer or on the role of art and spirituality in black women's lives. Lorde notes in the journal that both concepts are "grounded" in the same locus inside her: "I require the nourishment of art and spirituality in my life, and they lend strength and insight to all the endeavors that give substance to my living. It is the bread of art and the water of my spiritual life that remind me always to reach for what is highest within my capacities and in my demands of myself and others. Not for what is perfect but for what is the best possible."[32]

Along with her focus on experiencing and speaking of the world around her, the world of her senses, Lorde's later work demonstrates a growing consciousness of her own legacy as a writer. Just as she vowed in an early poem to "never leave her pen lying in someone else's blood" ("To the Poet Who Happens to Be Black and the Black Poet Who Happens to Be a Woman," 360), in the final poems, she has begun to think about what she leaves behind for those who would read her work. She noted in one of the interviews with Griffin and Parkerson that "[w]hen you open and read something that I wrote, the power that you feel from it doesn't come from me. That's a power that you own. The function of the words is to, [snaps her fingers] tick you into, 'Oh, hey, I can feel like that.' And then to go out and do the things that make you feel like that *more*." Later, in "October," she prays for the goddess Seboulisa to carry her heart to a shore that her feet "will not shatter" (346). She is concerned about how her work will represent her after she is dead. Lorde prays to Seboulisa for help in "re-member[ing] what I have learned" and in "attend[ing] with passion these tasks at my hand for doing" (346); she also analyzes her own mortality in terms of her political work: "Now I span my days like a wild bridge / . . . caught between poems like a vise / I am finishing my piece of this bargain / and how shall I return?" (346). She prays to Seboulisa for help in maintaining her intimacy with herself, her work, and her issues. In "Call," another prayer, this time to the "Rainbow Serpent, Aido Hwedo" (418),[33] Lorde uses the now familiar gesture of conflating her own past and present with the experiences of other powerful women, including Rosa Parks, Fannie Lou Hamer, Assata Shakur, and Yaa Asantewa.[34] She also discusses her writing as part of her spiritual calling, hoping her life will be "worth its ending," hoping that the commitment she has made to speaking her truth, the risks she has taken—for she has "offered up" safety—will be part of a positive transformation of the world she is preparing to leave behind:

> Rainbow Serpent who must not go
> unspoken
> I have offered up the safety of separations
> sung the spirals of power
> and what fills the spaces
> before power unfolds or flounders
> in desirable nonessentials
> I am a Black woman stripped down
> and praying
> my whole life has been an altar
> worth its ending . . .
>
> (418)

Essays and journal entries reveal the strength of this commitment to speaking her truth about both life and death as an extension of Lorde's erotics, which clearly heeds the womanist theological call to give voice to herself and to her sisters[35] and also to resistance activity.[36] Lorde wants to use the time that she has left to document the way of her passing, for use by others later, just as she had challenged readers earlier through her coming out about her sexuality and about her breast cancer and mastectomy. She is beginning to understand that, long after readers can no longer hear her actual voice in their ears, they will continue to seek her written counsel. As she noted in the essay, "My Words Will Be There," composed for a collection of black women writers published in 1984: "It was hard but very strengthening to remember that I could be silent my whole life long and then be dead, flat out, and never have said or done what I wanted to do, what I needed to do, because of pain, fear. . . . [M]y words will be there, something for her to bounce off, something to incite thought, activity."[37] A journal entry from several years later takes up the theme of her literary estate and ties it, as Lorde so often does, to womanist concerns with speech, politics, and living life fully, openly, and connected to her community. Especially relevant in this particular entry is her entreaty to Seboulisa, the goddess whom she clearly understands as the muse for her death journey, to protect her from "throwing any part of [her]self away."[38] She acknowledges her awareness that her writing performs a personal service for her but also a community service:

> Women who have asked me to set these stories down are asking me for my air to breathe, to use in their future, are courting me back to my life as a warrior. . . .
>
> I am going to write again from the world of cancer and with a different perspective—that of living with cancer in an intimate daily relationship. Yes, I'm going to say plainly, six years after my mastectomy, in spite of drastically altered patterns of eating and living, and in spite of my self-conscious living and increased self-empowerment, and in spite of my deepening commitment to using myself in the service of what I believe, . . . I have been diagnosed as having cancer of the liver, metastasized from breast cancer. . . .
>
> This fact does not make my last six years of work any less vital or important or necessary. The accuracy of that diagnosis has become less important than how I use the life I have.[39]

In this journal entry, Lorde's integration of the issues that preoccupied her early writings is stunningly complete. Conscious of the need to attend to her spiritual/emotional well-being regardless of her physical health, aware of the importance of not just her words but her presence to the women who have looked to her for guidance and strength, Lorde is also connecting with the strength that such sharing engenders in her. Bent on "using" the pain as well as the pleasure in her life, as her notion of the erotic requires, she will use her resistance to death just as she has used her resistance to the cultural push toward superficial eroticism and toward collusive silence, as an opportunity to seek truth from within. And of course, such a truth will be shared in the service of the creation of a new, "more possible" world.

Another late poem, "Beams," integrates this zest for life and her connection to other "sisters" with a growing sense of a future unbound by material or bodily concerns. She begins with images of the progression of seasons, "in the afternoon sun" with "autumn about to begin." Remembering past summers, "the sunset colors of Southampton Beach," and "red-snapper runs at Salina Cruz," where "for a few short summers / I too was delightful," she uses autumn's seasonal deaths as a metaphor for personal loss, where "desire for what is gone" is "sealed into hunger   like an abandoned mine" (415). Just as her days have begun their "inexorable dwindling," she is beginning to move from fear and longing for more earthly days into a timeless future. Desire in the present "to burn," and to "ride the flood" mixes with "desire for what is gone," re-creating Lorde's "emotional mathematic" as part of her record of the effects, both in power and in fear, of living with an intimate and immediate awareness of death. Slowly, seasonal images give way to connections with women warriors, "dark women clad in flat and functional leather," who offer "sisterly advice" and "the last Dahomean Amazons . . . three old Black women in draped cloths / holding hands" (416). In the final images, Lorde conjures another moment transformed, containing past, present, and future, beyond which "there is no telling" (366):

A knout of revelation   a corm of song
and love   a net of possible
surrounding all acts of life
one woman harvesting   all I have ever been . . .

sun   wind   come round again
seizing us in her arms like a warrior lover

or blowing us into shapes
we have avoided for years
as we turn
we forget what is not possible.
(416)

"Harvesting" all she has ever been, Lorde connects to her spiritual roots through a photograph of the last Dahomean Amazons. She pulls together revelations, songs, and loves in a "net of possible" as she envisions her journey beyond death. Making peace with the spinning seasons of earthly existence, Lorde prepares to embrace her future, the "turn," after which "we forget what is not possible" (416). This vision, which she presents to readers "for use," is an effort to make possible those things that seem impossible from a worldly perspective. Death is an experience that must be embraced because it provides another way for Lorde to teach and agitate for transformation.

Lorde poetically records her spiritual journey into death not as the end of her work but as its extension into a realm undefined by earthly "reckoning." In "The Night-Blooming Jasmine," the midnight flower blooms along the road between Lorde's house and "the tasks before" her. Calling what is "beyond" her vision not an "enemy / to be avoided / but a challenge / against which my neck grew strong" (466), Lorde acknowledges the strength that the struggle for life has engendered in her, noting her physical pain even as she celebrates its challenge to and enhancement of her life. Not yet ready to relinquish earthly existence, Lorde is beginning to understand that the border between bodily existence and nonexistence is not necessarily the difference between spiritual life and death. The call of death, the "fractured border through the center of my days" that she "patrols . ... sword drawn" (466), is one that she hears as a call to move through earthly existence, not leaving it behind but extending it beyond what can be known by creatures of the earth.

Another of Lorde's final poems, "The Electric Slide Boogie," completed on January 3, 1992, just ten months before she died, evidences her connection to the womanist concern for community as she celebrates the tension between her awareness of the richness of life and the pull of her imminent death. The scene is New Year's Day at 1:16 a.m.; Lorde is "weary beyond" and must leave the celebration to rest. She knows that her family and friends understand her physical weariness, "but community calls / right over the threshold" (474) as she hears the dancing, talk, and laughter of

the New Year's revelers. She closes reflectively, "How hard it is to sleep /
in the middle of life" (474). In this meditation Lorde is focused not on
what they will miss of her but on what she misses by responding to the call
of her illness. Instead of shrinking away from the pain, Lorde pauses to
record her observations of the peaceful celebration of the new year as she
must withdraw to rest her ravaged body. In the "middle" of all this living,
it is hard for her to rest; in the midst of all the work she wants to do, it is
"hard," she acknowledges, to know that she is dying. The acknowledgment,
though, as evidenced in her journals, is what keeps her focus clear and her
political priorities honed.

In her final poem, appropriately entitled "Today Is Not the Day," Lorde
continues to use her experience, her "patrol[ling] of that line" between life
and death, as a source of strength for herself and for her community. As in
the other poems about death, the intense, honest focus on the details of
her existence continues to call readers to understand the empowering potential of a heightened sense of mortality. Celebrating life through her relationships, her spiritual connections to ancient goddesses and women-
warriors, thinking about love and survival, positing a future that extends
beyond her life—with her existence "trailing behind" as a mere "comfort-
ing hum" (473)—Lorde is at peace with her life and her work. Moving as
a testament of her love for her children and her lover, and, in its preface,
of her desire to embrace even the experience of death fully, the poem also
worships the moment, made full and powerful by Lorde's heightened awareness of its fleeting nature:

> Today is not the day.
> It could be
> but it is not.
> Today is today
> in the early moving morning
> sun shining down upon
> the farmhouse in my belly . . .
>   (472)

Conscious of her literary legacy and of her desire that her work remind
readers to do ours, as well as to enjoy the doing, Lorde poetically asserts the
connections between loving and work that she articulated earlier in "Uses
of the Erotic":

By this rising
some piece of our labor
is already half-done
the taste of loving
doing a bit of work
having some fun
riding my wheels so close to the line
my eyelashes blaze. . .

(472)

Ending her poetic life with a return to "today," Lorde places before her readers a one-word emblem of the challenge that much of her life and work represents: We must first of all experience "today"—our lives, our pain, our pleasure—to our full, internally regulated capacity; we must share—verbally, artistically, creatively—this experience of "today" not as a way of distancing ourselves from it but in service of a vision of the future; we must use "today," as we can learn to use the past and the reality of our own mortality, to help guide us to an as yet unimagined tomorrow:

This could be the day.
I could slip anchor and wander
to the end of the jetty
uncoil into the waters
a vessel of light moonglade
ride the freshets to sundown . . .

But today
is not the day.
Today.

(472)

Lorde's extension of the erotic redefined and her claiming of the death journey as a personally and politically empowering spiritual experience in her late poetry mark a unique contribution to womanist spirituality. She says in A Litany for Survival, "What I leave behind has a life of its own. I've said this about poetry; I've said it about children. Well, in a sense I'm saying it about the very artifact of who I have been." The message that death, like the deep feeling of the erotic, can also be transformed into an experience of power and joy is one that Lorde would have her readers mark well, one that would take her earlier commitments to speaking her experience and to deepening the erotic and extend them in a "marvelous arithmetic" that would move systems as well as hearts and souls.

NOTES

1. Audre Lorde, "The Transformation of Silence into Language and Action," in *Sister/Outsider: Essays and Speeches* (Freedom, Calif.: Crossing Press, 1984), 40–44.

2. Ibid., 40–41.

3. Audre Lorde, "Uses of the Erotic: The Erotic as Power," in Lorde, *Sister/Outsider*, 53–59.

4. Judith Plaskow and Carol P. Christ, "Self in Relation" (section introduction), in *Weaving the Visions: New Patterns in Feminist Spirituality*, ed. Judith Plaskow and Carol P. Christ (San Francisco: HarperCollins, 1989), 173, 175.

5. Lorde, "Uses of the Erotic," 53, 54. Subsequent page citations to this essay will be given parenthetically in the text.

6. Teresa L. Fry Brown, "Avoiding Asphyxiation: A Womanist Perspective on Intrapersonal and Interpersonal Transformation," in *Embracing the Spirit: Womanist Perspectives on Hope, Salvation, and Transformation*, ed. Emilie Townes (Maryknoll, N.Y.: Orbis Books, 1997), 86.

7. Alice Walker, "Preface to the Tenth Anniversary Edition," in *The Color Purple*, 10th anniversary ed. (New York: Harcourt Brace Jovanovich, 1992), xi.

8. Alice Walker, "The Universe Responds," in *Living by the Word: Selected Writings, 1973–1987* (San Diego: Harcourt Brace, 1988), 192.

9. Walker's definition of *womanist* is given as the epigraph to her book *In Search of Our Mothers' Gardens: Womanist Prose* (San Diego: Harcourt Brace Jovanovich, 1983:

> *Womanist 1.* From *womanish.* (Opp. of "girlish," i.e. frivolous, irresponsible, not serious.) A black feminist or feminist of color. From the black folk expression of mothers to female children, "You acting womanish," i.e., like a woman. Usually referring to outrageous, audacious, courageous or *willful* behavior. Wanting to know more and in greater depth than is considered "good" for one. Interested in grown-up doings. Acting grown up. Being grown up. Interchangeable with another black folk expression: "You trying to be grown." Responsible. In charge. *Serious.*
>
> *2. Also:* A woman who loves other women, sexually and/or nonsexually. Appreciates and prefers women's culture, women's emotional flexibility (values tears as natural counterbalance of laughter), and women's strength. Sometimes loves individual men, sexually and/or nonsexually. Committed to survival and wholeness of entire people, male *and* female. Not a

separatist, except periodically, for health. Traditionally universalist, as in: "Mama, why are we brown, pink, and yellow, and our cousins are white, beige, and black? Ans.: "Well, you know the colored race is just like a flower garden, with every color flower represented." Traditionally capable, as in: "Mama, I'm walking to Canada and I'm taking you and a bunch of other slaves with me." Reply: "It wouldn't be the first time."

3. Loves music. Loves dance. Loves the moon. *Loves* the Spirit. Loves love and food and roundness. Loves struggle. *Loves* the Folk. Loves herself. *Regardless*.

4. Womanist is to feminist as purple to lavender. (xi)

10. Layli Phillips and Barbara McCaskill, "Who's Schooling Who? Black Women and the Bringing of the Everyday into Academe, or Why We Started *The Womanist*," *Signs: Journal of Women in Culture and Society* 20, no. 41 (1995): 1010.

11. Walker, *In Search*, xi.

12. Katie Geneva Cannon, *Katie's Canon: Womanism and the Soul of the Black Community* (New York: Continuum, 1995).

13. Ibid., 25.

14. Ula Y. Taylor, "Making Waves: The Theory and Practice of Black Feminism," *Black Scholar* 28, no. 2 (1998): 26.

15. Walker, *In Search*, xii.

16. Audre Lorde, *The Cancer Journals* (San Francisco: Aunt Lute, 1980), 53. This book and her later collection *A Burst of Light: Essays* (Ithaca, N.Y.: Firebrand, 1988) both clearly articulate Lorde's desire for her experience to be used by other women on their journeys toward empowerment, while at the same time closely scrutinizing the medical establishment, "cancer, inc.," breast implants, and many other personal/political aspects of her illness. In *The Cancer Journals*, she states that

> survival throughout these years has taught me how to value my own beauty, and how to look closely into the beauty of others. It has also taught me to value the lessons of survival, as well as my own perceptions. I feel more deeply, value those feelings more, and can put those feelings together with what I know in order to fashion a vision of a pathway toward true change. Within this time of assertion and growth, even the advent of a life-threatening cancer and the trauma of a mastectomy can be integrated into the life-force as knowledge and eventual strength, fuel for a more dynamic and focussed [sic] existence. Since the supposed threat of self-actualized women is one that our society seeks constantly to protect itself against, it is not coincidental that the sharing of this knowledge among women is diverted, in this case by the invisibility imposed by an insistence upon prosthesis as a norm for post-mastectomy women. (63)

A fuller analysis of Lorde's critique of prosthesis and breast reconstruction can be found in Sharon Barnes, "Marvelous Arithmetics: The Poetry and Prose of Audre Lorde" (Ph.D. diss., University of Toledo, 1998).

17. Alice Walker, *Anything We Love Can Be Saved* (New York: Random House, 1997), 82.

18. Lorde, *The Cancer Journals*, 77.

19. Lorde, *A Burst of Light*, 126.

20. Joy Bostic, "It's a Jazz Thang: Interdisciplinarity and Critical Imagining in the Construction of a Womanist Theological Method," in *Women's Studies in Transition: The Pursuit of Interdisciplinarity*, ed. Kate Conway-Turner et al. (Newark: University of Delaware Press, 1998), 138–55.

21. Audre Lorde, *The Collected Poems of Audre Lorde* (New York: W.W. Norton, 1997), 471. All of Lorde's poems reprinted in this essay are taken from this volume; subsequent page citations will be given parenthetically in the text.

22. Marjorie Pryse, "Introduction: Zora Neale Hurston, Alice Walker, and the 'Ancient Power' of Black Women," in *Conjuring: Black Women, Fiction, and the Literary Tradition*, ed. Marjorie Pryse and Hortense J. Spillers (Bloomington: Indiana University Press, 1985), 2, 22.

23. Lorde, *The Cancer Journals*, 46.

24. Lorde, *A Burst of Light*, 127. Both *The Cancer Journals* and *A Burst of Light* condense journal entries written over many years of Lorde's struggle with metastatic breast cancer. They present very personal discussions of her disease and treatment process as well as more political essays that analyze the medical establishment and Lorde's philosophical opposition to Western medical establishment practices, especially wearing prosthetic breasts. In the journals, Lorde's notion of the erotic as living enhanced by the power of deeply connected emotional response is connected to the potential power that can come from a heightened sense of mortality, a power she believes the western medical establishment seeks to deny women.

25. Lorde, *The Cancer Journals*, 53.

26. Barbara G. Walker, *The Woman's Encyclopedia of Myths and Secrets* (San Francisco: Harper and Row, 1983). The connection to creation comes through the classical image of Athene "with her totemic spider spinning the web of Fate" (957) and to death via Hindu myth, in which "the female spider's habit of devouring her mate led to identification of the spider with the death goddess" (957).

27. Ibid., 958.

28. Lorde, *A Burst of Light*, 120–21.

29. Ibid., 121.

30. As early as her 1978 volume of verse, *The Black Unicorn*, Lorde dedicated herself to Seboulisa, especially in the poem "125th Street and Abomey," in which she called herself Seboulisa's "severed daughter" (a reference to Lorde's mastectomy), who would laugh Seboulisa's name "into echo / all the world shall remember" (241). Entries in the journals, both *The Cancer Journals* and *A Burst of Light*, make consistent references to Seboulisa, whom I believe Lorde saw as the muse for her death journey.

31. Ada Gay Griffin and Michelle Parkerson, dirs., *A Litany for Survival: The Life and Work of Audre Lorde* (New York: Third World Newsreel, 1998).

32. Lorde, *A Burst of Light*, 122.

33. According to Lorde's note to this poem, Aido Hwedo is "The Rainbow Serpent; also a representation of all ancient divinities who must be worshipped but whose names and faces have been lost in time" (419).

34. According to Lorde's note, "An Ashanti Queen Mother in what is now Ghana, who led her people in several successful wars against the British in the nineteenth century" (332).

35. Geta Le Seur, "From Nice Colored Girl to Womanist: An Exploration of Development in Ntozake Shange's Writings," in *Language and Literature in the African-American Imagination*, ed. Carol Aisha Blackshire-Belay (Westport, Conn.: Greenwood Press, 1992), 167.

36. Bostic, "It's a Jazz Thang," 145.

37. Audre Lorde, "My Words Will Be There," in *Black Women Writers (1950–1980): A Critical Evaluation*, ed. Mari Evans (Garden City, N.J.: Anchor/Doubleday, 1984), 263.

38. Lorde, *A Burst of Light*, 111.

39. Ibid., 111–12.

10 THE SPIRIT OF A PEOPLE

The Politicization of Spirituality in
Julia Alvarez's *In the Time of the Butterflies*,
Ntozake Shange's *sassafrass, cypress & indigo*,
and Ana Castillo's *So Far from God*

HOLLY BLACKFORD

Literary critics have been reluctant to recognize the prominence of spiritual concerns in postmodern fiction. Typifying this reluctance, John A. McClure claims, is Fredric Jameson, who asserts that "spirituality virtually by definition no longer exists."[1] Indeed white male postmodern novelists such as John Barth, Donald Barthelme, William Burroughs, Don DeLillo, Thomas Pynchon, and Kurt Vonnegut represent the individual's search for meaning as an impossible quest. To formalize this thematic content, their novels employ self-reflexive narrative technique, "aleatory writing, parody and pastiche";[2] meaning, then, is a complete fiction. Ethnic women novelists write against this tradition. Their novels use self-reflexive storytelling to underscore the theme that within stories the individual *constructs* meaning. Their novels redefine the postmodern novel by responding to the secular bias of white male writers and literary critics. Their novels foreground the presence of spiritual healers, oracles, saints, martyrs, visions, conjurings, and allusions to myth. In novels by Julia Alvarez, Ntozake Shange, and Ana Castillo, individual characters achieve a spiritual consciousness that leads them to serve the spiritual and social needs of the ethnic community. Through their novels, communal

spiritual consciousness achieves postmodern form. Their narrative practices situate the spiritual realm within the everyday material world of the
community and the human character.

Postmodern ethnic women writers use self-reflexive storytelling to mirror the ethnic community's subjective experience and acceptance of supernatural and mythic reality. In Alvarez's novel *In the Time of the Butterflies*,
the Virgin Mary and various saints link female characters to the people of
the Dominican Republic and the enterprise of mothering.[3] In Shange's
novel *sassafrass, cypress & indigo*, female characters are linked to the spirits
of southern slaves, to women in Greek and African mythology, and to all
women across cultures.[4] In Castillo's novel *So Far from God*, various Catholic saints and Native American gods define women's relationship to the New
Mexican land, to themselves, and to community.[5] The novel's acceptance
of spiritual presences provides the context for individual characters to undergo a conversion experience through which they embrace a communal
purpose. In Alvarez's novel, Patria's spiritual growth enables her to decide
for herself what the church cannot decide for her and to lead a revolutionary
movement against the oppressive Dominican Republic dictator. In Shange's
novel, Indigo's connection with the spirit world leads her to recognize the
call to serve her people and to become a midwife and healer for the African
American community. In Castillo's novel, Sophi changes the future of her
New Mexican community after her four daughters are martyred. These female characters define their social and political role through their spiritual
identity and define the politics of the novel, which voices the spiritual identity of an ethnic community.

In the view of these contemporary ethnic women writers, the work of
the postmodern ethnic novel is to heal and transform the spirit of the ethnic community. The postmodern ethnic novel heals by first cleansing, in
the form of critiquing and remembering the past, and then restoring collective spirit by articulating a contemporary identity distinct from white
hegemony. When describing her goals for writing *In The Time of the Butterflies*, Julia Alvarez suggests that the ethnic novelist's imagination of the
past becomes a means of redemption: "I wanted to immerse my readers in
an epoch in the life of the Dominican Republic that I believe can only
finally be understood by fiction, only finally be redeemed by the imagination" (324). In the postmodern novel lies the promise of redemption. If
the past can be felt, experienced, and imagined by readers, then the past,
the author, the community of color, and the reader are redeemed. Only the
fictional novel can immerse readers in a particular past from the point of

view of the oppressed. Alvarez expresses the experiences of the Mirabal sisters during the reign of Trujillo, narrating their experiences in the voices of the four sisters. Shange employs magic realist narrative technique to imaginatively depict three sisters who struggle to express themselves as art-ists and women within the African American community. Similarly using magic realism, Castillo represents the experiences of a mother and her four daughters within the oppressed New Mexican community. Expressing the experiences of oppressed women, these novelists immerse their readers in the point of view of the ethnic community.

In all three novels, redemption is the result of the novelist's ability to imagine how a community can be transformed through spiritual leader-ship. As Carol Marsh-Lockett argues of Shange's novel, the novel with a spiritual purpose redefines European ideas of art: "A great achievement in [*sassafrass, cypress & indigo*] is Shange's ultimate displacement of the Euro-pean notion of art for art's sake with the traditional African perception of art's serving a functional and spiritual purpose in people's (here, Black women's) lives."[6] To redefine the purpose of art is to redefine European definitions of spirituality. Theologians have traditionally conceived of spirituality as an individual's personal relationship with God—as inner experience.[7] The notion that spirituality is an inner or individual quality, Carol Ochs argues, tends to reflect a male point of view.[8] Male spiritual writings tend to use the metaphor of the spiritual journey to suggest that spiritual maturity is movement toward individuation.[9] Kristina Groover argues that spirituality in many American women's writings involves com-munity, and both Ochs and Ursula King state that feminist theologians question spirituality as individuation and instead equate spiritual maturity with movement toward community.[10] Looking at women's novels, Groover feels that a more useful definition of spirituality is "positive transformative experience."[11] Ochs claims that spirituality entails "a transformation of our being and consciousness."[12] Inner transformation defines the conversion experiences of Patria, Indigo, and Sophi, but inner transformation always involves social transformation in these novels.

Novelists that seek social change construct the ethnic community as the site of the holy. Narrow definitions of spirituality as inner experience are only partial truths, given that people practice their spiritual truths. Their intuitions, emotions, thoughts, and social consciousness depend upon what they feel to be "holy, that is, of ultimate importance."[13] The individual character transforms in relation to the broader force of a spiritual commu-nity. The problem with traditional theological definitions of spirituality is that they divide the sacred from the profane, separating the spiritual from earthly existence. Inner, asocial transformations foreclose the possibility of changing the environment, as Margaret Chatterjee argues: "A spiritual landscape which relegates the everyday to a lower rung of the scale of existence can hardly provide a leverage for social transformation."[14] To claim that spirituality is inner experience and that it is concerned with another world rather than this world is to hold dear the status quo, since no political action based on spiritual truths can be effected.

Social transformation in the novels of Alvarez, Shange, and Castillo requires critique of church fathers and traditional notions of spiritual focus. Characters must think through their relationship to transcendent beings for themselves. To depend upon institutional dogmas would be to depend upon institutions bound up with oppression. Characters depend upon their own experiences as women, particularly as mothers and sisters, to understand their spiritual call to serve the community. In particular, theological divisions between spirit and flesh become a site of critique, largely because, as Susan Bordo argues, such a division has tended to equate women and female experience with the lower rung of the binarism—with flesh rather than spirit: "That which is not-body is the highest, the best, the noblest, the closest to God. . . . The scheme is frequently gendered, with woman cast in the role of the body. . . . Women *are* that negativity, whatever it may be: distraction from knowledge, seduction away from God, capitulation to sexual desire, violence or aggression, failure of will, even death."[15] These novels critique this dualistic philosophy that since the twelfth century has produced the spirit/corporeality divide.[16] These novels imagine a dynamic relationship between spirit and flesh, embracing female experiences such as menstruation, pregnancy, lactation, sexuality, and care of others' bodies (children, the sick, the dying, and the dead).

The novels of Alvarez, Shange, and Castillo feature a feminine spirituality that includes the body and female experience. They feature principles of connectivity between women and the natural universe, God, other women's bodies, the enterprise of mothering both children and the community, the land, and spirits. A reevaluation of the female body and of its natural cycles figures prominently in these novels, for they seek to celebrate a spirituality unique to women as well as to a particular ethnicity. The female body itself becomes an oracle of the spirits, a site of spiritual knowledge and intuition by virtue of its natural rhythms and connection with the land. David Ray Griffin makes clear that definitions of spirituality centered on the spirit/flesh dualism are actually invested in dividing the individual from nature: "Insofar as dualism proclaimed the essential independence of the soul from the body, it was simply individualism in relation to nature."[17] This dualism denies humanity's connections with nature. The anthropologist Sherry Ortner argues that domination of nature results in the domination of women because cross-culturally women have been interpreted as synonymous with nature and natural cycles.[18] Griffin defines a movement he calls "postmodern spirituality," including feminists, ecologists, and Eastern influenced spiritual leaders, which seeks to reevaluate the human connection to nature, past, family, body, environment, and culture as constitutive of identity and spirituality.[19] Seeking to reclaim the female body's relationship to generational continuity, spiritual knowledge, and nature, including land, the three novels discussed in this essay articulate this conception of postmodern spirituality. Women become the very expression of these spiritual connections by linking spiritual transformation with human female experience, the body, community, social activism, and storytelling.

PATRIA, THE WOMB OF REVOLUTION

In the Time of the Butterflies enacts a struggle against Catholicism's division between material and spiritual realms. The text resolves that struggle with Patria's recognition that spirituality allows for social transformation and serves the collective good. Ultimately the individual human being's relationship to God is embodied by Patria's relationship to her people. The novel indicts the ideology that divides the material from the spiritual by ironizing the Catholic Church for refusing to interfere in "temporal matters" (153) and speak out against the Dominican dictator. The novel critiques the patriarchs of the church not only for their inaction but also for their patriarchal symbolism, easily appropriated by Trujillo's regime. Minerva explains how the history books began to change when Trujllo took power, following "the plot of the Bible" and depicting Trujillo as "God's glory made flesh" (24). Required portraits of Christ and Trujillo hang side by side in Dominican houses. In Patria's mind the ideology of deified patriarchs begins to feel the same in church and state: "Beside [the picture of the Good Shepherd, talking to his lambs] hung the required portrait of El Jefe, touched up to make him look better than he was. . . . How could our loving, all-powerful Father allow us to suffer so? I looked up, challenging Him. And the two faces had merged!" (53). The novel critiques the deification of men. The idea of worshiping a Father merges into the rhetoric of the state, such that the two fathers of the nation seem to indicate one central paternalism to which the people owe allegiance. Recognizing the pervasive quality of paternalism as ideology raises Patria's critical consciousness, and she challenges the idea that man embodies the "image" of God. The portraits reveal that these faces are only images.

In her postscript, Alvarez directly attacks the ideology that separates temporal from spiritual concerns. She critiques the way in which the Mirabal sisters have been completely mythologized: "As for the sisters of legend, wrapped in superlatives and ascended into myth, they were finally also inaccessible to me. I realized, too, that such deification was dangerous, the same godmaking impulse that had created our tyrant [Trujillo]. And ironically, by making them myth, we lost the Mirabals once more, dismissing the challenge of their courage as impossible for us, ordinary men and women"(324). Ironically, Alvarez connects the dictator to the sisters who resisted his regime and led an underground movement; both were mythologized by the people. In fact, Alvarez represents the most religious of the sisters, Patria, as struggling against a tyranny within herself, "the tyranny of my spirit" (45). The tyranny that the novel fights is far greater than an abusive dictator; it is actually an ideology that separates deities from humans.

This tendency toward mythologizing is a thinly veiled impulse to dehumanize. Patria voices the novel's critique of deification by turning her attention to the people, who are in her view equally responsible for their own oppression because they accord a human being the status of myth: "Once the goat [Trujillo] was a bad memory in our past, that would be the real revolution we would have to fight: forgiving each other for what we had all let come to pass" (222). The separation of the realm of ethics from the realm of politics keeps the people passive. "Come to pass" echoes biblical language but reinforces the passivity implicit in this dangerous assumption that temporal matters and spiritual matters, flesh and spirit, are distinct and not equally bound up with collective good. Alvarez's representation of these four sisters as real women, who not only are heroes but also fear and wish to survive, seeks to undo an ideology that separates spirituality from possibilities for social transformation on earth.

When we are introduced to Patria, in Patria's own voice, she begins her story as if telling a biblical tale of origins, of the separation between her flesh and spirit. Her first passages encapsulate her story and recite the novel's position on spirituality. One should come down to earth and be a woman, rather than remain "in the clouds" as a spirit:

From the beginning, I felt it, snug inside my heart, the pearl of great price. No one had to tell me to believe in God or to love everything that lives. . . .

So you could say I was born, but I wasn't really here. One of those spirit babies, alelá, as the country people say. My mind, my heart, my soul in the clouds.

It took some doing and undoing to bring me down to earth. (44)

Patria's rhetoric echoes the narrative of Genesis, "in the beginning," and tells of birth, but emotionally, intellectually, and spiritually she feels otherworldly. In this novel, exclusive focus on spirit worlds creates the conditions in which an evil dictator can rise to power. Patria, which means "fatherland" or "homeland," is a metaphor for the nation and is initially like the Catholic Church, which refuses to get involved in "temporal matters," being more focused on the clouds than on the atrocities around it. Patria, however, has a distinct philosophy of faith, which serves as a basis for her subsequent conversion. To her, faith and love are intertwined, pointing toward a philosophy of connectedness between all living beings and God. For Patria this principle comes to be embodied by the female body's capacity to mother and embody connectivity between people. Patria finds that, instead of being called to become a nun, she experiences an awakening womanly body. She marries and becomes a mother. Her maternal body and identity become the cornerstones of spiritual experience and leadership, bringing Patria "down to earth" in the sense of connecting her both with natural rhythms and with her people's condition on earth.

The novel suggests that to turn toward earthly concerns with a maternal sensibility is an expansive act, enlarging the self and the very concept of soul. The scene in which Patria chooses an earthly path is initially troubling because Patria takes the posture of servant to her husband. Patria is washing the feet of penitents at church and feels an attraction to a certain set of feet, her future husband's. However, the image is couched in terms of maternal nurturing, and maternity becomes the principle of Patria's spiritual recognition that she must act for political change. While washing her future husband's feet, Patria embodies the posture of Mary Magdalene in the Bible, but in that moment she becomes a maternal caretaker and infantilizes the man, cleaning her husband's feet "as one does a baby's legs in cleaning its bottom" (48). At another point in the novel she gives her husband the breast milk meant for her child, who is stillborn. To participate in "earthy" relationships rather than lead the celibate life expands the female self into mother of more than just children: "At last, my spirit was descending into flesh, and there was more, not less, of me to praise God" (49). The novel suggests, then, that the flesh should triumph against "the tyranny of the spirit" and that through women's earthly experiences the self grows in its relationship to God, to nature, to land, and to community. Patria compares her feelings for her husband to feelings she would have for a wild bird or a stray cat who would eat out of her hand. A maternal relationship to all creatures great and small is thus already expressed by her choice to not be absorbed into the church but to marry.

Patria's maternal sensibility is mirrored by her choice of spiritual inspiration, the Virgin Mary. By looking to a female deity for spiritual guidance, Patria challenges the paternal tradition of the church and seeks a supernatural presence that is grounded in her own experience as a woman. The Virgin Mary embodies human and female experience, an underemphasized aspect of Christianity in white American theology. Because Patria's spiritual sense is bound up with maternal presence and Mary's ability to contain God's seed within her very body, Patria's loss of faith in church fathers is registered by her maternal body, and she gives birth to a stillborn child. The loss is of greater significance in the novel because it embodies faith in traditional institutions to do right and to effect leadership for the collective good: "I started noting the deadness in Padre Ignacio's voice, the tedium between the gospel and communion, the dry papery feel of the host in my mouth. My faith was shifting, and I was afraid. . . . I could feel the waters breaking, the pearl of great price slipping out, and I realized I was giving birth to something dead I had been carrying inside me" (52). Religious imagery and body imagery intertwine to produce connections between politics and spiritual truths. By burying her stillborn child, Patria buries her faith in the leadership of father figures and opens herself to the idea that Mary embodies a human experience of God and an alternative to faith in fathers.

The Virgin Mary becomes a symbol not only for the nurturing power of motherhood as a context for leading a revolutionary movement but for the true force of spirituality, the holy within the earthly and within the people. Patria's faith, always focused in the feelings of her womb, becomes alive again when she visualizes and hears the voice of the Virgin in the people: "I turned around and saw the packed pews, hundreds of weary, upturned faces, and it was as if I'd been facing the wrong way all my life. My faith stirred. It kicked and somersaulted in my belly, coming alive. . . . Here I am, Virgencita. Where are you? / And I heard her answer me with the coughs and cries and whispers of the crowd: *Here, Patria Mercedes, I'm here, all around you. I've already more than appeared*" (58–59) . This aural vision of Mary completes the reconnection between earthly and spiritual concerns in the novel and undoes the division the church makes between spiritual and temporal. Further, the vision asserts that women bridge these divisions. By giving birth and caring for the community, including the dead, women link earth and spirit, past and present, inner and social experience, emotion and faith. Mary becomes a model for how faith is expressed through administering to the bodies of others and caring for a collective good. Traditional faith faces the wrong way, the text argues, toward the wrong transcendent entity—the world beyond rather than the transcendent cultural body and political ideal that would save a community. Mary is actually an embodiment of the people in Patria's vision. She *is* their bodily sounds—their coughs, cries, and whispers.

Mary becomes the antidote to the stillborn image of dead faith that Patria has brought to fruition, the waters broken within her. The people are to be encompassed in Patria's spiritual concerns, and motherhood becomes the context for imagining that relationship: "Ever since I'd had my vision of the Virgencita, I knew spirit was imminent" (154). Patria's personal journey through crisis to transformative faith is an allegory for a collective journey as well, as Bados Ciria argues: "Patria is the only one who uses an allegorical relationship between personal and political narratives, one of the fundamental foundations of fiction in Latin American novels."[20] Patria's allegorical embodiment of the Virgin Mary symbolizes her embodiment of a collective human good. For example, as she debates about letting her son participate in the movement, she finds a model in Mary's willingness to become a collective mother by letting her son go: "She had clung to Jesus until He told her straight out, Mamá, I have to be about My Father's business. And she had to let him go, but it broke her heart because, though He was God, He was still her boy" (154). Patria's most significant conversion experience to revolutionary sentiment occurs at a retreat on the subject of Mary, at which their shelter becomes the center of gunfire as guerrilla fighters are gunned down by government armies. To protect herself from the gunfire, Patria topples a statue of the Virgin and hides in it, symbolically displacing and becoming one with the divine figure. The vision she sees from this position, however, forever links her to the slain in an intimate, familial way. As she looks into the eyes of a young man just before he is shot, she connects this man with the son she is carrying in her womb, "Oh my God, he's one of mine!" (162) Thereafter she feels she is carrying this man in her womb as well, and this recognition of her maternal connection with her suffering people instigates her vow: "I'm not going to sit back and watch my babies die, Lord, even if that's what You in Your great wisdom decide" (162). Motherhood, spirituality, and leadership for the collective good are now one and the same for her: "So it was that our house became the motherhouse of the movement" (166).

As we approach the end of the Mirabals' lives, Patria grows in spiritual strength, ultimately linked with the image of Christ. With this shift in spiritual imagery, we can conclude that Patria has actually birthed herself in the image of God, having chosen her spiritual path for herself. Next to Mary, Christ is the figure who perfectly bridges spirit and flesh, godliness and care for those on earth. Although Dede will compare all her sisters to Christ in their sacrifices, Patria becomes a Christ figure much earlier, as she begins to think of herself as Christ: "Oh my sisters, my Pedrito, oh my little lamb! / My crown of thorns was woven of thoughts of my boy. His body I had talcumed, fed, bathed. His body now broken as if it were no more than a bag of bones" (201). She begins to plead with God to take her instead of her son, a bargain repeated several times and one that foreshadows the sacrifice of herself that will be made. She thus bargains with God to take a woman rather than her son as Christ, subverting the order of gender. As if narrated by an outside narrative voice, the refrain "And on the third day He rose again" (200, 201) repeats throughout Patria's narrative, in which she describes her despair at the loss of her husband, son, and house. The spiritual power that Patria develops in the novel is politically persuasive. It sustains her more than the political ideals that motivate her sisters Minerva and Mate: "The captain held on to my hand too long, but this time I didn't pull away. I was no longer his victim, I could see that. I might have lost everything, but my spirit burned bright. Now that I had shined it on him, this poor blind moth couldn't resist my light" (217). The Patria of the end of the novel is a very different Patria from the beginning, less religious but more spiritual, more revolutionary, and more powerful. Her inner light reflects as well the growing spiritual and political strength of a country aware that Trujillo's days are numbered and that he is acting like a frightened animal.

The "inner light" that Patria represents is a progressive model for the church, which eventually follows suit and denounces the government's actions. But the "inner light" that Patria represents, as homeland, makes clear that the Mirabal sisters, as both myths and real women, embody the spirit of the nation in a way the church cannot. Their power is distinct from the church, as Trujillo reveals when he complains, "My only two problems are the damn church and the Mirabal sisters" (281). The Mirabal sisters are spiritualized figures and become national icons, people all over the country mourning their martyrdom and adopting the slogan "Bring back the butterflies!" (310). The image of the butterfly, the Mirabals' code name, brings to mind a transformation and transfiguration between earth and sky, a fluidity between worlds that such women make possible, as Elizabeth Martinez has suggested: "The butterflies provide the image of Latin America—of a people's hope—and even global awareness. Traditionally, the butterfly has been a metaphor for the transformations undergone by our own souls, which then ascend to the heavens reflecting hope for our lives here on earth."[21] While a metaphor for the soul, the butterfly links air and earth, symbolizing the potential relationship between the spiritual and material world.

Alvarez reevaluates the material world, female experience, and the maternal body to define them as contexts for a spiritual self; when female experience becomes a context for spirituality, women's role in communities, in the care of others, and in body-invested labor can become a means of social change. Throughout the text, images of the female body, particularly of pregnancy, are used to express principles of connectivity between unique individuals, politics, and spirituality. With all the sisters, the female body registers spiritual and intuitive knowledge of political ethics. For example, just as Patria's stillborn child is a sign of her knowledge of Trujillo, Minerva's menarche symbolizes her loss of faith in the nation's leadership. Minerva and Sinita, young girls at school, exchange secrets; while Minerva's secret is "about bleeding and having babies" (16), Sinita's is about how Trujillo murders those who oppose him. Minerva's "complications," her word for menstruation, begin the next morning, as if the pearl of great price slips from her as well as from Patria, but much earlier in life. Similarly, Patria's conception of her third child, she believes, occurs on the day Cuba is freed, thus linking her body with spiritual and political struggle. After the sisters' husbands are imprisoned, the sisters go to a doctor to speak with him about finding remaining revolutionary members; to circumvent recording devices, they speak of whether their "cycles" are still working and will still be active (code for revolutionary activity). The connections between Patria's house as the motherhouse of the revolution and the motherhouse of everyday domestic activity are made by repeated juxtapositions between the violence of the weaponry and the life-sustaining activities that occur at the very same sites (breakfast at the same table used to make bombs, tweezers used to twine wires, etc.). The sisters call the bombs they make nipples, and Dede's survival of her sisters results in breast cancer, the loss of her breast linked with the loss of her sisters and marked on her body, near her heart. Inherently connected, then, are bodies, spirits, and politics, through carefully orchestrated imagery that connects female experience with spirituality, community and social change. Locating spiritual and political leadership within the human experience of motherhood, Alvarez creates an archetype for feminine spirituality. Using the Virgin Mary to symbolize bridges between human and divine, body and spirit, individual and communal mothering, Alvarez self-reflexively invokes the saint's presence to further the novel's spiritual purpose.

INDIGO, THE FIDDLE OF THE SOUTH

Shange develops feminine spirituality into magic by situating her spiritual characters in the magic realist novel. The three sisters of *sassafrass, cypress & indigo* invoke Greek and African myths, the three fates, the Tree of Life in Creole mythology of Voudoun, the spirits of slaves, the Voodoo triple goddess, and women from different cultures who labor at similar crafts.[22] They are thus combinations of many mythological traditions and cultures, all of which suggest that women and the divine speak to one another and through that connection become powerful. However, the spiritual presences voiced by the novel support the material community. Although she is receptive to messages from spirits, Shange's character Indigo has to undergo changes in her relationship to spirits and a fundamental conversion experience to recognize that spiritual gifts are intended to serve the community. The novel's spiritual purpose depends upon the materialization of spiritual truth in the human world.

The novel critiques theological divisions between material and spiritual realms by suggesting that Indigo, "a consort of the spirits" (3), embodies the African American community: "[Indigo's] sisters were artists. Would they understand she just wanted where they came from to stay alive? Hilda Effania [Indigo's mother] knew Indigo had an interest in folklore. Hilda Effania had no idea that Indigo was the folks" (224). Indigo's embodiment of "the folks" parallels Patria's embodiment of her people through the Virgin Mary—the life represented by human coughs, cries, and whispers. Indigo's ultimate choice to use her spiritual gifts to serve human life and her people marks a spiritual journey similar to Patria's in that she must grow to recognize the pain of her people and her relationship to that pain. Spirituality is thus the dynamic force that expands the female self to assuage collective pain and work for the survival of a people, keeping alive "where [her sisters] came from" and facilitating the birth of new lives, for Indigo becomes a midwife and healer. By suggesting that she bridges folklore and "the folks," the narrator invites us to regard Indigo as a symbol for the magic realist novel, which evokes the spiritual community of the folk by telling their stories. The female character represents connectivity between spirit and flesh, past and future, nature and culture, folk and folklore, by ensuring the continuing life of African American stories.

By emphasizing that Indigo nurtures the origins of her sisters' lives as artists, the narrator suggests that Indigo's embodiment of "the folks" ensures the survival of communal art forms. Indigo's spiritual connection to the community stands for the form of the postmodern novel that voices the spiritual aspects of the ethnic community. Indigo achieves a spiritual voice when she receives the gift of a fiddle from Uncle John. This fiddle expresses a folk art form; Uncle John explains that it invokes the spiritual voice of an oppressed community:

> "Now, listen. Them whites what owned slaves took everythin' was ourselves & didn't even keep it fo' they own selves. Just threw it on away, ya heah. . . . Took off wit our spirits & left us with they Son. But the fiddle was the talkin' one. The fiddle be callin' our gods what left us/be givin' back some devilment & hope in our bodies worn down & lonely over these fields & kitchens. Why white folks so dumb, they was thinkin' that if we didn't have nothin' of our own, they could come controllin', meddlin', whippin' our sense on outta us. But the Colored smart, ya see. The Colored got some wits to em, you & me, we ain't the onliest ones be talkin' wit the unreal. What ya think music is, whatchu think the blues be, & them get happy church musics is about, but talkin' wit the unreal what's mo' real than most folks ever gonna know." (27)

Uncle John links African American spirituality with its art forms, including folk and church music. The fiddle defines the unique voice of ethnic art. We recognize in Uncle John's speech the thesis of W. E. B. DuBois regarding the souls of black folk, expressed through song, and thus Uncle John represents the voice of African American cultural leadership through his perspective on song.[23] As Indigo begins to play, "the slaves who were ourselves had so much to say, they all went on at once in the voices of the children: this child, Indigo" (27). Indigo conjures the souls of black folk to combat white oppression, continuing the tradition of folk art, which expresses the people's spirit without the oppressors' knowledge. As she welcomes the speech of the spirits and becomes a vessel for their speech, "She had many tongues, many spirits who loved her, real & unreal. / The South in her" (28). Indigo's spiritual voice is traced to African American southern history, expressing a pantheism of myths just as the novel does and thus standing for Shange's use of magic realism.

The novel's blend of classical, African, and crosscultural myth politicizes the spiritual center of the novel. African American spirituality draws upon many cultural traditions because of southern history and a past in which one specific vision of spirituality was imposed upon the community. Indigo becomes the voice of the magic realism novel, embodying the unique blend of myths and spiritual expressions that a particular cultural history shapes. The novel's pantheistic spiritual community critiques the dominance of Christian authority. Uncle John voices the novel's critique of Christian authority in the African American past by equating worship of Christ with white oppression. But he explains that forced religious ideas can never completely efface the authentic spiritual expressions of the people. The combination of spiritual traditions that Indigo embodies by fiddling allows her to become a healer of African American scars:

> She'd look at somebody. Say a brownskinned man with a scar on his cheek, leathery hands, and a tiredness in his eyes. Then she'd bring her soul all up in his till she'd ferreted out the most lovely moment in that man's life. & played that. You could tell from looking that as Indigo let notes fly from the fiddle, that man's scar wasn't quite so ugly; his eyes filling with energy, a tenderness tapping from those fingers now, just music. The slaves who were ourselves aided Indigo's mission, connecting soul & song, experience & unremembered rhythms. (45)

Indigo heals wounds by incarnating memory and storytelling, foregrounding certain past experiences and connecting those experiences with artistic expressions. She changes how this man looks, transforming his and the community's relationship to his scarred flesh and filling his soul as would a "mission(ary)." The postmodern ethnic novel heals by transforming the people's scars into art and beauty, restoring spirit by restoring lost connections. Yet the power of spiritual pantheism is not sanctioned by the community's preacher, Sister Mary, who feels that "too much of the Holy Ghost came out of Indigo & that fiddle. Sister Mary Louise swore even she couldn't stand that much spirit every day" (35). The church objects to the presence of the spiritual in the everyday life of the community.

Indigo's expression of an African American spirituality is counterpoised to Christian spiritual authority. Indigo turns away from Christian power, a power historically used to justify slavery and passivity (the meek shall inherit the earth). In the novel's view, worship of Jesus distracts from community by distracting focus from material needs: "Black people needed so many things. That's why Indigo didn't tell her mama what all she discussed with her friends [spirits]. It had nothing to do with Jesus. Nothing at all. Even her mama knew that, and she would shake her head the way folks do when they hear bad news, murmuring, 'Something's got hold to my child, I swear. She's got too much South in her'" (4). Indigo is filled with the historical power of the land rather than with the Savior, with the knowledge of her people and their needs rather than with Christian religion. The novel suggests that Indigo's spirituality is distinct from Christian worship because it embodies the material history of African Americans in the South: "When her father died, Indigo had decided it was the spirit of things that mattered. The humans come and go. Aunt Haydee said spirits couldn't be gone, or the planet would fall apart. / The South in her" (8). The land figures importantly in Indigo's spiritual identity, signifying that she stands for the collective conditions of the people and that the experiences of the community need to be the context for authentic spirituality.

Indigo finds her spiritual powers and knowledge in conflict with Sister Mary, who ironically voices Christianity's equation of women with material rather than spiritual concerns. In a pivotal scene, Indigo challenges Sister Mary. She feels that the passage Sister Mary reads, "And your sons will become shepherds in the wilderness. Numbers 14:33" (16), does not include her because she is a girl. Indigo is angry: "But that doesn't have anything to do with me. . . . I'm a girl, that's all. I want to know what I'm supposed to do" (16). Sister Mary tells her to help make the bread, and Indigo asks if that is what Christian girls do, bake bread. Sister Mary replies, "We tend after beauty in the world. The flowers and the children" (17), but Indigo is not satisfied. As if her anger cannot be contained, she begins to bleed. Menarche becomes the sign of her rage at the passage's neglect of girls and at the limitations the preacher places upon girls and women. The biblical passage implies that only boys obtain spiritual maturity, and Sister Mary implies that girls support bodily, earthly needs at home—"in the world," not beyond it.

Subtly, Indigo's spirituality critiques Sister Mary's view of a gendered division between spirit and flesh, suggesting that Sister Mary is not the only authority on women's place. Although Sister Mary offers a ritual to recognize Indigo's first blood, the novel allows Indigo the final word on rituals of menstruation. Just after this scene, Indigo's own recipes appear for "marvelous menstruating moments," including "flowing" and "for disturbance of the flow," signifying that Indigo has her own ideas about how menstruation should be ritualized and how menstruating women are especially in tune with spirituality. Indigo obtains her own path to womanhood, seeing spiritual implications in the material sign that she inhabits a womanly body. Her recipes assert the spiritual magic of the female body's role in reproduction.

Indigo revises the connection between spirit and flesh by recognizing Sister Mary's emphasis on female materiality and by deciding that women's material connections, symbolized by the body's blood, provide a context for feminine spirituality. Recommending that a woman flow in water, Indigo's healing recipe for menstrual flow links the female body with symbols of creation and life rather than symbols of domesticity. Because the character who represents Christian authority is a woman, Christian connections between women and earthly labor cannot be entirely rejected. Instead, those connections become the basis for Indigo's recognition of menarche as an empowering magic of womanhood. Although she voices Christian rhetoric, Sister Mary daringly revises the Garden of Eve myth to celebrate Indigo's first blood, telling Indigo to bleed into the garden, to "Speak, child, raise your voice that the Lord May Know You as the Woman You Are" (19), and to bathe in red, yellow, and white rose petals. The colors of the rose petals around Indigo's skin, Janice Crosby argues, suggest that all the races are represented in this initiatory moment.[24] Crosby further argues that both Eve and Mary are represented in this revision because Sister Mary returns Indigo to the garden "filled with grace" (19). Thus Sister Mary represents menarche as a positive, empowering, transformative rite of passage for Indigo, after which she should have voice and knowledge of God. Although Indigo expresses dissatisfaction with Christianity in this scene, she finds in Sister Mary a role model for spiritual womanhood. She bases her ideas of menstruation magic on Sister Mary's discourse of female earthiness and the preacher's embodiment of spiritual womanhood. The body and the material conditions of the people become the context for Indigo's spiritual conversion into a healer and midwife. She is called to serve the spirit of the community by recognizing and facilitating its material needs. Indigo needs to undergo a conversion experience that will solidify her understanding of spirituality as a collective action. Although she begins to play her fiddle for a club and conjure her listeners' pasts to heal their scars, she also joins a street gang and begins to lose sight of serving a collective good. After a conflict with Mabel, the girlfriend of the club owner, she hears Mabel being beaten and realizes that she is responsible because when Mabel told her not to play her fiddle Indigo reacted with hostility and left, which enraged Mabel's boyfriend (the club owner). Indigo has to undergo a radical conversion experience in which she recognizes her relationship to Mabel's cries, which come to stand for her people's cries of past and present pain:

> Indigo felt The Caverns [the space beneath the club] for the first time. The air was dark, heavy. The baking breads wafted thru her nostrils, leaden. Her fiddle, as she let it fall over her side, weighed down on her spirit. Shame crawled up her cheeks. She was going to see about Mabel. Mabel had gotten in trouble 'cause of Indigo's fiddle, 'cause Indigo was a Geechee Captain. Mabel was just some woman. One day Indigo would be a woman too. . . . The Caverns began to moan, not with sorrow but in recognition of Indigo's revelation. The slaves who were ourselves had known terror intimately, confused sunrise with pain, & accepted indifference as kindness. Now they sang out from the walls, pulling Indigo toward them. Indigo ran her hands along the walls, to get the song, getta hold to the voices. Instead her fingers grazed cold, hard metal rings. Rust covered her palms & fingers. She kept following the rings. Chains. Leg irons. The Caverns revealed the plight of her people, but kept on singing. The tighter Indigo held the chains in her hands, the less shame was her familiar. Mabel's tiny woeful voice hovered over the blood thick chorus of The Caverns. Indigo knew her calling. The Colored had hurt enough already. (49)

The Caverns represent Indigo's passage through a mythical yet real Hades, through the hell of history in which her people still suffer. The smell of baking breads permeating this space is reminiscent of the labor she is assigned by Sister Mary, a Christian symbol with which she is not content. But anger and resistance, she realizes, are not the answer. She must experience this vision of her people's hell to fully understand the connection between spirituality and community, signified by the female body and voice.

Once identification with the suffering of a people becomes the guiding principle of the spiritual character, the character's spiritual knowledge converts to communal insight. Indigo's recognition that she and Mabel are the same parallels Patria's recognition that the man she sees slaughtered is her own son, symbolically and collectively. In recognizing Mabel's voice as the people's voice, Indigo discovers what Patria discovers in church: the cries of the people represent a transcendent spirit, larger than any one person. This moment of identification is a "revelation," enacted in the cries of the people that both Indigo and Patria hear when they recognize their identification with the sufferers. In this moment Indigo hears the songs of others for the first time, even though she has been producing songs throughout the text. She confronts history, for which Mabel is a symbol, an incarnation, and a connector. Women signify a cultural past and future; Indigo must confront history by recognizing Mabel's cries as the cries of history and by understanding that Mabel's womanhood represents Indigo's future as a woman. As for Patria, this moment of recognizing self in "other" is a reaction to violence, for the self must see violence done to a person recognized as self in order to emerge with a new identity. This moment of identification with the victim of violence is a revision of the initiatory moment in Frederick Douglass's slave narrative in which the beaten body of a female slave (his aunt) serves as his "gateway into the hell of slavery."[25] Douglass's initiation depends upon difference, or disassociation, rather than identification. An initiation based upon difference creates the need to individuate from community, whereas identification drives characters to communal identity.

Indigo's moment of recognizing self-in-other expands her self into a symbolic mother who nourishes the spirit of a place, a people, a history, and a collective identity. After Indigo's conversion moment, she apprentices to Aunt Haydee, a midwife, and uses her powers to help women give birth and to heal their spirits. Indigo must assume responsibility for collective mothering and understand her calling. Both Patria and Indigo symbolically embody mothering as the principle of connectivity. Both have to achieve a new understanding of the past, their people, oppression, history, and themselves as incarnations of a people's spirit in order to become fully receptive to spiritual service and understand the purpose of their gifts. Although Indigo does not literally become a mother, she obtains the status of symbolic mother to a community, much like Patria, who, "aptly named for the mother country, trades in her traditional Dominican role as mother to become the symbolic mother of all children persecuted and victimized by the state."[26] In both novels, a woman is called upon to nourish the lives of the people who compose her very identity. Indigo literally goes underground to discover the same connections that bring Patria "down to earth."

Yet while she embodies the universal possibility of mothering, Indigo mothers a specific community of "folks" and comes to link past and future by embodying a mythological figure unique to the African American South. The text claims that Indigo, in helping women in labor and calling forth new lives with her fiddle, invokes the legendary slave figure Blue Sunday. Blue Sunday moved the sea with rage because her master and overseers repeatedly tried to rape her; yet, miraculously, she remained a virgin. Although whipped "before the indigo harvest, . . . no scars, no blood appeared on her back. . . . There was nothing could come between Indigo, Aunt Haydee, & new people of color" (222–23). Indigo is the "harvest" of African American spiritual expression and storytelling. Indigo represents the presence of spiritual art in life, symbolizing with her fiddle the role of the postmodern novel in restoring the integrity of a people. Indigo's choice to remain a virgin implies that although she is a symbolic mother, she is self-sufficient. She enjoys a connection with the divine that supersedes men and contains instead the powers of myth, legend, and story within the human female body. Her symbolic embodiment of the virgin sea goddess and Blue Sunday mirrors Patria's embodiment of the Virgin Mary, a figure miraculously "still a virgin" despite experiences that for others would reveal sexual experience.

With the language of myth, Shange creates an archetypal feminine spirituality, voicing women's inherent spiritual "magic" and signifying that Indigo represents that magic:

> Where there is a woman there is magic. If there is a moon falling from her mouth, she is a woman who knows her magic, who can share or not share her powers. A woman with a moon falling from her mouth, roses between her legs and tiaras of Spanish moss, this woman is a consort of the spirits.
>
> Indigo seldom spoke. There was a moon in her mouth. Having a moon in her mouth kept her laughing. Whenever her mother tried to pull the moss off her head, or clip the roses round her thighs, Indigo was laughing. (3)

Mythical or archetypal "woman" obtains spiritual knowledge through links to earthly rhythms and natural bodies—the sea, the moon, flowers, blood. These aspects of female experience make all women inherently magical. However, like Alvarez, Shange objects to mythologizing her female characters and removing them from the human realm. Thus a woman "can share or not share her powers"; the choice to use spiritual gifts to serve the community denotes Indigo's humanity. Indigo's powers in the novel can heal others, but they can also hurt. Before her conversion experience, in certain incidents she uses her supernatural powers in self-protection and in anger. For instance, she reverses a cockfight, putting razors in men's hands and watching them bleed; she also defends herself against the Geechee captains (a small, young gang) so that she is accepted rather than harmed. This distinction between spiritual knowledge and action based on that knowledge remains important throughout the text. Like *In the Time of the Butterflies*, Shange's novel asserts that the human and spiritual worlds must be bridged or the postmodern novel's spiritual purpose in real people's lives will be thwarted. The archetype of feminine spirituality that these writers create with spiritual characters and mythical novelistic universes must include the everyday world of the human community in its folds.

Sophia, the "Wisdom" of Communal Hope, Faith, and Charity

Like *In the Time of the Butterflies* and *sassafrass, cypress & indigo*, *So Far from God* revolves around the lives of sisters who are simultaneously real women and saints, martyrs, and/or spirits. Real women's experiences such as giving birth, mothering, and working coexist with miracles, visions, and spirits. Castillo creates a storytelling universe that features the mundane along with the sacred. Rather than represent one character who undergoes a spiritual transformation that ultimately leads to social service, Castillo's novel allegorically combines the spiritual values of four daughters, Fe (Faith), Esperanza (Hope), Caridad (Charity, synonymous with Love in Latin), and La Loca (Crazy), into the spiritual leadership of the mother Sophi (Wisdom). As in Shange's novel, we witness the spiritual transformation of a young woman, Caridad, as she becomes a community healer. However, Caridad's spiritual transformation is understated; although she undertakes a spiritual journey and obtains spiritual gifts, she can recall very little of the transformation, and the journey makes little difference to her self-identity. The characters must be understood in relationship to one another. The sisters represent the triad of hope, faith, and charity, traditionally represented as sisters in Western literature. The Bible favors the value of charity, or love, above all: "And now faith, hope, and love abide, these three; and the greatest of these is love. Pursue love and strive for the spiritual gifts, and especially that you may prophesy."[27] However, Castillo revises this triad by positing that wisdom is the greatest spiritual virtue, for Sophi becomes capable of spiritual leadership once her daughters die. Once faith, hope, and charity leave their human forms, the symbolic logic of the novel demonstrates that "Wisdom," in human form, is social activism. Sophi transforms her daughters into communal symbols of oppression, restoring faith, hope, and charity to the New Mexican community.

The mythical structure of the novel asks us to regard the stories of faith, hope, and charity as ultimately embodied in maternal wisdom. The narrator overtly links faith, hope, charity, and wisdom when she discusses Caridad as a *curandera*. Caridad longs for direct knowledge of God so she can understand her spiritual gifts: "Caridad had always been charitable. She had faith and hope. Soon, she would have wisdom from which she had sprung, and sooner still her own healing gifts would be revealed" (56). Although the narrator states that the daughter will obtain wisdom, Caridad dies. Castillo depicts Caridad's death as a return to the female spirit who first created life:

> Tsichtinako was calling! . . . The Acoma people heard it and knew it was the voice of the Invisible One who had nourished the first two humans, who were also both female, although no one had heard it in a long time and some had never heard it before. But all still knew who It was. . . . There were no morbid remains of splintered bodies tossed to the ground, down, down, like bad pottery or glass or old bread. There weren't even whole bodies lying peaceful. There was nothing. / Just the spirit deity Tsichtinako calling loudly with a voice like wind, guiding the two women back, not out toward the sun's rays or up to the clouds but down, deep within the soft, moist dark earth where Esmeralda and Caridad would be safe and live forever. (211)

Caridad's return to the Native American genesis myth suggests that she does not obtain wisdom but that the maternal "origin [wisdom] from which she had sprung" obtains charity, along with the faith, and hope that Caridad holds. Caridad's death signifies her spiritual return to the earth, figured as a womb, "down, deep within the soft, moist dark earth" and thus as a symbol for both her mother (Wisdom) and mother earth. Caridad leaves no traces of her human form, becoming a purely spiritual quality that can return to the womb. Death is a means to "live forever" and reconnect with the feminine creative principle of the land. In her death, she joins mother earth as a symbol for spiritual consciousness, for she has healing and spiritual gifts. Caridad is the last of the hope/faith/charity triad to die, and thus the imagery of return explains that her death returns all the spiritual values she "had" to the mother. Caridad paves the path for Sophi's social activism by returning the values of faith, hope, and charity to the maternal life principle. Toward the end of the novel Sophi bridges spirit and earth by providing spiritual leadership to the community and helping them improve material conditions. She founds a farming co-op, leads a procession that mourns the dead, and founds M.O.M.A.S.—Mothers of Martyrs and Saints.

By revising the Bible's view of hope, faith, and charity and by alluding to a non-Christian genesis myth, Castillo announces that her female characters reconstruct the spiritual community by revising biblical traditions. Though the land is "so far from God" (102), it contains the origin of the Invisible One, an older story that voices an insistent call to women, original creators of earthly life. The land embodies the genesis of the spirit itself in Castillo's text by embodying the oral myths, legends, and stories of the people. Spirit, land, and story come together in the Procession of the Cross, a tradition that Castillo revises by combining stories of the people's oppression with the martyrdom of Christ. Contemporary material conditions of the community become the focus of spiritual ritual:

> No, there had never been no procession like that one before.
>
> When Jesus was condemned to death, the spokesperson for the committee working to protest dumping radioactive waste in the sewer addressed the crowd.
>
> Jesus bore His cross and a man declared that most of the Native and hispano families throughout the land were living below poverty level. . . . Jesus met his mother, and three Navajo women talked about uranium contamination on the reservation, and the babies they gave birth to with brain damage and cancer. . . . The women of Jerusalem consoled Jesus. Children also played in those open disease-ridden canals. . . . Jesus fell a third time. . . . AIDS was a merciless plague indeed. . . . It was the Murder of the Innocents. . . . Jesus was stripped of his garments. . . . ¡Ayyy! Jesus died on the cross. (242–43)

Weaving together the story of Jesus' persecution with the stories of contemporary suffering told by the New Mexican people, the narrative voice depicts the people as martyrs and revises the meaning of the procession. The spiritual and material conditions of the people are an intertwined story; formally, the narrative forges mythical connections between individuals and community, past and contemporary events, political protest and spiritual consciousness. The narrative voice clearly emerges from the community, as an oracle of this spiritual consciousness, sharing the oral patterns of community storytellers and yet representing their stories. The narrative voice constructs Christ as a generalized figure for the oppressed, as if the voice protests from a spiritual plane. The women in the procession mirror the narrative voice. The role of women in the procession is to both protest and console, announcing the relationship between female characters and the postmodern novel as a project of protesting social conditions and consoling the spirit of the ethnic community. The women of the procession protest in the name of their children, displaying that women represent the spiritual and material continuity of a community; they achieve a voice by embracing that role.

Castillo revises the Catholic ritual of the procession by replacing the Virgin Mary with Sophi, a human mother, who carries her own vision of "faith" by carrying a photograph of her daughter Fe. Fe's picture represents collective mourning for and anger toward environmental racism because Fe is essentially murdered by a weapons company that forces her to work with a dangerous chemical. The company gives her neither information nor air circulation, and the investigators blame Fe instead of the company for using an illegal chemical. Fe signals the mother's protest and through the procession becomes a communal symbol of an oppressed land: "No brother was elected to carry a lifesize cross on his naked back. There was no 'Mary' to meet her son. Instead, some, like Sofi, who held a picture of la Fe as a bride, carried photographs of their loved ones who died due to toxic exposure hung around the necks like scapulars; and at each station along their route, the crowd stopped and prayed and people spoke on the so many things that were killing their land and turning the people of those lands into an endangered species" (241–42). The systematic oppression of the land and its people is given spiritual significance by the narrator's use of the Procession of the Cross to mark the daughters' deaths. With her human connection to "faith," Sophi embodies the principle of connectivity between spiritual and material conditions, signaling revision of Catholic divisions between spirit and flesh. By replacing Mary much as Patria does in her community, the mother of the oppressed constructs her daughters as communal Christ figures, demonstrating that women give birth to the community's connection to the divine and that the maternal principle restores hope, faith, and charity to the people.

Sophi's construction of her daughters' deaths as collective spiritual concerns stands for the novel's project to give characters' spiritual concerns communal significance. Mirroring Indigo's embodiment of "the folks" and slaves through her connection to folklore and African American art, Sophi embodies a collective story of past oppression, through her children, and future hope, given her expressions of protest and spiritual leadership. The daughters' deaths become collective deaths in that each death represents an affliction common to the oppressed New Mexican community and is thus memorialized by the procession. Fe dies from environmental toxins; Esperanza dies during the Persian Gulf War, which she covers as a journalist; Caridad, when young, suffers a brutal attack that the police ignore because of her racial and economic status; and Sophi's youngest daughter La Loca is pronounced dead at three years old, the result of a misdiagnosed medical condition, but miraculously revives and then later dies from AIDS as a young woman. Sophi transforms the meaning of her daughters' deaths from personal grief to social activism, learning the social lessons they teach. From La Loca Sophi learns the value of social change on the domestic front, for La Loca heals "her sisters from the traumas and injustices they were dealt by society" (27). From Esperanza Sophi learns to question "the system" as the force that keeps people oppressed. Esperanza's injunctions to her mother to change "the system" do not make sense to Sophi until after her daughters' deaths, when she thinks about what Esperanza meant.

When Sophi carries a picture of Fe in the procession, she voices the spiritual principle of the novel—that faith will transform the community but only if it can be revised to accommodate the needs of the community. As Roland Walter argues, faith in *So Far from God* "facilitates a dynamic relationship between human beings and their surroundings and an implicit magico-realist conception of the world. . . . This peculiar type of faith, which is revised and actualized through female 'agency,' is the driving force behind the collective activism and implicit alternative mode of living and relating outlined in the novel; a counterhegemonic mode conceived as possible solution to the postmodern fragmentation and dislocation experienced in the borderlands."[28] Castillo's revision of spiritual focus directly responds to the white male postmodern novel; not only does she revise traditional Catholic tenets, but she answers postmodern writers who assert the impossibility of finding meaning in the social world. Ironically, both the secularist bias of white male postmodern novelists and the spiritual bias of Catholicism foreclose the possibility for social transformation, always based upon ideals.

Like *In the Time of the Butterflies* and *sassafrass, cypress & indigo*, *So Far from God* uses women to critique patriarchal assumptions reflected by church fathers. Sophi confronts Father Jerome when he suspects that La Loca's resurrection is the devil's doing. In defense of her child, she challenges him: "Don't you dare start this about my baby! If our Lord in His heaven has sent my child back to me, don't you dare start this backward thinking against her; the devil doesn't produce miracles! And this is a miracle, an answer to the prayers of a brokenhearted mother" (23). In fact, she calls him a *pendejo* ("asshole"). The maternal voice is thus opposed to the paternal church voice. The maternal voice can express rage at indignity, even protesting against a church father. Although Sophi claims the resurrection to be an answer to her prayers, she has not been praying as much as questioning God himself, much as Patria questions God after her husband and son are arrested. Passive acceptance of God's will and of church fathers is antithetical to the spiritual values of the postmodern novel; the social consciousness of these novels requires that each woman's relationship to the spiritual realm be unmediated by the church.

Repeatedly, the female characters in the text question institutional dogma and find meaningful spirituality outside institutions. Not only do La Loca, Esperanza (deceased), and Caridad have direct relationships with the spirits, but Caridad's spiritual guide Dona Felicia claims that true faith, the most important component of a healer, is "based not on an institution but on the bits and pieces of the souls and knowledge of the wise teachers that she met along the way" (60). La Loca refuses to go to mass, and when Father Jerome threatens her with hell she tells her own story of having been to hell. She thus rejects the church's attempts to use hell as a threat and exert power over the people, relying on her own experience of hell rather than on Scripture. While drawing upon biblical images and rituals, the novel asserts that the meaning of spiritual stories must be interpreted by the people of a community. Moving away from a monastic vision of God toward a recognition of a broader spiritual community that includes Native American gods and Mexican legends, the novel argues for expanding the spiritual realm to encompass the diversity of the New Mexican community, particularly including female deities. La Loca, although she never leaves home, has more spiritual knowledge than Father Jerome, for all sorts of female spirits visit her. On her deathbed she reflects on the expansive sense of self one can achieve through opening the self to spiritual pantheism. She has experienced faraway places through the spirits' stories and songs while never leaving home: "[F]or a person who had lived her whole life within a mile radius of her home and had only traveled as far as Albuquerque twice, she certainly knew quite a bit about this world, not to mention beyond, too, and that made her smile as she closed her eyes" (245).

Visions of the spirit world must reflect the material experiences of the community, Castillo's novel asserts. The novel speaks for the need to revise spiritual myths through Sophi, who revises the Mexican myth of La Llorona, which she feels to be disjunctive with real women's experience:

> The land was old and the stories were older. Just like a country changed its name, so did the names of their legends change. Once, La Llorona may have been Matlaciuatl, the goddess of the Mexica who was said to prey upon men like a vampire! Or she might have been Ciuapipiltin, the goddess in flowing robes who stole babies from their cradles and left in their place an obsidian blade, or Cihuacoatl, the patron of women who died in childbirth, who all wailed and wept and moaned in the night air. These women descended to earth on certain days which were dedicated to them to appear at crossroads, and they were fatal to children.
>
> Her mother's mother had been from old Mexico and Sofi knew a little about the antiquity of this tale, but mostly she just knew what her father had told her, that La Llorona was a bad woman who had left her husband and home, drowned her babies to run off and have a sinful life, and God punished her for eternity, and she refused to repeat this nightmare to her daughters.
>
> Sofia had not left her children, much less drowned them to run off with nobody. On the contrary, she had been left to raise them by herself. And all her life, there had always been at least one woman around like her, left alone, abandoned, divorced, or widowed, to raise her children, and none of them had ever tried to kill their babies. (161)

Not only does Sophi revise the myth, but the narrative voice acts as her guiding spirit by suggesting other possibilities of the figure of La Llorona. Sophi compares the mythological figure to reality, and the narrator compares the mythological figure to spiritual goddesses who share a storytelling origin older than the land itself. Domino Renee Perez argues that Sophi's revision reflects the text's feminist agenda; each character's life parallels La Llorona's troubles in some way, but the myth is revised by "privileging female spirituality and subverting patriarchal Christian views of the weeping

woman."[29] The influence of feminist theology—its search for prepatriarchal goddesses—is also apparent. New stories of experience replace old ones
in postmodern interpretations of patriarchal religions. Mirroring Sophi's
revision of stories with the narrator's larger project to revise and subvert
Catholic stories, Castillo's novel asserts the philosophy that stories both
transform communal experience and change with the experiences of the
community.

Sophi's revision of La Llorona is thus a microcosm of the text's enterprise to change the myths and spirits of the land, mirrored by the procession's transformation of oppression into stories of protest and social change.
Communal experience is central to this process of revision because Castillo seeks a means by which her community of readers can connect its material conditions with a spiritual identity. Because the female experience of
motherhood is a crucial link between individuals and community, the narrator argues for expanding the spiritual world to include female deities; she
presumes that La Llorona is in fact a prepatriarchal female deity, whose
dwindled power and patriarchal use reflects the degradation of women and
the need to reclaim feminine spirituality: "Who better but La Llorona could
the spirit of Esperanza have found, come to think of it, if not a woman
who had been given a bad rap by every generation of her people since the
beginning of time and yet, to Esperanza's spirit-mind, La Llorona in the beginning (before men got in the way of it all) may have been nothing short
of a loving mother goddess" (162–63). Castillo thus evinces a common
feminist attraction to the idea of maternal goddesses and female deities
that originate in prepatriarchal history. In this passage the principle of a
maternal deity connects communities cross-culturally, since the maternal
deity predates historical time, suggesting that mothering as a bridge between spirit and flesh could be a universal connecting principle as well as
a means to make a specific ethnic community cohere. Castillo's attraction to a maternal goddess who both predates God and bridges divine and
earthly worlds is evident in her naming of Sophi. Wisdom, in the Bible, is
thought to be a vestige of an older goddess figure. She claims, in Proverbs 8,
to be present from the beginning of the Lord's work, "before the beginning
of the earth."[30] She is thus an originator of all being and claims throughout Proverbs to be instrumental to creation. Interpreting and alluding to
the Bible in her own way, while expanding the novel's spiritual community
to include Native American and Mexican folk legends, Castillo implicitly
proclaims that stories contain ideological power. Institutions that mediate
the meaning of spiritual myths separate rather than unite the ethnic com-

munity, while the postmodern ethnic novel redeems by inviting the spirits into the human world and, conversely, inviting human experience into the divine.

THE CONVERSION OF THE READER

The philosophy of these three postmodern novels is that a spiritual consciousness both *reflects* and *creates* a social consciousness. These writers ground spirituality in communal experience and yet suggest that the experience of the community is defined by, and thus can be transformed by, stories of the spiritual realm. While these novelists critique the limitations of Catholicism and Anglo-Protestantism, they reinvoke the central narrative of the Bible, believing in an inherent feminine spirituality that remains from pre-Fall times (prepatriarchal worship of goddesses and nature) and in a central plot toward redemption, after which the people will be saved. Through thematizing and formalizing communal spirituality, these novelists seek to change the future by healing the unseen wounds of the past and restoring the integrity of communal culture, which spiritual figures define, model, symbolize, and concretize.

Ultimately, spiritual characters model the conversion of the reader, who experiences transformation into spiritual consciousness with the character. Hence, postmodern ethnic women writers find the humanity of their characters as important as their connection to the spirit world. These novelists deify women's experiences by using mythical language to include *all* women in the spiritual realm. But they do not mythologize female characters and separate them from the human world of the reader. The use of spiritual connections, in all these novels, is a choice. The women of these novels are kept human by making choices and debating the effects of those choices. Just as Shange's Indigo can choose to "share or not share her powers" (3), Castillo's Caridad reveals that she is a true healer when she distinguishes spiritual knowledge from spiritual action; knowing and preventing the future, Dona Felicia asserts, embody "two important aspects of the laws of the universe" (54–55). As Alvarez puts it in her "Postscript" to *Butterflies*, characters are part of the reader's human community so that they mirror "us, ordinary men and women" (324).

Everyday women's experiences and the mythical, archetypal aspects of female experience exist side by side in the novel that features supernatural presence. The narrative technique of Alvarez, Shange, and Castillo invites readers to imagine women, women's bodies, women's labor, women's experiences, and women's communal role as spiritually powerful and insightful, as starting places for individual and social transformation. However, unique blends of myth and real voices or characters in these novels both elevate female characters and keep them real. Alvarez's butterflies are national and spiritual myths, but their voices feel real and human. Patria is Mary, even Christ, but also a woman who fears for her son and who will say what she must to save her husband and sisters. Indigo, though a woman who knows her magic, is also a young girl who has to negotiate with her mother to get a half cup of coffee on Christmas. Sophi, though solemnly heading the Procession of the Cross at one point in the novel, is also lending her sewing machine to a neighbor at another point. The female characters have both significant and mundane thoughts and experiences, and their conversations with each other make them real characters, distinct and unique rather than ethereal.

To capture the subjective experience of human characters, all of these novelists use multivoiced narration, refusing the isolation of the traditional narrator who views an empirical reality from above. Their novels critique Western, novelistic realism to heal divisions that traditional Western thought has engendered: divisions between flesh and spirit, science and experience, reason and intuition, mind and body, individuals and nature, humanity and God, and individual and community. Alvarez argues that the multivoiced quality of her novel reflects the ways women structure their lives, an alternative to the male plot of working toward a trajectory or solitary voyage.[31] Shange articulates the very same description of *sassafrass's* structure, saying that the plot "undulates," rather than moves forward, "with the flow of rivers and streams and tides and lakes."[32] Shange's narrator freely launches into mythical lyricism to provide insight into a scene, reflecting a multivoiced narrative discourse. Castillo's narrator is like an oral storyteller, rejecting linear narrative time and promising that she will connect everything "later." Sharing storytelling patterns of the community she depicts, the narrator emerges as a communal voice and has the authority to invite the human reader into its community. As Maria-Elena Angula explains, the magic realism form encourages the reader to accept the explanation of a transcendental reality and participate in the novel's spiritual community.[33] These novelists use multivoiced narration to mirror a pantheistic philosophy of spiritual reality.

To convert the reader, the narrative voice models the idea of a spiritual consciousness that redeems by rendering the past, present, and future of a people with vision and imagination. The past in these novels is composed of both a historical and a literary past, each defining and redefining the meaning of the other. For example, the Afro-Caribbean and Latin American roots of Shange's magic realism have been thoroughly traced by Jose David Saldivar, and Shange herself informed an interviewer that Indigo was a response to Garcia Marquez's character Remedios in *One Hundred Years of Solitude*.[34] However, a rich tradition of spiritual presence also exists in African American women's texts. Spirituality, Anne Dalke suggests, became a means for black women to distance themselves from oppressive conditions and write against the limitations of realism and naturalism, in which characters often lack agency.[35] Shange, Alvarez, and Castillo seek to redefine the postmodern novel by employing its self-reflexive allusions to literary traditions to reconstruct and imagine possibilities for the community rather than to demonstrate themes of existential alienation. Thus, we could say, the spirituality of the postmodern ethnic novel is a model of the Word made flesh. It strikes a relationship between the realm of the sacred and the reader's environment within which sacred literature dwells.

NOTES

1. Quoted in John A. McClure, "Postmodern/Post-Secular: Contemporary Fiction and Spirituality," *Modern Fiction Studies* 41, no. 1 (1995): 141.

2. J. A. Cuddon, *The Penguin Dictionary of Literary Terms and Literary Theory* (New York: Penguin Books, 1991), 734.

3. Julia Alvarez, *In the Time of the Butterflies* (New York: Penguin Books, 1994). Subsequent page citations will be given parenthetically in the text.

4. Ntozake Shange, *sassafrass, cypress & indigo* (New York: St. Martin's Press, 1982). Subsequent page citations will be given parenthetically in the text.

5. Ana Castillo, *So Far from God* (New York: Penguin Books, 1994). Subsequent page citations will be given parenthetically in the text.

6. Carol Marsh-Lockett, "A Woman's Art, a Woman's Craft: The Self in Ntozake Shange's *sassafrass, cypress & indigo*," in *Arms Akimbo: Africana Women in Contemporary Literature*, ed. Janice Lee Liddell and Yakini Belinda Kemp (Gainesville: University Press of Florida, 1999), 48.

7. Theologians describe spirituality as "personal communion with God" and the indwelling of the Holy Spirit in each individual; the "interior aspects of religious life"; and "the essence of religious phenomena for it is concerned with the nature and content of the relationship between an individual and God." See C. P. M. Jones, "Liturgy and Personal Devotion," in *The Study of Spirituality*, ed. Cheslyn Jones, Geoffrey Wainwright, and Edward Yarnold, S.J. (New York: Oxford

University Press, 1986), 4, 5–6; Margaret Chatterjee, *The Concept of Spirituality* (New Delhi: Allied Publishers, 1987), 3, 13; and Anthony Russell, "Sociology and the Study of Spirituality," in Jones et al., *The Study of Spirituality*, 34.

8. Carol Ochs, *Women and Spirituality* (Totowa, N.J.: Rowman and Allanheld, 1983).

9. Ibid., x.

10. Kristina Groover, *The Wilderness Within: American Women Writers and Spiritual Quest* (Fayetteville: University of Arkansas Press, 1999); Ursula King, *Women and Spirituality: Voices of Protest and Promise* (New York: New Amsterdam, 1989).

11. Groover, *The Wilderness Within*, 10.

12. Ochs, *Women and Spirituality*, 10.

13. David Ray Griffin, "Introduction: Postmodern Spirituality and Society," in *Spirituality and Society: Postmodern Visions*, ed. David Ray Griffin (Albany: State University of New York, 1988), 1.

14. Chatterjee, *The Concept of Spirituality*, 84.

15. Susan Bordo, *Unbearable Weight: Feminism, Western Culture, and the Body* (Berkeley: University of California Press, 1993), 5.

16. While early Christian ideology defined spirituality as how one lived one's life "according to the spirit of God," and while Christ himself placed great importance on the body and on body-service like healing and feeding, by the twelfth century "spiritualitas should be contrasted with materialitas, and later, with corporeality." Chatterjee, *The Concept of Spirituality*, 11.

17. Griffin, "Introduction," 4.

18. Sherry Ortner, "Is Female to Male as Nature Is to Culture?" in *Making Gender: The Politics and Erotics of Culture* (Boston: Beacon Press, 1996), 21–42.

19. Griffin, "Introduction," 14.

20. Bados Ciria, "*In the Time of the Butterflies* by Julia Alvarez: History, Fiction, Testimonio and the Domican Republic," *Monographic Review* 13 (1997): 412.

21. Elizabeth Conrod Martinez, "Recovering a Space for a History between Imperialism and Patriarchy: Julia Alvarez's *In the Time of the Butterflies*," *Thamyris* 5, no. 2 (1998): 265.

22. The three sisters embody the three fates Atropos, Clotho, and Lachesis in their roles as weavers, a metaphor for creation and life (Marsh-Lockett, "A Woman's Art," 48); they stand for the Greek figures Persephone (Sassafrass), Aphrodite (Cypress), and Artemis (Indigo), according to Jean Strandness, "Reclaiming Women's Language, Imagery, and Experience: Ntozake Shange's *sassafrass, cypress & indigo*," *Journal of American Culture* 10, no. 3 (1987): 11–17; the sisters also embody allegorical names of trees that have healing properties, thus reflecting the Tree of Life in Creole mythology of Voudoun—the Tree linking the mortal with the immortal (Strandness, "Reclaiming Women's Language," 12). Yet in addition to classical figures they also embody the spirits of slaves, African gods and goddesses, and the Voodoo goddess Oshun (the triple goddess, divided into Sassafrass as Wrath, Cypress as Generous Love, and Indigo as Virginity) (Strandness, "Reclaiming Women's Language," 16).

23. W. E. B. DuBois, *The Souls of Black Folk: Authoritative Text, Contexts, Criticism*, ed. Henry Louis Gates, Jr., and Terri Hume Oliver (New York: Norton, 1999).

24. Janice Crosby, *Cauldron of Changes: Feminist Spirituality in Fantastic Fiction* (Jefferson, N.C.: McFarland, 2000), 148.

25. Frederick Douglass, *Narrative of the Life of Frederick Douglass, an American Slave: Written by Himself,* ed. Houston A. Baker, Jr. (New York: Penguin Books, 1982).

26. Ibis GomezVega, "Metaphors of Entrapment: Caribbean Women Writers Face the Wreckage of History," *Journal of Political and Military Sociology* 25 (1997): 243.

27. 1 Corinthians 13:13, 14:1, *The New Oxford Annotated Bible with the Apocrypha,* ed. Bruce M. Metzger and Roland Murphy (New York: Oxford University Press, 1991).

28. Roland Walter, "Cultural Politics of Dislocation and Relocation," *MELUS* 23, no. 1 (1998): 89.

29. Domino Renee Perez, "Crossing Mythological Borders: Revisioning La Llorona in Contemporary Fiction," *Proteus* 16, no. 1 (1999): 51.

30. Proverbs 8:23, *New Oxford Annotated Bible.*

31. Bonnie Lyons and Bill Oliver, "A Clean Windshield," in *Passion and Craft: Conversations with Notable Writers* (Urbana: University of Illinois Press, 1998), 132.

32. Brenda Lyons, "Interview with Ntozake Shange," *Massachusetts Review* 28, no. 4 (1987): 691.

33. Maria-Elena Angula, *Magic Realism: Social Context and Discourse* (New York: Garland Publishing, 1995), 16.

34. Jose David Saldivar, "The Real and the Marvelous in Charleston, South Carolina: Ntozake Shange's *sassafrass, cypress & indigo,*" in *Genealogy and Literature,* ed. Lee Quinby (Minneapolis: University of Minnesota Press, 1995), 184.

35. Anne Dalke, "Spirit Matters: Re-Possessing the African-American Women's Literary Tradition," *Legacy* 12, no. 1 (1995): 1–2.

11 FACES OF THE VIRGIN IN SANDRA CISNEROS'S *WOMAN HOLLERING CREEK*

JACQUELINE DOYLE

> My *Virgen de Guadalupe* is not the mother of God. She is
> God. She is a face for a god without a face, an *indígena* for
> a god without ethnicity, a female deity for a god who is
> genderless, but I also understand that for her to approach
> me, for me to finally open the door and accept her, she had
> to be a woman like me.
>
> Sandra Cisneros,
> "Guadalupe the Sex Goddess"

"She is one of the few female figures to have attained the status of a myth," writes Marina Warner of the Virgin Mary, "—a myth that for nearly two thousand years has coursed through our culture, as spirited and often as imperceptible as an underground stream."[1] In *Alone of All Her Sex,* Warner substantially reconsiders the myth and cult of the Virgin as it is implicated in patriarchal theology and patriarchal institutions. Building on Warner, Julia Kristeva sees in the Virgin a locus both for "women's wishes for identification" and for those who "keep watch over the symbolic and social order," diagnosing "feminine paranoia" and repudiation of other women in the "virginal maternal."[2] Even Mary Daly, who famously recuperated the "Mary symbol" in *Beyond God the Father* as a

256

powerful expression of female autonomy and "women's becoming," later dismissed her as a mere "aftershadow" of earlier female deities: "Dutifully dull and derivative, drained of divinity, she merits the reward of perpetual paralysis in patriarchal paradise."[3]

Yet Eurocentric feminist assumptions concerning "our culture" and "woman's experience" may obscure some of the Virgin's most "spirited" manifestations in contemporary feminist literature. In both the Old World and the New, apparitions and representations of the Virgin in different countries, in different regions, and at different points in history have taken on a range of political, national, ethnic, class, and gender identifications that significantly alter their meanings. Marian apparitions the world over, observe Victor and Edith Turner, have persistently been associated with the poor, the marginalized, and the colonized.[4] In Hormigueros, Puerto Rico, devotees still ascend on their knees to the hilltop sanctuary of the black *Virgen de Monserrata,* who appeared "floating above a treetop" back in Spanish colonial times. "Being a woman and black," writes Judith Ortiz Cofer, "made Our Lady the perfect depository for the hopes and prayers of the sick, the weak and the powerless."[5] The Spanish possession of Manila in 1571 coincided with a miraculous apparition of the Virgin in a *pandam* tree. Today in the Philippines a black Virgin is said to appear amidst the devastation after typhoons, "seeking to comfort those who cannot be comforted."[6] When Ezili appeared in the image of the Virgin in the branches of a palm tree to a crowd of Haitian worshippers outside Ville-Bonheur, she was visible to all but the white Catholic priest.[7] In Haiti, the Virgin, as the *Mater salvatoris, Maria dolorosa del Monte Calvario,* the *Virgin de los dolores,* is syncretized with the shifting personae of Ezili, Vodou goddess of love—and in Cuba and Puerto Rico, she is syncretized with the Yoruba-derived *orisha* Yemaya. The *Virgen de la Caridad del Cobre,* who appeared to Cubans under Spanish colonial rule in 1604, syncretizes aboriginal, European, and African deities, who themselves derive from multiple sources. The dark-skinned *Virgen's* nickname *la Virgen mulata* emphasizes her hybridity.[8] Implicit in religious syncretism, observes Jacques Lafaye, is the "notion of challenge," whereby the "substitutions and reinterpretations of beliefs borrowed from the dominant culture by the dominated culture in the last analysis represent efforts at salvaging the latter."[9]

In Tepeyac, Mexico, the apparition of the brown-skinned Virgin of Guadalupe in 1531 to the peasant Juan Diego prompted unprecedented numbers of Mexican Indians to convert to Spanish Catholicism. In the well-known image left on Juan Diego's cloak, now exhibited over the altar at La Basílica de Nuestra Señora de Guadalupe, *la Morenita* (the Dark One) stands on a black crescent moon, surrounded by a spiky halo of golden light, clothed in rose-colored robes, a sash signifying her pregnancy, and a midnight-blue mantle strewn with stars. Her shrine, built on the site of her apparition, reconsecrates a former temple to the Aztec mother goddess To-nantzín, a deity who also manifests herself under many names and guises.[10] The "multi-iconicity" of Guadalupe's shifting Christian and pre-Christian identities locates her somewhere between the intercessor sanctioned by the church and the deity beloved of the people.[11] Gloria Anzaldúa calls her "the single most potent religious, political and cultural image of the Chicano/ *mexicano*," "more venerated than Jesus or God the Father."[12] At once the "chaste protective mother" of the church's teachings and the "poor people's agent" and front-line "guerrilla fighter," *la Guadalupana* on both sides of the border functions as a symbol of ethnic identity and women's spirituality.[13] "Beloved by Indians, creoles, mestizos, blacks, and mulattoes, all those who identified with the color of her skin," Margaret Randall observes, *la Virgen de Guadalupe* over the centuries has become as well "a highly visible icon for women whose own lives are too often invisible or shamed."[14]

In *Weaving the Visions: New Patterns in Feminist Spirituality*, Judith Plaskow and Carol P. Christ point out that "different experiences of op-pression, and also a diversity of positive religious, racial, ethnic, national and cultural identities that shape our lives as women," function in very spe-cific and particular ways as feminist spiritual resources that provide "knowl-edge, strength, and possible visions for social change."[15] Thus, while Warner ultimately reads the Virgin as a patriarchal construct "likely," under the "new circumstances of sexual equality," to "recede into legend,"[16] the re-readings of the Virgin in the work of Sandra Cisneros and her contempo-raries are charged with very different historical and cultural energies, en-ergies that challenge not only traditional religious doctrines but also Anglo feminist assumptions, energies directed in specific ways toward "possible visions for social change."

"I see the spiritual and political in some ways being the same thing," Cis-neros explained in an interview.[17] Throughout the stories in *Woman Holler-ing Creek and Other Stories*, Cisneros rewrites cultural myths central to Mexi-can American female identity in order to redefine the possibilities available to her diverse array of female characters: Patricia Chávez, an unrepentant runaway from Our Lady of Sorrows High School. Cleófilas Sánchez, a bat-tered wife who flees across the border. "One of those Mexican saints, I guess," says the woman who helps her, "A martyr or something."[18] Michele, uneasy captive at a Mexican church where her grandmother prays endlessly to *la Virgen de Guadalupe*. "If I stare at the eyes of the saints long enough," she tells us, "they move and wink at me, which makes me a sort of saint too."[19] Rosario De Leon, who leaves her braid in the church as a *milagrito* for *la Virgen de Guadalupe*. Clemencia, a painter who plots revenge on her married lover and his wife, lighting candles to the Virgin and the saints. Guadalupe Arredondo, who parodically invokes the Catholic prayer to her namesake as she sighs over an all too brief love affair: "Who knows why the universe singled me out. Lupe Arredondo, stupid art thou amongst all women."[20]

The Virgin of Guadalupe has always taken on significance from the communities she has nourished; she has accrued vital significance for contemporary Chicana writers within the community of women. "*La Diosa*'s face is resurrected in all the faces of all the mothers, of all the young women and children of our *gente*," writes Luis J. Rodriguez.[21] Cisneros explores the many faces of the Virgin in the stories in *Woman Hollering Creek*, particularly in "Mericans" and "Little Miracles, Kept Promises," re-creating *la Madrecita* in dynamic relation to a series of "real women," the kind that Cisneros's Lupe says she can't find in the books or magazines or *telenovelas*.[22] "If we don't help her, who will?" says Graciela to her *comadre* Felice as they plot to free the pregnant Cleófilas from her abusive husband. It is only through the feminine intercession of such *comadres* that the motherless Cleófilas can undergo her spiritual transformation from suffering to grace.[23]

I

It is through the particular suffering evoked by the Virgin that the
basis for women's chastity is generated. It is suffering, explicitly expressed
in a form of self-sacrifice, which serves to transcend sexuality and becomes
the mark of motherhood. Thus suffering becomes a virtue, and women are
its victims.

Marit Melhuus,
"Power, Value and the Ambiguous Meanings of Gender"

In one of Frida Kahlo's most haunting self-portraits, a full-grown woman emerges in a pool of blood from the spread legs of a woman in labor, whose upper torso and head are shrouded by a white sheet. The doleful face of the *Mater Dolorosa*, bristling with daggers,[24] looks on from a painting above the bed, its centrality emphasized by the diagonal lines of the floorboards, the bed, and the woman's lower legs. It is clear from Kahlo's comments on "My Birth" that she identified herself both with the hidden mother and with the child, whose face resembles her own. There are no visible attendants to the birth. Both the child and the mother appear to be dead. Kahlo explained that the Virgin was a "memory image" of her own mother's bedroom, not meant to be "symbolic,"[25] but *Nuestra Señora de los Dolores* (Our Lady of Sorrows) appropriately oversees this domestic scene of female suffering. The single vertical axis formed by the heads of the three women may suggest their unity in suffering, or it may suggest that the stillbirth was produced by this Catholic icon of long-suffering motherhood, whose countenance appears to replace the faceless mother's. Hayden Herrera points out that the blank scroll extending the full length of the bottom of the painting places "My Birth" in the popular Mexican folk tradition of *retablos*, or "votive paintings" to the Virgin and the saints. Here, however, no miraculous intervention by the Virgin is described on the scroll, and no thanks are given.[26] Within the silence of this broken connection between the Virgin Mother and her daughters, this deliberate erasure of the message expected on the scroll, *la Virgen* seems to reign as a cultural sign of the female artist's failed self-birth.

This broken connection continues to haunt contemporary Chicana artists and writers, engaged in what Sandra Cisneros calls the "trauma" of "'reinventing ourselves,' revising ourselves." Part of the difficulty, she remarked in an interview in 1988, is "our religion, because there's so much guilt. . . . Mexican religion is half western and half pagan; European Catholicism and Precolumbian religion all mixed in. It's a very strange Catholicism like nowhere else on the planet." The figure of the Virgin, so central to Mexican Catholicism, poses particular problems for feminists who, like Cisneros, have felt they "could not inherit [their] culture intact without revising some parts of it."[27] In *Loving in the War Years* Cherríe Moraga describes how she was moved to tears by the devotion of the Mexican women at the Basilica of *la Virgen de Guadalupe* in Mexico, "knowing how for so many years I had closed my heart to the passionate pull of such faith that promised no end to pain." Yet she also shudders at the price of this pain as she watches the female pilgrims crawl on their hands and knees to the Virgin's shrine. When, she wonders, will those "dusty knees begin/to crack," when will the "red blood of the women" begin to stain the road? At her grandmother's deathbed, Moraga moves to free herself from the doleful stare of *Nuestra Señora de los Dolores*. "Stop the chain of events. La procesión de mujeres, sufriendo. Dolores my grandmother, Dolores her daughter, Dolores her daughter's daughter. Free the daughter to love her own daughter."[28]

Chayo, in Cisneros's story "Little Miracles, Kept Promises," must look beyond "all that self-sacrifice, all that silent suffering," to achieve her own freedom through a new vision of the Virgin. For years she blamed her for "all the pain my mother and her mother and all our mother's mothers have put up with in the name of God." "For a long time," Chayo tells *la Virgencita*, "I wouldn't let you in my house. . . . Couldn't let you in my house."[29] Cisneros has explained that she also once thought "that writing was a way to exorcise those ghosts that inhabit the house that is ourselves." Chayo finds what Plaskow and Christ term "positive identities" in her reconstitution of *la Virgen de Guadalupe*, and a powerful reconnection to her mother, her grandmother, her Catholic and Indian heritages, her own spirituality. "The big ghosts still live inside you, . . . and you make your peace with those ghosts," concludes Cisneros.[30] Writing thus becomes an act of recognition and exploration rather than an act of exorcism, a speaking in multiple mother tongues rather than a severance from the mother.

The issue of "redefining myself or controlling my own destiny or my own sexuality," Cisneros said in 1988, is the "ghost I'm still wrestling with."[31] In *Woman Hollering Creek and Other Stories*, Cisneros joins the larger community of *comadres* engaged in liberating women from oppressive symbols, in cultural revision, self-invention, and the creation of new myths. "I write the myths in me, the myths I am, the myths I want to become," explains Anzaldúa. In *Borderlands/La Frontera* she claims the freedom to overstep laws, institutions, territories, and borders, to "claim my space, making a new culture—*una cultura mestiza*—with . . . my own feminist architecture." The new *mestiza* inhabits multiple borderlands— an "actual physical borderland" between the United States and Mexico, and also "psychological borderlands," "sexual borderlands," and "spiritual borderlands . . . not particular to the Southwest."[32] In the multiple contradictions and crossings of these shifting terrains, Anzaldúa discerns an emerging new *mestiza* consciousness and the birth of a new culture: "I am cultureless because, as a feminist, I challenge the collective cultural/ religious male-derived beliefs of Indo-Hispanics and Anglos; yet I am cultured because I am participating in the creation of yet another culture, a new story to explain the world and our participation in it, a new value system with images and symbols that connect us to each other and to the planet."[33] *Borderlands/La Frontera* closes with a vision of the rebirth of *la Raza* and opens with a prayer to *la Virgen de Guadalupe*, "our spiritual, political, and psychological symbol," a figure central to the *mestiza's* "new story" and self-birth.[34]

When Ana Castillo dedicates her anthology of contemporary responses to the Virgin of Guadalupe to the "Goddess of the Americas," "who has never abandoned us," she explicitly acknowledges a broken and renewed connection to the Virgin Mother: "Mother, we have returned / Forgive our absence, neglect, / and ingratitude please."[35] Cisneros offers her stories in *Woman Hollering Creek* as a tribute to *la Virgen* and *nuestra gente* ("our people"). "*Virgen de Guadalupe Tonantzín,*" she writes in her acknowledgments, combining her with the Aztec deity formerly worshipped at Tepeyac, "*infinitas gracias. Estos cuentitos te los ofrezco a tí, a nuestra gente. A toditos. Mil gracias.* A thousand thanks from *el corazón.*"

II

Call Her the first mestiza, the original Chicana. And because she crosses so many borders—walls erected and kept in place by American nativists and Mexican nationalists who refuse to see we already live in a borderless time—call Her the Undocumented Virgin.

Rubén Martínez,
"The Undocumented Virgin"

In *Borderlands/La Frontera,* Anzaldúa voices the urgent necessity to "reinterpret history," to break with "all oppressive traditions of all cultures and religions," and to "shape new myths." The "first step" for the new *mestiza* is "to take inventory": "Just what did she inherit from her ancestors? This weight on her back—which is the baggage from the Indian mother, which is the baggage from the Spanish father, which the baggage from the Anglo?"[36]

Visions of the Virgin, in Mexico and elsewhere, have always been highly charged with nationalist and political energies and with shifting ethnic, class, and gender identifications. Victor and Edith Turner, who are particularly attentive to the "multivocality" and "polysemy" of religious icons, uncover a "populist, anarchical, even anticlerical" element in the underground stream nourishing Marian apparitions and pilgrimages. Symbols of the Virgin "take on life of their own" within complex fields of signification: "New significance may . . . be generated as devotees associate the particularized personalized image with their own hopes and sorrows as members of a particular community with a specific history. . . . The 'new' signified may not in fact be historically new, but may represent a resurgence of archaic ideas and beliefs. It is . . . the creation of a semantic arena in which a multiplicity of signifieds—original, new, archaic—are for a time in conflict."[37] The figure of the Virgin of Guadalupe stands at just such a critical crossroads within Mexican and Mexican American Catholic culture—central and marginal, oppressive and liberating, baggage from the colonizers and yet pre- and postcolonial in her aspects. "It is she who integrates the folk and mainstream cultures of Mexico," writes Ena Campbell, "It is the Virgin of Guadalupe who expresses the sociopolitical uniqueness of the entire Mexican population."[38]

In Cisneros's short story "Mericans," the young girl Michele/Micaela waits outside the Mexican national shrine to *la Virgen de Guadalupe* with her brothers while her "awful grandmother" offers endless prayers for all those in the family who "never attend mass." "It doesn't matter," Michele tells us, "Like La Virgen de Guadalupe, the awful grandmother intercedes on their behalf."[39] *La Virgen* eclipses Christ inside the church, where Michele sees "la Virgen de Guadalupe on the main altar because she's a big miracle," and "the crooked crucifix," damaged but not destroyed by a bomb, "on a side altar because that's a little miracle" (18). Outside, "women with black shawls" are crawling to the church on their knees, "crossing and uncrossing themselves," while Michele resists and debates competing gender definitions with her brothers, who assign her subordinate roles in their games and use *"girl"* as their "favorite insult now instead of 'sissy'" (18).

Mexican, Mexican American, and American cultures cross and uncross here as well. Inside the church their Mexican grandmother "knits the names of the dead and the living into one long prayer fringed with the grandchildren born in that barbaric country with its barbarian ways" (19). Outside the church American tourists give white Chiclets to Junior, mistaking him for a native Mexican whose photo will serve as souvenir of their trip.

> "But you speak English!"
> "Yeah," my brother says, "we're Mericans."
> We're Mericans, we're Mericans, and inside the awful grandmother prays. (20)

The word *Mericans* contains a cross-cultural self-definition, an "r" substituted for the "x" crossing borders, the "awful" Mexican grandmother "inside" inspiring awe and possibly shame as well. Michele's brother Keeks reinscribes cultural stereotypes of the Indian when he wants Michele to play Tonto to his Lone Ranger. To the grandmother all Americans are "barbarians." Even Michele observes that the tourists are dressed inappropriately. "Ladies don't come to church dressed in pants," she tells us. "And everybody knows men aren't supposed to wear shorts" (20). "Everybody" constitutes a civilized community excluding the barbaric American tourists, for whom, in turn, the brown-skinned little boy "squatting against the entrance" (20) could only be native, that is, barbarian. Perceptions of the "civilized" and the "barbaric" ironically "cross and uncross themselves" at a point of intersection where "everybody" is "American."

The group of Americans stands outside on the threshold of the church. Inside, the *Virgen de Guadalupe* functions as a threshold between human and divine, the living and the dead, and as mediator between competing cultures and languages. Both Michele and her little brother would like to be male Aztec "flying feather dancers," "like the ones we saw swinging high up from a pole on the Virgin's birthday" (18). For centuries Aztec dances such as the *volador* have been performed in honor of the dark Virgin who appeared to the Indian peasant on ground sacred to the pre-Christian *Tonantzín*, also worshipped as "Our Mother."[40] These complex cultural crossings are evident in the "deterritorialization" of the English of "Little Miracles, Kept Promises" through vernacular, multilingual prayers, even private codes.[41] "Mericans" also dramatizes multiple cultural and linguistic crossings. The narrator is Michele to her brothers, Micaela to her Mexican grandmother, whose Spanish she can understand if she's "paying attention" (19). Her grandmother's whispered prayers in Spanish are always faintly audible, though curtained from the English of the text, for she prays "behind the heavy leather outer curtain and the dusty velvet inner" (18). One step removed from the grandmother's Spanish, and two steps removed from the English of the Americans outside La Basílica de Nuestra Señora are the words of the *Virgen de Guadalupe* herself, who spoke to the humble peasant Juan Diego in Nahuatl, his vernacular tongue.

Anzaldúa suggests that while *Guadalupe* has traditionally been used within Mexican American society and the church to reinforce a feminine ethos of humility, subservience, and devotion, *la Virgen* has also become a revolutionary "symbol of ethnic identity" and a crucial cultural and linguistic "mediator":

> *Guadalupe* unites people of different races, religions, languages: Chicano protestants, America Indians and whites. "*Nuestra abogada*

siempre serás/Our *mediatrix* you will always be." She mediates between the Spanish and the Indian cultures (or three cultures as in the case of *mexicanos* of African or other ancestry) and between Chicanos and the white world. She mediates between humans and the divine, between this reality and the reality of spirit entities. *La Virgen de Guadalupe* is the symbol of ethnic identity and of the tolerance for ambiguity that Chicanos-*mexicanos*, people of mixed race, people who have Indian blood, people who cross cultures, by necessity possess.[42]

In 1810 the priest Miguel Hidalgo y Costilla rallied Indian peasants in a revolt against the Spanish with *la Virgen de Guadalupe* as their protectress. She was a symbol of Mexican revolution for Emiliano Zapata, whose followers decorated their sombreros with facsimiles of her figure. In 1965, her image fluttered on the banners of striking farmworkers led by César Chavez in Delano, California. Building on these precedents, Andrés G. Guerrero mobilizes *Guadalupe* as part of a contemporary Chicano liberation theology: "Guadalupe historically has been, can, and ought to be used as part of the *grito* (cry, shout) to unify Chicanos in their struggle toward liberation."[43] He includes the feminist struggle as part of the *Guadalupan grito*, although Norma Alarcón in 1982 noted a "telling absence of poems by women to the Virgin of Guadalupe, while poems by men to her are plentiful," concluding that "blind devotion is not a feasible human choice" for the feminist writer.[44]

III

Did you ever notice, Felice continued, how nothing around here is named after a woman? Really. Unless she's the Virgin.[45]

Sandra Cisneros, "Woman Hollering Creek,"
in *Woman Hollering Creek and Other Stories*

In an interview in 1988, Cisneros spoke of the difficulties of growing up as a Mexican American woman, "always straddling two countries . . . but not belonging to either culture," "trying to define some middle ground" where revision and reinvention of cultural and sexual roles might be possible—and being "told you're a traitor to your culture."[46] In particular, the roles defined for women by the church invite heretical feminisms. "The culture expects women to show greater acceptance of, and commitment to, the value system than men," observes Anzaldúa, "The culture and the Church insist that women are subservient to males. If a woman rebels she is a *mujer mala*."[47] Chayo in Cisneros's "Little Miracles, Kept Promises" is called "heretic," "atheist," "traitor," "*Malinchista*," "*Malinche*," when she turns from the female roles supplied by tradition and Catholicism and insists on her artistic vocation. "Certainly that black-white issue, good-bad, it's very prevalent in my work and in other Latinas," Cisneros commented in 1988, "We're raised with a Mexican culture that has two role models: *La Malinche y la Virgen de Guadalupe*. And you know that's a hard route to go, one or the other, there's no in-betweens."[48] Both figures represent "baggage from the Spanish fathers": Cortés's Indian mistress and interpreter *Malinche* and the Indian Virgin whom the Spaniards named *Guadalupe*, *puta* and *virgen*, cultural symbols of betrayal and purity at once ethnic, national, linguistic, cultural, and sexual.

Alarcón has compellingly argued that highly charged "symbolic figures" such as *la Virgen* and *la Malinche* have been used as "reference point[s] not only for controlling, interpreting, or visualizing women" in Mexican American culture "but also to wage a domestic battle of stifling proportions."[49] Most obviously, the Virgin has been used to represent the importance of chastity and obedience for young girls and of humility, self-sacrifice, and long-suffering motherhood for women.

In Cisneros's "My *Tocaya*," the narrator Patricia suffers through coed assemblies at her Catholic school on topics like "The Blessed Virgin: Role Model for Today's Young Women." The nuns called them "Youth Exchanges," she tells us, but the girls called them "Sex Rap Crap." When her errant schoolmate and "namesake" Trish (another Patricia) disappears, she is not surprised: "[A] girl who wore rhinestone earrings and glitter high heels to school was destined for trouble that nobody—not God or correctional institutions—could mend." Sister Virginella announces that "one of our youngest and dearest students has strayed from home"; her mother's "weepy message" appears in the newspaper; a funeral is held when a body is found in a drainage ditch. It would seem that girls who stray from the route of *la Virgen* risk the perdition of *la Malinche*. But the two mirror-image Patricias and the banner on the student body's floral offering to Trish, "Virgencita Cuídala," also suggest the interdependence of *la Virgen/la Malinche*. Both Patricias attend Our Lady of Sorrows High School, and before her disappearance Trish is last sighted "in the vicinity of Dolorosa and

Soledad," two aspects of the *Mater Dolorosa* (*Nuestra Señora de los Dolores*, Our Lady of Sorrows, and *la Virgen de la Soledad*, the Virgin of the Lonely).[50] Trish turns out not to be dead after all, just a runaway from Our Lady of Sorrows and from a father who probably beat her.

Melhuus sees the "female discourse of suffering and motherhood" associated with the Virgin as "parallel to a male discourse of dominance and power."[51] The implicit connection between Our Lady of Sorrows, Trish's abusive father, and the anonymous female corpse buried in Trish's grave becomes more explicit in other stories in the collection. In "One Holy Night," a pregnant eighth-grader sees a newspaper photo of her thirty-seven-year-old boyfriend being led away by the police: "*[O]n the road to* Las Grutas de Xtacumbilxuna, *the Caves of the Hidden Girl*," authorities discovered "*eleven female bodies.*"[52] Cleófilas in "Woman Hollering Creek" crosses the border from Mexico to Texas to find herself trapped in an abusive marriage: "There is no place to go. Unless one counts the neighbor ladies. Soledad on one side. Dolores on the other." Cleófilas absorbs the message of fidelity and suffering from her neighbors, her religion, her romance novels and soap operas. In the words of her favorite *telenovela* in Mexico, "[T]o suffer for love is good. The pain all sweet somehow. In the end." She is haunted by the mute and nameless women whose stories flood the newspapers: "Was Cleófilas exaggerating as her husband always said? It seemed the newspapers were full of such stories. This woman found on the side of the interstate. This one pushed from a moving car. This one's cadaver, this one unconscious, this one beaten blue. Her ex-husband, her husband, her lover, her father, her brother, her uncle, her friend, her co-worker. Always. The same grisly news in the pages of the dailies." The two women who rescue Cleófilas speculate that she's named after "one of those Mexican saints . . . a martyr or something" but that she'll name her new child after them. The pregnant Cleófilas undergoes a spiritual rebirth with her second border crossing, turning from Soledad and Dolores (loneliness and sorrow) through the intercession of the aptly named Felice and Graciela (happiness and grace).[53]

Guadalupe, the artist in "*Bien* Pretty," becomes addicted to the *telenovelas* as she broods over the departure of her lover, but she rebels against their message of suffering and passivity. "I started dreaming of these Rosas and Briandas and Luceros. And in my dreams I'm slapping the heroine to her senses, because I want them to be women who make things happen, not women who things happen to." Not women who are simply evil or good. Not women who weep. "Not loves that are *tormentosos.*"[54]

While Octavio Paz described both *la Virgen* and *la Malinche* as essentially passive, Anzaldúa and Cisneros are among the Chicana feminists who resurrect what Anzaldúa calls "the virgin mother who has not abandoned us" and "the raped mother whom we have abandoned" as borderland figures surrounded by ambiguities and filled with subversive energies.[55] The "symbol of symbols in Chicano experience," according to Guerrero, *Guadalupe* has wrongly been exploited as Virgin Mother and maternal haven for men, "in opposition to the violated mother" *Malinche*.[56] Working within the Catholic Church, Guerrero redefines both *la Malinche* and *la Virgen* as redemptive symbols, much as Anzaldúa's *mestiza*—inside and largely outside the church—re-creates her foremothers, "questions the definition of light and dark and gives them new meanings."[57] If the Spaniards and their church artificially separated light from dark, transforming "*la Virgen de Guadalupe/Virgen María* into chaste virgins and *Tlazolteotl/Coatlicue/la Chingada [Malinche]* into *putas*," then the "first step" for the new *mestiza* must be to heal this split. The Virgin Mother takes on aspects not only of her predecessor, the earth mother Tonantzín, but also of the openly sexual Aztec mother goddess Tlazolteotl, patron of fertility and sexuality, and of the bloodthirsty mother goddess Coatlicue, depicted in a well-known statue with defiantly bared breasts, a skirt of writhing snakes, and a necklace of human hands and hearts.[58]

"To me *la Virgen de Guadalupe* is also Coatlicue," Cisneros writes in her essay "Guadalupe the Sex Goddess": "When I think of the Coatlicue statue . . . I think of a woman enraged, a woman as tempest, a woman *bien berrinchuda*, and I like that. *La Lupe* as *cabrona*. Not silent and passive, but silently gathering force."[59]

IV

Thus each historical moment is capable of giving a sacred "recharge" to a pious image, by endowing it with a new power adapted to new aspirations.

Jacques Lafaye, *Quetzalcóatl and Guadalupe:
The Formation of a Mexican National Consciousness 1531–1813*

Cisneros extends Anzaldúa's project to reclaim *la Virgen*'s powers and origins in "Little Miracles, Kept Promises," where the "mumbling, mumbling, mumbling" of the grandmother's prayers to *la Virgen de Guadalupe* in

"Mericans" becomes audible. More than half of Cisneros's text consists of letters, *exvotos* (offerings in fulfillment of promises), *retablos* (votive paintings depicting miracles), *milagritos* (charms, tokens, "little miracles") offered to Catholic saints, healers, and to *la Virgen* in thanks or supplication. Chayo's feminist revision of the Blessed Virgin and her *milagrito*, a braid of hair, follows a polyvalent, polyvocal chorus of braided voices addressing *la Virgencita de Guadalupe, Niño Fidencio, San Martín de Porres, San Antonio de Padua*, the Miraculous Black Christ of Esquipulas, *la Virgen de los Remedios*, the Seven African Powers, the Mexican faith healer *Don Pedrito Jaramillo*, Saint Jude, *Santísima Señora de San Juan de los Lagos*. Young, old, sick, healthy, single, married, male, female, the petitioners write in Spanish and in English, and one even addresses the "Bɪlck Chr3st" in secret code, signing himself "B2njlm3n T."[60]

Their letters reveal poverty, displacement, sorrows, and hardships ranging from the profound to the quotidian. A husband of forty-eight years watches his wife suffer in the hospital and asks the Blessed *Virgen de los Remedios* to "intercede on her behalf," for we "don't know whether she should die or continue this life" (124). A teenage boy worries about his pimples. Several grandparents pray for grandchildren addicted to alcohol or drugs. César Escandón hopes for a job. Leocadia writes on behalf of her two-and-a-half-year-old granddaughter, suffering from cancer. Moises Ildefonso Mata hopes the "Seven African Powers that surround our Savior" will bring him luck and help him win the lottery (119). Arnulfo Contreras begs the *Virgencita* to help him collect the $253.72 owed him for two weeks' work at a tortilleria, for his family and in-laws in Mexico "all depend on what I send home." "We are humble people, Virgencita," he tells her, closing his plea: "There is no one else I can turn to in this country" (120).

Shifting gender relations within Mexican and Mexican American culture also emerge in these prayers. When Adelfa Vásqez complains to *San Martín de Porres* of the difficulty of starting over after a fire, she prays that her daughter be reminded of her traditional duties: "Zulema would like to finish school but I says she can just forget about it now. She's our oldest and her place is at home helping us out I told her. Please make her see some sense" (117). A petitioner signing herself Ms. Barbara Ybañez blames her mother for spoiling her brothers and aggressively demands a real man from *San Antonio de Padua*, patron of unmarried girls. A petitioner signing herself "s." writes briefly and poignantly: "Teach me to love my husband again. Forgive me" (119). Another petitioner whose request to *Santísima Señora de San Juan de los Lagos* was granted for "a guy who would love only me" now desires only freedom: "Please, Virgencita. Lift this heavy cross from my shoulders and leave me like I was before, wind on my neck, my arms swinging free, and no one telling me how I ought to be" (122). Others thank the *Madrecita* for the birth of their child. A mother thanks the *Santo Niño de Atocha* that her son has stopped drinking: "Raquel and the kids are hardly ever afraid of him anymore" (116).

Within this Bakhtinian dialogic space,[61] Chayo constructs her own fluid and multiple identity as she reconstructs the Mother's, addressing her intimately as *Virgencita*, offering her hair as tribute.[62] Chayo sloughs her braid "like a snakeskin" (125), giving birth to a new self, and reinvesting the dark-skinned *Virgencita* with the powers of the pre-Christian snake goddesses. Her previous estrangement from *la Virgen* mirrored her distance from her mother and grandmother, for in *la Virgen de Guadalupe* she at one time saw only the pain suffered by her mother and mother's mothers "in the name of God" (127), fathers and sons. "I couldn't see you without seeing my ma each time my father came home drunk and yelling. . . . I couldn't look at your folded hands without seeing my *abuela* mumbling, 'My son, my son, my son'" (127). Instead, she explains, she wanted a powerful, female-centered goddess filled with sexual energies: "I wanted you bare-breasted, snakes in your hands. I wanted you leaping and somersaulting the backs of bulls. I wanted you swallowing raw hearts and rattling volcanic ash. I wasn't going to be my mother or my grandma. All that self-sacrifice, all that silent suffering. Hell no. Not here. Not me" (127). When Chayo's mother tearfully compares the cutting off of her braid to Saint Lucy's plucking out her eyes, the identities of female saint and young female artist are momentarily braided together. Another voice chimes in to bewail the loss of Chayo's braid: "*Chayito, how could you ruin in one second what your mother took years to create?*" (125). Unbraiding herself as her mother's creation, Rosario (Chayo) De Leon rebraids the strands of her matrilineal inheritance in a tribute to the goddess she now names "Mighty Guadalupana Coatlaxopeuh Tonantzín" (129): "I'm a snake swallowing its tail. I'm my history and my future. All my ancestors' ancestors inside my own belly. All my futures and all my pasts" (126).

Alarcón writes of the marginalization of the Chicana within her own culture: "When our subjection is manifested through devotion we are saints and escape direct insult. When we are disobedient, hence undevout, we are equated with Malintzin [*la Malinche*]." It is particularly when "Chicanas embrace feminism," she writes, that "they are charged with betrayal *a la Malinche*."[63] Chayo is condemned as an outsider, accused both of unnatural devotions such as St. Lucy's and of unnatural disobedience and *Malinchisme*.

"Don't think it was easy going without you," she tells the *Virgencita*, "Don't think I didn't get my share of it from everyone. Heretic. Atheist. *Malinchista*" (127). When she is indignantly pulled from the solitude of her dark room, where she is "just . . . thinking," she wonders about the accommodations required of her: "Do boys think, and girls daydream? Do only girls have to come out and greet the relatives and smile and be nice and *quedar bien?*" (126). The values that she is expected to embrace if she remains within her culture are clearly expressed in the collective chorus of her relatives' voices:

> *It's not good to spend so much time alone.*
> *What she do in there all by herself? It don't look right.*
> *Chayito, when you getting married? Look at your cousin Leticia.*
> *She's younger than you.*
> *How many kids you want when you grow up?* (126)

"I don't want to be a mother," thinks Chayo, thanking the Blessed Virgin that her pregnancy was false. While a man might be both artist and father, a woman is not allowed that freedom: "I wouldn't mind being a father. At least a father could still be artist, could love some*thing* instead of some*one*, and no one would call that selfish" (127). Anzaldúa outlines the prescribed behavior and restrictive gender roles sanctioned by Chayo's church and culture: "If a woman doesn't renounce herself in favor of the male, she is selfish. If a woman remains a *virgen* until she marries, she is a good woman. For a woman of my culture there used to be only three directions she could turn: to the Church as a nun, to the streets as a prostitute, or to the home as a mother."[64]

In *la Virgencita*, Chayo plaits together female roles, cultures, and religions normally seen as at odds with each other. St. Lucy, who fiercely preserved her virginity and refused all marriage offers, despite the efforts of her family, is the patron saint of eyes, associated with Chayo's resistance to domestication and perhaps also her artistic vocation.[65] "*A painter!*" exclaims one of the relatives, "*Tell her I got five rooms that need painting*" (126). *La Malinche*, associated with voice or tongue in her capacity as translator/interpreter, speaks in Chayo's "mouth," "always getting me in trouble" (127)[66] and in her pre-Christian, pre-Conquest Indian spirituality. "The worst kind of betrayal lies in making us believe that the Indian woman in us is the betrayer," writes Anzaldúa of *la Malinche*, "We, *indias y mestizas*, police the Indian in us, brutalize and condemn her. Male culture has done a good job on us."[67] Rethinking the split between *Tlazolteotl/Coatlicue/la Malinche* and *la Virgen de Guadalupe,* Anzaldúa and Cisneros recover the Indian deities in the Catholic icon and the "serpent/sexuality" repressed in *Guadalupe* after the Conquest.[68] Rosario (Chayo) learns new names to describe her namesake, "Our Lady of the Rosary" (128), and thereby reconstitutes her own identity as well as the *Virgencita's.*[69]

Drawing on and revising a Catholic tradition of litanies to the Virgin that is centuries old,[70] Chayo's new *mestiza* litany interweaves *la Virgen's* Spanish, English, and hidden Indian names, in the process reweaving the strands of her own identity with her mother's, her grandmothers', her female ancestors':

> When I learned your real name is Coatlaxopeuh, She Who Has Dominion over Serpents, when I recognized you as Tonantzín, and learned your names are Teteoinnan, Toci Xochiquetzal, Tlazolteotl, Coatlicue, Chalchiuhtlicue, Coyolxauhqui, Huixtocihuatl, Chicome-coatl, Cihuacoatl, when I could see you as Nuestra Señora de la Soledad, Nuestra Señora de los Remedios, Nuestra Señora del Perpetuo Socorro, Nuestra Señora de San Juan de los Lagos, Our Lady of Lourdes, Our Lady of Mount Carmel, Our Lady of the Rosary, Our Lady of Sorrows, I wasn't ashamed, then, to be my mother's daughter, my grandmother's granddaughter, my ancestors' child. (128)[71]

Chayo opens a flexible cross-cultural field for new values where she crosses borders freely and rewrites old connections. Crossing gender lines, picket lines, national boundaries, and historical periods, Chayo rediscovers *la Virgen's* "power to rally a people" in the Mexican Revolution, the civil war, the farmworkers' strike in Delano, and so redefines the suffering of her mother and mother's mother, finding new "power in my mother's patience, strength in my grandmother's endurance" (128). Her braid "shed like a snakeskin," Chayo sheds the shame she felt "to be my mother's daughter, my grandmother's granddaughter" (128) and feels her "heart buoyant again" (125). At this new crossroads for *la Virgen,* "I could love you, and, finally, learn to love me" (128). Her litany of "facets" of the Virgin is multiplied well beyond Christianity and Aztec religion, for she sees in her "all at once the Buddha, the Tao, the true Messiah, Yahweh, Allah," and the natural sources of creation myths the world over (128).

Like each of the earlier petitioners, Chayo prays to a deity who mirrors her own deepest values and who offers support when she is displaced and disowned. *Nuestra Señora, la Virgen de Guadalupe,* speaks to her as a

mother who does not require that Chayo sacrifice her vocation to motherhood, as a virgin who understands the integrity of solitude.[72]

> I leave my braid here and thank you for believing what I do is
> important. Though no one else in my family, no other woman, nei-
> ther friend nor relative, no one I know, not even the heroine in the
> *telenovelas*, no woman wants to live alone.
>   I do. (127)

Chayo's "I do" is a vow that both mirrors and subverts the "I do" of the wife
and mother and the alternative "I do" of the nun, bride of Christ. Neither
mother, nun, nor prostitute, Chayo feels betrayed herself when she is accused by her own family of betrayal. "*Malinche*. Don't think it didn't hurt
being called a traitor. Trying to explain to my ma, to my *abuela*, why I didn't
want to be like them" (128). Chayo meets her mother, her grandmother,
and *la Virgen* in a borderland maternal terrain that allows her to sidestep
and combine the routes prescribed for her, to erase the boundaries that
confine her, and to remap the familiar. "A borderland is a vague and unde-
termined place created by the emotional residue of an unnatural boundary,"
writes Anzaldúa, "It is in a constant state of transition."[73]

V

We've been taught that the spirit is outside our bodies or above our
heads somewhere up in the sky with God.

                                        Gloria Anzaldúa,
                        Borderlands/La Frontera: The New Mestiza

[Women writers] look at or into, but not up at, sacred things;
we unlearn submission.

                                Alicia Ostriker, *Stealing the Language:
                        The Emergence of Women's Poetry in America*

As Anzaldúa bodily incorporates the U.S./Mexico border in the opening poem of *Borderlands/La Frontera*, a "1,950 mile long open wound" that
runs the length of her own body,[74] so Cisneros's Chayo straddles multiple
cultures, with her physical sex marking the borderline: "A woman with one

foot in this world and one foot in that. A woman straddling both. This thing between my legs, this unmentionable" (125). Exploring sexuality as a zone of conflict, Cisneros gives voice to the "unmentionable," what Luce Irigaray has memorably figured as "two lips" that speak together to express a female "geography of . . . pleasure" that is "always at least double, is in fact *plural*."[75] Anzaldúa also resists the domestication of her plural identities, her "wild tongue," her transgressive sexuality. "I will have my voice," she asserts: "Indian, Spanish, white. I will have my serpent's tongue—my woman's voice, my sexual voice, my poet's voice. I will overcome the tradition of silence."[76] In a 1996 essay on Guadalupe's multiple identities, Cisneros explores the connections between spirituality, sexuality, and writing, breaking the "[overwhelming] silence regarding Latinas and our bodies." Through the erotic history of her own body, Cisneros traces the history of the ancient goddesses within Guadalupe and uncovers a powerful new Virgin of Guadalupe of the present, the *Lupe* "of the 1990s who has shaped who we are as Chicanas/ *mexicanas* today, the one inside each Chicana and *mexicana*."[77]

Working through the often painful collisions between languages, cultures, classes, genders, and religious identities, "*la mestiza* undergoes a struggle of flesh, a struggle of borders, an inner war." Occupying multiple positions, she must simultaneously defend and dismantle the myths and practices of her home culture.[78] Anzaldúa and Cisneros defend and reclaim their cultural inheritances by reconstructing home as a place they can inhabit. Redefining "Our Mothers" *la Virgen* and *la Malinche*,[79] they "deterritorialize and reterritorialize" the symbolic landscape of "home,"[80] exploring its sexual and spiritual ambiguities and in-betweens, making it anew. Tapping the power that Audre Lorde calls the "erotic,"[81] Cisneros reconnects spiritual and physical experience in *la Virgen* to rewrite the possibilities for Chicana identity. "If the spirit and sex have been linked in our oppression," writes Cherríe Moraga, "then they must also be linked in the strategy toward our liberation."[82]

Seventy years ago, the baleful gaze of *la Virgen* dominated her mother's bedroom in Frida Kahlo's rendition of her own nativity, mother to sorrow and suffering, offering no possibility of salvation. This unblinking image of the Virgin is replaced in Cisneros's *Woman Hollering Creek and Other Stories* by a shape-changing deity connecting a series of female characters to each other and to lost and undiscovered parts of themselves.[83] The artist Lupe in "*Bien* Pretty" turns to the Virgin for strength and independence when her lover disappears, leaving no return address. At the "Mexican voodoo store on South Laredo," where "Church-sanctioned powers" are lined up "on one aisle," "folk powers on another," she selects something from both: "a Yo Puedo Más Que Tú from the pagan side and a Virgen de Guadalupe from the Christian."[84] In "The Eyes of Zapata," his mistress gives thanks for his letter with "a prayer in *mexicano* to the old gods, an Ave María in Spanish to La Virgen."[85] The female narrator of "Anguiano Religious Articles . . ." visits Anguiano's store on Soledad in quest of a *Virgen de Guadalupe* for her girlfriend Tencha, who is in the hospital. "I looked at all the Virgen de Guadalupes he had," she tells another friend, "The statues, the framed pictures, the holy cards, and candles," without finding what it was she wanted: "A statue is what I was thinking, or maybe those pretty 3-D pictures, the ones made from strips of cardboard that you look at sideways and you see the Santo Niño de Atocha, and you look at it straight and it's La Virgen, and you look at it from the other side and it's Saint Lucy with her eyes on a plate or maybe San Martín Caballero cutting his Roman cape in half with a sword and giving it to a beggar, only I want to know how come he didn't give that beggar *all* of his cape if he's so saintly, right?"[86] With humor and pointed irreverence toward the received wisdom of the Church, Cisneros multiplies the faces of *la Virgen* in *Woman Hollering Creek* to create a protean, decidedly three-dimensional figure reflecting the many faces of what Guadalupe's *tocaya* (namesake) in "*Bien* Pretty" calls "real women": "The ones I've loved all my life. *If you don't like it* lárgate, *honey*. Those women. The ones I've known everywhere except on TV, in books and magazines. *Las* girlfriends. *Las comadres*. Our mamas and *tías*. Passionate *and* powerful, tender and volatile, brave. And, above all, fierce."[87]

NOTES

1. Marina Warner, *Alone of All Her Sex: The Myth and Cult of the Virgin Mary* (New York: Alfred A. Knopf, 1976), xxv.

2. Julia Kristeva, "Stabat Mater," trans. Léon S. Roudiez, in *The Kristeva Reader*, ed. Toril Moi (New York: Columbia University Press, 1986), 180–84. Roudiez points to the strong presence of Warner in Kristeva's 1977 essay (160, 186 n. 1).

3. See Mary Daly, *Beyond God the Father: Towards a Philosophy of Women's Liberation* (Boston: Beacon Press, 1973), 82–90, and *Gyn/Ecology: The Metaethics of Radical Feminism* (Boston: Beacon Press, 1978), 88. In "An Open Letter to Mary Daly," Audre Lorde forcefully objected to the implicit dismissal of nonwhite spiritual traditions in *Gyn/Ecology*, questioning Daly's "assumption that the herstory and myth of white women is the legitimate and sole herstory of all women to call

upon for power and background, and that nonwhite women and our herstories are noteworthy only as decorations, or examples of female victimization." Audre Lorde, "An Open Letter to Mary Daly," in *Sister/Outsider: Essays and Speeches* (Freedom, Calif.: Crossing Press, 1984), 69.

4. Victor Turner and Edith Turner, *Image and Pilgrimage in Christian Culture: Anthropological Perspectives* (New York: Columbia University Press, 1978), 213.

5. Judith Ortiz Cofer, "The Black Virgin," in *Silent Dancing: A Partial Remembrance of a Puerto Rican Childhood* (Houston: Arte Público Press, 1990), 44.

6. See Jean Mallat, *The Philippines: History, Geography, Customs, Agriculture, Industry and Commerce of the Spanish Colonies in Oceania*, trans. Pura Santillan-Castrence and Lina S. Castrence (1846; reprint, Manila: National Historical Institute, 1983), 24; quote is from Jessica Hagedorn, *Gangster of Love* (New York: Houghton Mifflin, 1996), 290. For a powerful revision of the *Mater dolorosa/* indigenous Virgin, see Hagedorn's novel *Dogeaters* (New York: Penguin Books, 1990), particularly the closing "Kundiman."

7. See Leslie G. Desmangles, *The Faces of the Gods: Vodou and Roman Catholicism in Haiti* (Chapel Hill: University of North Carolina Press, 1992), 135–36.

8. See Antonio Bénitez-Rojo, *The Repeating Island: The Caribbean and the Postmodern Perspective*, trans. James Maraniss (Durham, N.C.: Duke University Press, 1992), 12–16, 26.

9. Jacques Lafaye, *Quetzalcóatl and Guadalupe: The Formation of a Mexican National Consciousness 1531–1813*, trans. Benjamin Keen (Chicago: University of Chicago Press, 1976), 308.

10. Burr Cartwright Brundage observes, "We may group a constellation of the many names applied to the goddess around that of Tonantzin, literally Our Holy Mother. Cihuatzin, Revered Lady; Toci, Our Grandmother; Ilama, Old Woman; Tocenan, All Mother; and Teteoinnan, Mother of the Gods—all speak to the same effect. As Tonan the goddess was simply the Mother. To each of her apotheoses were ascribed a flavor and sometimes a very definite geographical provenience and a characteristic cult, but they were all the same divinity underneath; their names shift like quicksilver, and one is often identified with another." Burr Cartwright Brundage, *The Fifth Sun: Aztec Gods, Aztec World* (Austin: University of Texas Press, 1979), 154. See also Lafaye, *Quetzalcóatl and Guadalupe*, 211–14.

11. Susanna Rostas applies the term *multi-iconicity* to the Virgin of Guadalupe in "The Production of Gendered Imagery: The Concheros of Mexico," in *Machos, Mistresses, Madonnas: Contesting the Power of Latin American Gender Imagery*, ed. Marit Melhuus and Kristi Anne Stølen (New York: Verso, 1996), 226. Margaret Randall cites "a 1969 poll showing almost half the working-class population of Zamora and Saltillo reporting the Virgin Mary as their most important deity. (Only twenty-three percent named God!)" Margaret Randall, "Guadalupe, Subversive Virgin," in *Goddess of the Americas/La Diosa de las Américas: Writings on the Virgin of Guadalupe*, ed. Ana Castillo (New York: Riverhead Books, 1996), 115. The official church position, however, holds that she is not to be "venerated in isolation, but always (at least implicitly) on account of her relation to Christ" (Turner and Turner, *Image and Pilgrimage*, 154). Officially, Catholics pray to the Blessed Virgin as intercessor rather than as deity.

12. Gloria Anzaldúa, *Borderlands/La Frontera: The New Mestiza* (San Francisco: Spinsters/Aunt Lute, 1987), 30, 29.

13. For "chaste protective mother," see Anzaldúa, *Borderlands*, 28. Luis J. Rodríguez calls Guadalupe the "poor people's agent" in "'Forgive Me, Mother, for My Crazy Life,'" in Castillo, *Goddess of the Americas*, 130, and Randall calls her a "guerrilla fighter" in "Guadalupe, Subversive Virgin," 119.

14. Randall, "Guadalupe, Subversive Virgin," 115, 119.

15. Judith Plaskow and Carol P. Christ, introduction to *Weaving the Visions: New Patterns in Feminist Spirituality*, ed. Judith Plaskow and Carol P. Christ (New York: Harper and Row, 1989), 3–4.

16. Warner, *Alone of All Her Sex*, 338–39.

17. Reed Way Dasenbrock, "Sandra Cisneros," in *Interviews with Writers of the Post-Colonial World*, ed. Feroza Jussawalla and Reed Way Dasenbrock (Jackson: University Press of Mississippi, 1992), 306.

18. Sandra Cisneros, "Woman Hollering Creek," in *Woman Hollering Creek and Other Stories* (New York: Random House, 1991), 54.

19. Sandra Cisneros, "Mericans," in *Woman Hollering Creek*, 19.

20. Sandra Cisneros, "*Bien* Pretty," in *Woman Hollering Creek*, 138. Lupe, named for the Virgin of Guadalupe, mimics the lines from the "Hail Mary": "Hail Mary . . . blessed art thou among women." See Rev. Hugh H. Hoever, ed., *The Saint Joseph Daily Missal* (New York: Catholic Book Publishing, 1957), 1292, and Luke 1:28.

21. Rodriguez, "'Forgive Me, Mother,'" 130–31.

22. Cisneros, "*Bien* Pretty," 161. *Madrecita* (the diminutive for "mother") is another of the many affectionate nicknames for the Virgin of Guadalupe.

23. Cisneros, "Woman Hollering Creek," 54. Graciela calls Felice *comadre* at the end of their phone call. The term *comadre*, which literally translates as "co-mother," traditionally refers to the woman a mother has chosen as godmother for her child, a very important member of the extended family in Mexican American culture. Today it is also used simply as a term of respect and affection for a female friend. Francisco A. Lomeli discusses the importance of the journals *El Grito* and *Comadres* for emerging Chicana feminists in the 1970s. (Felice's joyful *grito* as she crosses Women Hollering Creek opens new possibilities for independence and expression for Cleófilas.) Francisco A. Lomali, "Chicana Novelists in the Process of Creating Fictive Voices," in *Beyond Stereotypes: The Critical Analysis of Chicana Literature*, ed. María Herrera-Sobek (Binghamton, N.Y.: Bilingual Press, 1985), 29–30.

24. The *Mater Dolorosa* ("Our Lady of Sorrows") is traditionally depicted in full figure, with seven swords piercing her heart, which is hidden. Kahlo depicts her face only, with two daggers piercing her throat. In Mexican folk retablos she typically appears with one dagger piercing her chest or throat. See Elizabeth N. C. Zarur, "Catalogue Raisonné," in *Art and Faith in Mexico: The Nineteenth-Century Retablo Tradition*, ed. Elizabeth Netto Calid Zarur and Charles Muir Lovell (Albuquerque: University of New Mexico Press, 2001), 315, plates 67–78. On the cult surrounding the *Mater Dolorosa* (the Virgin as Pietà, mother grieving her dead son), see Warner, *Alone of All Her Sex*, 206–23.

25. Hayden Herrera quotes Kahlo: "'My head is covered,' Frida told a friend, 'because, coincidentally with the painting of the picture, my mother died.' 'My head,' Frida said, indicating that the dead woman is herself as well as her mother. Thus in My Birth Frida not only is born but gives birth to herself." Hayden Herrera, Frida Kahlo: The Paintings (New York: HarperCollins, 1991), 9. (A color reproduction of the painting appears on the facing page.)

26. Ibid., 10.

27. Pilar E. Rodríguez Aranda, "On the Solitary Fate of Being Mexican, Female, Wicked and Thirty-Three: An Interview with Writer Sandra Cisneros," Americas Review, 18, no. 1 (1990): 66–67. For further discussion of the Virgin of Guadalupe and Chicana writers and artists, see Tey Dina Rebolledo, Women Singing in the Snow: A Cultural Analysis of Chicana Literature (Tucson: University of Arizona Press, 1995), 52–57; Charlene Villaseñor Black, "Sacred Cults, Subversive Icons: Chicanas and the Pictorial Language of Catholicism," in Speaking Chicana: Voice, Power, and Identity, ed. D. Letticia Galindo and María Dolores Gonzales (Tucson: University of Arizona Press, 1999), 134–35, 161–68; and Jacqueline Doyle, "Assumptions of the Virgin and Recent Chicana Writing," Women's Studies 26 (1997): 171–201.

28. Cherríe Moraga, Loving in the War Years (Boston: South End Press, 1983), ii, 18.

29. Sandra Cisneros, "Little Miracles, Kept Promises," in Woman Hollering Creek, 127.

30. Aranda, "On the Solitary Fate," 67; Plaskow and Christ, introduction.

31. Aranda, "On the Solitary Fate," 67. For an intriguing study of ghosts, possession, exorcism, haunting, and redefined ethnicities, see Kathleen Brogan, Cultural Haunting: Ghosts and Ethnicity in Recent American Literature (Charlottesville: University Press of Virginia, 1998).

32. Anzaldúa, Borderlands, 71, 22; Gloria Anzaldúa, preface to Borderlands, vii.

33. Anzaldúa, Borderlands, 80–81.

34. Ibid., 203, 3, 30.

35. Ana Castillo, Goddess of the Americas.

36. Anzaldúa, Borderlands, 82.

37. Turner and Turner, Image and Pilgrimage, 32, 143–44.

38. Andrés G. Guerrero, A Chicano Theology (Maryknoll, N.Y.: Orbis Books, 1987), 96; Ena Campbell, "The Virgin of Guadalupe and the Female Self-Image: A Mexican Case History," in Mother Worship: Theme and Variations, ed. James J. Preston (Chapel Hill: University of North Carolina Press, 1982), 5.

39. Cisneros, "Mericans," 17. Subsequent page citations to this story will be given parenthetically in the text.

40. Many continue to worship under the name Guadalupe-Tonantzín. See Alan R. Sandstrom, "The Tonantsi Cult of the Eastern Nahua," in Preston, Mother Worship, on the contemporary worship of this dual deity, and chap. 2 of Turner and Turner, Image and Pilgrimage, for a rich analysis of the Marian shrines in Mexico as they assimilate Aztec and pre-Aztec deities and as they figure in changing nationalist discourses.

41. I borrow this term from Gilles Deleuze, who suggests that "there is no mother tongue, only a power takeover by a dominant language" that may be challenged or made "minor," "deterritorialized" from within. Gilles Deleuze, *The Deleuze Reader,* ed. Constantin V. Boundas (New York: Columbia University Press, 1993), 149. See also Harryette Mullin, "'A Silence between Us Like a Language': The Untranslatability of Experience in Sandra Cisneros' *Woman Hollering Creek,*" MELUS 21, no. 2 (1996): 3–20.

42. Anzaldúa, *Borderlands,* 30.

43. Guerrero, *A Chicano Theology,* 147.

44. Norma Alarcón, "Chicana's Feminist Literature: A Re-vision through Malintzin/or Malintzin: Putting Flesh Back on the Object," in *This Bridge Called My Back: Writings by Radical Women of Color,* ed. Cherríe Moraga and Gloria Anzaldúa (Watertown, Conn.: Persephone Press, 1982), 187. José E. Limón points to the doubleness of Guadalupe as both a "symbol of popular resistance" and a symbol of "possibly repressive standards of purity" and like Alarcón remarks the "absence" of "revisionist effort[s] on behalf of La Virgen de Guadalupe" akin to feminist recuperations of *la Malinche* on both sides of the border. José E. Limón, "La Llorona, the Third Legend of Greater Mexico: Cultural Symbols, Women, and the Political Unconscious," in *Between Borders: Essays on Mexicana/Chicana History,* ed. Adelaida R. Del Castillo (Encino, Fla.: Floricanto Press, 1990), 404–5. In recent years this has changed considerably, however, so much so that the Mexican writer Elena Poniatowska observes that while the Virgin of Guadalupe and *la Malinche* are "hardly mentioned" by Mexican women writers, "for Chicanas, the Virgin of Guadalupe is an obsession." Elena Poniatowska, "Mexicanas and Chicanas," *MELUS* 21, no. 3 (1996): 48.

45. The hidden name or names behind "Woman Hollering," "a name no one from these parts questioned, little less understood," form an important subtext in the story (Cisneros, "Woman Hollering Creek," 46). Cisneros chooses not to disclose that the major river in Seguín, which like Woman Hollering Creek often overflows its banks, is named for the very Virgin to whom she dedicates her stories: the Guadalupe River.

46. Aranda, "On the Solitary Fate," 65–66.

47. Anzaldúa, *Borderlands,* 17. On behavior circumscribed by the woman's sphere, see Marit Melhuus, "Power, Value and the Ambiguous Meanings of Gender," in Melhuus and Stølen, *Machos, Mistresses, Madonnas,* 243–49.

48. Cisneros, "Little Miracles, Kept Promises," 127–28; Aranda, "On the Solitary Fate," 65.

49. Alarcón, "Chicana's Feminist Literature," 182, 189 n. 1.

50. Cisneros, "My Tocaya," in *Woman Hollering Creek,* 36, 37. *La Virgen de la Soledad* and *Nuestra Señora de los Dolores* have many churches dedicated to them in Mexico (most notably in Oaxaca and Soriano, Querétaro), where their feast days are celebrated widely. See Joseph L. Cassidy, *Mexico: Land of Mary's Wonders* (Patterson, N.J.: St. Anthony Guild Press, 1958), 92–102, and Frances Toor, *A Treasury of Mexican Folkways* (New York: Crown Publishers, 1947), 246.

51. Melhuus, "Power, Value," 248.

52. Sandra Cisneros, "One Holy Night," in *Woman Hollering Creek*, 34.

53. Cisneros, "Woman Hollering Creek," 51, 45, 52, 54. For a fuller discussion of Cleófilas's spiritual transformation, see Jacqueline Doyle, "Haunting the Borderlands: La Llorona in Sandra Cisneros's 'Woman Hollering Creek,'" *Frontiers* 16 (1996): 53–70, reprinted in *Women, America, and Movement: Narratives of Relocation*, ed. Susan L. Roberson (Columbia: University of Missouri Press, 1998), 62–78.

54. Cisneros, "*Bien* Pretty," 161.

55. Octavio Paz, "The Sons of La Malinche," in *The Labyrinth of Solitude: Life and Thought in Mexico*, trans. Lysander Kemp (New York: Grove Press, 1961), 85; Anzaldúa, *Borderlands*, 30–31.

56. Guerrero, *A Chicano Theology*, 146–47.

57. Ibid., 113–14; Anzaldúa, *Borderlands*, 81. Her "*choice to be queer,*" Anzaldúa writes, leads her on "an interesting path . . . that continually slips in and out of the white, the Catholic, the Mexican"(19). She retains her grandmother's and mother's devotion to *la Virgen de Guadalupe*, whom she also invokes as *la Virgen de Coatlalopeuh*. But she writes emphatically of the church: "In my own life, the Catholic Church fails to give meaning to my daily acts." Anzaldúa, *Borderlands*, 37. Cisneros also professes to be "very, very much devoted to the Virgin of Guadalupe, but not exactly the same figure celebrated in Church." Dasenbrock, "Sandra Cisneros," 292.

58. Anzaldúa, *Borderlands*, 28, 27–28, 84.

59. Sandra Cisneros, "Guadalupe the Sex Goddess," in Castillo, *Goddess of the Americas*, 49–50. Anzaldúa also writes of the significance of the goddess, and of the well-known statue in the National Museum in Mexico City, in *Borderlands*, 41–51.

60. Cisneros, "Little Miracles, Kept Promises," 122–23. Subsequent page citations to this story will be given parenthetically in the text. The Seven African Powers are each identified with Catholic saints in Santería, a Yoruba-derived religion with strong New World, Catholic overtones that is practiced widely in Latin America, most prominently in Cuba and Puerto Rico, and among Hispanic immigrants to the United States. See Migene González-Wippler, *Santería: The Religion* (New York: Harmony Books, 1989), 268. Devotions to the miraculous Black Christ of Esquipulas originated in Guatemala, but he is popular throughout Central America and Mexico, and his shrines have spread as far as the U.S. Southwest. See Edith Hoyt, *The Silver Madonna: Legends of Shrines, Mexico-Guatemala* (Mexico City: Editorial Letras, 1963), 257–63, who also devotes chapters to *la Virgen de Guadalupe, la Virgen de los Remedios*, and *la Virgen de San Juan de los Lagos*. For a useful survey of the functions of individual Catholic saints in Mexican worship, see Gloria Kay Giffords, *Mexican Folk Retablos: Masterpieces on Tin* (Tucson: University of Arizona Press, 1974).

61. See M. M. Bakhtin, *The Dialogic Imagination*, ed. Michael Holquist, trans. Caryl Emerson and Michael Holquist (Austin: University of Texas Press, 1981).

62. Chayo's *milagrito* intertwines with Catholic and Indian practices surrounding worship of the *Virgen de Guadalupe* in Mexico. Richard M. Dorson notes the significance of hair in the cult of *la Virgen* in the village of Tecospa in the Valley of Mexico: "In the Tecospan synthesis of Aztec and Christian beliefs in heaven and hell, the Virgin again has her role. Women who die in childbirth ascend to the

sky world and are sent to the Virgin, who asks them, 'Where is the hair I lent you?' If they have cut their tresses and failed to save the cut hair, the Virgin commands them to return to earth as spirits until they have collected their hair. Hence the women of Tecospa keep their hair cuttings in pillows, to be placed beneath their heads at burial and offered to the Virgin." Richard M. Dorson, foreword to *Folktales of Mexico*, ed. Américo Paredes (Chicago: University of Chicago Press, 1970), xxx.

63. Alarcón, "Chicana's Feminist Literature," 187, 188. María Herrera-Sobek connects this cultural backlash against feminism with the conservative devotions to the Virgin of Guadalupe: "We are cognizant of patriarchal influence in the over-glorification of a female deity, the Virgin of Guadalupe, while males continue to oppress a large part of the female population. The patriarchal order shines through the violence directed at recalcitrant women who challenge male authority at a dance or in the privacy of the home. Women who are different from the 'good' daughter, wife, or mother pay with their lives for their audacity in deviating from established patterns of feminine behavior." María Herrera-Sobek, *The Mexican Corrido: A Feminist Analysis* (Bloomington: Indiana University Press, 1990), 117. See also Jean Wyatt, "On Not Being La Malinche: Border Negotiations of Gender in Sandra Cisneros' 'Never Marry a Mexican' and 'Woman Hollering Creek,'" *Tulsa Studies in Women's Literature* 14, no. 2 (1995): 243–71.

64. Anzaldúa, *Borderlands*, 17.

65. See David Hugh Farmer, *The Oxford Dictionary of Saints* (Oxford, England: Clarendon Press, 1978), 250–51. In Cisneros's "Never Marry a Mexican," in *Woman Hollering Creek*, the artist narrator paints the married lover who spurned her: "Making the world look at you from my eyes. And if that's not power, what is?" She lights candles to *la Virgen de Guadalupe* and an array of saints: "especially, Santa Lucía, with her beautiful eyes on a plate" (75).

66. On *Malinche* and tongue, see Edward Garcia Kraul and Judith Beatty, foreword to *The Weeping Woman: Encounters with La Llorona*, ed. Edward Garcia Kraul and Judith Beatty (Sante Fe, N.M.: Word Process, 1988), xi.

67. Anzaldúa, *Borderlands*, 22.

68. Ibid., 27–28.

69. Chayo's full name, Rosario, constitutes a tribute to the Virgin in itself; the rosary, a "garland of *Aves* for the Queen of Heaven," consists of one hundred and fifty "Hail Marys." Marina Warner reports that numerous "visions of the Virgin confirmed her special love of the rosary" and increased the belief of the devout in its "miracle-working" capacities. See Warner's *Alone of All Her Sex*, 306–9. In an apt crossing of cultures and spiritual traditions, the shrine of *la Virgen del Rosario* in Talpa, Mexico, is said to occupy the site where the Aztec goddess Cihuacoatl was formerly worshipped in earlier centuries. Hoyt, *The Silver Madonna*, 181–82.

70. The oldest litany, the Litany of Loreto, dates from 1200 and contains seventy-three invocations. See Geoffrey Ashe, *The Virgin* (London: Routledge and Kegan Paul, 1976), 218.

71. When the Virgin appeared to Juan Diego, speaking in Nahuatl, she identified herself as María Coatlaxopeuh, or Coatlalopeuh. Anzaldúa writes: "*Coatl* is the Nahuatl word for serpent. *Lopeuh* means 'the one who has dominion over serpents.' . . . Because *Coatlalopeuh* was homophonous to the Spanish *Guadalupe*, the

Spanish identified her with the dark Virgin, *Guadalupe*, patroness of West Central Spain." Anzaldúa, *Borderlands*, 29.

72. Adrienne Rich defines virginity in this way: "The ancient meaning of the word 'virgin' (she-who-is-unto-herself) is obscured by connotations of the 'undeflorated' or intact hymen, or of the Roman Catholic Virgin Mother, defined entirely by her relationship to God the Son." Adrienne Rich, *Of Woman Born: Motherhood as Experience and Institution* (New York: W. W. Norton, 1976), 249.

73. Anzaldúa, *Borderlands*, 3.

74. "Los Tigres del Norte," in Anzaldúa, *Borderlands*, 1.

75. Luce Irigaray, "This Sex Which Is Not One," trans. Claudia Reeder, in *New French Feminisms: An Anthology*, ed. Elaine Marks and Isabelle De Courtivron (New York: Schocken Books, 1980, 1981), 102–3.

76. Anzaldúa, *Borderlands*, 59.

77. Cisneros, "Guadalupe the Sex Goddess," 48, 50.

78. Anzaldúa, *Borderlands*, 18. Anzaldúa writes of her painfully divided loyalties inside and outside Mexican American culture: "So yes, though 'home' permeates every sinew and cartilage in my body, I too am afraid of going home. Though I'll defend my race and culture when they are attacked by non-*mexicanos*, *conosco el malestar de mi cultura*, I abhor some of my culture's ways, how it cripples its women, *como burras*, our strengths used against us, lowly *burras* bearing humility with dignity. . . . I do not buy all the myths of the tribe into which I was born" (*Borderlands*, 21). Cisneros speaks in similar terms of the difficult "balancing act" between culture and self-determination in her interview with Aranda, "The Solitary Fate," 66.

79. When Anzaldúa uses the phrase "Our Mothers" in *Borderlands*, she invokes three mothers: *la Virgen de Guadalupe*, *la Malinche*, and *la Llorona*, the legendary weeping woman who drowned her own children (*Borderlands*, 31). Cisneros devotes attention to all three figures in *Woman Hollering Creek*, most prominently in her revision of *la Virgen* in "Little Miracles, Kept Promises," of *la Malinche* in "Never Marry a Mexican," and of *la Llorona* in the title story "Woman Hollering Creek."

80. See Caren Kaplan's feminist application of Gilles Deleuze and Felix Guattari's terms. Kaplan advises first-world feminists to "leave home, as it were, since our homes are often sites of racism, sexism, and other damaging social practices. Where we come to locate ourselves in terms of our specific histories and differences must be a place with room for what can be salvaged from the past and what can be made new. What we gain is a reterritorialization; we reinhabit a world of our making." Caren Kaplan, "Deterritorializations: The Rewriting of Home and Exile in Western Feminist Discourse," in *The Nature and Context of Minority Discourse*, ed. Abdul R. JanMohamed and David Lloyd (New York: Oxford University Press, 1990), 364–65.

81. See Audre Lorde, "The Uses of the Erotic: The Erotic as Power," in *Sister/Outsider*, 53–59. Plaskow and Christ include Lorde's essay in their second anthology on women and spirituality, *Weaving the Visions*. In the introduction they discuss Lorde and other feminist writers who move beyond the "traditional association of women with nature and the body" and beyond "mind/body dualism" to consider the

theological implications of women's emphasis on "embodied experience": "Moreover, since embodied experience is always spatially located, the emphasis on embodiment connects with . . . the 'pull to relation' among women—relation to particular others, to communities of origin and choice, and to a wider web of connectedness that encompasses the earth." Plaskow and Christ, introduction, 11.

82. Moraga, *Loving in the War Years*, 132.

83. I borrow here from Kaplan's definition of a feminist poetics that "points towards a rewriting of the connections between different parts of the self in order to make a world of possibilities out of the experience of displacement." Kaplan, "Deterritorializations," 368.

84. Cisneros, "*Bien* Pretty," 158–59.

85. Sandra Cisneros, in "Eyes of Zapata," in *Woman Hollering Creek*, 99.

86. Sandra Cisneros, "Anguiano Religious Articles . . . ," in *Woman Hollering Creek*, 115, 114.

87. Cisneros, "*Bien* Pretty," 161.

12   BEGINNINGS ARE EVERYTHING

The Quest for Origins in Linda Hogan's *Solar Storms*

ELLEN L. ARNOLD

> Beginnings, I know now, are everything.
>
> Linda Hogan, *Solar Storms*

In a seminal 1987 essay, William Bevis argues that novels written by Native Americans are characterized by incentric "homing-in" plots that take their protagonists home to community and tradition for a recovery of identity and healing of spirit that are "transpersonal" and deeply connected to the natural world, a pattern that offers a distinct contrast to and critique of mainstream American fiction.[1] As Bevis points out, Euro-American heroes are most often "lighting out for the territories";[2] in keeping with America's four-hundred-year history of colonial expansion, these primarily male protagonists leave family, community, and tradition behind in the interests of a competitive individualism that objectifies and subordinates nature, separating it from the realm of spirit. Chickasaw writer Linda Hogan's first novel, *Mean Spirit* (1990), in many ways conforms to Bevis's scheme.[3] A historical novel set during the Oklahoma oil boom of the 1920s, *Mean Spirit* depicts a world torn apart by conflicting worldviews and the violence of capitalist greed. Ultimately, the novel's Osage Indian characters are forced to retreat from the threat of murder for their oil wealth and the destruction of the earth to the hidden community of the traditional Hill Indians in order to preserve their lifeways and the spiritual beliefs that structure them.

Like many of the novels of the Native American renaissance of the 1970s on which Bevis focuses, *Mean Spirit* is a novel of resistance that reclaims Native American histories and traditions from a dominant culture that would obliterate or assimilate them. In particular, *Mean Spirit* exposes the genocidal policies and practices that underlie American expansionism and rejects the individualist ideologies and Christian "dominion theology"[4] that awarded Euro-American males dominion over all of life and served as both justifications for and instruments of manifest destiny. Kimberly Blaeser's important essay "Pagans Rewriting the Bible" explores the way *Mean Spirit*, like much of the literature written by Native Americans in the twentieth century, challenges the "vertical understanding" and authoritarian dogma of Christianity, contrasting Christianity to and replacing it with indigenous spiritual visions based in values of interconnection and participation.[5] As Catherine Rainwater points out, *Mean Spirit* is like the ancient medicine bundle that belongs to one of its characters;[6] it contains an "older world, wanting out," and *The Book of Horse*, a "missing book of the Bible" being composed by Osage healer Michael Horse throughout the course of the novel, prophesies a time when "all the people [will] return and revere the earth and sing its praises."[7]

Hogan's second novel, *Solar Storms* (1995), maps the way to the "older world" that still exists within the present, fragmented world, through a restored connection between humans and the earth.[8] Inspired by indigenous protests to the James Bay HydroQuebec Project in the early 1970s, *Solar Storms* adopts a mediational approach[9] that moves toward a healing of the ruptures between Euro-American and Native American cultures that *Mean Spirit* so vividly describes. While it never fails to illuminate the practices and systems of thought that serve the interests of the dominant culture, *Solar Storms* also performs what Arnold Krupat terms "anti-colonial translation," engaging the narratives of the dominant culture not so much to reject them as to rewrite and expand them.[10] *Solar Storms* layers an incentric, "homing-in" narrative with an "eccentric" or centrifugal[11] wilderness quest more typical of Euro-American literature to produce a complex revisioning of both. In the process, Hogan explores commonalities, resonances, and connections between the beliefs and stories of Native American and Western religious traditions, opening on a new spiritual vision in their intersections that foregrounds Christianity's "others"—women, animals, indigenous peoples, the earth itself—and redeems elements of Christianity and its God by regrounding, feminizing, and "heterarchicalizing"[12] them. *Solar Storms* suggests a new spirituality that is not "regressive," as Bevis terms Native American homing narratives,[13] but evolving, enfolding Western conceptualizations of reality and identity within ancient indigenous understandings of interconnectivity and process.

THE BODY IN THE SPIRIT

Nothing sings in our bodies.

Linda Hogan, *The Book of Medicines*

Like the nineteenth- and twentieth-century women novelists whose work Kristina Groover explores in her study *The Wilderness Within: American Women Writers and Spiritual Quest*, Hogan deconstructs the male quest narrative by locating the sacred in the mundane and expressing the spiritual development of its primarily female protagonists "in terms of increased engagement with the everyday world."[14] At the same time, *Solar Storms* performs a sort of double subversion by appropriating and reconstructing the solitary male quest model—the "linear journey . . . toward wilderness, individual achievement, and autonomy" that Groover contrasts to the female quest[15]—by retelling it from a feminine and communal point of view. *Solar Storms'* central narrative follows young mixedblood Angela Jensen on a multidimensional search for her origins that achieves both individuation and a complex renegotiation of the boundaries of self, in relationship not only with other humans but with the natural and spirit worlds as well. Angela's journey moves in many directions at once—inward and outward across the surfaces that separate individual from world and cosmos, backward and forward in time—destabilizing conventional Western divisions between nature and culture, spirit and matter, past and future, time and space.

Raised in foster care in Oklahoma, Angela returns at age seventeen to her birthplace in the Boundary Waters region between Minnesota and Canada, an area inhabited by indigenous Crees and Anishnabeg,[16] and the descendants of European and Native immigrants brought there by the fur trade, including an invented tribe Hogan names the "Fat Eaters." Hoping to find the mother who abandoned her and the secrets of her personal history, written on her body in a map of scars, Angela seeks out her great grandmother Agnes Iron, a descendant of the Fat Eaters, "with religious fervor, . . . thinking she would . . . be my salvation" (27). Arriving at Adam's Rib, a finger of land extending into Lake Grand, Angela takes her birth name, Angel, and steps into the space of her absence, the "place that holds her life" (23). At Adam's Rib—the site where Adam's wounding gave birth to Eve—Angel begins her journey into mature womanhood and wholeness. Hogan's choices of names and terms signal from the outset that Angel's quest for history and identity will also be a spiritual transformation, one that will combine and transform her dual spiritual heritages as well.

When Angel arrives at Adam's Rib, she is in many ways like the "sky-worshiping" Christians who built "boxlike," small-windowed houses there, afraid to look out "at the threatening miles of frozen lake on one side of them, and on the other, at the dense, dark forest with its wolves" (27). She describes herself as "the element of air, light and invisible, moving from place to place" (89); she fears the dark, silence, stillness, the earth world of water and trees, even sleep. Angel is contained by surfaces, "care[s] only about what [she] looked like" (147). The scars that divide her face into halves—one "perfect," the other "hated"—and "the red hair so unusual above dark skin" (17) that marks her as a mixedblood, reflect back to her a history of violence and victimization. "Scars had shaped my life," Angel says (25); "I was nothing more than emptiness covered with skin" (74). She claims only a "room of fear" and "the fire-red room of anger" as home (26–27), but she comes to Adam's Rib set on "constructing and inhabiting [a] new room" (27) by entering her fears.

Angel's great-grandmother Agnes and Agnes's ancient mother Dora-Rouge impart to Angel what they can of her story, then send her to Bush, the mixedblood Chickasaw woman who helped care for her as an infant. On remote Fur Island, through a dark and silent winter filled with the constant tasks of daily survival, Bush helps Angel put the pieces of her life together, like the skeletons of dead turtles and wolverines Bush restores for museums. This skeleton provides a framework for Angel's self-re-creation: "People say that in the beginning was the word. But they have forgotten the loneliness of God, the yearning for something that shaped itself into the words. *Let there be*. It was this same desire in me, this same longing for creation, and Bush's spare words were creation itself. I was finding a language, a story, to shape myself by" (94). Though she arrives at Adam's Rib longing for an "unbroken line between me and the past" (77), Angel soon comes to understand that her own broken life is part of a larger brokenness, "fragments and pieces left behind by fur traders, soldiers, priests, and schools" (77). By the time Bush finally recounts the story of Angel's birth and her mother Hannah's physical abuse and rejection of her (113), Angel has come to understand this beginning as one of many, a mirror reflecting an entire complex of historical, social, and environmental events: "My beginning was Hannah's beginning, one of broken lives, gone animals, trees felled and kindled. Our beginnings were intricately bound up in the history of the land," with the "broken connections of people to the world and its many gods" (96).

Having traced this narrative line to its origins, Angel has finished with piecing fragments together and can begin the process of making a new identity, like the ribbon shirts—symbols of an emerging pan-Indian identity in the 1970s—that she and Bush begin to sew for sale at the local trading post. Angel recalls, "One night I dreamed of a woman in a white-walled cave sewing together pieces of humans, an arm to a trunk, a foot to a leg. When I told her this, Bush said, 'Wouldn't it be wonderful if we could piece together a new human, a new kind of woman and man? . . . Start with bones, put a little meat on them, skin, and set them to breathing. We'd do it right this time. They'd be love-filled, the way we were meant to be all along'" (86). That her quest will take Angel deep into the chaos of creation is foreshadowed by events before she leaves Adam's Rib. A question about the origin of her scars and the smell of blood from a cut finger bring back memories of wounds and hospitals, and in her anger and pain, Angel strikes out at the reflection of her scarred face in Agnes's bathroom mirror. The fragments of the mirror reflect her own fragmentation and bring its origins to consciousness, and "the girl who never cried" (53) finally weeps. Afterwards, she dreams:

> I fell over the edge of land, fell out of order and knowing into a world dark and primal, seething, and alive as creation, like the beginning of life.

> I began to form a kind of knowing at Adam's Rib. I began to feel that if we had no separate words for inside and out and there were no boundaries between them, no walls, no skin, you would see me . . . not the mask of what had happened to me, not the evidence of violence. . . . Some days you would see fire, other days, water. Or earth. . . . You would see the dust of sun, the turning of creation taking place. But the night I broke my face there were still boundaries

and I didn't yet know I was beautiful as the wolf, or that I was a new order of atoms. Even with my own eyes I could not see deeper than my skin or pain. (54)

Angel shatters the surface that reflects back to her the brokenness of her history, and her grief makes her permeable to the world, opening her to be filled by the forces of creation.

Finally, on Fur Island Angel breaks the last small mirror she possesses and "g[ives] up on all surfaces." Her vision "shifts" and she sees "inside water," begins to read people's eyes "to see what kind of souls they had" (85). She overcomes her fear of water, teaching herself to swim by imagining herself turtle. Entering silence, she discovers it "full and caring" (116), "loud" with "soundless walkings, . . . quiet flying, . . . absent voices" (115), learns there is no empty space, that even air is a "soup of love and pollen and stars" (164). Angel comes to understand that her scars are not just the record of a violent past but also "proof . . . that there is healing" (125), visible evidence of the ongoing processes of creation, her skin a mirror revealing the continuity of inner and outer worlds, a site of deep interconnection. As she recognizes that "everything [is] alive," that "[w]e are seen, our measure taken, not only by the animals and spiders but even by the alive galaxy in deep space " (80), Angel becomes fluent in the languages of a sentient world, learns to read its stories with her body. And in that embodied conversation, time collapses and an "older world" enters her awareness: "On Fur Island a person could feel and hear where the faraway and ancient began" (93).

In her quest for self, Angel has found herself "traveling backward in time toward myself at the same time I journeyed forward, like the new star astronomers found that traveled in two directions at once." As Agnes's part-ner Husk tells Angel, "Einstein believed time would bend and circle back to itself" (64), and it is that circling, connecting Angel's quest for her origins to the history of her people and the land, to the birth of life in the fire and dust of solar storms, that ultimately brings about her spiritual healing. The arduous canoe journey through the wilderness that takes Angel and the three older women north to the site of the hydroelectric project that is "drowning" the land (58) repeats this circular pattern. The four women, each with her own mission—Angel, to find her mother; Bush, to join the protestors; Agnes, to accompany her mother Dora-Rouge home to die among the Fat Eaters—reverse the destructive path of the fur traders south into lake country, moving back in time as they journey toward the future. In this circularity, time is spatialized, and the women "enter" it: "The time

we'd been teasing apart, unraveled. And now it began to unravel us as we
entered a kind of timelessness" (170). In "a place between worlds" where
"[e]verything merged and united," the four women become "like one animal," hear "inside each other in a tribal way" (177) as they struggle to survive. They communicate as the parts of the body communicate, through
the circulation of breath and blood, through their shared embodied merger
with the world. "[A]rticulate in the languages of land, water, animal, even
in the harder languages of one another" (193), the women hear, understand,
and speak the languages of the wilderness through and with their bodies.
"Held" by the world, they move "out from the narrowed circle of our history the way rays of light grow from the sun" (93), unraveling the history
that has contained them to participate in the creation of a new world, a
world that enfolds an older world of human integrality with nature, a time
when "humans and animals . . . spoke the same language" (82).

In this boundary world, Angel is baptized into a new spirituality that
lives in the intersections of new and old worlds. As the women travel, they
come upon ancient pictographs of wolf and wolverine, a wolverine with
wings that are invisible until rain on the rockface makes them appear. Here
Angel dives below the surface of the water into a mirror world of submerged
trees and more pictographs of deer and fish: "Two parts hydrogen, one part
oxygen. . . . When I was inside water, I understood how these simple elements married and became a third thing. . . . I remembered being fish. I remembered being hydrogen and oxygen" (179). In this act, Angel, formerly
"the element of air" (89), of rootlessness and flight, remakes her connection
with water, the water that signifies for Hogan the spirit that suffuses everything, binds all life together. Later, Dora-Rouge leads the women to other
rock paintings of moon and lynx reflected in the water, "the lynx gazing
down at itself, looking at its twin . . . as if it could step away from stone, enter
water, its own reflection, and come alive, the way spirit meets matter" (182),
mirroring the healing of the split between Angel's body and spirit.

However, Angel's evolution toward wholeness is not simply a restoration of divided parts but a recognition that matter and spirit are mirrors to
each other, twinned (but not identical) aspects of a greater whole, which
have separated in the creation of life. Angel has come to a crucial understanding of the nature of life; mind and body, spirit and matter, time and
space are abstracted out of the "soup" of creation by surfaces—skin, language, maps, the surface of water, the "skin of time" (247)—and can re-
join in the way that the dust of solar storms and the light of the sun,
originally one, come together again to create life. By dispersing subjec-

tivity throughout the universe, Hogan situates matter within spirit, history within timelessness, culture within nature, in concentric interwoven layers that extend through the realm of tangible realities and historical events into "the between" (31)—the intangible realms of interconnection and transformation—as well.

Understanding that her self comes into being in its intersections with the world, Angel can make a conscious choice to enter "the dreams of earth, . . . the language that animals and humans had in common" (170), to speak with land and become a "plant dreamer." Having undertaken the solitary mission into the wilderness to find the healing plants that can save the dying Agnes—her first independent act on this journey and one that bears similarities to the vision quest in which traditional Anishnabeg received spirit guides and knowledge of their life's work—Angel is no longer driven by the quest for salvation outside herself. Though she still longs to find her mother, she has learned that "what matters is living in the body, knowing the current of water" (204).

The Mother's Body

Pain had a way of changing the body. Human skin became
something else, a wall, a membrane between the worlds of
destruction and creation.

Linda Hogan, *Mean Spirit*

Angel's first meeting with her mother occurs after she has experienced a second baptism at Two-Town Post, near the site of the dam construction. Shedding her clothes to enter the icy water, she steps out of her "rational mind" and enters myth, reliving the traditional Anishnabe story of Eho, the woman who fell in love with a whale and became "keeper of the animals" (229), told to her by Dora-Rouge. Emerging from the water naked, Angel sees the mother who cut and bit and abandoned her walking toward her; reborn, Angel also re-creates Hannah's arrival at Adam's Rib icy cold from water, washed ashore in violent storms, raped and mutilated by the men who came to strip the land of its resources. Thus Angel remakes her own history through her new covenant with water. But Hannah turns away from her daughter, and instead of the reconciliation she desires, Angel makes a new relationship with the earth, in the recognition that her mother's body, her own body, and the body of earth are the same. In the heart of a new community, amidst the chaos of the dam construction, Angel remembers, "[W]e were shaped out of this land by the hands of gods. . . . [W]e embodied the land" (228). She learns she must "live by feeling" on land, as well as in water; she begins to understand how the Anishnabe and Cree people hunted by "dreaming the maps" to their prey and feels "the rhythm of it" herself, "My heart and the beat of the land . . . becoming the same thing" (236).[17]

Angel does not see her mother again in life; soon after their meeting, she receives word that Hannah is dying. Angel realizes, "Her desperation and loneliness was my beginning. Hannah had been my poison, my life, my sweetness and pain, my beauty and homeliness. And when she died, I knew that I had survived in the best of ways for I was filled with grief and compassion" (251). Her search for her personal beginnings in the body of her mother finds only that body, a shell of skin emptied out long ago, the ultimate consequence of the splitting of body and spirit inherent in Western systems of power over world and others. Angel and Bush lay Hannah's body out on newspaper, on "words of war, obituaries, stories of carnage and misery" (253), and the words merge with her scars, the legacies of conquest and genocide written doubly on her flesh. These signs mark the wall that Hannah's skin became, allowing no exchange between her internal landscape and the external world, preventing her participation in the cyclical interchange of genesis and loss. But earth's cycles enfold her and continue, and from Hannah's flesh, from acts that resembled "something akin to love" (251), came Angel, and a new baby born shortly before Hannah's death, the "[n]ew skin, straight from mystery" that holds a different future (255). Angel hears the baby's first cry as "death speaking" (244), her life called into being out of the hunger that holds the universe together and finds expression in the "desperate" baby's "will to live" (244). Angel names her new sister Aurora, for the dawn sun and the northern lights that are the reflection of sunlight off the dust of solar storms, a doubled name that reflects the wholeness of creation and destruction.

The search for her mother takes Angel to other beginnings as well—the origins of Hannah's death in history, the origins of genocide and ecocide. Angel comes to understand that Hannah "walked out of the rifles of our killers. She was born of knives, the skinned-alive beaver and marten and the chewed-off legs of wolves. She hurt me because I was part of her and she hated herself" (345). Literally cut from the world, "contained" but not "held" in it (242), Hannah's body is emptied. She is "a skin that others wore" (77), inhabited by the demons of capitalist greed and the cannibal windigo spirits of Anishnabe tradition, who dismember and consume their victims to satisfy the terrible hungers born of harsh winters or transform their victims into beings of ice with insatiable cravings of their own.[18]

Hannah's designation as a "black hole" (251) suggests that while Hannah is the victim of the historical destruction of local economy and place and the specific acts of white men who inscribed that history on both land and the bodies of women, she is also an impersonal force of the universe, participant in its ongoing cycles of destruction and creation, like the Hungry Mouth of Water that swallows everything that comes near or the angry Se Nay River that bargains with Dora-Rouge for Agnes's life. As Angel comes to understand, "[A] person can't blame the wind for how it blows and Hannah was like that. . . . [W]hat possessed my mother was a force as real as wind, as strong as ice, as common as winter" (115). Similarly, the men who participate in the building of the dams, white and Indian alike, act out of fear and hunger, the need to feed themselves and their families in a system of neocolonial production that uses hunger to turn people away from a contextual ethic of mutual support to a system that pits every-man-for-himself against the natural world. At the same time, the building of the dam participates in the same cycles of change as the re-creation of land by the beavers. Human history, which in Western thought is constructed with the world's resources and occurs against the backdrop of a "natural" history of earth and cosmos, in Hogan's vision is enfolded, "held" within the larger histories of nature's cycles and the universe's evolution. Hannah's death and Aurora's birth reflect a "hundred-year-old history . . . breaking itself apart and trying to reform" (249), and in the midst of the chaos of the dam site, "the world seemed to be breaking open . . . like the beginning of a universe." "In time," Angel comes to know, "all things would break and would become whole again" (325). The cannibals who consume the earth separate themselves and their victims from the webs and cycles of interdependence. In the end, they destroy only themselves and each other; creation continues.

Angel's reunion with the body of earth is no more a joyful reconciliation with a nurturing mother than is her reunion with Hannah; her arrival at Two-Town, where she will remake her covenant with land, is heralded by the terrible scene of the moose being swallowed by the earth. Earth has her own histories, her own hungers. Angel returns to an ancestral home that is scarred, torn, and angry; it is as displaced as she. But it is home nonetheless, and Angel has learned she is already part of earth and can make herself at home in it through her body's permeability. Like the roots of plants, she takes in earth and remakes it, growing into, becoming place.

For Hogan, healing is no seamless erasure of wounds, no restoration of harmonious balance, but a dynamic process grounded in the interdependency of destruction and creation. The healing of individuals, communities, land, earth, and cosmos demands that humans make a conscious choice to enter, not only what is beautiful and whole, but what has been wounded and destroyed, the way Bush sings herself into Hannah, steps into the "ruins of humans" inside her (103) to understand what had happened to her. The covenant between humans and the natural world, between the colonizers and the indigenous people they have assigned to the category "nature" apart from them, cannot be remade without acknowledging and passing through the dismemberment and pain of our violent pasts, individual and collective. Hogan traces the unnecessary and unfeeling violence of what she terms a "death-loving culture"[19] to the fear and denial of the dependence of life on death, the inevitable cycling of destruction and creation. The body of earth, the body that is the source of all lives, must, like Hannah's body, be respected and cared for in its destructive as well as its creative manifestations.

THE BODY OF GOD

Skin is the closest thing to god,
touching oil, clay
intimate with the foreign land of air
and other bodies
places not in light, lonely
for its own image.

Linda Hogan,
The Book of Medicines

Angel's multidimensional quest for identity unfolds outward from her own skin to mother, grandmothers, community, nation, earth, God, and universe—and simultaneously inward, through muscle and bone, blood and cells, iron and water, atoms and particles, until it again opens on the universe—"infinity" in "its circular flight" (345). Angel's search for her own origins takes her back to the creation of world, ending in the recognition that she *is* creation, like Dora-Rouge, "born new every day . . . the closest thing to God" (182), and re-creates the world anew in herself every day as well. Physical fathers are significantly missing in this novel. Angel's grandfather Harold is only a memory, and her own father is never considered; hers is a virgin birth. Similarly, God's role as creator is subsumed in the daily lives of women and a few men, like Husk, Tulik, and Tommy, who also embody sensitivity, tenderness, nurturing, and caretaking. For Hogan, male and female are "kindred spirits" split off from the same body "like Pangaea" (66), which mirror and balance each other.[20] *Solar Storms* restores that balance, lost in Western patriarchy, by privileging mothering over fathering, sustaining and cultivating over begetting and production.[21] Hogan rewrites the Christian myth of origins from indigenous and female points of view, reinserting women into the stories of men, regrounding and feminizing the masculine god of the "sky worshiping" Christians (27), the god who "wouldn't stoop to the level of humans" (276).

Hogan's method layers indigenous stories with biblical and scientific stories of creation, allowing them to intertwine, complement, and correct each other, paralleling the lives of many contemporary Ojibwe people, who, according to Theresa Smith's 1995 study *The Island of the Anishnaabeg*, practice Catholicism without experiencing conflict with traditional beliefs and practices. On the basis of conversations with her Ojibwe consultants, Smith concludes that many Ojibwe have a kind of "global consciousness," believing that

> cross-cultural references strengthen rather than dilute Ojibwe beliefs. . . . Without surrendering their identity and what they consider to be the uniqueness of their own symbols, contemporary Ojibwes tend toward a holistic understanding of both . . . religions. Inasmuch as they hold that all things and persons in their own world are interconnected, they extend this web of relations to the whole earth. They see themselves to be, in a way, like the lakes of their own lifeworld, connected by unseen passages, first to one another, then to other tribes and peoples, and ultimately, as rivers and underground channels reach the oceans, to the entire population of the world.[22]

In a similar way, the lives of the five generations of women in *Solar Storms* are patterned within and reiterate many different indigenous stories that link with and reshape biblical narratives. The flooding and destruction surrounding the James Bay project repeat cycles of destruction and re-creation recounted in the biblical story of Noah and the earth-diver stories of the Northeast Indians, in which a trickster god (Nanabush among the Anishnabeg) and animal helpers re-create the world after a catastrophic flood. At Angel's first visit to Fur Island, she finds the island rising from the water, with Bush standing in newly exposed mud, "as if she'd just been created, . . . as if she'd risen up like First Woman, still and awed by the creation" (67). When Bush and Angel return to Adam's Rib after the protest at the Canadian dam site, Angel "knew we walked into another day of creation" (334). Like Noah, they and Tommy remove the animals by boat from the now flooding Fur Island, and Angel's role in the whole narrative is that of a new Nanabush, the Anishnabe trickster god who brings up the mud from beneath the waters from which a new world and new humans will be formed. At the same time, each woman is referred to as God: Dora-Rouge is the "closest thing to God" (182); Bush "created light" as "God had done in one day" (73) and wants to redo God's creation of human beings and "do it right this time" (86); Angel experiences "the same longing for creation" as God (94); even Hannah participates "in the same life-creating act as God" (251), bringing Angel into being out of her loneliness, as God creates the world. Bush herself epitomizes a kind of holism that is more than pluralism, yet does not obliterate difference—she is both God and "goddess" (75), "neither Catholic nor Protestant" but a "person of the land," whose altar of "statues of saints and crosses alongside eagle feathers, tobacco, and photographs of loved ones" (71) assembles the signs of both earth and sky religions, and even the religion of technology.

Hogan traces the breaking of the covenant between humans and animals that was part of Native American participation in the fur trade back to yet another origin—Christianity's patriarchal "dominion theology" and the hierarchical institution it created, which requires practices of exclusion and domination of women and animals. Hogan reinstates the power of women within Christianity by blending its stories not only with indigenous ones but also with earlier versions of Christianity's own narratives. The name "Adam's Rib," where Angel's journey both begins and ends, suggests one of two accounts of creation in Genesis, one that makes woman subordinate to man; Hogan's narrative, however, incorporates the other, more gender-balanced version. According to Elaine Pagels,

> Genesis contains not one but two distinct accounts of creation, of
> which the first begins with the opening chapter of Genesis and tells

how God created the world in six days, crowning his achievement by creating *adam*—that is, humanity—in his image (Genesis 1:26). But this account ends with Genesis 2:3; and the following verse, Genesis 2:4, begins a different narrative. This second story tells how the Lord made a man out of earth, and, after making all the animals and finding none of them a suitable companion for Adam, he put Adam to sleep, brought woman out of his side, and presented her to Adam as his wife. The woman then persuaded her husband to dis-obey divine law and earned with him their expulsion from Paradise.[23]

Hogan's retelling of Genesis—"People say that in the beginning was the word. But they have forgotten the loneliness of God, the yearning for some-thing that shaped itself into the words, Let there be. Out of that loneliness, light was conceived, water opened across a new world, and people rose up from clay" (94)—infuses the act of creation with the imagery of female creative processes of conception and opening. It also comes closer to the first creation story that appears in Genesis, which tells of the equal creation of man and woman, rather than the chronologically earlier second version that brings Eve forth from the body of Adam, marking her as subordinate and flawed.[24] Left behind in the wake of the fur trade, "The first women at Adam's Rib had called themselves the Abandoned Ones" (28), a choice of words that also evokes the story of Adam's first wife Lilith, whom God ban-ished from the Garden of Eden for refusing to submit to Adam.[25]

In addition, in Hogan's narrative, God is not a primary unity, prior, complete, and transcendent, but co-creator with the world. Creation is born of God's desire, the word God speaks from loneliness speaks others into being, from whom new desires and new lives emerge. Angel and her grandmothers are part of God, and God inhabits the world the way the women do. God's identity is articulated within the processes of creation, processes born of the splitting of wholeness and the hunger for comple-tion. In such a system, human suffering, the pain of death and birth, are not the wages of original sin, visited by a jealous god for the misuse of free will, but are inextricable from creation, part of the cycle of wholeness within which no creation is possible that does not also entail loss. As Hogan puts it in an interview, Angel's spirituality is a spirituality of dailiness, acquired "not by any tricks of instant waking, but by hard work, by loss, by learning from life about pain and hurt, death and wisdom."[26] "[G]rowth takes time," Hogan observes elsewhere; "And for women, it happens when we give

ourselves up to the process of it, the uprooting, the limbo world of the unknown we cannot control."[27]

Angel's arrival at Adam's Rib in the fall inverts the biblical Fall; Angel's
"innocence"—her lack of knowledge of personal and tribal histories—
distances her from herself and the world, and her "fall" into history and
knowing restores her to paradise, a paradise that has been refigured, not as
a static originary oneness with God, but as a flowing wholeness, a cyclical
interpenetration of creation and destruction. Angel's interior journey includes the struggle to come to terms with a God and Christianity that she
can accept as consistent with her own experience. As she learns the traditional beliefs (everything is alive) and oral creation stories of the Cree and
Anishnabe, she revises the notions of God and creation she has received
from institutional Christianity. Angel negotiates her own relationship with
God, piecing together a new God as she reassembles the fragments of her
self. Passing God Island, Angel "had a feeling of intimacy. It was open and
inviting. . . . Or," she thinks, "perhaps it was the word 'God' that was inviting to me" (169).[28] After Agnes's death Angel hates God and wishes that
"the mysteries of, the fire of stars were a nature separate from that of death"
(211). She comes to recognize that "the world was alive and that all creatures were God" (139), that God "was everything beneath my feet, everything surrounded by water; it was in the air, and there was no such thing as
empty space" (170). The numerous repetitions of the word *God* in the text
connect to form a fluid web, which takes shape in Angel's realization that
the name "does not refer to any deity, but means simply to call out and pray,
to summon" (169). Hogan thus links Christianity to its gnostic roots, part
of a pattern in the novel that makes a circle of Western traditions, tying
them back to their "origins."[29] Orthodox Christianity, Pagels points out in
her examination of gnostic branches of early Christianity, "insist[s] that a
chasm separates humanity from its creator,"[30] a chasm that mirrors Western
splits between mind and body, subject and object, humanity and nature.
Solar Storms, like the gnostic gospels, suggests that "self-knowledge is knowledge of God; the self and the divine are identical."[31]

Solar Storms continues the project of rewriting the Bible begun by the
Osage healer and firekeeper Michael Horse in *Mean Spirit*, a project that
Kimberly Blaeser notes challenges "the exclusiveness of religious experience [and] the privileging of text over oral tradition," marking a shift from
the fixed system of religion to "spirituality, which involves the interactive
formation of relationships."[32] At the end of *Mean Spirit* we are introduced

to the "Gospel according to Horse," in which Horse corrects the Christian "mistake" that gives man dominion over the animals, and adds the "missing" commandments:

> Honor father sky and mother earth. Look after everything. Life resides in all things, even the motionless stones. Take care of the insects for they have their place, and the plants and trees for they feed the people. Everything on earth, every creature and plant wants to live without pain, so do them no harm. Treat all people in creation with respect; all is sacred, especially the bats.
>
> Live gently with the land. We are one with the land. We are part of everything in our world, part of the roundness of cycles of life. The world does not belong to us. We belong to the world. And all life is sacred.
>
> Pray to the earth. Restore your self and voice. Remake your spirit, so that it is in harmony with the rest of nature and the universe. Keep peace with all your sisters and brothers. Humans whose minds are healthy desire such peace and justice. . . . This is the core of all religion.[33]

In *Solar Storms*, Dora-Rouge adds the lost and forgotten days of creation: on the eighth day, "human beings were given their place with the earth," on the ninth day "was the creation of stories," and on the tenth day was given the knowledge to communicate with the "voices of the world" (181). Other days were devoted to crawling things and insects, the creation of singing and songs, since "Creation, according to Dora-Rouge, was an ongoing thing" (181), kept alive and moving through story and song.

Like Horse in *Mean Spirit*, Hogan writes as if "to write away the appearances of things, all the way back down to the bare truth."[34] *Solar Storms* patiently deconstructs "appearances"—the "parts" that are singular identities given form out of chaos by skins and words and maps—and restructures them to demonstrate their inherence in the whole of creation, an inherence that is mappable in the journeys of particles, atoms and diatoms, dust and light. Hogan "writes away" the notion that the identity of inside and out, human and land, human and animal, human and god is an "idea," a metaphoric or metonymic equivalence, "down to the truth" that these equivalencies are material, as material as the specks of dust around which infinitely varied snowflakes form, as material as the hydrogen and oxygen that combine to form vast bodies of water. Thus the myths of creation tell the literal, material histories of life on earth, collapsing time into timefulness, where the "time between histories falls away" (303).

As Vine Deloria argues in *God Is Red*, the West's obsession with time, with history and progress, allows "time to consume place" and leaves Christianity with nothing but abstract rules divorced from context, a concept of a creation that "determined all other facts of . . . existence."[35] In *Solar Storms*, origins are "everything," and, as in Genesis, each "word shaped what would follow. . . . It determined the kind of world that would be created" (37). But Hogan does not shift "from a temporal to a spatial framework," as Deloria suggests that religion must do,[36] but rather re/spatializes time, regrounding the abstract in place and demonstrating that place and person are always in process. Salvation lives in the telling and retelling of the stories that speak our interconnectedness into being. There is no beyond, just as there is "no empty space." What humans hunger for and imagine to be elsewhere (the mother, identity, wholeness, God, salvation) is already within us, and we are held within it.

Conclusion: The Covenant of the Flesh

When she arrives at Adam's Rib, Angel is lost from place and community, lost from the old ways, as a result of historical violence and displacement. Similarly lost and even more violently abused, Hannah is emptied of self and becomes a "meeting place" (101) inhabited by the shadows and voices of her torturers. While Hannah's living body is a "house of lament and sacrifice" (250), and only a second sacrifice (her murder) can free her and restore a kind of balance to the world, Angel re-creates with her body the ancient pact with the living world that Hannah was unable to make. Thus Angel becomes not sacrifice but "sacrament" (16), her flesh uniting her community and her two cultures, the human and nonhuman worlds. Her body becomes a site of healing where the old world enters the new world that is coming into being. Angel's consciously re-created self comes into being in relationship with all of life, and simultaneously the universe comes into being through her, re-creating itself anew in her. Angel is herself the remade covenant between humans and animals, humans and earth.

Returning to Adam's Rib with Aurora, after the protestors have temporarily halted the dam project, Angel's journey circles once again. She performs both a heroic journey of individuation, the recovery of a unified sense of self, identity, and agency formed in opposition to destructive forces—*and* a communal subjectivity within a relational field that includes both the human and nonhuman world. Hogan has commented elsewhere on the destructiveness of Western individualism, which often sacrifices other people and nature to the needs of the individual.[37] Yet *Solar Storms* demonstrates the importance of recovering an individual identity, of remapping a securely bounded ego, out of the chaos of destruction—the loss of personal and communal histories, the repetition of abuse of self and others—that is the legacy of Conquest. Early in the narrative, Agnes tells Angel, "Nobody knows where it began, your story," but Angel also knows that "[b]eginnings were important to my people" (37). In fact, she observes later, "Beginnings . . . are everything" (334); in an evolving universe, origins may be both everywhere and nowhere, infinitely deferred, but the quest for them is crucial to piecing back together the skeletons of lost and stolen histories and identities, so that each agent's participation in ongoing creation can be conscious and response-able.[38]

Hogan makes it clear that the terrible destruction visited upon the earth and bodies in the name of power and progress has its source in the splitting of matter and spirit, the "removal of spirit from everything" that was the "legacy" of the Europeans, who "trapped themselves inside their own destruction of [the world]" (180). In her 1994 essay "Department of the Interior," Hogan observes, "We [humans] are what is missing from the equation of wholeness."[39] Western culture, seeking objective knowledge and a "pure" spirituality that transcends the material, has abstracted itself from that equation. *Solar Storms* foregrounds women, Natives, and nature—historically objectified and commodified—and the associated participatory knowledges of body and deep ecological interdependencies suppressed by Enlightenment materialism and Christianity's demonization of flesh. Yet in Hogan's work there is no simplistic replacement of one model for another. Hogan merges the Judeo-Christian God of omniscience and omnipotence with an indigenous spirituality, the "God's-eye view" of objectivity with embodied knowledges. Hogan's novel also shifts perspectives to recognize the sentience of the natural world. As Angel puts it, "no one lives in full humanity" without the elements of "land, water, animals, trees" (324); humans do not fully come into being unless "the eyes of land . . . and creatures tak[e] our measure" (177). This shift of vision, like the one that allows Angel to see inside water, re-embodies God's eye in the individual and the collective soma from which it emerges.

NOTES

1. William Bevis, "American Indian Novels: Homing In," in *Recovering the Word: Essays on Native American Literature,* ed. Brian Swann and Arnold Krupat (Berkeley: University of California Press, 1987), 590.

2. Ibid., 581.

3. Linda Hogan, *Mean Spirit* (New York: Ivy Books, 1990).

4. See Jace Weaver, "Introduction: Notes from a Miner's Canary," in *Defending Mother Earth: Native American Perspectives on Environmental Justice,* ed. Jace Weaver (Maryknoll, N.Y.: Orbis Books, 1996), 14–15, and Vine Deloria, *God Is Red: A Native View of Religion* (Golden, Colo.: Fulcrum, 1994), 78–97, for discussions of dominion theology.

5. Kimberly Blaeser, "Pagans Rewriting the Bible: Heterodoxy and the Representation of Spirituality in Native American Literature," *Ariel* 25, no. 1 (1994): 18.

6. Catherine Rainwater, *Dreams of Fiery Stars: The Transformations of Native American Fiction* (Philadelphia: University of Pennsylvania Press, 1999), 47.

7. Hogan, *Mean Spirit,* 138, 362.

8. Linda Hogan, *Solar Storms* (New York: Scribner, 1995). Subsequent page citations to this work will be given parenthetically in the text.

9. For an exploration of cultural mediation in contemporary Native American fiction, see James Ruppert, *Mediation in Contemporary Native American Fiction* (Norman: University of Oklahoma Press, 1995).

10. Arnold Krupat, *The Turn to the Native: Studies in Criticism and Culture* (Lincoln: University of Nebraska Press, 1996), 8.

11. Bevis, "American Indian Novels," 582.

12. I borrow this term from Patrick D. Murphy, *Literature, Nature, and Other: Ecofeminist Critiques* (New York: State University of New York Press, 1995). Murphy defines a heterarchy as a "continuum in which difference exists without binary opposition and hierarchichal valorization" (5).

13. Bevis, "American Indian Novels," 589.

14. Kristina Groover, *The Wilderness Within: American Women Writers and Spiritual Quest* (Fayetteville: University of Arkansas Press, 1999), 124.

15. Ibid., 123.

16. Here I use the term and spelling *Anishnabe* that Hogan uses. Spelled variously, including *Anishnaabe, Anishinabe,* or *Anishinaabe,* the name refers to the people also known as Ojibway, Ojibwa, or Ojibwe. *Anishnabeg* is the plural form.

17. See Hugh Brody, "Maps of Dreams," in *Out of the Background: Readings on Canadian Native History,* ed. Robin Fisher and Kenneth Coates (Toronto: Copp Clark Pitman, 1988), 256–66. In this essay, Brody recounts his experiences among the Indians of British Columbia, who were still hunting by dreaming maps in the 1980s.

18. See Basil Johnston, *The Manitous: The Supernatural World of the Ojibway* (New York: HarperCollins, 1995), 222–27, for a discussion of windigo spirits.

19. Linda Hogan, "Department of the Interior," in *Minding the Body: Women Writers on Body and Soul,* ed. Patricia Foster (New York: Doubleday, 1994), 161.

20. Pangaea is the name given to the original single landmass from which the continents we know now broke away.

21. See Murphy, *Literature, Nature, and Other*, 5, for a discussion of the privileging of engendering in the history of Western culture.

22. Theresa S. Smith, *The Island of the Anishnaabeg: Thunderers and Water Monsters in the Traditional Ojibwe Life-World* (Moscow: University of Idaho Press, 1995).

23. Elaine Pagels, *Adam, Eve, and the Serpent* (New York: Vintage Books, 1989), xxi–xxii.

24. Ibid., xxii.

25. Lilith's story is recorded in the Kabbalah; see also Barbara Walker, *The Woman's Encyclopedia of Myths and Secrets* (San Francisco: HarperCollins, 1983), 541–42.

26. Laura Coltelli, *Winged Words: American Indian Writers Speak* (Lincoln: University of Nebraska Press, 1990), 76. In this interview, Hogan describes an earlier version of the novel, in which Angel's character is called Roberta.

27. Hogan, "Department of the Interior," xii.

28. God Island has been renamed Smith's Island, another of the novel's pervasive signs of the continuing desacralization of the world, which Angel resacralizes as she moves through it.

29. And to even earlier roots in Jewish mysticism; see, e.g., David A. Cooper's exploration of the Kabbalah and practices of mystical Judaism, *God Is a Verb: Kabbalah and the Practice of Mystical Judaism* (New York: Riverhead Books, 1997).

30. Elaine Pagels, *The Gnostic Gospels* (New York: Vintage Books, 1989), xx.

31. Ibid.

32. Blaeser, "Pagans Rewriting the Bible," 21, 23.

33. Hogan, *Mean Spirit*, 361–62.

34. Ibid., 341.

35. Deloria, *God Is Red*, 74, 87.

36. Ibid., 68.

37. Hogan, "Department of the Interior."

38. Both Hogan and Blaeser use the hyphenated term *response-ability* to alter the meaning of the word toward a more embodied and interconnected sense of commitment to the world.

39. Hogan, "Department of the Interior," 168.

13

NUALA NÍ DHOMHNAILL AND WOMEN'S SENSUAL SPIRITUALITY

KIMBERLY R. MYERS

In a conversation published in *Sleeping with Monsters*, Nuala Ní Dhomhnaill claims that "for poetry to occur it has to come from a deeper level of the psyche. I call it the *lios* or 'faery fort,' . . . where the fairies live. My attitude is that the *lios* is not [in the Irish countryside] at all. It's within, the subconscious, which generally you can't get into, and poetry is bringing stuff from that other world into this world. Anything that comes from there will be imbued with an extraordinary charge, a luminous quality that will make it jump off the page."[1] Elsewhere, in an interview with Lucy McDiarmid and Michael Durkin, Ní Dhomhnaill links herself and the poetic process to another spiritual domain: "I never get over my fascination with the Annunciation, the virgin birth, and parthenogenesis. When I write a poem I have experienced inspiration and that is being impregnated by the divine. There is no other explanation."[2] These two statements reveal that Ní Dhomhnaill clearly regards herself and her poetic process as inherently spiritual and that that spirituality embraces both influences from her childhood in the West Kerry Gaeltacht: "pagan" preternaturalism and Christianity. In fact, one of the hallmarks of Ní Dhomhnaill's poetry is that she juxtaposes these pagan and Christian impulses to great effect, producing images that are sometimes quietly reverent and at other times exceedingly humorous. Whatever the tone, it is clear that she means to challenge traditional perceptions of the nature of spirituality. In this way, her work can be viewed as a literary complement to feminist revisionary theology; and it is in that context that I wish to begin.

To discuss spirituality in Ní Dhomhnaill's poetry, one must first adopt a working definition whose open-endedness Ní Dhomhnaill herself would endorse. Critic Kristina Groover provides a helpful beginning, characterizing spirituality as any "positive transformative experience."[3] Such an experience enables a person to realize the beauty and power of self and others — mind, body, and soul — within an increasingly broad context. What was hidden becomes clear, often in epiphanic fashion. Simply put, at its most basic level spirituality is an apprehension of or a belief in something greater than human beings normally are or perceive ourselves to be, and it may or may not involve a deity apart from the divine impulse within us. Ní Dhomhnaill's poems that reveal a luminosity of soul (the *lios*), as well as those that directly address codified religion, support this interpretation. Fittingly, this working definition is also well suited to feminist revisionary theology — alternatively known as feminist liberation theology.

The main goal of this field of study is to articulate an understanding of God that more fully incorporates and validates the experiences of women. In a contribution to *Literature and Theology at Century's End,* Judith Lee identifies two major directions in feminist revisionary theology. On the one hand are theologians who embrace non-Christian traditions of spirituality, such as earth religions and goddess worship, in order to be free from the oppressiveness of conventional patriarchal religions. On the other hand are theologians who immerse themselves in traditional religions — Judaism and Christianity in particular — in order to rewrite them, inscribing or excavating views that more fully accommodate the needs of those people typically disenfranchised by patriarchal religions — the poor and people of color, for instance.[4]

A key issue that feminist theologians challenge is the belief that ultimate spiritual growth occurs only by transcending the natural world and the things that bind us to it — most notably our corporeal bodies. Gender roles perpetuated in and by traditional religions are based in part on the essentialist belief that women are, because of the female body's natural rhythms and reproductive capabilities, more closely tied to the physical world than men. By contrast, men are the more rational creatures, who could, if it weren't for women who tempt them to sins of the flesh, achieve godlike transcendence. Feminist theology reverses this thinking, advocating the full expression and experience of a bodily existence that celebrates our "earthly relatedness."[5] As Elizabeth Dodson Gray explains, "Instead of distancing ourselves and withdrawing from the reality of life to find sacredness, we go toward that reality—toward bodies, toward nature, toward food, toward dust, toward transitory moments in relationships."⁶ In this way, we honor the "presence of the sacred embodied in earthly experience."⁷ This holistic perspective on body and spirit is precisely what we discover in the poetry of Nuala Ní Dhomhnaill.

The situation Nuala Ní Dhomhnaill finds herself in as a woman in a country that for centuries has been dominated by Catholicism is exactly what feminist theologians find objectionable. Catholicism's male, celibate priesthood promotes unrealistic images of female sexuality, consigning women to either the role of virgin or that of mother. Mary Condren explains this situation in her book *The Serpent and the Goddess: Women, Religion, and Power in Celtic Ireland:*

> Women have been identified with Eve, the symbol of evil, and can only attain sanctity by identifying with the Virgin Mary, the opposite of Eve. But this is an impossible task since we are told that Mary herself "was conceived without sin" and when she gave birth to Jesus remained a virgin. To reach full sanctity then, women have to renounce their sexuality, symbol of their role as Temptresses and the means by which they drag men down from their lofty heights. For this reason most of the women saints of the Catholic church have been either virgins, martyrs, widows, or married women who have taken a perpetual vow of continence. Sex and spirituality have become polar opposites in Christian teaching.⁸

So pervasive is the Catholic perspective that the (1937) Constitution of Ireland itself—framed in the preamble as a religious document—offers women a "right" to motherhood but to no other occupation, prescribing their role as reproducers of culture and nation and thus confining them to the domestic sphere while also denying them sexual freedom by outlawing contraceptive aids. Given this persistent religio-political climate, Irish women have had an especially difficult time claiming their full humanity as sexual and spiritual beings. Ní Dhomhnaill, however, artfully rejects this dualism by reuniting the sacred and the sensual in her poetry.

In some poems, Ní Dhomhnaill addresses the dualism within Christianity head on, exposing the shortsightedness of antifeminist portrayals of women as either licentious or asexual. Especially in her earliest (1986) volume, *Selected Poems: Rogha Danta*, she rewrites the characters of two principal biblical women, Eve and Mary, by revealing their human complexities and contradictions. "We Are Damned, My Sisters" is Ní Dhomhnaill's corrective to those who view Eve as the one-dimensional mother of (sexual) sin. In this poem, Ní Dhomhnaill creates a community of Eves past, present, and future who exult in the pleasures of the body and are "no longer concerned" with the patriarchy that condemns them:

> We spent nights in Eden's fields
> eating apples, gooseberries; roses
> behind our ears, singing songs
> around the gipsy bon-fires
> drinking and romping with sailors and robbers:
> and so we're damned, my sisters.[9]

Ní Dhomhnaill counters the view of pleasure as sinful with images of childlike exuberance, as the women

> swam at night
> . . . .
> with the stars
> laughing with us
> . . . .
> without shifts or dresses
> as innocent as infants.

Although such lawless behavior will result in their being served "as food to the parish dogs," the women will continue to subvert the oppressiveness of those who continue to damn them: "They'll find apple seeds and gooseberry skins / in the remains of our vomit / when we are damned, my sisters."

In "Poem for Melissa," presumably for the poet's daughter of that name, the speaker is even more defiant of patriarchal religions' cruelties toward women. She vows:

> Oh white daughter here's your mother's word:
> I will put in your hand the sun and moon
> I will stand my body between the millstones
> in God's mills so you are not totally ground.[10]

Ní Dhomhnaill fashions a new Eden that is freely offered without prohibitions and thus without a fall into bodily shame:

> I grant you all on this delicate earth.
> . . . .
> The garden gates forever wide open
> no flaming swords in hands of cherubim
> no need for a fig-leaf apron here
> in the pristine world I would delicately give.

Similar to the way in which Ní Dhomhnaill rewrites sexual shame into celebration—exuberant or gentle—in these Eve poems, she provides Mary with a healthy sexuality in "Annunciations," humanizing her without invalidating her impact on the world as mother of Christ. Ní Dhomhnaill writes:

> She remembered to the very end
> the angelic vision
> in the temple:
> the flutter of wings
> about her—
> noting the noise of doves,
> sun-rays raining
> on lime-white walls—
> the day she got the tidings.[11]

The description of the annunciation in this first stanza easily preserves the Christian tradition; Ní Dhomhnaill retains the images of the angel who delivers the tidings and of the Holy Spirit (often portrayed iconographically as a dove) descending to impregnate Mary. But the third stanza undercuts the traditional "sanctity" of the annunciation, as the speaker admonishes:

> Remember
> o most tender virgin Mary
> that never was it known
> that a man came to you
> in the darkness alone,
> his feet bare, his teeth white
> and roguery swelling in his eyes.

In retrospect, then, the "angelic vision" of the initial stanza is not to be taken literally; it is merely a way of describing a sexually charged human encounter. That Mary enjoyed a fully corporeal moment, however, does not alter the course of history or the power of the Christ she conceived. As Ní Dhomhnaill indicates in the middle stanza,

> two thousand years
> of carrying a cross
> two thousand years
> of smoke and fire

still occurred, despite the fact that "He"—whoever "He," the father of Christ, really was—"went away / and perhaps forgot" the encounter with Mary.

This poem affirms what feminist theologian Rosemary Radford Ruether calls the "critical principle of feminist theology": the "promotion of the *full* humanity of women" (emphasis mine). Ruether writes, "Whatever denies, diminishes, or distorts the full humanity of women is . . . appraised as not redemptive" in that it does not reflect the divine or bear an "authentic relation to the divine." The converse is also true: "what does promote the full humanity of women is of the Holy, it does reflect true relation to the divine, it is the true nature of things."[12] A woman's sexuality, then, is sacred because it is a natural, *integral* part of who she is. In "Annunciations," Ní Dhomhnaill forces us to rethink the assumption that Mary's identity as mother of God somehow hinges on her virginity. Indeed, the very humanity in Mary's susceptibility to a rogue with bare feet and white teeth makes her all the more capable of interceding on behalf of similarly vulnerable human beings. From this perspective, sexuality is an advantage, not a liability. In her book *Touching Our Strength: The Erotic as Power and the Love of God*, feminist theologian Carter Heyward clarifies the salvific nature of sexuality, claiming that "our erotic power is sacred" because it is at once fully human and, paradoxically, transcendent. Our erotic power "connects us in our most profoundly human, most deeply embodied, soulful places, making us who we are: a relational body of incarnate love. Through the real, daily presence and yearnings of our bodyselves, this sacred power is involved intimately in the lives of both women and men. God is not, therefore, above sex or gender, but rather is immersed in our gendered and erotic particularities."[13]

Because flesh and spirit are not pitted against each other in "pagan" religions as they are in Christianity, Ní Dhomhnaill celebrates the sacred power of the erotic even more fully in poems whose imagery is not exclusively Christian. Sacred and sensual impulses are beautifully conflated in the poem "Carnival," for example, in which Ní Dhomhnaill depicts a sexual union in images drawn from both Christian and earth religions. Ní Dhomhnaill herself says of the poem that it is "a 'mimesis' of lovemaking, of its sacramental quality and its ecstatic joy and pain."[14] The eleven-section poem begins:

When you rise in the morning
and pour into me
an unearthly music
rings in my ears.
A ray of sunshine comes
slender and spare
down the dark passageway
and through the gap
in the lintel
to trace a light-scroll
on the mud floor
in the nethermost
sealed chamber.
Then it swells
and swells until a golden glow
fills the entire oratory

From now on
the nights will be getting shorter
and the days longer and longer.[15]

The controlling image is that of a passage tomb—Newgrange here, during the rare minutes during the year when the sun is positioned just right at the winter solstice to flood the innermost darkness of the tomb, anticipating new life. Indeed, given the "Irish belief that death is a passageway into a new incarnation or a new enlightenment,"[16] the tomb is also paradoxically a womb, a place of generation. Whether one chooses to read the section literally—as the womb/tomb speaking to and of the sunlight—or metaphorically—as an open mound of earth and penetrating sunlight representing human sexual intercourse—Ní Dhomhnaill's point is clear: the coming together of human lovers, like that of the earth and sun, effects a radiance that is both physical and spiritual.

But another element is also at work in this section: a description of the poetic process, which Ní Dhomhnaill considers, as we recall, "divine." In early Irish literature, Newgrange is the residence of major figures of the Tuatha De Danaan (the divinities of pagan Ireland), including Oengus, famous lover and god of poetry. Because Irish mythology maintains the belief that humans can access two Otherworlds, one of which may by entered via an ancient burial mound, or passage grave,[17] surely part of this erotic experience is the contemporary poet's imaginative union with the archetypal poetic spirit of Oengus. And, as literary critic Deborah Consalvo says, it is "at the intersection of the natural world and the supernatural world—the temporal realm and the imaginative realm—that the potential for *self-recovery* is made possible through the powers of Otherworldly beings" (emphasis mine).[18] Such a union, then, would result not only in poetic inspiration but also in significant edification of the poet herself. In classical terms, this is a kairotic moment: the intersection of divine and mortal time, when life-altering changes are possible.

Even though the erotic relationship in the poem "Carnival" ends with a cavernous pain on the part of the speaker, she has nevertheless been opened to the *magnum mysterium*—the power greater than she is, which is beyond her understanding or control. And to be awakened to such a power—even with enormous distress—is what makes her at once human and transcendent. As feminist theologian Carol P. Christ says, "Eros reminds us of our embodiment, our finitude, our mortality, our inability fully to control the circumstances of our lives. But this is precisely its form of transcendence: eros gives meaning through depth of feeling, through our physicality, to our finite, mortal lives," and "Sexuality can make us intensely aware of our immersion in the rhythms of the universe, our ties to the whole web of life."[19]

Mircea Eliade explains this relationship between micro- and macrocosm more fully in his book *The Sacred and the Profane,* where he writes of religious festivals. Although Paul Muldoon translates Ní Dhomhnaill's original Irish title *Feis* as "Carnival," it can also be translated as "Festival," which is arguably more in keeping with the tone of the overall poem. Reading Ní Dhomhnaill's poem with the connotations of "festival" in mind, we find Eliade's discussion germane to the meaning Ní Dhomhnaill wants to convey. Eliade writes, "Every religious festival, any liturgical time, represents the reactualization of a sacred event that took place in a mythical past, 'in the beginning.' Religious participation in a festival implies emerging from ordinary temporal duration and reintegration of the mythical time reactualized by the festival itself. Hence sacred time is indefinitely recoverable, indefinitely repeatable. . . . [I]t neither changes nor is exhausted."[20]

Ní Dhomhnaill herself explains that the word *feis* comes from the Old Irish *fo-aid*, which means "sleeping with."[21] Understandably, then, Ní Dhomhnaill portrays the specific moment of reactualizing a sacred event in erotic terms. The lovemaking is a kairotic instant in which time as the lovers know it is suspended because it is somehow infused with a divinity they can touch, though only briefly.

In the second section of the poem, Ní Dhomhnaill writes:

such is the depth of emotion
we share
that neither of us speaks
as much as a word
for ages and ages

and later, in the third section, "The heavenly bodies stop / only for a single, transitory moment."[22] Ní Dhomhnaill's double entendre works especially well: the heavenly bodies of sun and moon suspend their diurnal round as the bodies of the lovers, made heavenly in their passion, experience complete unity. The paradox is rich: the suspension of time is only momentary, yet "ages and ages" are telescoped in the instant that the lovers lie together. God and the universe have become incarnate; and, reciprocally, the lovers have become part god. Significantly, theologian Carter Heyward describes this sort of erotic experience in just those terms. She writes, "Sex is a process of godding, of moving physically, emotionally, and spiritually together into a strengthening of our capacities to respect and delight in ourselves and others. Crossing boundaries erotically in this way can be a fully incarnate experience of transcendence, in which God comes with us, touching and touched in her deepest places."[23]

Ní Dhomhnaill depicts such erotic godding not only in Celtic and Christian terms but also in the context of classical mythology. In the poem "Daphne and Apollo" from her most recent volume, *The Water Horse*, the divine presence is that of Apollo, god of poetry; and Ní Dhomhnaill speculates what might have happened if Daphne had opened herself sexually instead of metamorphosing into a laurel. Underscoring the "mortal[ity]" of Daphne's soul, Ní Dhomhnaill depicts her body as fully sensual, capable of mutual passion with a god who, in this revision of the myth, is gentle and loving. In reminding Daphne of her sensuality, the speaker suggests a very different scenario than is legendarily true: "a lacy skin coated your breasts, leaves / flowed in the branches of your hair . . . / your mortal soul floated where the tree shone."[24] Re-envisioning an encounter in which "the immortal traced even the grain of your timber / sensing your frightened pulse in the warm boughs," the speaker asks Daphne:

> . . . just say, for the laugh, you had played
> along; that the door-leaves of your heart
> had jammed wide open, instead of their floodgates
> locking against that epiphanic assault—
> what would have been the result?

Especially with the use of the word *epiphanic*, Ní Dhomhnaill implies that the coupling of Daphne and Apollo could have effected another kind of transformation than the legend presents—one that would be positive for both characters in that the union would be at once fully sensual and fully spiritual. Indeed, in the final stanza, Ní Dhomhnaill again employs imagery that suggests a creativity, a kind of inspiration and new life born of such a sensual/spiritual encounter:

> He wasn't the liver-tearing, date-rape type,
> but the sun-god pouring inspiration-grace,
> displaying himself at such a morning peak,
> he would rouse the wind that moved over
> the face of the deep. When this harpist
> tautens his strings, the water snake
> stands to attention; at this dawn
> chorus, silence spills like a swan.

Ní Dhomhnaill's poeticizing the sacramental, life-giving quality of erotic love in the natural world reflects feminist theologian Rosemary Radford Ruether's belief that "[t]he liberating encounter with God/dess is always an encounter with our authentic selves resurrected from underneath the alienated self. It is not experienced against, but in and through relationships, healing our broken relations with our bodies, with other people, with nature."[25] This belief is evident in the poem "Island," for instance, where the speaker's lover

> . . . gave me a cooling drink
> when I was burning
> a healing drink
> when I was feverish . . .[26]

clearly referring to Christ's exhortation to minister to one in need that appears in Matthew 25:35. Christ says, "For I was hungry and you gave me food; I was thirsty and you gave me drink; I was a stranger and you made me welcome."[27] In this poem, such sharing of food and drink is depicted in sensual imagery that, if read metaphorically, suggests the healing power of sexual intercourse to cool burning, feverish flesh.

In "Labysheedy" (or "The Silken Bed"), Ní Dhomhnaill alludes to the Old Testament Promised Land of "milk and honey," which she makes explicitly sensual through comparisons to her lover's skin and the evening air:

> Skin which glistens
> shining over your limbs
> like milk being poured
> from jugs at dinnertime
> . . . .
> And your damp lips
> would be as sweet as sugar
> at evening and we walking
> by the riverside
> with honeyed breezes
> blowing over the Shannon. . . .[28]

The speaker says *sotto voce* to her lover:

> I'd make a bed for you
> in Labysheedy
> in the tall grass
> under the wrestling trees
> where your skin
> would be silk upon silk

in the darkness
when the moths are coming down.
. . . .
and what a pleasure it would be
to have our limbs entwine
wrestling
while the moths are coming down.

Echoing the sacredness that feminist theology ascribes to ordinary experiences and domestic spaces, Ní Dhomhnaill casts her poem in images of "mak[ing] a bed," eating dinner, and taking a postprandial stroll by the river.

"Blodewedd" is arguably the most interesting of these poems that unify humanity, divinity, and nature in an erotic way, for it both glorifies love and love's regenerative potential and humanizes it to the most basic, even "unpoetic" level. The first four stanzas portray human touch metaphorically as sunshine, as in "Carnival." Here, however, the tone is even more effusive:

At the least touch of your fingertips
I break into blossom,
my whole chemical composition
transformed.
I sprawl like a grassy meadow
fragrant in the sun;
at the brush of your palm, all my herbs
and spices spill open
. . . .
Your sun lightens my sky
and a wind lifts, like God's angel,
to move the waters,
every inch of me quivers
before your presence. . . .[29]

After this "blossoming," "sprawling," inspired awakening to the godlike power of love, we find the speaker in the ladies' toilet, lingering:

a sweet scent wafting
from all my pores,
proof positive, if a sign
were needed, that at the least

touch of your fingertips
I break into blossom.

The effect is at once bathetic and exalted and reinforces the idea that the most human, bodied connection is also the most divine. Ní Dhomhnaill cautions the contemporary reader against interpreting this scenario as somehow "dirty," explaining that "the attitude to the body enshrined in Irish remains extremely open and uncoy. It is almost impossible to be 'rude' or 'vulgar' in Irish. The body, with its orifices and excretions, is not treated in a prudish manner but is accepted as *an naduir,* or nature."[30] Because Christian teaching has traditionally vilified the body, discovering that sexuality can be liberating also positively alters the view that the body and its excretory processes are filthy and shameful—a change in perspective that results in a healthy acceptance of one's full self.

In an attempt to clarify the precise nature of Ní Dhomhnaill's revisionist agenda in poems such as these, interviewers McDiarmid and Durkan suggest that she is "prefeminist, not postfeminist,"[31] despite the fact that her initial volumes appear in the mid- to late-1980s and early 1990s, squarely within what is generally considered post- (or third-wave) feminism. The poet responds, "I don't know what I am, but I know my grandmother was a feminist and my mother was a feminist and sometimes I am a feminist, but what feminism has to do changes from generation to generation. . . . It seems to me in my generation that an inner change is taking place."[32] Ní Dhomhnaill's retort is indeed in line with third-wave feminists' aversion to a prescriptive political agenda; and examining Ní Dhomhnaill's poetry in light of recent feminist trends deepens our understanding of the nuances of her depiction of women's sensual spirituality.

Echoing Hegel and affirming a basic tenet of third-wave feminism, Ruether cautions that, in an effort to assert woman's full humanity, "women cannot simply reverse the sin of sexism. Women cannot simply scapegoat males for historical evil in a way that makes themselves only innocent victims. Women cannot affirm themselves as *imago dei* and subjects of full human potential in a way that diminishes male humanity."[33] In the same spirit, postfeminist Naomi Wolf claims that women can "hate sexism without hating men. . . . A true radical is not content to just tear down and turn away; these are the skills of the weak. She assumes the responsibilities of the strong, and builds up. If a system is morally incoherent, she builds it up better, builds it into the light. . . . True radicalism . . . is a woman who is thinking under nobody's control, and reaching no one's conclusions but her own."[34] In short, women do not have to choose between a healthy "feminist" self-image and the pleasures of heterosexual relationships; rather, they can choose to pursue "both/and" thinking. And this is what is so refreshing about Ní Dhomhnaill's work: she is not apologetic about casting her female personae in powerful heterosexual relationships that depict men as worthy of the love of women. Nor is she bashful about showing the power struggle between women and men, for she assumes that women are strong enough to "hold their own" with powerful men.

Although characterized—along with Katie Roiphe, Rene Denfeld, Camille Paglia, and Christina Hoff Sommers—as a "feminist dissenter"[35] and often dismissed by academic feminists as anti-intellectual and reductive, Naomi Wolf is nevertheless an important voice to consider in a study of Ní Dhomhnaill's poetry. Both writers appeal (though not exclusively) to popular audiences, and both use blunt language and bold tones—even overstatement—for shock effect; the "unholy glee"[36] that these women share at flying in the face of convention is a source of power. In these ways, Wolf and Ní Dhomhnaill adopt a third-wave stance. Philosophers Leslie Heywood and Jennifer Drake point out in their volume *Third Wave Agenda: Doing Feminism, Being Feminist* that third-wave feminism "contains elements of second wave critique of beauty culture, sexual abuse, and power structures" but also acknowledges and makes use of the "pleasure, danger, and defining power of those structures."[37] Both Wolf and Ní Dhomhnaill reveal how power in women is increasingly perceived as erotic—as it has been perceived for generations in men. In her book *Fire with Fire: The New Female Power and How It will Change the 21st Century*, Wolf urges women to move beyond what she calls "victim feminism" to a healthier "power feminism," and she offers some important psychological strategies for women who want to facilitate that shift. One of the most interesting challenges she provides is for women to "claim our dark side and take responsibility for it."[38] In the strong female personae she creates, Ní Dhomhnaill certainly acknowledges Wolf's contention that "aggression, competitiveness, the wish for autonomy and separation, even the danger of selfish and violent behavior, are as much a part of female identity as are nurturant behaviors."[39] Maire Mhac an tSaoi points out that Ní Dhomhnaill frequently adopts the alter ego of the archetypal Mother-goddess, which "allows her to voice all the suppressed evil in the female principle . . . [the] basic element, of which all women are aware, although it chills the blood when it is 'so set down.'"[40] According to

Barbara Walker, unlike later patriarchal societies, which admitted a goddess figure only as "the passive, humble, ever-benevolent Mother . . . like
Mary, prepatriarchal societies frankly envisioned" the actively sexual and destructive aspect of the goddess energy as natural: "In nature, they reasoned,
destruction is as necessary to cosmic balance as creation."[41] It is often in the
context of Ní Dhomhnaill's sensual spirituality that this darker female energy emerges as some sort of threat to the male lover.

Ní Dhomhnaill creates this scenario at times through subtle wordplay
and imagery that suggest beguiling danger or entrapment. The finest example of this form is "The Shannon Estuary Welcomes the Fish." As in
"Carnival" and "Daphne and Apollo," sexual passion is depicted metaphorically in images of the natural world; here, however, the female principle is
neither the womb/tomb of Newgrange nor the fecund laurel tree but an estuary of the River Shannon that beckons the phallic salmon as a lover. The
salmon—

> All meat
> . . . . . .
> Almost nothing of bone
> Less of entrail
> Twenty packed pounds
> Of tensed muscle
> Straining . . .[42]

is visually likened to the erect penis—especially in light of the first stanza
where, pink-fleshed, it leaps in darkness, bare. Although the estuary "sing[s]
a lullaby / To [her] darling" as he nests naively "among the neat mosses,"
she is not merely "welcoming" but also implicitly *luring* the salmon to his
demise; for the estuary is fraught with snares, "net- / Draped and slippery /
Full of seaweed." Inasmuch as the nets have been placed by fishermen and
seaweed is a natural part of waterways, the estuary cannot perhaps at this
point be viewed as willfully destructive to her lover. But Ní Dhomhnaill
concludes the poem by focusing on the estuary's volition in this erotic
enterprise. As natural femme fatale, she names the salmon her "chosen
one, drawn from afar," a detail that can be read either merely as indica-
tive of pointed desire *or* as having sinister malice aforethought. It is interesting that Ní Dhomhnaill depicts the salmon as a "bare [or "naked"
in her own translation from the Irish][43] blade"; for this suggests that he too
has the potential for cruelty. That the estuary is nevertheless destined to

better him through her "softness," however, heightens the tension of the seduction/destruction.

The salmon in this poem also functions in a spiritual capacity. In Celtic mythology, the white-and-red-speckled Salmon of Knowledge provides the hero Fionn with divine insight and the gift of poetry. Because Fionn accesses this otherworldly wisdom by chewing on the thumb burned by the Salmon as Fionn was cooking it for his druid teacher,[44] we infer that ingesting or otherwise incorporating the Salmon into one's own body enables that person to transcend the mortal realm. The integration of salmon into river—like the merging of two lovers—effects a momentary union with the divine, a positive experience that is desirable despite any potential pain or danger.

Ní Dhomhnaill sometimes casts this threateningly sensual transformative experience in explicitly Christian terms. In "Monk," for instance, Ní Dhomhnaill's Eve retains her biblical identity as temptress; but the temptation is toward sensual and spiritual life and beauty—toward salvation, not damnation. The speaker's tone is at once reverential, racy, and subtly ominous as she says quietly:

> You are St Anthony
> or some other saint
> sitting in your rocky
> hermitage.
> You make the sign of the cross—
> wind and sea no longer toss.
> Your hands are full of larks.
>
> I am Temptation.
> You know me.
> Sometimes I'm Eve,
> sometimes the snake:
> I slide into your reverie
> in the middle of brightest day.
> I shine like the sun in an orchard.
>
> But its not to torment you
> every day I rise—
> but to drown you
> in love's delights.
> . . . .

That's the only reason I haunt you:
my monk, my apostle, my priest.[45]

Though at first it seems undesirable, perhaps it is good for this ascetic to "drown" in the watery depths of a woman's sexual love. Perhaps to do so would be a greater "spiritual" experience than all of his prayer and fasting—even if it is fatal on some level, even if he experiences the loss of (separate) self that one would hope for in the process of erotic "godding." Audre Lorde's observation in "Uses of the Erotic: The Erotic as Power" is directly pertinent to Ní Dhomhnaill's suggestion in this poem. Lorde writes, "[W]e have attempted to separate the spiritual and the erotic, thereby reducing the spiritual to a world of flattened affect, a world of the ascetic who aspires to feel nothing. But nothing is farther from the truth. For the ascetic position is one of the highest fear, the gravest immobility. The severe abstinence of the ascetic becomes the ruling obsession. And it is one not of self-discipline but of self-abnegation."[46] By contrast, when we begin to live in full recognition of the erotic power within us we "begin to give up, of necessity, being satisfied with suffering and self-negation, and with the numbness that so often seems like their only alternative in our society. Our acts against oppression become integral with self, motivated and empowered from within."[47]

Expanding her spiritual vision to include Eastern religion, Ní Dhomhnaill provides another version of this kind of transformative but dangerous erotic encounter in her poem "Kundalini." The ideas here are based on Hinduism and Tantric sex, where sexuality is the very vehicle for spiritual enlightenment and union with the divine. As the psychosexual energy found in everyone, Kundalini is often associated with the power of Shakti, the female principle, because of its location at the base of the spine in the "root chakra." Visually, Kundalini manifests in the form of a coiled serpent, alternately a symbol of wisdom and of danger—and perhaps both simultaneously, depending upon one's theological perspective. It resides in a triangular bone called the Sacrum, which suggests that it is a holy or "sacred" part of the body, the seat of supernatural powers. Practitioners of Tantric sex use special methods of breathing, meditation, and touch to awaken this energy by uniting male and female principles. The feminine, sexual, creative energy (Shakti) rises up and merges with the male consciousness (Shiva) in the chakra at the crown of the head. This union of male and female energies enables partners to achieve supreme liberation of thought and body, thereby experiencing the divine.

Ní Dhomhnaill writes:

Don't unblock your heart—
in there a serpent
lies in loops.

. . . .
She rises up behind you
sharp and terrible her voice
throughout the land.

Hot coals and glowing fires
her swollen candle eyes
freezing your pulse's blood.

. . . .
She swells, spines on her back:
she'd eat five-sixths of the world
without permission.

She's there indeed—
sempiternally.
!Ay! Senor—c'est la vie.[48]

The magnitude of terror that Ní Dhomhnaill depicts in this poem certainly
seems plausible if one considers what a staggering psychological feat it would
be to enter the realm of the divine. Indeed, one could argue that no merging of mortal and immortal worlds could occur *without* such fear. But in her
lighthearted twist in the last line, Ní Dhomhnaill also dismisses the terror as
merely a part of life—for those who choose to live fully, body and soul.

While Ní Dhomhnaill's female personae in "The Shannon Estuary
Welcomes the Fish," "Monk," and "Kundalini" use their erotic power in a
somewhat sinister way, it is important to recognize that their doing so does
not deprive the man of sexual pleasure. The domination is neither complete
nor final; it is merely one step in the dance of Eros. Contemporary feminists might well conclude with Mhac an tSaoi that "we are immeasurably
in [Ní Dhomhnaill's] debt" for her willingness to poeticize this darker side
of women; for "she has restored to us something of our lost wholeness;
there can be no transcendent virtue without some inkling of the abyss."[49]

As if to balance this potency in women and their sexuality, third-wave feminists also advocate levity, thereby resisting the stereotype of feminists as "humorless, . . . angry . . . and fanatically invested in 'political correctness.'"[50] Wolf, for instance, urges that we "abandon the notion that the fight for equality has to be gloomy" and that we "take every opportunity to make it playful, witty, sexy, and fun."[51] One who practices power feminism is aware of her own innate power and can dispense with the all-encompassing sobriety that leaves no room for celebration of that power. This attitude is a healthy complement to the earnestness of feminist liberation theology, and one that Ní Dhomhnaill embraces with irreverent exuberance in some of her poetic depictions of transformative erotic experiences.

Among Ní Dhomhnaill's finest poems are those in which erotic wit is an invitation to or description of mutually gratifying sexual activity in which unabashed sexual passion poses no threat to either partner. These poems reveal a healthy realignment of power between the sexes: the woman is sure enough of herself to meet her partner as an equal; she has no need to subjugate the male lover, only enjoy what they create together. "Celebratory" and often "bawdy"[52] in their boisterous punning and double entendres, these poems reveal personae who exult in carnal pleasure for its own sake. In *Sleeping with Monsters*, Ní Dhomhnaill says that in addition to the more destructive side of female energy, "Sometimes I write love poems through the female muse and that feels right. The veritable experience of that female energy, which is not particularly goal-directed, is to do with the joy of being."[53]

At first glance, these poems are not ostensibly spiritual at all. But if one accepts the premise that sharing physical love is in itself a spiritual experience that transforms the ordinary into the extraordinary, then the poems are spiritual in the truest sense; for as Carter Heyward argues, "Lovemaking turns us simultaneously *into* ourselves and *beyond* ourselves. In experiencing the depths of our power in relation as pleasurable and good, we catch a glimpse of the power of right relation in larger, more complicated configurations of our life together," and we "are called forth more fully into becoming who we are—whole persons with integrity, together. Our shared power is sacred power, and it is erotic."[54]

In "Looking at a Man," Ní Dhomhnaill conveys a single-minded intensity that she modulates elsewhere, in "Nude." What in the former had been a lover's ardent appreciation—

Man, so long
In your limbs,

So broad-shouldered,
Fine-waisted,
Fair, masculine
From hair to toenails
And your sex
Perfect in its place,

You're the one they should praise
In public places . . .[55]

becomes in the latter an outrageously flirtatious invitation to "dance." Although the voyeuse praises her lover in ways similar to those in the previous poem—she again notes his shoulders, flank, back, waist, penis—this time she seduces him with playfulness, which is evident in musical words like *brolly, oxter, snazzy,* and *la-di-da.*[56] In this poem, Ní Dhomhnaill is, by her own admission, "a woman writer 'returning the compliment' to males who, inspired by a female muse, have written in praise of the female body,"[57] and she does so excellently simply by advising her lover that, since *his* body is so utterly tempting, "it would probably be best / for you to pull on your pants and vest / rather than send half the women of Ireland totally round the bend." The conclusion is archly flirtatious and overstated, all for the mutual pleasure of the speaker and her lover. Ní Dhomhnaill clearly believes that a woman's sexuality—and the spiritual power inherent therein—is not diminished in the least for "admitting" her powerful attraction to a man and his psychosexual energy. Nor is her lover emasculated by "offer[ing] himself up to a sexually evaluating gaze"; for, as Susan Bordo reasons in *The Male Body: A New Look at Men in Public and in Private,* thinking of such "receptive pleasures as 'passive' [and thus "effeminate"] . . . is just plain inaccurate. 'Passive' hardly describes what's going on when one person offers himself or herself to another. Inviting, receiving, responding—these are active behaviors too, and rather thrilling ones."[58]

The poem "Duil" (translated as "Desire") features the goddess Mor, who allows herself to be swept off her feet—literally—by a man's irresistible sexuality. The poem's brevity is central to its effectiveness:

"This man
with his hamper
makes me hungry,
his fresh fruits

before my eyes
drawing juice
from my thighs
and marrow
from my very joints
weakening my knees
to falling-point."

Oop-la!
She stumbles.
Mor is down.[59]

Here, going down before the *magnum mysterium* takes on new meaning! But there's no reason that it should be viewed as any less powerful just because it is humorous. Indeed, Mor's ability to laugh at her clumsiness (implied by the exclamation "Oop-la!") is a healthy complement to the raw, intensely focused desire that so moves her in the first stanza.

In "Rainbow" Ní Dhomhnaill even casts the humor in pointedly spiritual images. As in "Duil," the speaker literally "falls" for the man with whom she's suddenly infatuated. She begins by noticing

Showers about,
skyline glimmer,
velleities of light,
two pigeons clattered
from the mangels —
I looked again —
a rainbow owned
half the world,

so with you,
one to commence
like all the rest,
wouldn't give you
a second glance,

till I tripped
on the landing,
spun heels-over-head —

looked up—
the god loosed
his *coup de foudre* . . .

now you saddle cherubim,
coast the wind,
I watch rainbows stream
from the tips of your fingers.[60]

This poem highlights the power of a new love interest to quicken the life force within us, the "creative energy empowered," as Lorde calls it. This is the erotic evoking the numen, the divinity within us. It is a process of hierophany, as Eliade discusses it, whereby the sacred shows itself to us in epiphanic fashion—only this time, it occurs in the context of laughter.

As these poems amply illustrate, Nuala Ní Dhomhnaill exemplifies what Naomi Wolf calls a "psychology of abundance"[61] in which women reunify what was severed in the dualism upheld by Western patriarchal religion. Reinscribing sensuality and power in images of women's spirituality, Ní Dhomhnaill has accomplished primary goals of both feminist theology and third-wave feminism. We rightly imagine that Ní Dhomhnaill could say with Carol Christ, "I have learned that my writing is most powerful, most capable of influencing change in the world, when it is most in touch with the power of the erotic. . . . I have learned not to fear, but to celebrate, the rooting of my insight in the story of my life. I have learned to trust that when my writing is most open and vulnerable, it is also most powerful, most likely to touch a chord and to influence change in others."[62] It is because of this very vulnerability, courage, and passion that "her work is in the truest sense a work of piety."[63]

Notes

1. Gillean Somerville-Arjat and Rebecca E. Wilson, "Nuala Ní Dhomhnaill," in *Sleeping with Monsters: Conversations with Scottish and Irish Women Poets*, ed. Gillean Somerville-Arjat and Rebecca E. Wilson (Dublin: Wolfhound Press, 1990), 149–50.

2. Lucy McDiarmid and Michael Durkan, "Q. & A.: Nuala Ní Dhomhnaill," *Irish Literary Supplement* 6 (Fall 1987): 41–43.

3. Kristina K. Groover, *The Wilderness Within: American Women Writers and Spiritual Quest* (Fayetteville: University of Arkansas Press, 1999), 10.

4. Judith Lee, "'A New Interiority': Feminist Theologians, Women Writers, and Questions of Salvation," in *Literature and Theology at Century's End*, ed. Gregory Salyer and Robert Detweiler (Atlanta: Scholars Press, 1995), 43–68.

5. Ibid., 51.

6. Elizabeth Dodson Gray, *Sacred Dimensions of Women's Experience* (Wellesley, Mass.: Roundtable Press, 1988), 2.

7. Groover, *The Wilderness Within*, 9.

8. Mary Condren, *The Serpent and the Goddess: Women, Religion, and Power in Celtic Ireland* (San Francisco: HarperCollins, 1989), 5.

9. Nuala Ní Dhomhnaill, *Selected Poems: Rogha Danta*, trans. Michael Hartnett (Dublin: New Island Books, 2000), 15.

10. Ibid., 137.

11. Ibid., 45.

12. Rosemary Radford Ruether, *Sexism and God-Talk: Toward a Feminist Theology* (Boston: Beacon Press, 1983), 18–19.

13. Carter Heyward, *Touching Our Strength: The Erotic as Power and the Love of God* (San Francisco: Harper and Row, 1989), 103.

14. Nuala Ní Dhomhnaill, "Mother Ireland, Gaming and the Ard Fheis," *Yeats: An Annual of Critical and Textual Studies* 10 (1992): 196.

15. Nuala Ní Dhomhnaill, *The Astrakhan Cloak*, trans. Paul Muldoon (Winston-Salem, N.C.: Wake Forest University Press, 1993), 11.

16. Deborah McWilliams Consalvo, "The Lingual Ideal in the Poetry of Nuala Ní Dhomhnaill," *Eire-Ireland* 30 (Summer 1995): 159.

17. A. C. Partridge, *Language and Society in Anglo-Irish Literature* (Totowa, N.J.: Barnes and Noble, 1984), 24.

18. Consalvo, "The Lingual Ideal," 158.

19. Carol P. Christ, "In Praise of Aphrodite: Sexuality as Sacred," in *Sacred Dimensions of Women's Experience*, ed. Elizabeth Dodson Gray (Wellesley, Mass.: Roundtable Press, 1988), 226; Carol P. Christ, *Rebirth of the Goddess: Finding Meaning in Feminist Spirituality* (Reading, Mass.: Addison-Wesley Press, 1997), 147.

20. Mircea Eliade, *The Sacred and the Profane: The Nature of Religion*, trans. Willard R. Trask (New York: Harcourt Brace Jovanovich, 1959), 68–69.

21. Ní Dhomhnaill, "Mother Ireland," 196.

22. Ní Dhomhnaill, *The Astrakhan Cloak*, 13.

23. Heyward, *Touching Our Strength*, 150.

24. Nuala Ní Dhomhnaill, *The Water Horse*, trans. Medbh McGuckian and Eilean Ní Chuilleanain (Winston-Salem, N.C.: Wake Forest University Press, 2000), 65.

25. Ruether, *Sexism and God-Talk*, 71.

26. Ní Dhomhnaill, *Selected Poems*, 71.

27. *The New Testament of the Jerusalem Bible* (Garden City, N.Y.: Doubleday, 1996).

28. Ní Dhomhnaill, *Selected Poems*, 155.

29. Nuala Ní Dhomhnaill, *Pharaoh's Daughter*, rev. ed. (Winston-Salem, N.C.: Wake Forest University Press, 1993), 117.

30. Nuala Ní Dhomhnaill, "Why I Choose to Write in Irish, the Corpse That Sits up and Talks Back," in *Representing Ireland: Gender, Class, Nationality*, ed. Susan Shaw Sailer (Gainesville: University Press of Florida, 1997), 51.

31. McDiarmid and Durkan, "Q & A," 43.

32. Ibid.

33. Ruether, *Sexism and God-Talk*, 20.

34. Naomi Wolf, *Fire with Fire: The New Female Power and How It Will Change the 21st Century* (New York: Random House, 1993), 138, 115, 117.

35. Catherine M. Orr, "Charting the Currents of the Third Wave," *Hypatia: A Journal of Feminist Philosophy* 12, no. 3 (1997): 35, and Deborah L. Siegel, "The Legacy of the Personal: Generating Theory in Feminism's Third Wave," *Hypatia: A Journal of Feminist Philosophy* 12, no. 3 (1997): 47.

36. McDiarmid and Durkan, "Q & A," 42; Consalvo, "The Lingual Ideal," 156.

37. Leslie Heywood and Jennifer Drake, introduction to *Third Wave Agenda: Doing Feminism, Being Feminist*, ed. Leslie Heywood and Jennifer Drake (Minneapolis: University of Minnesota Press, 1998), 11.

38. Wolf, *Fire with Fire*, 318.

39. Ibid.

40. Maire Mhac an tSaoi, introduction to *Selected Poems: Rogha Danta*, by Nuala Ní Dhomhnaill, trans. Michael Hartnett (Dublin: New Island, 2000), 11.

41. Barbara G. Walker, *The Crone* (San Francisco: Harper and Row, 1985), 27.

42. In Patrick J. Crotty, trans. and ed., *Modern Irish Poetry: An Anthology* (Belfast: Blackstaff Press, 1995), 373.

43. Nuala Ní Dhomhnaill, *Selected Poems*, 159.

44. Robert Welch, ed., *The Oxford Companion to Irish Literature* (Oxford, England: Clarendon Press, 1996), 194.

45. Ní Dhomhnaill, *Selected Poems*, 57.

46. Audre Lorde, "Uses of the Erotic: The Erotic as Power," in *Weaving the Visions: New Patterns in Feminist Spirituality*, ed. Judith Plaskow and Carol P. Christ (San Francisco: Harper and Row, 1989), 210.

47. Ibid., 212.

48. Ní Dhomhnaill, *Selected Poems*, 77.

49. Mhac an tSaoi, introduction.

50. Cathryn Bailey, "Making Waves and Drawing Lines: The Politics of Defining the Vicissitudes of Feminism," *Hypatia: A Journal of Feminist Philosophy* 12, no. 3 (1997): 22.

51. Wolf, *Fire with Fire*, 318.

52. Mary O'Connor, "Lashings of the Mother Tongue: Nuala Ní Dhomhnaill's Anarchic Laughter," in *The Comic Tradition in Irish Women Writers*, ed. Theresa O'Connor (Gainesville: University Press of Florida, 1996), 153.

53. Somerville-Arjat and Wilson, "Nuala Ní Dhomhnaill," 153.

54. Heyward, *Touching Our Strength*, 4, 99.

55. Ní Dhomhnaill, *Pharoah's Daughter*, 141–43.

56. Ibid., 91–93.

57. Patricia Boyle Haberstroh, *Women Creating Women: Contemporary Irish Women Poets* (Syracuse, N.Y.: Syracuse University Press, 1996), 186.

58. Susan Bordo, *The Male Body: A New Look at Men in Public and in Private* (New York: Farrar, Straus and Giroux, 1999), 190.

59. Ní Dhomhnaill, *Selected Poems*, 31.

60. Ní Dhomhnaill, *Pharoah's Daughter*, 115.

61. Wolf, *Fire with Fire*, 138.

62. Christ, "In Praise of Aphrodite," 223.

63. Mhac an tSaoi, introduction, 12.

BIBLIOGRAPHY

Ackerman, Jane. "Teresa and Her Sisters." In *The Mystical Gesture: Essays in Medieval and Early Modern Spiritual Culture in Honor of Mary E. Giles*, edited by Robert Boenig. Aldershot, England: Ashgate, 2000.

Addison, Jane. "Christina Rossetti Studies, 1974–1991: A Checklist and Synthesis." *Bulletin of Bibliography* 2 (1995): 73–93.

Ahlgren, Gillian T. W. *Teresa of Avila and the Politics of Sanctity*. Ithaca, N.Y.: Cornell University Press, 1996.

Alarcón, Norma. "Chicana's Feminist Literature: A Re-vision through Malintzin/ or Malintzin: Putting Flesh Back on the Object." In *This Bridge Called My Back: Writings by Radical Women of Color*, edited by Cherríe Moraga and Gloria Anzaldúa. Watertown, Conn.: Persephone Press, 1982.

Alvarez, Julia. *In the Time of the Butterflies*. New York: Penguin Books, 1994.

Anderson, Peggy. "The Bride of the White Election: A New Look at Biblical Influence on Emily Dickinson." In *Nineteenth-Century Women Writers of the English-Speaking World*, edited by Rhoda B. Nathan, 1–11. New York: Greenwood Press, 1986.

Angula, Maria-Elena. *Magic Realism: Social Context and Discourse*. New York: Garland Publishing, 1995.

Anzaldúa, Gloria. *Borderlands/La Frontera: The New Mestiza*. San Francisco: Spinsters/Aunt Lute, 1987.

Aranda, Pilar E. Rodríguez. "On the Solitary Fate of Being Mexican, Female, Wicked and Thirty-Three: An Interview with Writer Sandra Cisneros." *Americas Review* 18, no. 1 (1990): 64–80.

Arseneau, Mary. "Incarnation and Interpretation: Christina Rossetti, the Oxford Movement, and 'Goblin Market.'" *Victorian Poetry* 31 (1993): 79–93.

Ashe, Geoffrey. *The Virgin*. London: Routledge and Kegan Paul, 1976.

Bailey, Cathryn. "Making Waves and Drawing Lines: The Politics of Defining the Vicissitudes of Feminism." *Hypatia: A Journal of Feminist Philosophy* 12, no. 3 (1997): 17–28.

Bakhtin, M. M. *The Dialogic Imagination.* Edited by Michael Holquist. Translated by Caryl Emerson and Michael Holquist. Austin: University of Texas Press, 1981.

Barroll, Leeds. "Looking for Patrons." In *Aemilia Lanyer: Gender, Genre, and the Canon,* edited by Marshall Grossman, 29–48. Lexington: University Press of Kentucky, 1998.

Baym, Nina. *Woman's Fiction: A Guide to Novels by and about Women in America, 1820–70.* Ithaca, N.Y.: Cornell University Press, 1978.

Beilin, Elaine V. *Redeeming Eve: Women Writers of the English Renaissance.* Princeton, N.J.: Princeton University Press, 1987.

Bellah, Robert N. "Civil Religion in America." *Daedalus* 96 (1967): 1–21.

Bénitez-Rojo, Antonio. *The Repeating Island: The Caribbean and the Postmodern Perspective.* Translated by James Maraniss. Durham, N.C.: Duke University Press, 1992.

Bennett, Mary Angela. *Elizabeth Stuart Phelps.* Philadelphia: University of Pennsylvania Press, 1939.

Benson, Pamela Joseph. "To Play the Man: Aemilia Lanyer and the Acquisition of Patronage." In *Opening the Borders: Inclusivity in Early Modern Studies,* edited by Peter C. Herman and Edward W. Tayler, 243–64. Newark: University of Delaware Press, 1999.

Bentley, D. M. R. "The Metricious and the Meritorious in 'Goblin Market': A Conjecture and Analysis." In *The Achievement of Christina Rossetti,* edited by David Kent, 57–81. Ithaca, N.Y.: Cornell University Press, 1987.

Bevington, David. "A. L. Rowse's Dark Lady." In *Aemilia Lanyer: Gender, Genre, and the Canon,* edited by Marshall Grossman, 10–28. Lexington: University Press of Kentucky, 1998.

Bevis, William. "American Indian Novels: Homing In." In *Recovering the Word: Essays on Native American Literature,* edited by Brian Swann and Arnold Krupat. Berkeley: University of California Press, 1987.

Bilinkoff, Jodi. *The Avila of Saint Teresa: Religious Reform in a Sixteenth-Century City.* Ithaca, N.Y.: Cornell University Press, 1989.

Bingham, Millicent Todd. *Emily Dickinson's Home: Letters of Edward Dickinson and His Family.* New York: Harper, 1955.

Black, Charlene Villaseñor. "Sacred Cults, Subversive Icons: Chicanas and the Pictorial Language of Catholicism." In *Speaking Chicana: Voice, Power, and Identity,* edited by D. Letticia Galindo and María Dolores Gonzales, 134–74. Tucson: University of Arizona Press, 1999.

Blaeser, Kimberly M. "Pagans Rewriting the Bible: Heterodoxy and the Representation of Spirituality in Native American Literature." *Ariel* 25, no. 1 (1994): 12–31.

Blondel, Nathalie. *Mary Butts: Scenes from the Life.* Kingston, N.Y.: McPherson, 1998.

Bordo, Susan. *The Male Body: A New Look at Men in Public and in Private.* New York: Farrar, Straus and Giroux, 1999.

————. *Unbearable Weight: Feminism, Western Culture, and the Body.* Berkeley: University of California Press, 1993.

Bostic, Joy. "It's a Jazz Thang: Interdisciplinarity and Critical Imagining in the Construction of a Womanist Theological Method." In *Women's Studies in Transition: The Pursuit of Interdisciplinarity,* edited by Kate Conway-Turner, Suzanne Cherrin, Jessica Schiffman, and Kathleen Doherty Turkel. Newark: University of Delaware Press, 1998.

Bowen, Barbara. "Aemilia Lanyer and the Invention of White Womanhood." In *Maids and Mistresses, Cousins and Queens: Women's Alliances in Early Modern England,* edited by Susan Frye, Karen Robertson, and Jean E. Howard, 274–303. New York: Oxford University Press, 1999.

Bradstreet, Anne. *The Works of Anne Bradstreet.* Edited by Jeannine Hensley. Cambridge, Mass.: Harvard University Press, 1967.

Brown, Teresa L. "Avoiding Asphyxiation: A Womanist Perspective on Intrapersonal and Interpersonal Transformation." In *Embracing the Spirit: Womanist Perspectives on Hope, Salvation, and Transformation,* edited by Emilie Townes, 72–94. Maryknoll, N.Y.: Orbis Books, 1997.

Brundage, Burr Cartwright. *The Fifth Sun: Aztec Gods, Aztec World.* Austin: University of Texas Press, 1979.

Bushnell, Horace. *Christian Nurture.* 1861. Reprint, New Haven, Conn.: Yale University Press, 1967.

Butts, Mary. Afterword to *Ashe of Rings,* by Mary Butts. London: Wishart, 1933.

————. *Ashe of Rings and Other Writings* (includes *Warning to Hikers* and *Traps for Unbelievers*). Kingston, N.Y.: McPherson, 1998.

————. *The Classical Novels: The Macedonian/Scenes from the Life of Cleopatra.* Kingston, N.Y.: McPherson, 1998.

————. *The Crystal Cabinet: My Childhood at Salterns.* London: Carcanet Press, 1988.

————. "The Real Wordsworth." Review of *The Later Life of Wordsworth,* by Edith Batho. *Time and Tide* 14 (December 2, 1923): 1446, 1448.

Byington, Robert. "The Writings and the World of Mary Butts." Tape 5, Proceedings of a Conference at the University of California, Davis, November 23–24, 1984.

Byington, Robert H., and Glen E. Morgan. "Mary Butts." *Art and Literature,* 1965, 163–79.

Bynum, Caroline Walker. *Holy Feast and Holy Fast: The Religious Significance of Food to Medieval Women.* Berkeley: University of California Press, 1987.

————. *Jesus as Mother: Studies in the Spirituality of the High Middle Ages.* Berkeley: University of California Press, 1982.

Cabbibo, Mia, and Sarah Davis. Introduction to "Excerpt, Joseph Swetman's *The Arraignment of Lewd, Idle, Froward, and Unconstant Women.*" Retrieved October 27, 2003, from the Early Modern Texts Project Web site: www.valpo.edu/english/emtexts/sweetnam1.html.

Campbell, Donna M. "Domestic or Sentimental Fiction, 1830–1860." *Literary Movements,* October 5, 2002. Retrieved October 30, 2002, from www.gonzaga.edu/faculty/campbell/enl311/domestic.htm.

————. "Sentimental Conventions and Self-Protection: *Little Women* and *The Wide, Wide World.*" *Legacy* 11, no. 2 (1994): 118–29.

Campbell, Elizabeth. "Of Mothers and Merchants: Female Economics in Christina Rossetti's 'Goblin Market.'" *Victorian Studies* 33 (Spring 1990): 393–410.

Campbell, Ena. "The Virgin of Guadalupe and the Female Self-Image: A Mexican Case History." In *Mother Worship: Theme and Variations*, edited by James J. Preston, 5–24. Chapel Hill: University of North Carolina Press, 1982.

Campbell, W. Gardner. "The Figure of Pilate's Wife in Aemilia Lanyer's *Salve Deus Rex Judaeorum*." *Renaissance Papers*, 1995, 1–13.

Cannon, Katie Geneva. *Katie's Canon: Womanism and the Soul of the Black Community*. New York: Continuum, 1995.

Carpenter, Mary. "'Eat Me, Drink Me, Love Me': The Consumable Female Body in Christina Rossetti's 'Goblin Market.'" *Victorian Poetry* 29 (1991): 415–34.

Carter, Paul. "'If a Man Die, Shall He Live Again?'" In *Passing: The Vision of Death in America*, edited by Charles O. Jackson, 112–33. Westport, Conn.: Greenwood, 1977.

Casey, Janet Calligani. "The Potential of Sisterhood: Christina Rossetti's 'Goblin Market.'" *Victorian Poetry* 29 (1991): 63–78.

Cassidy, Joseph L. *Mexico: Land of Mary's Wonders*. Patterson, N.J.: St. Anthony Guild Press, 1958.

Cassirer, Ernst. *The Individual and the Cosmos in Renaissance Philosophy*. New York: Barnes and Noble, 1964.

Castillo, Ana. *So Far from God*. New York: Penguin Books, 1994.

Cavanagh, Sheila T. *Cherished Torment: The Emotional Geography of Lady Mary Wroth's 'Urania.'* Pittsburgh, Pa.: Duquesne University Press, 2001.

———. "'The Great Cham': East Meets West in Lady Mary Wroth's *Urania*." *Meridian* 18, no. 2 (2000): 87–103.

Chapman, Alison. "The Afterlife of Poetry: 'Goblin Market.'" In *The Afterlife of Christina Rossetti*, 131–56. New York: St. Martin's Press, 2000.

Chatterjee, Margaret. *The Concept of Spirituality*. New Delhi: Allied Publishers, 1987.

Christ, Carol P. *Diving Deep and Surfacing: Women Writers on Spiritual Quest*. 3d ed. Boston: Beacon Press, 1995.

———. "In Praise of Aphrodite: Sexuality as Sacred." In *Sacred Dimensions of Women's Experience*, edited by Elizabeth Dodson Gray, 220–27. Wellesley, Mass.: Roundtable Press, 1988.

———. *Rebirth of the Goddess: Finding Meaning in Feminist Spirituality*. Reading, Mass.: Addison-Wesley Press, 1997.

———. "Rethinking Theology and Nature." In *Weaving the Visions: New Patterns in Feminist Spirituality*, edited by Judith Plaskow and Carol P. Christ. San Francisco: Harper San Francisco, 1989.

Christian, William A., Jr. *Local Religion in Sixteenth-Century Spain*. Princeton, N.J.: Princeton University Press, 1981.

Ciria, Bados. "*In the Time of the Butterflies* by Julia Alvarez: History, Fiction, Testimonio and the Dominican Republic." *Monographic Review* 13 (1997): 406–16.

Cisneros, Sandra. "Guadalupe the Sex Goddess." In *Goddess of the Americas/La Diosa de las Américas: Writings on the Virgin of Guadalupe*, edited by Ana Castillo. New York: Riverhead Books, 1996.

———. *Woman Hollering Creek and Other Stories*. New York: Random House, 1991.

Cofer, Judith Ortiz. "The Black Virgin." In *Silent Dancing: A Partial Remembrance of a Puerto Rican Childhood*, 38–50. Houston: Arte Público Press, 1990.

Collins, Joseph B. *Christian Mysticism in the Elizabethan Age with Its Background in Mystical Methodology*. Folcroft, Pa.: Folcroft Press, 1969.

Coltelli, Laura. *Winged Words: American Indian Writers Speak*. Lincoln: University of Nebraska Press, 1990.

Colton, Calvin. *History and Character of American Revivals of Religion*. London: Frederick Westley and A. H. Davis, 1832.

Condren, Mary. *The Serpent and the Goddess: Women, Religion, and Power in Celtic Ireland*. San Francisco: HarperCollins, 1989.

Consalvo, Deborah McWilliams. "The Lingual Ideal in the Poetry of Nuala Ní Dhomhnaill." *Eire-Ireland* 30 (Summer 1995): 148–61.

Cooper, David A. *God Is a Verb: Kabbalah and the Practice of Mystical Judaism*. New York: Riverhead Books, 1997.

Cott, Nancy F. *The Bonds of Womanhood: "Woman's Sphere" in New England, 1780–1835*. New Haven, Conn.: Yale University Press, 1977.

Crosby, Janice. *Cauldron of Changes: Feminist Spirituality in Fantastic Fiction*. Jefferson, N.C.: McFarland, 2000.

Crotty, Patrick, trans. and ed. *Modern Irish Poetry: An Anthology*. Belfast: Blackstaff Press, 1995.

Cunningham, J. V. "Sorting Out: The Case of Dickinson." In *The Collected Essays of J. V. Cunningham*, 353–74. Chicago: Swallow, 1976.

Dalke, Anne. "Spirit Matters: Re-Possessing the African-American Women's Literary Tradition." *Legacy* 12, no. 1 (1995): 1–16.

Daly, Mary. *Beyond God the Father: Towards a Philosophy of Women's Liberation*. Boston: Beacon Press, 1973.

———. *Gyn/Ecology: The Metaethics of Radical Feminism*. Boston: Beacon Press, 1978.

Dasenbrock, Reed Way. "Sandra Cisneros." In *Interviews with Writers of the Post-Colonial World*, edited by Feroza Jussawalla and Reed Way Dasenbrock. Jackson: University Press of Mississippi, 1992.

Davies, Gareth Alban. "St Teresa and the Jewish Question." In *Teresa de Jesus and Her World*, edited by Margaret A. Rees. Leeds, England: Trinity and All Saints' College, 1981.

Deleuze, Gilles. *The Deleuze Reader*. Edited by Constantin V. Boundas. New York: Columbia University Press, 1993.

Deloria, Vine, Jr. *God Is Red: A Native View of Religion*. Golden, Colo.: Fulcrum, 1994.

Desmangles, Leslie G. *The Faces of the Gods: Vodou and Roman Catholicism in Haiti*. Chapel Hill: University of North Carolina Press, 1992.

Dicken, E. E. Trueman. "Teresa of Jesus and John of the Cross." In *The Study of Spirituality*, edited by Cheslyn Jones, Geoffrey Wainwright, and Edward Yarnold, S.J., 373–76. New York: Cambridge University Press, 1992.

Dickinson, Emily. *The Letters of Emily Dickinson*. 3 vols. Edited by Thomas H. Johnson and Theodora Ward. Cambridge, Mass.: Belknap Harvard University Press, 1958.

———. *The Poems of Emily Dickinson*. 3 vols. Edited by Thomas H. Johnson. Cambridge, Mass.: Belknap Harvard University Press, 1951.

Dickinson, Susan Huntington Gilbert. "Obituary." *Springfield Republican*, May 18, 1886.

Diehl, Joanne Feit. *Dickinson and the Romantic Imagination*. Princeton, N.J.: Princeton University Press, 1981.

Doriani, Beth Maclay. *Emily Dickinson: Daughter of Prophecy*. Amherst: University of Massachusetts Press, 1996.

Dorson, Richard M. Foreword to *Folktales of Mexico*, edited by Américo Paredes. Chicago: University of Chicago Press, 1970.

Douglas, Ann. *The Feminization of American Culture*. 1977. Reprint, New York: Anchor, 1988.

———. "Heaven Our Home: Consolation Literature in the Northern United States, 1830–1880." *American Quarterly* 26 (1974): 496–515.

Douglass, Frederick. *Narrative of the Life of Frederick Douglass, An American Slave: Written by Himself*. Edited by Houston A. Baker, Jr. New York: Penguin Books, 1982.

Dowell, Susan, and Linda Hurcombe. *Dispossessed Daughters of Eve: Faith and Feminism*. London: SCM, 1981.

Doyle, Jacqueline. "Assumptions of the Virgin and Recent Chicana Writing." *Women's Studies* 26 (1997): 171–201.

———. "Haunting the Borderlands: La Llorona in Sandra Cisneros's 'Woman Hollering Creek." *Frontiers* 16 (1996): 53–70. Reprinted in *Women, America, and Movement: Narratives of Relocation*, edited by Susan L. Roberson, 62–78. Columbia: University of Missouri Press, 1998.

DuBois, W. E. B. *The Souls of Black Folk: Authoritative Text, Contexts, Criticism*. Edited by Henry Louis Gates, Jr., and Terri Hume Oliver. New York: W. W. Norton, 1999.

Duffy, Maureen. *The Erotic World of Faery*. London: Hodder and Stoughton, 1972.

Eliade, Mircea. *Myths, Rites, Symbols: A Mircea Eliade Reader*. Vol. 1. Edited by Wendell C. Beane and William G. Doty. New York: Harper and Row, 1975.

———. *The Sacred and the Profane: The Nature of Religion*. Translated by Willard R. Trask. New York: Harper and Row, 1959.

Eliot, T. S. "*Ulysses*, Order and Myth." In *Selected Prose of T. S. Eliot*, edited by Frank Kermode. New York: Harcourt Brace Jovanovich, 1975.

Eller, Cynthia. *Living in the Lap of the Goddess: The Feminist Spirituality Movement in America*. New York: Crossroad Press, 1993.

Elyot, Thomas. *The Defense of Good Women*. 1545. SCT. 7658. In *Early English Books: 1475–1600*. Ann Arbor, Mich.: University Microforms, 1938–. Microform.

England, Martha Winburn. "Emily Dickinson and Isaac Watts: Puritan Hymnodists." In *Critical Essays on Emily Dickinson*, edited by Paul J. Ferlazzo, 123–31. Boston: Hall, 1984.

Farmer, Sharon A. Introduction to *Embodied Love: Sensuality and Relationship as Feminist Values*, edited by Paula M. Cooey, Sharon A. Farmer, and Mary Ellen Ross. San Francisco: Harper and Row, 1987.

Faust, Drew Gilpin. *Mothers of Invention: Women of the Slaveholding South in the American Civil War*. Chapel Hill: University of North Carolina Press, 1996.

Ficino, Marsilio. *Three Books on Life*. Edited by Carol V. Kaske and John R. Clark. Binghamton: Center for Medieval and Early Renaissance Studies, State University of New York, 1989.

Fludd, Robert. *The Origin and Structure of the Cosmos*. Translated by Patricia Tahill. Edinburgh: Magnum Opus Hermetic Sourceworks, 1982.

Fowler, James. *Stages of Faith: The Psychology of Human Development and the Quest for Meaning*. San Francisco: Harper and Row, 1981.

Foy, Roslyn Reso. *Ritual, Myth, and Mysticism in the Work of Mary Butts: Between Feminism and Modernism*. Fayetteville: University of Arkansas Press, 2000.

Giffords, Gloria Kay. *Mexican Folk Retablos: Masterpieces on Tin*. Tucson: University of Arizona Press, 1974.

Goldenberg, Naomi R. "Archetypal Theory and the Separation of Mind and Body: Reason Enough to Turn to Freud?" In *Weaving the Visions: New Patterns in Feminist Spirituality*, edited by Judith Plaskow and Carol P. Christ, 244–54. New York: HarperCollins, 1989.

———. *Changing of the Gods: Feminism and the End of Traditional Religions*. Boston: Beacon Press, 1979.

Gomez-Vega, Ibis. "Metaphors of Entrapment: Caribbean Women Writers Face the Wreckage of History." *Journal of Political and Military Sociology* 25 (1997): 231–47.

González-Wippler, Migene. *Santería: The Religion*. New York: Harmony Books, 1989.

Gray, Elizabeth Dodson. *Sacred Dimensions of Women's Experience*. Wellesley, Mass.: Roundtable Press, 1988.

Greer, Germaine. Introduction to *Goblin Market*, by Christina Rossetti. New York: Stonehill, 1975.

Griffin, David Ray. "Introduction: Postmodern Spirituality and Society." In *Spirituality and Society: Postmodern Visions*, edited by David Ray Griffin. Albany: State University of New York, 1988.

Grigg, Richard. *When God Becomes Goddess: The Transformation of American Religion*. New York: Continuum, 1995.

Grimes, Ronald. *Beginnings in Ritual Studies*. Washington, D.C.: University Press of America, 1982.

Groover, Kristina K. *The Wilderness Within: American Women Writers and Spiritual Quest*. Fayetteville: University of Arkansas Press, 1999.

Guerrero, Andrés G. *A Chicano Theology*. Maryknoll, N.Y.: Orbis Books, 1987.

Guibbory, Achsah. "The Gospel According to Aemilia." In *Aemilia Lanyer: Gender, Genre, and the Canon*, edited by Marshal Grossman, 191–211. Lexington: University Press of Kentucky, 1998.

Haberstroh, Patricia Boyle. *Women Creating Women: Contemporary Irish Women Poets*. Syracuse, N.Y.: Syracuse University Press, 1996.

Hagedorn, Jessica. *Dogeaters*. New York: Penguin Books, 1990.

———. *Gangster of Love*. New York: Houghton Mifflin, 1996.

Hamilton, Alastair. *Heresy and Mysticism in Sixteenth-Century Spain: The Alumbrados*. Cambridge, England: James Clark, 1992.

Hannay, Margaret P. "How I These Studies Prize": The Countess of Pembroke and Elizabethan Science. In *Women, Science, and Medicine 1500–1700: Mothers and Sisters of the Royal Society*, edited by Lynette Hunter and Sarah Hutton, 108–22. Gloucestershire, England: Sutton Publishing, 1997.

Harrison, Beverly Wildung. *Making the Connections: Essays in Feminist Social Ethics*. Boston: Beacon Press, 1985.

———. "The Power of Anger in the Work of Love: Christian Ethics for Women and Other Strangers." In *Weaving the Visions: New Patterns in Feminist Spirituality*, edited by Judith Plaskow and Carol P. Christ, 214–25. New York: HarperCollins, 1989.

Harrison, Jane Ellen. *Epilogomena to the Study of Greek Religion and Themis: A Study of Social Origins of Greek Religion*. New York: University Books, 1962.

Hart, James D. "Platitudes of Piety: Religion and the Popular Modern Novel." *American Quarterly* 6 (1954): 311–22.

Heilbrun, Carolyn G. *Writing a Woman's Life*. New York: Ballantine Books, 1988.

Henderson, Katherine Usher, and Barbara F. McManus, eds. *Half Humankind: Contexts and Texts of the Controversy about Women in England, 1540–1640*. Urbana: University of Illinois Press, 1985.

Herrera, Hayden. *Frida Kahlo: The Paintings*. New York: HarperCollins, 1991.

Herrera-Sobek, María. *The Mexican Corrido: A Feminist Analysis*. Bloomington: Indiana University Press, 1990.

Herz, Judith Scherer. "Aemilia Lanyer and the Pathos of Literary History." In *Representing Women in Renaissance England*, edited by Claude J. Summers and Ted-Larry Rebworth, 121–35. Columbia: University of Missouri Press, 1997.

Heyward, Carter. *Touching Our Strength: The Erotic as Power and the Love of God*. San Francisco: Harper and Row, 1989.

Heywood, Leslie, and Jennifer Drake, eds. *Third Wave Agenda: Doing Feminism, Being Feminist*. Minneapolis: University of Minnesota Press, 1998.

Hoberman, Ruth. *Gendering Classicism: The Ancient World in Twentieth-Century Women's Historical Fiction*. Albany: State University of New York, 1997.

Hogan, Linda. *The Book of Medicines*. Minneapolis: Coffee House Press, 1993.

———. "Department of the Interior." In *Minding the Body: Women Writers on Body and Soul*, edited by Patricia Foster, 159–74. New York: Doubleday, 1994.

———. *Mean Spirit*. New York: Ivy Books, 1990.

———. *Solar Storms*. New York: Scribner, 1995.

Holt, Terrence. "'Men Sell Not Such in Any Town': Exchange in 'Goblin Market.'" *Victorian Poetry* 28 (1990): 51–67.

Homans, Margaret. "'Oh, Vision of Language!': Dickinson's Poems of Love and Death." In *Feminist Critics Read Emily Dickinson*, edited by Suzanne Juhasz, 114–33. Bloomington: Indiana University Press, 1983.

Hoyt, Edith. *The Silver Madonna: Legends of Shrines, Mexico-Guatemala*. Mexico City: Editorial Letras, 1963.

Hunt, Mary E. *Fierce Tenderness: A Feminist Theology of Friendship*. New York: Crossroad, 1991.

Irigaray, Luce. "This Sex Which Is Not One." Translated by Claudia Reeder. In *New French Feminisms: An Anthology*, edited by Elaine Marks and Isabelle De Courtivron. New York: Schocken Books, 1981.

Johnson, Elizabeth A. *She Who Is: The Mystery of God in Feminist Theological Discourse*. New York: Crossroad, 1993.

Johnston, Basil. *The Manitous: The Supernatural World of the Ojibway*. New York: HarperCollins, 1995.

Jones, C. P. M. "Liturgy and Personal Devotion." In *The Study of Spirituality*, edited by Cheslyn Jones, Geoffrey Wainwright, and Edward Yarnold, S.J., 3–9. New York: Oxford University Press, 1986.

Judd, Catherine. *Bedside Seductions: Nursing and the Victorian Imagination*. New York: St. Martin's Press, 1998.

Juhasz, Suzanne. "Reading Emily Dickinson's Letters." *ESQ: Journal of the American Renaissance* 30 (1984): 170–92.

Julian of Norwich. *A Book of Showings: Long Text*. Edited by Edmund Colledge and James Walsh. Toronto: Pontifical Institute of Medieval Studies, 1978.

Kaplan, Caren. "Deterritorializations: The Rewriting of Home and Exile in Western Feminist Discourse." In *The Nature and Context of Minority Discourse*, edited by Abdul R. JanMohamed and David Lloyd, 357–68. New York: Oxford University Press, 1990.

Keble, John. "Tract No. 89: On the Mysticism Attributed to the Early Church Fathers." In *The Evangelical and Oxford Movements*, edited by Elisabeth Jay. New York: Cambridge University Press, 1983.

Keller, Karl. *The Only Kangaroo among the Beauty: Emily Dickinson and America*. Baltimore: Johns Hopkins University Press, 1979.

Kelly, Joan. *Women, History, and Theory*. Chicago: University of Chicago Press, 1984.

Kelly, Lori Duin. *The Life and Works of Elizabeth Stuart Phelps, Victorian Feminist Writer*. Troy, N.Y.: Whitson Publishing, 1983.

Kessler, Carol Farley. *Elizabeth Stuart Phelps*. Boston: Twayne, 1982.

King, Ursula. *Women and Spirituality: Voices of Protest and Promise*. New York: New Amsterdam, 1989.

Knox, John. *The Political Writings of John Knox: The First Blast of the Trumpet against the Monstrous Regiment of Women and Other Selected Works*. Edited by Marvin A. Breslow. Cranbury, N.J.: Associated University Presses, 1985.

Kooistra, Lorraine Janzen. "The Representation of Violence/The Violence of Representation: Housman's Illustrations to Rossetti's 'Goblin Market.'" *English Studies in Canada* 19 (September 1993): 305–28.

Koole, Boudewijn. *Man en vrouw zijn een: De androgynie in het Christendom in het bijzonder bij Jacob Boehme. Or, Man and woman are one: Androgyny in Christianity, particularly in the works of Jacob Boehme*. Summary in English. Utretcht: HES Publishers, 1986.

Kouffman, Avra. "The Cultural Work of Stuart Women's Diaries." Ph.D. diss., University of Arizona, 2000.

Kraul, Edward Garcia, and Judith Beatty. Foreword to *The Weeping Woman: Encounters with La Llorona*, edited by Edward Garcia Kraul and Judith Beatty. Sante Fe, N. M.: Word Process, 1988.

Kristeva, Julia. *In the Beginning Was Love: Psychoanalysis and Faith*. New York: Columbia University Press, 1987.

————. *New Maladies of the Soul*. New York: Columbia University Press, 1995.

————. "Stabat Mater." Translated by Léon S. Roudiez. In *The Kristeva Reader*, edited by Toril Moi. New York: Columbia University Press, 1986.

————. "Women's Time." In *The Kristeva Reader*, edited by Toril Moi, 187–213. New York: Columbia University Press, 1986.

Krupat, Arnold. *The Turn to the Native: Studies in Criticism and Culture*. Lincoln: University of Nebraska Press, 1996.

Lafaye, Jacques. *Quetzalcóatl and Guadalupe: The Formation of a Mexican National Consciousness 1531–1813*. Translated by Benjamin Keen. Chicago: University of Chicago Press, 1976.

Lamb, Mary Ellen. *Gender and Authorship in the Sidney Circle*. Madison: University of Wisconsin Press, 1990.

————. "Patronage and Class in Aemilia Lanyer's *Salve Deus Rex Judaeorum*." In *Women Writing and the Reproduction of Culture in Tudor and Stuart Britain*, edited by M. E. Burke, Jane Donawerth, Linda L. Dove, and Karen Nelson, 38–57. Syracuse, N.Y.: Syracuse University Press, 2000.

Lanyer, Aemelia. "Salve Deus Rex Judaeorum." In *The Poems of Shakespeare's Dark Lady: Salve Deus Rex Judaeorum by Emelia Lanier*, edited by A. L. Rowse. New York: Clarkson N. Potter, 1978.

————. "To the Vertuous Reader." In *The Poems of Shakespeare's Dark Lady: Salve Deus Rex Judaeorum by Emilia Lanier*, edited by A. L. Rowse. New York: Clarkson N. Potter, 1978.

Lanyi, Ronald. "'My Faith that Dark Adores—': Calvinist Theology in the Poetry of Emily Dickinson." *Arizona Quarterly* 32 (1976): 264–76.

Le Seur, Geta. "From Nice Colored Girl to Womanist: An Exploration of Development in Ntozake Shange's Writings." In *Language and Literature in the African American Imagination*, edited by Carol Aisha Blackshire-Belay, 167–80. Westport, Conn.: Greenwood Press, 1992.

Lead, Jane. *A Fountain of Gardens: or, A Spiritual Diary of the Wonderful Experiences of a Christian Soul under the Conduct of Heavenly Wisdom*. 3 vols. London, 1697–1701.

Lee, Judith. "'A New Interiority': Feminist Theologians, Women Writers, and Questions of Salvation." In *Literature and Theology at Century's End*, edited by Gregory Salyer and Robert Detweiler, 43–68. Atlanta: Scholars Press, 1995.

Leonard, Douglas Novich. "Emily Dickinson's Religion: An Ablative Estate." *Christian Scholar's Review* 13 (1984): 333–48.

Levin, Carole. "John Foxe and the Responsibilities of Queenship." In *Women in the Middle Ages and the Renaissance: Literary and Historical Perspectives*, edited by Mary Beth Rose, 113–31. Syracuse, N.Y.: Syracuse University Press, 1986.

Lewalski, Barbara K. "Imagining Female Community: Aemilia Lanyer's Poems." In *Writing Women in Jacobean England*, 213–42. Cambridge, Mass.: Harvard University Press, 1993.

————. "Of God and Good Women: The Poems of Aemilia Lanyer." In *Silent but for the Word: Tudor Women as Patrons, Translators, and Writers of Religious*

Works, edited by Margaret Patterson Hannay, 203–24. Kent, Ohio: Kent State University Press, 1985.

———. "Seizing Discourses and Reinventing Genres." In *Aemilia Lanyer: Gender, Genre, and the Canon*, edited by Marshal Grossman, 49–59. Lexington: University Press of Kentucky, 1998.

Limón, José E. "La Llorona, the Third Legend of Greater Mexico: Cultural Symbols, Women, and the Political Unconscious." In *Between Borders: Essays on Mexicana/Chicana History*, edited by Adelaida R. Del Castillo. Encino, Fla.: Floricanto Press, 1990.

Llamas Martínez, Enrique. *Santa Teresa de Jesús y la Inquisición española*. Madrid: Instituto Francisco Suárez, 1972.

Lomeli, Francisco A. "Chicana Novelists in the Process of Creating Fictive Voices." In *Beyond Stereotypes: The Critical Analysis of Chicana Literature*, edited by María Herrera-Sobek, 29–46. Binghamton, N.Y.: Bilingual Press, 1985.

López Baralt, Luce. *Huellas de Islam en la literatura española: De Juan Ruiz a Juan Goytisolol*. Madrid: Hiperión, 1985.

Lorde, Audre. *A Burst of Light: Essays*. Ithaca, N.Y.: Firebrand, 1988.

———. *The Cancer Journals*. San Francisco: Aunt Lute, 1980.

———. *The Collected Poems of Audre Lorde*. New York: W. W. Norton, 1997.

———. "My Words Will Be There." In *Black Women Writers (1950–1980): A Critical Evaluation*, edited by Mari Evans, 261–68. Garden City, N.J.: Anchor-Doubleday, 1984.

———. "An Open Letter to Mary Daly." In *Sister/Outsider: Essays and Speeches*, 69–70. Freedom, Calif.: Crossing Press, 1984.

———. "The Transformation of Silence into Language and Action." In *Sister/Outsider: Essays and Speeches*, 40–44. Freedom, Calif.: Crossing Press, 1984.

———. "Uses of the Erotic: The Erotic as Power." In *Sister/Outsider: Essays and Speeches*, 53–59. Freedom, Calif.: Crossing Press, 1984. Reprinted in *Weaving the Visions: New Patterns in Feminist Spirituality*, edited by Judith Plaskow and Carol P. Christ, 208–13. San Francisco: Harper and Row, 1989.

Lyons, Bonnie, and Bill Oliver. "A Clean Windshield." In *Passion and Craft: Conversations with Notable Writers*, 128–44. Urbana: University of Illinois Press, 1998.

Lyons, Brenda. "Interview with Ntozake Shange." *Massachusetts Review* 28, no. 4 (1987): 687–96.

Mack, Phyllis. *Visionary Women: Ecstatic Prophecy in Seventeenth-Century England*. Berkeley: University of California Press, 1992.

Maclean, Ian. *The Renaissance Notion of Woman: A Study in the Fortunes of Scholasticism and Medical Science in European Intellectual Life*. New York: Cambridge University Press, 1980.

Mailloux, Steven. "Cultural Rhetorical Studies: Eating Books in Nineteenth-Century America." In *Reconceptualizing American Literary/Cultural Studies: Rhetoric, History, and Politics in the Humanities*, edited by William E. Cain, 21–33. New York: Garland Publishing, 1996.

Mairs, Nancy. *Ordinary Time: Cycles in Marriage, Faith, and Renewal*. Boston: Beacon Press, 1993.

Manley, Frank, ed. *The Anniversaries*. Baltimore: Johns Hopkins University Press, 1963.

Marsh, Jan. *Christina Rossetti: A Writer's Life*. New York: Viking, 1994.

Marsh-Lockett, Carol. "A Woman's Art, a Woman's Craft: The Self in Ntozake Shange's *sassafrass, cypress & indigo*." In *Arms Akimbo: Africana Women in Contemporary Literature*, edited by Janice Lee Liddell and Yakini Belinda Kemp, 46–57. Gainesville: University Press of Florida, 1999.

Martin, Wendy. *An American Triptych: Anne Bradstreet, Emily Dickinson, Adrienne Rich*. Chapel Hill: University of North Carolina Press, 1984.

Martinez, Elizabeth Conrod. "Recovering a Space for History between Imperialism and Patriarchy: Julia Alvarez's *In the Time of the Butterflies*." Thamyris 5, no. 2 (1998): 263–79.

Martínez, Rubén. "The Undocumented Virgin." In *Goddess of the Americas/La Diosa de las Américas: Writings on the Virgin of Guadalupe*, edited by Ana Castillo. New York: Riverhead Books, 1996.

Martz, Louis L. *The Poetry of Meditation: A Study in English Religious Literature of the Seventeenth-Century*. 1954. Rev. ed. New Haven, Conn.: Yale University Press, 1962.

Matar, Nabil. *Islam in Britain: 1558–1685*. New York: Cambridge University Press, 1998.

Mayberry, Katherine J. *Christina Rossetti and the Poetry of Discovery*. Baton Rouge: Louisiana State University Press, 1989.

McClure, John A. "Postmodern/Post-Secular: Contemporary Fiction and Spirituality." *Modern Fiction Studies* 41, no. 1 (1995): 141–63.

McDannell, Colleen. *The Christian Home in Victorian America, 1840–1900*. Bloomington: Indiana University Press, 1986.

McDiarmid, Lucy, and Michael Durkan. "Q. & A.: Nuala Ní Dhomhnaill." *Irish Literary Supplement* 6 (Fall 1987): 41–43.

McGrath, Lynette. "'Let Us Have Our Libertie Againe': Amelia Lanier's 17th Century Feminist Voice." *Women's Studies* 20 (1992): 331–38.

———. "Metaphoric Subversions: Feasts and Mirrors in Amelia Lanier's *Salve Deus Rex Judaeorum*." *Literature Interpretation Theory* 3 (1991): 101–13.

Melhuus, Marit. "Power, Value and the Ambiguous Meanings of Gender." In *Machos, Mistresses, Madonnas: Contesting the Power of Latin American Gender Imagery*, edited by Marit Melhuus and Kristi Anne Stølen, 230–59. New York: Verso, 1996.

Menke, Richard. "The Political Economy of Fruit." In *The Culture of Christina Rossetti: Female Poetics and Victorian Contexts*, edited by Mary Arseneau, Antony H. Harrison, and Lorraine Janzen Kooistra, 105–35. Athens: Ohio University Press, 1999.

Mermin, Dorothy. "Heroic Sisterhood in 'Goblin Market.'" *Victorian Poetry* 21 (1983): 107–18.

Mhac an tSaoi, Maire. Introduction to *Selected Poems: Rogha Danta*, by Nuala Ní Dhomhnaill. Translated by Michael Hartnett. Dublin: New Island, 2000.

Michie, Helena. "'There Is No Friend Like a Sister': Sisterhood as Sexual Difference." *ELH* 56 (1989): 401–21.

Miller, Cristanne. *Emily Dickinson: A Poet's Grammar*. Cambridge, Mass.: Harvard University Press, 1987.

Miller, Naomi J. "(M)other Tongues: Maternity and Subjectivity." In *Aemilia Lanyer: Gender, Genre, and the Canon*, edited by Marshal Grossman, 143–66. Lexington: University Press of Kentucky, 1998.

Moraga, Cherríe. *Loving in the War Years*. Boston: South End Press, 1983.

Mueller, Janel. "The Feminist Poetics of 'Salve Deus Rex Judaeorum.'" In *Aemilia Lanyer: Gender, Genre, and the Canon*, edited by Marshal Grossman, 99–127. Lexington: University Press of Kentucky, 1998.

Mullin, Harryette. "'A Silence between Us Like a Language': The Untranslatability of Experience in Sandra Cisneros' *Woman Hollering Creek*." *MELUS* 21, no. 2 (1996): 3–20.

Murphy, Patrick D. *Literature, Nature, and Other: Ecofeminist Critiques*. New York: State University of New York Press, 1995.

Nelson, Karen L. "Annotated Bibliography: Texts and Criticism of Aemilia Bassano Lanyer." In *Aemilia Lanyer: Gender, Genre, and the Canon*, edited by Marshal Grossman, 235–54. Lexington: University Press of Kentucky, 1998.

New, Elisa. *The Regenerate Lyric: Theology and Innovation in American Poetry*. New York: Cambridge University Press, 1993.

Newman, Barbara. *From Virile Woman to WomanChrist: Studies in Medieval Religion and Literature*. Philadelphia: University of Pennsylvania Press, 1995.

Ní Dhomhnaill, Nuala. *The Astrakhan Cloak*. Translated by Paul Muldoon. Winston-Salem, N.C.: Wake Forest University Press, 1993.

———. "Mother Ireland, Gaming and the Ard Fheis." *Yeats: An Annual of Critical and Textual Studies* 10 (1992): 193–96.

———. *Nuala Ní Dhomhnaill Selected Poems: Rogha Danta*. Translated by Michael Hartnett. Dublin: New Island Books, 2000.

———. *Pharaoh's Daughter*. Rev. ed. Winston-Salem, N.C.: Wake Forest University Press, 1993.

———. *The Water Horse*. Translated by Medbh McGuckian and Eilean Ní Chuilleanain. Winston-Salem, N.C.: Wake Forest University Press, 2000.

———. "Why I Choose to Write in Irish, the Corpse That Sits up and Talks Back." In *Representing Ireland: Gender, Class, Nationality*, edited by Susan Shaw Sailer, 45–56. Gainesville: University Press of Florida, 1997.

Norton, Mrs. Charles Eliot. "'The Angel in the House' and 'The Goblin Market.'" *Macmillan's Magazine*, September 1863, 401.

Obbard, Elizabeth Ruth. *Land of Carmel: The Origins and Spirituality of the Carmelite Order*. Gloucester, England: MPG Books, 1999.

Oberhaus, Dorothy Huff. "'Tender Pioneer': Emily Dickinson's Poems on the Life of Christ." In *Emily Dickinson: A Collection of Critical Essays*, edited by Judith Farr, 105–18. Upper Saddle River, N.J.: Prentice Hall, 1996.

Ochs, Carol. *Women and Spirituality*. Totowa, N.J.: Rowman and Allanheld, 1983.

———. *Women and Spirituality*. 2d ed. Lanham, Md.: Rowman and Littlefield, 1997.

O'Connor, Mary. "Lashings of the Mother Tongue: Nuala Ní Dhomhnaill's Anarchic Laughter." In *The Comic Tradition in Irish Women Writers*, edited by Theresa O'Connor, 149–70. Gainesville: University Press of Florida, 1996.

O'Neill, Patrick. *Fictions of Discourse: Reading Narrative Theory*. Toronto: University of Toronto Press, 1994.

Orr, Catherine M. "Charting the Currents of the Third Wave." *Hypatia: A Journal of Feminist Philosophy* 12, no. 3 (1997): 29–45.

Ortner, Sherry. "Is Female to Male as Nature Is to Culture?" In *Making Gender: The Politics and Erotics of Culture*, 21–42. Boston: Beacon Press, 1996.

Ostriker, Alicia Suskin. *Stealing the Language: The Emergence of Women's Poetry in America*. Boston: Beacon Press, 1986.

Pagels, Elaine. *Adam, Eve, and the Serpent*. New York: Vintage Books, 1989.

———. *The Gnostic Gospels*. New York: Vintage Books, 1989.

Palazzo, Lynda. *Christina Rossetti's Feminist Theology*. New York: Palgrave Press, 2002.

Paludan, Phillip Shaw. *"A People's Contest": The Union and Civil War, 1861–1865*. 2d ed. Lawrence: University Press of Kansas, 1996.

Parkerson, Michelle, dir., and Ada Gay Griffin, dir./prod. *A Litany for Survival: The Life and Work of Audre Lorde*. Edited by Holly Fisher. Videocassette. Third World Newsreel, 1995.

Parsons, Susan Frank, ed. *Cambridge Companion to Feminist Theology*. New York: Cambridge University Press, 2002.

Partridge, A. C. *Language and Society in Anglo-Irish Literature*. Totowa, N.J.: Barnes & Noble, 1984.

Patterson, W. B. *King James VI and I and the Reunion of Christendom*. New York: Cambridge University Press, 1997.

Paz, Octavio. "The Sons of La Malinche." In *The Labyrinth of Solitude: Life and Thought in Mexico*, translated by Lysander Kemp. New York: Grove Press, 1961.

Pearson, Jacqueline. "Women Writers and Women Readers: The Case of Aemilia Lanier." In *Representing Women in Renaissance England*, edited by Claude J. Summers and Ted-Larry Rebworth, 45–54. Columbia: University of Missouri Press, 1997.

Perez, Domino Renee. "Crossing Mythological Borders: Revisioning La Llorona in Contemporary Fiction." *Proteus* 16, no. 1 (1999): 49–54.

Petroff, Elizabeth Alvida. *Medieval Women's Visionary Literature*. New York: Oxford University Press, 1986.

Phelps, Elizabeth Stuart. *Chapters from a Life*. Boston: Houghton, Mifflin, 1896.

———. *The Gates Ajar*. Edited by Helen Sootin Smith. 1868. Reprint. Cambridge, Mass.: Belknap, 1964.

———. "Our Thanksgiving." *Harper's New Monthly Magazine* 32 (December 1865): 81–85.

Phillips, Layli, and Barbara McCaskill. "Who's Schooling Who? Black Women and the Bringing of the Everyday into Academe, or Why We Started *The Womanist*." *Signs: Journal of Women in Culture and Society* 20, no. 41 (1995): 1007–18.

Plaskow, Judith, and Carol P. Christ, eds. *Weaving the Visions: New Patterns in Feminist Spirituality*. San Francisco: HarperCollins, 1989.

Poniatowska, Elena. "Mexicanas and Chicanas." *MELUS* 21, no. 3 (1996): 35–51.

Powell, Brenda J. " 'Witness Thy Wife (O *Pilate*) Speaks for All': Aemilia Lanyer's Strategic Self-Positioning." *Christianity and Literature* 46, no. 1 (1996): 5–23.

Prentiss, Elizabeth. *Stepping Heavenward*. 1869. Reprint, Amityville, N.Y.: Calvary Press, 1998.

Prentiss, George L. *The Life and Letters of Elizabeth Prentiss*. New York: Anson D. F. Randolph, 1882.

Pryse, Marjorie, "Introduction: Zora Neale Hurston, Alice Walker, and the 'Ancient Power' of Black Women." In *Conjuring: Black Women, Fiction, and Literary Tradition*, edited by Marjorie Pryse and Hortense J. Spillers. Bloomington: Indiana University Press, 1985.

Purkiss, Diane. "Producing the Voice, Consuming the Body: Women Prophets of the Seventeenth Century." In *Women, Writing, History: 1640–1740*, edited by Isobel Grundy and Susan Wiseman. London: B. T. Batsford, 1992.

Rable, George C. *Civil Wars: Women and the Crisis of Southern Nationalism*. Urbana: University of Illinois Press, 1989.

Rabuzzi, Kathryn Allen. *The Sacred and the Feminine: Toward a Theology of Housework*. New York: Seabury Press, 1982.

Rainwater, Catherine. *Dreams of Fiery Stars: The Transformations of Native American Fiction*. Philadelphia: University of Pennsylvania Press, 1999.

Randall, Margaret. "Guadalupe, Subversive Virgin." In *Goddess of the Americas/La Diosa de las Américas: Writings on the Virgin of Guadalupe*, edited by Ana Castillo. New York: Riverhead Books, 1996.

Ranft, Patricia. *A Woman's Way: The Forgotten History of Women Spiritual Directors*. New York: Palgrave Press, 2000.

Rebolledo, Tey Diana. *Women Singing in the Snow: A Cultural Analysis of Chicana Literature*. Tucson: University of Arizona Press, 1995.

"Review of *Goblin Market and Other Poems*." *Saturday Review*, May 24, 1862, 595–96.

Reynolds, David S. *Faith in Fiction: The Emergence of Religious Literature in America*. Cambridge, Mass.: Harvard University Press, 1981.

Rich, Adrienne. *Of Woman Born: Motherhood as Experience and Institution*. New York: W. W. Norton, 1976.

Rich, Mary. *Memoir of Lady Warwick, also her diary from a.d. 1666–1672*. Edited by Antony Walker. London: Religious Tract Society, 1847.

Ricoeur, Paul. *Fallible Man*. Translated by Charles A. Kelbley. New York: Fordham University Press, 1986.

Roberts, Josephine, ed. *The Poems of Lady Mary Wroth*. Baton Rouge: Louisiana State University Press, 1983.

Rodríguez, Luis J. "'Forgive Me, Mother, for My Crazy Life.'" In *Goddess of the Americas/La Diosa de las Américas: Writings on the Virgin of Guadalupe*, edited by Ana Castillo. New York: Riverhead Books, 1996.

Romero, Lora. *Home Fronts: Domesticity and Its Critics in the Antebellum United States*. Durham, N.C.: Duke University Press, 1997.

Rossetti, Christina G. *Annus Domini: A Prayer for Each Day of the Year, Founded on a Text of Holy Scripture*. Oxford, England: James Parker, 1874.

———. *The Complete Poems of Christina Rossetti*. 3 vols. Edited by R. W. Crump. Baton Rouge: Louisiana State University Press, 1979–90.

———. *The Face of the Deep: A Devotional Commentary on the Apocalypse*. London: Society for Promoting Christian Knowledge, 1892.

———. *Letter and Spirit*. London: Society for Promoting Christian Knowledge, 1883.

———. *The Letters of Christina Rossetti*. Vol. 1. *1843–1873*. Edited by Antony Harrison. Charlottesville: University Press of Virginia, 1997.

———. *Time Flies: A Reading Diary*. London: Society for Promoting Christian Knowledge, 1885.

Rossetti, Dante Gabriel, Christina Rossetti, and William Michael Rossetti. *The Rossetti-Macmillan Letters: Some 133 Unpublished Letters Written to Alexander Macmillan, F. S. Ellis, and Others, by Dante Gabriel, Christina, and William Michael Rossetti, 1861–1889*. Edited by Lona Mosk Packer. Berkeley: University of California Press, 1963.

Rossetti, William Michael, ed. *Poetical Works of Christina Georgina Rossetti, with Memoir and Notes*. London: Macmillan, 1906.

———., ed. *Ruskin: Rossetti: Pre-Raphaelitism. Papers 1854 to 1862*. New York: Dodd, Mead, 1899.

Rostas, Susanna. "The Production of Gendered Imagery: The Concheros of Mexico." In *Machos, Mistresses, Madonnas: Contesting the Power of Latin American Gender Imagery*, edited by Marit Melhuus and Kristi Anne Stølen, 207–29. New York: Verso, 1996.

Rowse, A. L., ed. *The Poems of Shakespeare's Dark Lady: Salve Deus Rex Judaeorum by Emilia Lanier*. New York: Clarkson N. Potter, 1978.

Ruether, Rosemary Radford. "The Emergence of Christian Feminist Theology." In *Cambridge Companion to Feminist Theology*, edited by Susan Frank Parsons, 3–22. New York: Cambridge University Press, 2002.

———. "Motherearth and the Megamachine: A Theology of Liberation in a Feminine, Somatic and Ecological Perspective." In *Womanspirit Rising: A Feminist Reader in Religion*, edited by Carol P. Christ and Judith Plaskow, 43–52. San Francisco: Harper and Row, 1979.

———. *Sexism and God-Talk: Toward a Feminist Theology*. 2d ed. Boston: Beacon Press, 1993.

———. *Women and Redemption: A Theological History*. Minneapolis: Fortress Press, 1998.

Ruppert, James. *Mediation in Contemporary Native American Fiction*. Norman: University of Oklahoma Press, 1995.

Russell, Anthony. "Sociology and the Study of Spirituality." In *The Study of Spirituality*, edited by Cheslyn Jones, Geoffrey Wainwright, and Edward Yarnold, S.J., 33–38. New York: Oxford University Press, 1986.

Saldivar, Jose David. "The Real and the Marvelous in Charleston, South Carolina: Ntozake Shange's *sassafrass, cypress & indigo*." In *Genealogy and Literature*, edited by Lee Quinby, 175–92. Minneapolis: University of Minnesota Press, 1995.

Sandstrom, Alan R. "The Tonantsi Cult of the Eastern Nahua." In *Mother Worship: Theme and Variations*, edited by James J. Preston, 25–50. Chapel Hill: University of North Carolina Press, 1982.

Schechner, Richard. *Essays on Performance Theory, 1970–1976*. New York: Drama Book Specialists, 1977.

Schechner, Richard, and Willa Appel. *By Means of Performance: Intercultural Studies of Theatre and Ritual*. New York: Cambridge University Press, 1990.

Schnell, Lisa. "Breaking 'the Rule of Cortezia': Aemilia Lanyer's Dedications to *Salve Deus Rex Judaeorum.*" *Journal of Medieval and Renaissance Studies* 27, no. 1 (1997): 77–101.

Schnog, Nancy. "'The Comfort of My Fancying': Loss and Recuperation in *The Gates Ajar.*" *Arizona Quarterly* 49, no. 3 (1993): 127–54.

Sells, Michael A. *Mystical Languages of Unsaying.* Chicago: University of Chicago Press, 1994.

Sewall, Richard B. *The Lyman Letters: New Light on Emily Dickinson and Her Family.* Amherst: University of Massachusetts Press, 1965.

Shalkhauser, Marian. "The Feminine Christ." *Victorian Newsletter* 10 (Autumn 1956): 19–20.

Shange, Ntozake. *Sassafrass, cypress & indigo.* New York: St. Martin's Press, 1982.

Siegel, Deborah L. "The Legacy of the Personal: Generating Theory in Feminism's Third Wave." *Hypatia: A Journal of Feminist Philosophy* 12, no. 3 (1997): 46–75.

Slee, Nicola. "The Holy Spirit and Spirituality." In *The Cambridge Companion to Feminist Theology,* edited by Susan Frank Parsons, 171–89. New York: Cambridge University Press, 2002.

Small, Judy Jo. *Positive as Sound: Emily Dickinson's Rhyme.* Athens: University of Georgia Press, 1990.

Smith, Catherine. "Jane Lead: Mysticism and the Woman Cloathed with the Sun." In *Shakespeare's Sisters: Feminist Essays on Women Poets,* edited by Sandra Gilbert and Susan Gubar. Bloomington: Indiana University Press, 1979.

———. "Jane Lead: The Feminist Mind and Art of a Seventeenth-Century Protestant Mystic." In *Women of Spirit: Female Leadership in the Jewish and Christian Traditions,* edited by Rosemary Ruether and Eleanor McLaughlin. New York: Simon and Schuster, 1979.

———. "Jane Lead's Wisdom: Wisdom and Prophecy in Seventeenth-Century England." In *Poetic Prophecy in Western Literature,* edited by Jan Wojcik and Raymond-Jean Frontain, 55–63. Cranbury, N.J.: Associated University Presses, 1984.

Smith, Martha Nell. *Rowing in Eden: Rereading Emily Dickinson.* Austin, University of Texas Press, 1992.

Smith, Theresa S. *The Island of the Anishnaabeg: Thunderers and Water Monsters in the Traditional Ojibwe Life-World.* Moscow: University of Idaho Press, 1995.

Smith, Wilfred Cantwell. *Faith and Belief.* Princeton, N.J.: Princeton University Press, 1979.

Somerville-Arjat, Gillean, and Rebecca E. Wilson, eds. "Nuala Ní Dhomhnaill." In *Sleeping with Monsters: Conversations with Scottish and Irish Women Poets,* edited by Gillean Somerville-Arjat and Rebecca E. Wilson, 148–57. Dublin: Wolfhound Press, 1990.

St. Armand, Barton Levi. "Paradise Deferred: The Image of Heaven in the Work of Emily Dickinson and Elizabeth Stuart Phelps." *American Quarterly* 29 (1977): 55–78.

Stansell, Christine. "Elizabeth Stuart Phelps: A Study in Female Rebellion." *Massachusetts Review* 13 (1972): 239–56.

Stone, Merlin. *When God Was a Woman*. New York: Harcourt Brace, 1976.

Strandness, Jean. "Reclaiming Women's Language, Imagery, and Experience: Ntozake Shange's *sassafrass, cypress & indigo*." *Journal of American Culture* 10, no. 3 (1987): 11–17.

Stuart, D. M. *Christina Rossetti*. London: Macmillan, 1930.

Swietlicki, Catherine. *Spanish Christian Cabala: The Works of Luis de León, Santa Teresa de Jesús, and San Juan de la Cruz*. Columbia: University of Missouri Press, 1986.

Taylor, Ula Y. "Making Waves: The Theory and Practice of Black Feminism." *Black Scholar* 28, no. 2 (1998): 18–29.

Teresa de Jesús. *Obras completas*. Edited by Efren de la Madre de Dios, O.C.D., and Otger Steggink, O. Carm. Madrid: Biblioteca de Autores Cristianos, 1997.

Teresa of Avila. *Interior Castle: St. Teresa of Avila*. Translated by E. Allison Peers. New York: Image Doubleday, 1989.

———. *Teresa of Avila: The Interior Castle*. Translated by Kieran Kavanaugh, O.C.D., and Otilio Rodriguez, O.C.D. New York: Paulist Press, 1979.

Thickstun, Margaret Olofson. *Fictions of the Feminine: Puritan Doctrine and the Representation of Women*. Ithaca, N.Y.: Cornell University Press, 1988.

Thorp, Willard. "The Religious Novel as Best Seller in America." In *Religious Perspectives in American Culture*, vol. 2, edited by James Ward Smith and A. Leland Jamison, 195–242. Princeton, N.J.: Princeton University Press, 1961.

Toor, Frances. *A Treasury of Mexican Folkways*. New York: Crown Publishers, 1947.

Travitsky, Betty. "The Lady Doth Protest: Protest in the Popular Writings of Renaissance Englishwomen." *English Literary Renaissance* 14, no. 3 (1984): 255–73.

———. *The Paradise of Women: Writings by Englishwomen of the Renaissance*. Westport, Conn.: Greenwood Press, 1981.

Turner, Victor, and Edith Turner. *Image and Pilgrimage in Christian Culture: Anthropological Perspectives*. New York: Columbia University Press, 1978.

Underhill, Evelyn. *Mysticism: A Study in the Nature and Development of Man's Spiritual Consciousness*. New York: World Publishing, 1955.

———. *Mysticism: The Preeminent Study in the Nature and Development of Spiritual Consciousness*. New York: Doubleday, 1990.

Van de Wetering, Maxine. "The Popular Concept of 'Home' in Nineteenth-Century America." *Journal of American Studies* 18 (1984): 5–28.

Venn, Anne. *A Wise Virgin's Lamp Burning: The experiences of Mrs. Anne Venn (Daughter to Col. John Venn & member of the Church of Christ at Fulham): written by her own hand, and found in her closet after her death*. London: E. Cole, 1658.

Versluis, Arthur. *Wisdom's Book: The Sophia Anthology*. St. Paul, Minn.: Paragon House, 2000.

Vigil, Mariló. *La vida de las mujeres en los siglos XVI y XVII*. 2d ed. México: Siglo Veintiuno Editores, 1994.

Walker, Alice. *Anything We Love Can Be Saved*. New York: Random House, 1997.

———. *In Search of Our Mothers' Gardens: Womanist Prose*. San Diego: Harcourt Brace Jovanovich, 1983.

———. *Living by the Word: Selected Writings, 1973–1987*. San Diego: Harvest (Harcourt Brace), 1988.

————. "Preface to the Tenth Anniversary Edition." In *The Color Purple*, 10th ed. New York: Harcourt Brace Jovanovich, 1992.

Walker, Barbara G. *The Crone*. San Francisco: Harper and Row, 1985.

————. *The Woman's Encyclopedia of Myths and Secrets*. San Francisco: Harper-Collins, 1983.

Wall, Wendy. "Our Bodies/Our Texts? Renaissance Women and the Trials of Authorship." In *Anxious Power: Reading, Writing, and Ambivalence in Narrative by Women*, edited by Carol J. Singley and Susan Elizabeth Sweeney, 51–71. Albany: State University of New York Press, 1993.

Walter, Roland. "Cultural Politics of Dislocation and Relocation." *MELUS* 23, no. 1 (1998): 81–97.

Warner, Marina. *Alone of All Her Sex: The Myth and Cult of the Virgin Mary*. New York: Alfred A. Knopf, 1976.

Weathers, Winston. "Christina Rossetti: The Sisterhood of Self." *Victorian Poetry* 3 (1965): 81–89.

Weaver, Jace, ed. *Defending Mother Earth: Native American Perspectives on Environmental Justice*. Maryknoll, N.Y.: Orbis Books, 1996.

Weber, Alison. "Saint Teresa, Demonologist." In *Culture and Control in Counter-Reformation Spain*, edited by Anne J. Cruz and Mary Elizabeth Perry, 171–95. Minneapolis: University of Minnesota Press, 1992.

————. *Teresa of Avila and the Rhetoric of Femininity*. Princeton, N.J.: Princeton University Press, 1990.

Weigle, Luther A. Introduction to *Christian Nurture*, by Horace Bushnell, xxxi–xl. New Haven, Conn.: Yale University Press, 1967.

Welch, Robert, ed. *The Oxford Companion to Irish Literature*. Oxford, England: Clarendon Press, 1996.

Welter, Barbara. *Dimity Convictions: The American Woman in the Nineteenth Century*. Athens: Ohio University Press, 1976.

————. "The Feminization of American Religion: 1800–1860." In *Clio's Consciousness Raised: New Perspectives on the History of Women*, edited by Mary S. Hartman and Lois Banner, 137–57. New York: Harper Torchbooks, 1974.

Westerholm, Joel. "'I Magnify Mine Office': Christina Rossetti's Authoritative Voice in Her Devotional Prose." *Victorian Newsletter* 84 (1992): 11–17.

Williams, Isaac, B.D. *The Autobiography of Isaac Williams*. Edited by Sir George Prevost. London: Longmans, Green, 1892.

Williamson, Hugh Ross. "Three Letters." In *A Sacred Quest: The Life and Writings of Mary Butts*, edited by Christopher Wagstaff. Kingston, N.Y.: McPherson, 1995.

Wolf, Naomi. *Fire with Fire: The New Female Power and How It Will Change the 21st Century*. New York: Random House, 1993.

Wolff, Cynthia Griffin. *Emily Dickinson*. Reading, Mass.: Addison-Wesley Press, 1988.

————. "[Im]pertinent Constructions of Body and Self: Dickinson's Use of the Romantic Grotesque." In *Emily Dickinson: A Collection of Critical Essays*, edited by Judith Farr, 119–29. Upper Saddle River, N.J.: Prentice Hall, 1996.

Wolosky, Shira. "Rhetoric or Not: Hymnal Tropes in Emily Dickinson and Isaac Watts." *New England Quarterly* 61 (1988): 214–32.

Woodbridge, Linda. *The Paradise of Women: Writings by Englishwomen of the Renaissance*. Westport, Conn.: Greenwood Press, 1981.

———. *Women and the English Renaissance: Literature and the Nature of Womankind, 1540–1620*. Urbana: University of Illinois Press, 1987.

Woods, Susanne. "Aemilia Lanyer and Ben Johnson: Patronage, Authority, and Gender." *Ben Jonson Journal: Literary Contexts in the Age of Elizabeth, James and Charles* 1 (1994): 15–30.

———. "Vocation and Authority: Born to Write." In *Aemilia Lanyer: Gender, Genre, and the Canon*, edited by Marshal Grossman, 83–98. Lexington: University Press of Kentucky, 1998.

———. "Women at the Margins in Spenser and Lanyer." In *Worldmaking Spenser: Exploration in the Early Modern Age*, edited by Patrick Gerard Cheney and Lauren Silberman. Lexington: University of Kentucky Press, 2000.

Wright, Patrick. *On Living in an Old Country: The National Past in Contemporary Britain*. London: Verso, 1985.

Wroth, Mary. *The First Part of the Countess of Montgomery's Urania*. Edited by Josephine A. Roberts. Binghamton, N.Y.: Center for Medieval and Early Renaissance Studies, State University of New York at Binghamton, 1995.

———. "Love's Victory." In *Renaissance Drama by Women: Texts and Documents*, edited by S. P. Cerasano and Marion Wynne-Davies, 91–126. London: Routledge, 1996.

———. *The Second Part of the Countess of Montgomery's Urania*. Edited by Josephine A. Roberts, Suzanne Gossett, and Janel Mueller. Tempe: Arizona Center for Medieval and Renaissance Studies.

———. "The Second Part of the Countesse of Montgomery's Urania." Newberry Library manuscript, Case MSfY 1565. W95, n.d.

Wyatt, Jean. "On Not Being La Malinche: Border Negotiations of Gender in Sandra Cisneros' 'Never Marry a Mexican' and 'Woman Hollering Creek.'" *Tulsa Studies in Women's Literature* 14, no. 2 (1995): 243–71.

Zarur, Elizabeth N. C. "Catalogue Raisonné." In *Art and Faith in Mexico: The Nineteenth-Century Retablo Tradition*, edited by Elizabeth Netto Calid Zarur and Charles Muir Lovell. Albuquerque: University of New Mexico Press, 2001.

Zemon Davis, Natalie, and Arlette Farge, eds. *A History of Women in the West*. Vol. 3. *Renaissance and Enlightenment Paradoxes*. Cambridge, Mass.: Harvard University Press, 2000.

CONTRIBUTORS

ELIZABETH J. ADAMS earned a Ph.D. in world religions from Temple University; her dissertation is entitled "Windows of Desire: Narrative Discourse in Teresa of Avila's *Interior Castle* (1577)." She teaches women's studies, writing, and world religions at several universities in the Philadelphia area and online. Her academic interests include prayer and postmodernism, women and mysticism, narratology, and interreligious dialogue, especially among Jewish, Christian, and Muslim traditions. She is an activist in several organizations, including the Women's International League for Peace and Freedom and a pacifist religious group of secular Franciscans.

ELLEN L. ARNOLD holds a Ph.D. in interdisciplinary studies from Emory University. She is Assistant Professor of English at East Carolina University, where she teaches courses in multicultural literature, ethnic studies, and women's studies. She is editor of *Conversations with Leslie Marmon Silko* (University of Mississippi Press, 2000) and has published essays on Linda Hogan, Leslie Marmon Silko, and Carter Revard. She is currently working on a study of emerging worldviews in contemporary Native American literature.

SHARON BARNES holds a Ph.D. in English and a graduate minor in women's studies. Her primary research focuses on twentieth-century American women poets. She is Assistant Professor of Interdisciplinary and Special

Programs and an affiliated faculty member in the Department of Women's and Gender Studies at the University of Toledo.

HOLLY BLACKFORD (Ph.D., University of California, Berkeley) is Assistant Professor of English at Rutgers University, Camden. She teaches and researches nineteenth- and twentieth-century multicultural American literature/culture, women's studies, film, and children's literature. Her book on the reading practices of girls is forthcoming (*Out of This World: Why Literature Matters to Girls* [Teachers College Press, 2004]). She has also published articles on *Little Women*, *Incidents in the Life of a Slave Girl*, *Redwall*, and female rites of passage in American culture. She is a member of the American Studies Faculty and the Center for Children and Childhood Studies.

SHEILA T. CAVANAGH is Masse-Martin/National Endowment for the Humanities (NEH) Distinguished Teaching Professor at Emory University. She is the author of *Cherished Torment: The Emotional Geography of Lady Mary Wroth's Urania* (Duquesne University Press, 2001), *Wanton Eyes and Chaste Desires: Female Sexuality in The Faerie Queene* (Indiana University Press, 1994), and numerous articles on Renaissance literature and pedagogy. She is also Director of the Emory Women Writers Resource Project, a Web site that was recently awarded $314,000 by the NEH.

DEBRA CUMBERLAND is an assistant professor of English at Winona State University in Winona, Minnesota. Her work has appeared in the journals *American Literary Realism* and the *Nebraska English Journal* and in the collection *Virginia Woolf: Texts and Contexts* (Pace University Press, 1996), among others.

RORY DICKER earned her Ph.D. in English at Vanderbilt University, where she currently teaches in the Women's Studies Program. Her research focuses on nineteenth-century American women's literature. *Catching a Wave: Reclaiming Feminism for the 21st Century*, a collection of essays she edited with Alison Piepmeier, was published in 2003 by Northeastern University Press.

JACQUELINE DOYLE is Professor of English at California State University-Hayward, where she teaches American literature and women's literature. Her recent publications on ethnic American women's writing have appeared in *Critique: Studies in Contemporary Fiction*, *Hitting Critical Mass: A Journal of Asian American Cultural Criticism*, *Women's Studies*, *Frontiers*, and *MELUS*, and in the anthologies *The Immigrant Experience in North America: Carving out a Niche*, edited by Katherine B. Payant and Toby Rose (Greenwood Press, 1999) and *Women, America, and Movement: Narratives of Relocation*, edited by Susan L. Roberson (University of Missouri Press, 1998).

ROSLYN RESO FOY received her Ph.D. from the University of Connecticut and teaches twentieth-century British literature and classics at the University of New Orleans. She is the author of *Ritual, Myth, and Mysticism in the Work of Mary Butts: Between Feminism and Modernism* (University of Arkansas Press, 2000), the first full-length study on the work of Mary Butts, as well as numerous articles on modernist writers.

KRISTINA K. GROOVER is Associate Professor of English at Appalachian State University in Boone, North Carolina, where she teaches twentieth-century British and American literature, African American literature, and women writers. She is author of *The Wilderness Within: American Women Writers and Spiritual Quest* (University of Arkansas Press, 1999) and of essays on Sarah Orne Jewett, Harriette Arnow, and Kaye Gibbons.

ROXANNE HARDE is currently finishing her dissertation on the theologies of Anne Bradstreet, Emily Dickinson, and Elizabeth Stuart Phelps at Queen's University, Ontario. She will begin a postdoctoral fellowship at Cornell University in fall 2004, and her research will focus on Phelps and early feminist theologies. Her work has appeared in the journals *Legacy: A Journal of American Women Writers*, *Critique*, and *Contemporary Verse II* and in several collections. She is currently guest-co-editing a special "girlpower" issue of *Femspec*.

AVRA KOUFFMAN received her Ph.D. in seventeenth- and eighteenth-century literary studies from the University of Arizona. She has taught literature and language on three continents—most recently, to grant-winning professors from the former USSR on a faculty development program in Moldova. As a London-based performance poet, she has performed on British television and radio and at many UK festivals and venues. Her publications include poetry, journalism, diary scholarship, and autobiographical prose.

SUE MATHESON teaches literature, film, and popular culture at Red Deer College in Alberta, Canada. Her research interests include popular culture, Jungian psychology, and cultural and classical anthropology, as well as early modern literature. Her essays have appeared in *BESTIA*, *Dalhousie Review*, *Mythlore*, and the *Doris Lessing Newsletter*.

KIMBERLY R. MYERS is Associate Professor of English at Montana State University, where she teaches nineteenth- and twentieth-century British literature, Irish literature, pedagogy, and specialty courses that she designs, including one on literature and medicine. She has won several awards for university teaching, including the 2002 President's Award for Excellence in Teaching and four MSU Alumni Association/Bozeman Chamber of Commerce Awards for Excellence. She was also named Distinguished Educator for 2002 by Montana's Association of Teachers of English Language Arts. Her forthcoming book, *Illness in the Academy: A Collection of Pathographies by Academics*, grew out of her experience in the National Endowment for the Humanities 2002 Summer Institute on "Medicine, Literature and Culture."

SOURCES AND CREDITS

N.C.: Wake Forest University Press, 1993); "Looking at a Man," "Nude," "Blode-wedd," and "Rainbow" in *Pharaoh's Daughter*, rev. ed. (Winston-Salem, N.C.: Wake Forest University Press, 1993); "Daphne and Apollo," in *The Water Horse*, trans. Medbh McGuickian and Eilean Ní Chuilleanain (Winston-Salem, N.C.: Wake Forest University Press, 2000).

Poetry excerpts, reprinted by permission of New Island Books, from Nuala Ní Dhomhnaill, *Selected Poems: Rogha Danta*, trans. Michael Hartnett (Dublin: New Island Books, 2000).

Excerpts from "The Shannon Estuary Welcomes the Fish," by Nuala Ní Dhomhnaill, reprinted by permission of Patrick J. Crotty, from Patrick J. Crotty, trans. and ed., *Modern Irish Poetry: An Anthology* (Belfast: Blackstaff Press, 1995).

Portions of chapter 11 are based on Jacqueline Doyle, "Assumptions of the Virgin and Recent Chicana Writings," *Women's Studies* 26, no. 2 (1997): 171–201, and are used courtesy of *Women's Studies*.

INDEX